The Official Lladró Collection Identification Catalog and Price Guide

Second Edition: 1994

by Dr. Glenn S. Johnson

**The Lladró Dealer Advisory Board
and The Staff of the Lladró Collectors Society**
New York, New York

The Official Lladró Identification Catalog and Price Guide
Published in the United States of America in 1994
by the Lladró Collectors Society
43 West 57th Street
New York NY 10019
1-800-634-9088
© 1994 by Lladró Collectors Society

Library of Congress Catalog Card Number: 92-97380
ISBN Number: 1-882738-01-2
Designed and produced by Glenn S. Johnson, Wayland MA 01778
Printed by Grafacon, Inc., Hudson MA 01749
Printed in the United States

The first edition of the Lladró Identification Catalog and Price Guide was a compendium of the entire creative output of the Lladró Studios beginning from the early years. This informative tool for collectors sold over 50,000 copies making it a best seller among book selections from the collectibles' press.

The second edition updates that volume. In it you will find that the 1993 retirements are indicated and the 1994 introductions are included. All 136 new figurines from the '94 collection appear as a group in the front of the book. This edition then continues to list selections as they appeared in the first edition, with corrections made of typographical errors that were missed the first time around.

The cataloging system allows collectors to locate figurines by identifying basic characteristics. The best way to acquaint yourself with the system is to flip through the book at your leisure.

The rarity codes key figurines with an approximation of their availability in current circulation. Without actual production records from the early years, one can only estimate. But, if a figurine had limited distribution or was produced for only one or two years, it is safe to assume that very few of those pieces exist. On the other hand, figurines that have remained in the collection for 12 or more years are likely to be widely circulated.

A final note: Please be aware that the "LCS Estimates" are established by an independent researcher and an appraiser's estimate based on rarity and public auction results. They are frankly educated opinions from sources independent of the Lladró Society.

Figurines Produced Exclusively for Disney by Lladró
(These co-branded figurines include both the Lladró Logo and the Disney Trademark)

Disneyana Convention Exclusives

The *Disneyana Convention* for collectors of Disneyana memorabilia is conducted in alternating sites every year, Disneyland in Anaheim, California and Walt Disney World in Lake Buena Vista, Florida. Lladró is one of the select companies commissioned to produce limited edition Disney merchandise to be sold exclusively at the conventions. *Tinkerbell*, the 1992 exclusive was priced at $350 and was recently auctioned for $3,200. *Peter Pan*, 1993, was sold for $400 and auctioned for $3,400.

The 1994 exclusive is *Cinderella and the Fairy Godmother*.

No.: 7518
Name: Tinker Bell
Height: 7
Current status: Limited edition, fully subscribed "Disneyana Exclusive"
Original issue year: 1992
Edition limit: 1500
Issue price: $350
High auction price: $3,200

No.: 7529
Name: Peter Pan
Height: 9.5
Current status: Limited edition, fully subscribed "Disneyana Exclusive"
Original issue year: 1993
Edition limit: 2000
Issue price: $400
High auction price: $3,400

No.: 7553
Name: Cinderella and the Fairy Godmother
Height: 8.5
Current status: Limited edition "Disneyana Exclusive"
Original issue year: 1994
Edition limit: 2,500
Issue price: $875

Snow White and the Seven Dwarfs
Available Only at Theme Parks

The *Snow White and the Seven Dwarfs* series by Lladró was commissioned by Walt Disney Attractions Merchandise for sale at both US Disney theme parks, Disneyland and Walt Disney World.

No.: 7555
Name: Snow White
Height: 9.5
Current status: Open issue, Available
 Exclusively at Disney Theme Parks
Original issue year: 1994
Issue price: $295

No.: 7533
Name: Doc
Height: 6.25
Current status: Open issue, Available
 Exclusively at Disney Theme Parks
Original issue year: 1994
Issue price: $195

No.: 7534
Name: Dopey
Height: 5.5
Current status: Open issue, Available
 Exclusively at Disney Theme Parks
Original issue year: 1995

No.: 7535
Name: Sneezy
Height: 6
Current status: Open issue, Available
 Exclusively at Disney Theme Parks
Original issue year: 1995

No.: 7536
Name: Bashful
Height: 6.5
Current status: Open issue, Available
 Exclusively at Disney Theme Parks
Original issue year: 1994
Issue price: $175

No.: 7537
Name: Happy
Height: 6.5
Current status: Open issue, Available
 Exclusively at Disney Theme Parks
Original issue year: 1994
Issue price: $195

No.: 7538
Name: Grumpy
Height: 6
Current status: Open issue, Available
   Exclusively at Disney Theme Parks
Original issue year: 1994
Issue price: $175

No.: 7539
Name: Sleepy
Height: 5.75
Current status: Open issue, Available
   Exclusively at Disney Theme Parks
Original issue year: 1994
Issue price: $175

New in 1994

No.: 7532
Name: 1994 Limited Edition Egg
Height: 4
Current status: Limited edition, exclusive US distribution
Original issue year: 1994
Edition limit: 1994 only
Issue price: $ 150

No.: 6043
Name: Doves Cup and Saucer
Height: 2.25
Current status: Open issue, currently active
Original issue year: 1994
Issue price: $ 160

No.: 6046
Name: Cautious Friends Cup and Saucer
Height: 2.25
Current status: Open issue, currently active
Original issue year: 1994
Issue price: $ 175

No.: 6050
Name: Rose Cup and Saucer
Height: 2.25
Current status: Open issue, currently active
Original issue year: 1994
Issue price: $ 145

No.: 6053
Name: Daisy Cup and Saucer
Height: 2.25
Current status: Open issue, currently active
Original issue year: 1994
Issue price: $ 145

No.: 6045
Name: Ducklings Cup and Saucer
Height: 2.25
Current status: Open issue, currently active
Original issue year: 1994
Issue price: $ 160

No.: 6051
Name: Blue Bell Cup and Saucer
Height: 2.25
Current status: Open issue, currently
active
Original issue year: 1994
Issue price: $ 145

No.: 6047
Name: Springtime Pals Cup and
Saucer
Height: 2.25
Current status: Open issue, currently
active
Original issue year: 1994
Issue price: $ 175

No.: 6044
Name: Kittens Cup and Saucer
Height: 2.25
Current status: Open issue, currently
active
Original issue year: 1994
Issue price: $ 175

No.: 6052
Name: Calla Lily Cup and Saucer
Height: 2.25
Current status: Open issue, currently
active
Original issue year: 1994
Issue price: $ 145

No.: 6048
Name: Orchid Cup and Saucer
Height: 2.25
Current status: Open issue, currently
active
Original issue year: 1994
Issue price: $ 145

No.: 6042
Name: Playful Pals Cup and Saucer
Height: 2.25
Current status: Open issue, currently
active
Original issue year: 1994
Issue price: $ 175

No.: 6049
Name: Pansy Cup and Saucer
Height: 2.25
Current status: Open issue, currently active
Original issue year: 1994
Issue price: $ 145

No.: 6040
Name: Creamer
Height: 3.75
Current status: Open issue, currently active
Original issue year: 1994
Issue price: $ 270

No.: 6041
Name: Sugar
Height: 5.5
Current status: Open issue, currently active
Original issue year: 1994
Issue price: $ 335

No.: 6039
Name: Beverage Server
Height: 8
Current status: Open issue, currently active
Original issue year: 1994
Issue price: $ 520

No.: 6160
Name: Turtledove
Height: 4
Current status: Open issue, currently active
Original issue year: 1994
Issue price: $ 32

No.: 6159
Name: Apple Picking
Height: 4
Current status: Open issue, currently active
Original issue year: 1994
Issue price: $ 32

No.: 6158
Name: Friends
Height: 4
Current status: Open issue, currently active
Original issue year: 1994
Issue price: $ 32

No.: 6162
Name: Resting
Height: 4
Current status: Open issue, currently active
Original issue year: 1994
Issue price: $ 32

No.: 6161
Name: Flamingo
Height: 4
Current status: Open issue, currently active
Original issue year: 1994
Issue price: $ 32

No.: 6139
Name: 1994 Christmas Bell
Height: 3
Current status: Limited edition
Original issue year: 1994
Edition limit: Available in 1994 only
Issue price: $ 39.50

No.: 7542
Name: 1994 Limited Edition Bell, Eternal Love
Height: 7.25
Current status: Limited edition, exclusive US distribution
Original issue year: 1994
Edition limit: Available in 1994 only
Issue price: $ 95

No.: 1781
Name: Allegory of Time
Height: 19.75
Current status: Limited edition, currently active
Original issue year: 1994
Edition limit: 5000
Issue price: $ 1290

No.: 6105
Name: 1994 Christmas Ornament
Height: 3.25
Current status: Limited edition
Original issue year: 1994
Edition limit: Available in 1994 only
Issue price: $ 55

No.: 6138
Name: Globe Paperweight
Height: 4.75
Current status: Open issue, currently active, exclusive US distribution
Original issue year: 1994
Issue price: $ 95

No.: 1795
Name: Natural Beauty
Height: 3
Current status: Limited edition, currently active
Original issue year: 1994
Edition limit: 500
Issue price: $ 650

No.: 1792
Name: Fluvial Cup with Roses
Height: 5.5
Current status: Limited edition, currently active
Original issue year: 1994
Edition limit: 500
Issue price: $ 1150

No.: 1793
Name: Fluvial Cup with Branch
Height: 6.25
Current status: Limited edition, currently active
Original issue year: 1994
Edition limit: 500
Issue price: $ 1590

No.: 1794
Name: Fluvial Cup with Water Lily
Height: 6.25
Current status: Limited edition, currently active
Original issue year: 1994
Edition limit: 500
Issue price: $ 1350

No.: 1790
Name: Neoclassic Cup (Color)
Height: 6.25
Current status: Limited edition,
  currently active
Original issue year: 1994
Edition limit: 500
Issue price: $ 1370

No.: 1791
Name: Neoclassic Cup (Bisque)
Height: 6.25
Current status: Limited edition,
  currently active
Original issue year: 1994
Edition limit: 500
Issue price: $ 1250

No.: 1789
Name: Large Neoclassic Cup
Height: 7
Current status: Limited edition,
  currently active
Original issue year: 1994
Edition limit: 300
Issue price: $ 2695

No.: 1786
Name: Romantic Vase - Blue
Height: 8.5
Current status: Limited edition,
  currently active
Original issue year: 1994
Edition limit: 300
Issue price: $ 2250

No.: 1787
Name: Romantic Vase - White
Height: 9.5
Current status: Limited edition,
  currently active
Original issue year: 1994
Edition limit: 300
Issue price: $ 2598

No.: 1788
Name: Floral Figure
Height: 9.75
Current status: Limited edition,
  currently active
Original issue year: 1994
Edition limit: 300
Issue price: $ 2198

No.: 3028
Name: Modesty
Height: 20.5
Current status: Limited edition,
  currently active
Original issue year: 1994
Edition limit: 300
Issue price: $ 1295

No.: 3027
Name: Ebony
Height: 20.75
Current status: Limited edition,
  currently active
Original issue year: 1994
Edition limit: 300
Issue price: $ 1295

No.: 3571
Name: At the Helm
Height: 17.25
Current status: Limited edition,
  currently active
Original issue year: 1994
Edition limit: 3500
Issue price: $ 1495

No.: 3569
Name: A Moment's Pause
Height: 20.5
Current status: Limited edition,
  currently active
Original issue year: 1994
Edition limit: 3500
Issue price: $ 1495

No.: 3564
Name: Gentle Moment
Height: 15.75
Current status: Limited edition,
  currently active
Original issue year: 1994
Edition limit: 1000
Issue price: $ 1795

No.: 3565
Name: At Peace
Height: 15.75
Current status: Limited edition,
  currently active
Original issue year: 1994
Edition limit: 1000
Issue price: $ 1650

No.: 1778
Name: Pegasus
Height: 18
Current status: Limited edition,
  currently active
Original issue year: 1994
Edition limit: 1500
Issue price: $ 1950

No.: 6097
Name: Sleeping Bunny with Flowers
Height: 2.5
Current status: Open issue, currently
  active, exclusive US distribution
Original issue year: 1994
Issue price: $ 110

No.: 6099
Name: Preening Bunny with Flowers
Height: 4
Current status: Open issue, currently
  active, exclusive US distribution
Original issue year: 1994
Issue price: $ 140

No.: 6098
Name: Attentive Bunny with Flowers
Height: 4.25
Current status: Open issue, currently
  active, exclusive US distribution
Original issue year: 1994
Issue price: $ 140

No.: 6100
Name: Sitting Bunny with Flowers
Height: 5.5
Current status: Open issue, currently
  active, exclusive US distribution
Original issue year: 1994
Issue price: $ 110

No.: 7543
Name: Spike
Height: 3
Current status: Open issue, currently
  active, exclusive US distribution
Original issue year: 1994
Issue price: $ 95

No.: 7545
Name: Rocky
Height: 3.75
Current status: Open issue, currently
active, exclusive US distribution
Original issue year: 1994
Issue price: $ 110

No.: 7547
Name: Rex
Height: 4.75
Current status: Open issue, currently
active, exclusive US distribution
Original issue year: 1994
Issue price: $ 125

No.: 7544
Name: Brutus
Height: 7.25
Current status: Open issue, currently
active, exclusive US distribution
Original issue year: 1994
Issue price: $ 125

No.: 7546
Name: Stretch
Height: 7.5
Current status: Open issue, currently
active, exclusive US distribution
Original issue year: 1994
Issue price: $ 125

No.: 6104
Name: Finishing Touches
Height: 8.5
Current status: Open issue, currently
active, exclusive US distribution
Original issue year: 1994
Issue price: $ 240

No.: 6127
Name: Sweet Dreamers
Height: 7
Current status: Open issue, currently
active, exclusive US distribution
Original issue year: 1994
Issue price: $ 280

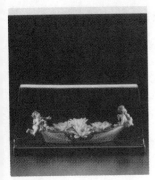

No.: 1796
Name: Floral Enchantment
Height: 5.5
Current status: Limited edition,
   currently active
Original issue year: 1994
Edition limit: 300
Issue price: $ 2990

No.: 6126
Name: Angelic Violinist
Height: 7
Current status: Open issue, currently
   active
Original issue year: 1994
Issue price: $ 150

No.: 6125
Name: Joyful Offering
Height: 8.25
Current status: Open issue, currently
   active
Original issue year: 1994
Issue price: $ 245

No.: 6146
Name: Spring Angel
Height: 9
Current status: Open issue, currently
   active, exclusive US distribution
Original issue year: 1994
Issue price: $ 250

No.: 6148
Name: Summer Angel
Height: 9.25
Current status: Open issue, currently
   active, exclusive US distribution
Original issue year: 1994
Issue price: $ 220

No.: 6085
Name: Angelic Harmony
Height: 10
Current status: Open issue, currently
   active
Original issue year: 1994
Issue price: $ 495

No.: 6149
Name: Winter Angel
Height: 11.25
Current status: Open issue, currently active, exclusive US distribution
Original issue year: 1994
Issue price: $ 250

No.: 6147
Name: Fall Angel
Height: 11.25
Current status: Open issue, currently active, exclusive US distribution
Original issue year: 1994
Issue price: $ 250

No.: 6131
Name: Angel of Peace
Height: 12
Current status: Open issue, currently active, exclusive US distribution
Original issue year: 1994
Issue price: $ 345

No.: 6133
Name: Angel with Garland
Height: 12.25
Current status: Open issue, currently active, exclusive US distribution
Original issue year: 1994
Issue price: $ 345

No.: 3570
Name: Ethereal Music
Height: 14.25
Current status: Limited edition, currently active
Original issue year: 1994
Edition limit: 1000
Issue price: $ 2450

No.: 1784
Name: Flower Wagon
Height: 11.5
Current status: Limited edition, currently active
Original issue year: 1994
Edition limit: 3000
Issue price: $ 3290

No.: 2258
Name: Family Love
Height: 13.25
Current status: Open issue, currently active
Original issue year: 1994
Issue price: $ 450

No.: 1783
Name: Circus Fanfare
Height: 18.25
Current status: Limited edition, currently available
Original issue year: 1994
Edition limit: 1500
Issue price: $ 14240

No.: 1785
Name: Cinderella's Arrival
Height: 24
Current status: Limited edition, currently available
Original issue year: 1994
Edition limit: 1500
Issue price: $ 25950

No.: 2260
Name: Arctic Friends
Height: 7
Current status: Open issue, currently active
Original issue year: 1994
Issue price: $ 345

No.: 6112
Name: Medieval Lord
Height: 8.5
Current status: Open issue, currently active
Original issue year: 1994
Issue price: $ 285

No.: 6115
Name: Medieval Prince
Height: 8.5
Current status: Open issue, currently active
Original issue year: 1994
Issue price: $ 295

No.: 6096
Name: The Sportsman
Height: 8.75
Current status: Open issue, currently
active, exclusive US distribution
Original issue year: 1994
Issue price: $ 495

No.: 6129
Name: Little Friends
Height: 9.5
Current status: Open issue, currently
active
Original issue year: 1994
Issue price: $ 225

No.: 2257
Name: Constant Companions
Height: 13.25
Current status: Open issue, currently
active
Original issue year: 1994
Issue price: $ 575

No.: 6164
Name: Wedding Bells
Height: 8.25
Current status: Open issue, currently
active, exclusive US distribution
Original issue year: 1994
Issue price: $ 175

No.: 6116
Name: Medieval Majesty
Height: 9
Current status: Open issue, currently
active
Original issue year: 1994
Issue price: $ 315

No.: 1779
Name: High Speed
Height: 10.5
Current status: Limited edition,
currently active
Original issue year: 1994
Edition limit: 1500
Issue price: $ 3830

No.: 6128
Name: Christmas Melodies
Height: 10.5
Current status: Open issue, currently
active
Original issue year: 1994
Issue price: $ 375

No.: 6086
Name: Allow Me
Height: 11.75
Current status: Open issue, currently
active, exclusive US distribution
Original issue year: 1994
Issue price: $ 1625

No.: 1776
Name: Conquered by Love
Height: 15.25
Current status: Limited edition,
currently active
Original issue year: 1994
Edition limit: 2500
Issue price: $ 2850

No.: 1777
Name: Farewell of the Samurai
Height: 16.75
Current status: Limited edition,
currently active
Original issue year: 1994
Edition limit: 2500
Issue price: $ 3950

No.: 6154
Name: African Love
Height: 7.75
Current status: Open issue, currently
active, exclusive US distribution
Original issue year: 1994
Issue price: $ 225

No.: 6140
Name: Springtime Friends
Height: 6.25
Current status: Open issue, currently
active
Original issue year: 1994
Issue price: $ 485

No.: 6087
Name: Loving Care
Height: 6.5
Current status: Open issue, currently active
Original issue year: 1994
Issue price: $ 250

No.: 6109
Name: Meal Time
Height: 7.5
Current status: Open issue, currently active
Original issue year: 1994
Issue price: $ 495

No.: 6157
Name: Polynesian Love
Height: 8
Current status: Open issue, currently active, exclusive US distribution
Original issue year: 1994
Issue price: $ 225

No.: 6102
Name: Mother's Little Helper
Height: 8.25
Current status: Open issue, currently active
Original issue year: 1994
Issue price: $ 275

No.: 6141
Name: Kitty Cart
Height: 8.25
Current status: Open issue, currently active, exclusive US distribution
Original issue year: 1994
Issue price: $ 750

No.: 6134
Name: Birthday Party
Height: 8.25
Current status: Open issue, currently active, exclusive US distribution
Original issue year: 1994
Issue price: $ 395

No.: 6110
Name: Medieval Maiden
Height: 8.5
Current status: Open issue, currently active
Original issue year: 1994
Issue price: $ 150

No.: 6153
Name: American Love
Height: 8.75
Current status: Open issue, currently active, exclusive US distribution
Original issue year: 1994
Issue price: $ 225

No.: 6113
Name: Medieval Lady
Height: 9
Current status: Open issue, currently active
Original issue year: 1994
Issue price: $ 225

No.: 6093
Name: Songbird
Height: 9
Current status: Open issue, currently active
Original issue year: 1994
Issue price: $ 395

No.: 6101
Name: Follow Us
Height: 9
Current status: Open issue, currently active, exclusive US distribution
Original issue year: 1994
Issue price: $ 198

No.: 6114
Name: Medieval Princess
Height: 9.25
Current status: Open issue, currently active
Original issue year: 1994
Issue price: $ 245

No.: 6106
Name: Spring Joy
Height: 10.25
Current status: Open issue, currently active, exclusive US distribution
Original issue year: 1994
Issue price: $ 795

No.: 2256
Name: Solitude
Height: 13.25
Current status: Open issue, currently active
Original issue year: 1994
Issue price: $ 398

No.: 1780
Name: Indian Princess
Height: 18.5
Current status: Limited edition, currently active
Original issue year: 1994
Edition limit: 3000
Issue price: $ 1630

No.: 6090
Name: Baseball Player
Height: 7
Current status: Open issue, currently active
Original issue year: 1994
Issue price: $ 295

No.: 6137
Name: Baseball Star
Height: 7
Current status: Open issue, currently active, exclusive US distribution
Original issue year: 1994
Issue price: $ 295

No.: 6124
Name: Traveler's Rest
Height: 7.25
Current status: Open issue, currently active, exclusive US distribution
Original issue year: 1994
Issue price: $ 275

No.: 6107
Name: Football Player
Height: 7.5
Current status: Open issue, currently active
Original issue year: 1994
Issue price: $ 295

No.: 6088
Name: Communion Prayer - Boy
Height: 7.5
Current status: Open issue, currently active
Original issue year: 1994
Issue price: $ 194

No.: 6108
Name: Hockey Player
Height: 7.5
Current status: Open issue, currently active
Original issue year: 1994
Issue price: $ 295

No.: 2259
Name: Little Fisherman
Height: 7.75
Current status: Open issue, currently active
Original issue year: 1994
Issue price: $ 298

No.: 6123
Name: Out For a Stroll
Height: 8.25
Current status: Open issue, currently active, exclusive US distribution
Original issue year: 1994
Issue price: $ 198

No.: 6119
Name: Musketeer Aramis
Height: 8.25
Current status: Open issue, currently active
Original issue year: 1994
Issue price: $ 275

No.: 6118
Name: Musketeer Portos
Height: 8.5
Current status: Open issue, currently active
Original issue year: 1994
Issue price: $ 220

No.: 6122
Name: A Great Adventure
Height: 8.5
Current status: Open issue, currently active, exclusive US distribution
Original issue year: 1994
Issue price: $ 198

No.: 6111
Name: Medieval Soldier
Height: 8.5
Current status: Open issue, currently active
Original issue year: 1994
Issue price: $ 225

No.: 6121
Name: Musketeer Athos
Height: 8.75
Current status: Open issue, currently active
Original issue year: 1994
Issue price: $ 245

No.: 6120
Name: Musketeer Dartagnan
Height: 8.75
Current status: Open issue, currently active
Original issue year: 1994
Issue price: $ 245

No.: 6135
Name: Football Star
Height: 8.75
Current status: Open issue, currently active, exclusive US distribution
Original issue year: 1994
Issue price: $ 295

No.: 6091
Name: Basketball Player
Height: 8.75
Current status: Open issue, currently active
Original issue year: 1994
Issue price: $ 295

No.: 6136
Name: Basketball Star
Height: 9
Current status: Open issue, currently active
Original issue year: 1994
Issue price: $ 295

No.: 6084
Name: Saint James
Height: 10
Current status: Open issue, currently active
Original issue year: 1994
Issue price: $ 310

No.: 6092
Name: The Prince
Height: 10.5
Current status: Open issue, currently active
Original issue year: 1994
Issue price: $ 325

No.: 3567
Name: Trapper
Height: 12.25
Current status: Limited edition, currently active
Original issue year: 1994
Edition limit: 3000
Issue price: $ 950

No.: 7528
Name: Dr. Martin Luther King, Jr.
Height: 12.5
Current status: Open issue, currently active
Original issue year: 1994
Issue price: $ 345

No.: 3568
Name: American Cowboy
Height: 13.25
Current status: Limited edition,
  currently active
Original issue year: 1994
Edition limit: 3000
Issue price: $ 950

No.: 3566
Name: Indian Chief
Height: 13.25
Current status: Limited edition,
  currently active
Original issue year: 1994
Edition limit: 3000
Issue price: $ 1095

No.: 3563
Name: Saint James The Apostle
Height: 16
Current status: Limited edition,
  currently active
Original issue year: 1994
Edition limit: 1000
Issue price: $ 950

No.: 6089
Name: Communion Prayer - Girl
Height: 7.5
Current status: Open issue, currently
  active
Original issue year: 1994
Issue price: $ 198

No.: 6151
Name: Bearing Flowers
Height: 7.5
Current status: Open issue, currently
  active
Original issue year: 1994
Issue price: $ 175

No.: 6150
Name: Playing the Flute
Height: 7.75
Current status: Open issue, currently
  active
Original issue year: 1994
Issue price: $ 175

No.: 6155
Name: European Love
Height: 7.75
Current status: Open issue, currently active, exclusive US distribution
Original issue year: 1994
Issue price: $ 225

No.: 6152
Name: Flower Gazer
Height: 7.75
Current status: Open issue, currently active
Original issue year: 1994
Issue price: $ 175

No.: 6156
Name: Asian Love
Height: 8
Current status: Open issue, currently active, exclusive US distribution
Original issue year: 1994
Issue price: $ 225

No.: 6103
Name: Beautiful Ballerina
Height: 8.5
Current status: Open issue, currently active, exclusive US distribution
Original issue year: 1994
Issue price: $ 250

No.: 6142
Name: Indian Pose
Height: 8.75
Current status: Open issue, currently active
Original issue year: 1994
Issue price: $ 475

No.: 6117
Name: Constance
Height: 9.25
Current status: Open issue, currently active
Original issue year: 1994
Issue price: $ 195

No.: 7622
Name: Basket of Love
Height: 9.5
Current status: Limited edition,
    currently active
Original issue year: 1994
Issue price: $ 225
Comments: LCS Special

No.: 6143
Name: Indian Dancer
Height: 13.25
Current status: Open issue, currently
    active
Original issue year: 1994
Issue price: $ 475

No.: 6145
Name: Heavenly Prayer
Height: 17.25
Current status: Open issue, currently
    active
Original issue year: 1994
Issue price: $ 675

No.: 3029
Name: Danae
Height: 25.5
Current status: Limited edition,
    currently active
Original issue year: 1994
Edition limit: 300
Issue price: $ 2880

No.: 6168
Name: The Apollo Landing (25th
    anniversary)
Height: 16.25
Current status: Limited edition,
    currently active
Original issue year: 1994
Edition limit: July 1994 to July 1995
Issue price: $ 450

Contents

To Elaine —
Yes, it's done.

Acknowledgments

Except for the creation of the complex classification system for the 2,911 objects making up the complete Lladró collection, this is not a creative book. It is, instead, an objective report and listing of already existing artistic images and facts, some of which go back to the early 1940s. As such, the book required the work of many other more creative people.

First, we thank the brothers Lladró — Juan, Jose and Vicente — and their heirs. It is they who have given us, and continue to give us, their important focussed, discrete and identifiable legacy within the much larger one-thousand-year history of artistic hard-paste porcelain.

There might be skeptics who say: "Their achievement is not that special; it probably would have happened somewhere, sometime, under someone else's creativity if the Lladró brothers hadn't done it." People who say this would know nothing of the rare combination of artistic vision, aesthetic sensibility, business acumen and courage, ceaseless labor, inspirational leadership and, for over forty years now, of the cooperation, dedication and perseverance required to create a 3,000-piece collection of consistently excellent porcelain art.

In the history of music, Mozart's legacy of 626 inspired musical compositions could only have been created by Wolfgang Amadeus himself. In the entire history of fine porcelain, no single institution has ever given us the wealth of superb figurine art given us by the Lladró brothers. What makes their achievement especially remarkable is the fact that it was accomplished within a period measured by the lifetimes of three men who lived at the same time. Knowing them and their attitudes towards their work, their company and their own lives, they are probably as amazed at what they have been able to create as we are.

We thank the past collectors, curators, encyclopedists and scholars who, over the centuries, have given us the body of historical information we use today to place the Lladró collection in its proper perspective. "Museum-quality" porcelain art in the home has only recently been affordable by ordinary working people. We know the early historian was motivated mainly by his love of the field and a generous desire to share his findings.

We thank the people in Spain who, in preparing the Lladró *Collectors Catalogue* and 1991 and 1992 annual sales catalogs, have researched and photographed every object in the collection that has been identified up to this moment and have assembled the mammoth collection now on display in the Lladró Museum on 57th Street in New York City. We have researched and photographed other collections "from scratch" ourselves and know the work and dedication involved.

We thank the staff of the Lladró Collector Society in New York City for their appreciation of what we were trying to do, their unfailingly swift responses to our many requests and, not the least of their required qualities, their senses of humor (you should have seen some of our requests; you would know what we mean!).

We thank the seven Lladró dealers in the United States who, experts all in the rapidly developing secondary market, so graciously volunteered their expertise and guidance.

Finally, our thanks to Hugh Robinson, first director of the U.S. Collectors Society. A pioneer in fine porcelain art collectibles since the late 1940s, Mr. Robinson was essential in opening all the Lladró doors and records we needed to succeed with this book.

Dr. Glenn S. Johnson
Wayland, Massachusetts
November, 1992

The Lladró Dealer Advisory Board

The following authorized Lladró dealers stand out for their contributions to the development of the secondary market in the United States for fully subscribed limited editions and permanently retired open issues.

[Both Rostand and Thalheimer conduct well-prepared and heavily attended annual public

West Coast

Herb Rostand
Rostand Jewelers
8349 Foothill Blvd.
Sunland CA 91040
818-352-7814

South

Bruce Thalheimer
Thalheimers Jewelers
PO Box 7255
2095 E. Tamiami Trail
Naples FL 33914
813-774-4666

Lladró auctions. We could not have assigned LCS price estimates to the entire collection without these statistical anchors.]

Southwest

Barry Harris
Amanda's Gifts
279 Central Park Mall
San Antonio TX 78216
512-525-0412

Central Midwest

David May
The Hummel Shop
Garfield Road
New Springfield OH
216-540-3728

New England

Craig Edwards
Stacy's Gifts
E. Walpole Mall, Rt.1
Walpole MA
508-668-4212

Midwest

Ed Delgan
European Imports
7900 N. Milwaukee Ave.
Niles IL 60714
312-561-2871

Northeast

Buddy Savitt and Ruth Wolfe
Limited Edition
2170 Sunrise Highway
Merrick NY
516-623-4400

Although these dealers' efforts have contributed significantly to the wealth of information reported in this volume, the author alone is responsible for all errors and omissions.

A Request For Your Help

The Lladró families in Valencia and New York City and the volunteer members of the Lladró Dealer Advisory Committee have worked long hours to make this *Identification Catalog and Price Guide* as accurate as humanly possible. Unfortunately, certain errors will occur when compiling a factual history of this size and scope. The errors will be of two general types:

One, because of the scattered introduction of the Lladró collection to the American scene, many objects illustrated and documented in this volume were never available in the U.S. marketplace. They were distributed only in Spain and neighboring European countries. Many prices were available only in pesetas, Deutschmarks, francs and lire. We have had to extrapolate from these currencies to arrive at comparable American prices.

Two, because of Lladró's necessary focus on the day-to-day artistic, production and commercial aspects of the collection, several inconsistencies prior to the formation of the Lladró Collectors Society in 1985 pop up. These inconsistencies are not important in the job of starting and building a successful business enterprise. They are *very important* to collectors who must understand the rules of the game and the boundaries of the playing field before they make their investment decisions.

We can assure you that the data in this volume have been researched, checked and rechecked and that there are not many of these errors. The pages that follow paint a remarkably honest and accurate picture of the Lladró collection as it exists in 1993. However, we know that some collectors know far more about their specialized areas than do those of us who work with the whole.

Given all the above, when you *do* spot an error or omission in this volume, such as a lower issue price, a different year of introduction, or such, we request that you drop us a card and let us know about it.

One word of warning: please do not rely on your memory alone. We have worked very hard to get to this point and we must insist on proper documentation of all your claims. Send your facts and documentation to:

> *Collector Guide*
> Lladró Collectors Society
> 43 West 57th Street
> New York NY 10019

We promise to take immediate action on your changes and will personally credit your contribution in subsequent revisions of this study.

Thank you,

Glenn S. Johnson
Wayland, Massachusetts

How to Use This Book

IMPORTANT: Please Read This Brief Section Carefully

The entire Lladró Collection through the start of 1993 consists of 2,911 separate porcelain objects. To make it as easy as possible for you to find your way through this dense forest of objects, we've developed a display system based on common sense and widely understood characteristics. The way the collection is displayed, you will never have to flip through more than 14 pages of photographs to spot your piece. However, it is vital you understand how we've arranged the photographs or you'll be quickly lost again.

Lladró began distributing porcelain in the United States in the late 1960s. Save for a few theoretical collectors and dealers who have kept up with the three Lladró brothers' amazing productivity (theoretical because we haven't identified them yet), most of us are stunned by the sheer magnitude of what has become *The Lladró Collection*.

When discussing this project with the Lladró Collectors Society, they charged us with two forbidding challenges:

1. Make it easy for new or old collectors to identify their Lladró piece quickly and without a great deal of expertise, and
2. Give them an idea of what it's worth.

To discover the fair market value for your Lladró, all you have to do is identify it by photo.

1. Identification

The new collector encountering the immensity of the Lladró Collection for the first time is quickly intimidated by the sheer variety of the ways the brothers Lladró have chosen to demonstrate their porcelain virtuosity.

There is so much, and in so many different forms . . .

Young ballerinas, dancing or preparing for the dance,
Collector spoons bearing the Lladró crest,
Deer, pursued by hunting dogs,
Majestic cranes, perched in a base of rushes and cattails,
Clowns upon clowns,
The virgin Mary and her infant Jesus,
Wedding scenes,
Marvelously complex automobiles, filled with young couples
and chased by barking dogs or honking geese,
Lamps, surrounded by exquisite figures,
Little girls, with birds, cats and bushels of delicate flowers,
Little beagle puppies, and
Japanese vases and on and on and on.

Then, as we study the literature, we read intimidating terms, many of which we're not confident with, terms such as . . .

> Valencian,
>> Gres,
>>> Don Quixote,
>>>> "Sculpture" (versus figurines?)
>>>>> Caprichos,
>>>>>> Goyescas,
>>>>>>> "Pastorals",
>>>>>>>> Harlequins and on and on and on.

We decided to do the hard work and leave the easy part up to you. We knew you could tell a collector spoon from a

> candleholder from a
>> vase from a
>>> full-figured female from a
>>>> head of a female from a
>>>>> ceramic tile from a
>>>>>> lamp from an
>>>>>>> animal figurine . . .

. . . so we divided the 2,911 objects into nine major chapters we knew a collector was comfortable with. Then we divided those chapters into what we considered commonsense categories.

We request that you determine if your Lladró falls into one of nine major shapes. Then we ask you to turn to that chapter and read the further breakdowns required to limit your search.

The 2,911 objects are in far different **SHAPES,** our first classifier:

Shape	Objects In Collection
26 "Miscellaneous" shapes	201
Bowls	39
Lamps	89
Flowers (bouquets and stems)	98
Vases (and jugs)	230
Figurines	(2254)
Birds	114
Human busts, heads and torsos	152
Animals	212
Full head-to-toe human figures	1776

Miscellaneous Forms

Two-hundred-and-one Lladró porcelain objects are in 27 different minor identifiable shapes. Since none of these categories are large enough to warrant further classification, we've displayed them together. Once you understand the shape below, you will be able to flip through just a few pages to locate your piece. The Miscellaneous Forms are:

Bowls

Designs: 39   **Pages:** 37-44

Bowls and centerpieces are distinguished from Lladró vases when the top rim is as large or larger than the body of the bowl. We classify vases and jugs as "vases" when the neck is smaller than the body.

Lamps

Designs: 87   **Pages:** 45-60

Lamps are divided into two further categories:
  Figurines: as an integral part of the lamp base
  Designs: where a design covers a solid surface

Flowers

Designs: 98   **Pages:** 61-78

All Lladró porcelain flowers, bouquets and floral displays are classed into three further categories:
Single Flowers or Stems
Bouquets or arrangements, not in a porcelain container
Bouquets or arrangements, in a porcelain container

Bird Figurines

Designs: 114   **Pages:** 79-98

Bird figurines are further classified into three categories:
Figurines of two or more birds
Single-bird figurines up to 5-1/2" in height
Single-bird figurines 6" in height and higher

Busts, Heads and Torsos

Designs: 152   **Pages:** 99-127

Lladró figurines portraying people are classified into full-figured people, portrayed from head to toe, and heads, busts and partial torsos. Of the latter group, 152 figures are further classified into:
Single females
Single males
Figures portraying more than a single female or male

Animal Figurines

Designs: 212   **Pages:** 129-165

Lladró animal figurines portray seven major species and a variety of others. We classify them as:
Dogs and puppies
Deer, elk, gazelles and antelopes
Horses
Rabbits
Bears
Bulls, cows, oxen and bison
Cats and kittens
Others, listed by species

Vases

Designs: 231   **Pages:** 167-206

Lladró vases are distinct from Lladró bowls and centerpieces. Whether they're named "vases," "jugs" or "urns," vases' necks are smaller than their bodies.
If porcelain flowers are an integral part of the vase, the object is classified under "Flowers."
Vases are classified by height:
3" to 6-1/2"
7" to 9-3/4"
10" to 11-3/4"
12" to 18-1/2"
19" and taller

Full-figured Humans

Designs: 1,776   **Pages:** 207-502

Of the 2,911 porcelain objects, 1,776, or more than 60%, are of full-figured humans and fantasy figures (angels, cupids, centaurs, and so on). Since we have attempted to keep your search to as few a number of pages as possible, we've made some very narrow distinctions and then we've broken these down further by height. All other classifications are rather easy (such as distinguishing between a spoon, vase, lamp, bowl, dog and Christmas ornament). This category requires a more careful analysis. As such, it requires the greatest study.

The opening pages of the chapter, beginning on page 207, explain and illustrate the nine sub-classifications we use.

2. Price Guide

Once you've identified your piece, each photo is followed by a Fact Box listing:

1. The 4-digit production number Lladró has assigned to it
2. Its name (or title)
3. Its height in inches
4. The year it was issued
5. Its current status:
    Open issue, currently active (without any preannounced limits) and available through authorized dealers at suggested retail prices
    Open issue, permanently retired, available only on the secondary market
    Limited edition (either by preannounced number or time period), currently active and available through authorized dealers at suggested retail prices
    Limited edition, fully subscribed, available only on the secondary market
6. The year it was permanently retired
7. Its rarity (relative to the other objects in the collection)
8. Its original issue price
9. If active (open or limited) its current suggested retail price
10. If auctioned previously, the highest price paid for it during the past two years
11. If permanently retired, the Lladró Collectors Society Estimate of its fair market value
12. Comments on factors otherwise affecting its value

This information, possible with only single source "closed" collections (versus "Depression glass", "Disneyana", Coca-Cola memorabilia and so on where hundreds of different producers have contributed to the whole), provides you with enough price information for you to be comfortable when trading in the secondary market (see page xxix, *The Art and Logic of Collecting for Pleasure and Profit*) or deciding on which currently active pieces to purchase.

History of Hard-paste Porcelain

[Ed. Note: This volume has been compiled to help Lladró collectors identify their collection and discover its fair market value. It is not intended as an academic discourse on the 1,000-year history of fine porcelain. That subject is treated in thousands of books, many exploring the most minute of details. The subject is abridged nicely in a series of *Expressions* magazines (the Lladró Collectors Society quarterly publication) in the Fall 1989, Winter 1989 and Spring 1990 issues, and an excellent short history also appears in another Lladró book, *Lladró: The Magic World of Porcelain* (1989, Salvat Editores, S.A.). We've included these few pages to try to give you a quick idea of the Lladró collection's place in all of this and where you now stand in the past-future continuum.]

Figure of Meissen *Harlequin* from the *Commedia dell' Arte* painted in colors from a model by Johann Joachim Kaendler, 1738, 7.5", Fitzwilliam Museum, Cambridge, England.

Most of us are familiar with the Lladró of the "Now". The "Now" is a world made up of creative art, craftsmanship, technology and a constantly changing commercial interaction between the factory, its tens of thousands of dealers worldwide and its millions of collectors. It's a world of urgency, introductions, retail prices, glitzy store displays and catalogs, promotions, quotas, warehouses, inventories, sales and profits.

Most of us are not inclined to think of the Lladró of the "Future". This perspective requires us to ignore the present

Lladró's *Troubadour*, sculpted by F. Garcia, 1969, 9.5".

and, paradoxically, project ourselves into the "Past". Yet, this volume is compiled as the first of the collection histories that will be available to many millions of Lladró collectors far into the future.

One Century Ago

To appreciate how far we have to project ahead, we have to look back. One hundred years ago, roughly during the Gay Nineties, the porcelain world was already teeming with European and American factories producing beautiful and distinctive ware for increasing numbers of middle class families that were just starting to emerge from the Industrial and Political Revolutions. A porcelain collector like us, trying to project the future, might ask:

"What factory made this figurine?"

"Is it possible the piece we just bought might end up in a museum?"

"Will objects made in this factory be famous and prized or will they disappear, smashed and forgotten in the attics of history"?

"Should we buy it?"

Two Centuries Ago

Two hundred years ago, in 1790, less than 35 European porcelain houses had broken China's eight-hundred-year (or longer?) monopoly of hard-paste porcelain. They were producing objects that could be afforded only by Europe's heads of state, nobility and the ultrarich. A middle class had not yet emerged. Printing technology was still so new that literacy was reserved for a precious few. There were few "museums", only "royal collections", not open to "the public" (or whatever they called us then).

Sevres vases painted with mythological subjects in panels reserved against *blue-de-roi* grounds and gilt with jewelled decoration, 1781. Mark, crossed "L's" enclosing date — letters "DD", 12.5". British Museum, London.

Attempting to get into the collectors' minds of this period, we can quickly sense there are no questions to be asked. For the sake of illustration, however, let's dream up an imaginary collector and attribute some questions to him:

"Does the Duke realize that the Meissen he's eating off (and of which two of his unruly guests have already broken several pieces this evening) will be fit to rest in the world's finest museums and art galleries just a few hundred years from now? Can't he be more careful?"

"I wonder how the recent discovery of new clay at Limoges is going to affect the history of French porcelain?"

"I know England's Bow porcelain factory just closed but will their addition of pulverized animal bones to the mix have any affect on other English porcelains?"

We can go back 300 years, to 1692, but Europe's discovery of the formula for hard-paste porcelain lies some twenty years in the future. No European has the vaguest idea of what lies ahead.

Some elitists reading this story so far may have already started shuddering, sensing that we're headed toward a favorable comparison of the Lladró collection and the collections of China's Ching-te Chen and Fukien province, Germany's Meissen, France's Sevres and the other hallowed names of porcelain. Well, we *are* headed that way. These elitists, we suggest, may be blinded by the "Now" of the Lladró business, forgetting that all those other factories also had their "Nows", now long gone.

Urn, by Juan Lladró, 1953, 14.5".

Ceramics and Hard-paste Porcelain

The world of ceramics has been defined by producers and collectors into many classes of product and levels of prestige. Most of these classifications are based on the clays used, the methods of decoration and the heat at which the ceramic body is fired. Some are known to us by such names as *faience, maiolica,* soft-paste porcelain, stoneware and English bone china (almost all the great English porcelain houses use a soft-paste body mixed with crushed calcified animal bone). Each class is worthy of its own scholarship and museum display and each has thrilled and delighted millions of collectors and users.

Hoechst figure, *The Medicine Seller,* painted in colors from a model by Simon Feilner, 1753, 6.25", British Museum, London.

The acknowledged Queen of the ceramic world has come to be known as hard-paste (or high-fired, or "true" porcelain). Lladró uses this porcelain.

The Chinese were the first to produce hard-paste, probably well over a thousand years ago. Its successful development was a gradual and probably accidental series of progressions from the manufacture of simple earthenware. Although Europeans didn't know it at the time, hard-paste porcelain consisted of a very special and very secret formula of two clays called *kaolin* and *petuntse* and traces of other earth elements. The distinction of this mixture is that it is fired at approximately 1450 degrees Centigrade and vitrifies the porcelain in the firing.

Marco Polo, at the end of the 13th century, wrote of China's fine porcelains, although his first writings did not appear until 1477. The Venetian is reputed to be the first to use a version of the term "porcelain" when he likened the white luxurious surface to that of the cowrie shells which in Italy were called *porceletta*. The English used the term "china ware," shortened to "china".

Porcelain found its way from China to Europe in very small quantities from at least the 1300s. It was so difficult to obtain it was very rare and highly prized. Some of it was set into metal settings, like jewels.

The flow of porcelain into Europe on a commercial scale gathered momentum in the late 1500s. The Portuguese held a near-monopoly in the trade. Chinese porcelains shipped by Portugese sailors were mainly useful wares (plates, dishes, bowls, small bowls, saucers, and so on) and were mainly painted in underglaze blue (cobalt painted on the "biscuit", then painted with a protective coat of "glaze" and then fired). Since so much of this blue-and-white porcelain was subsequently shipped from warehouses in Canton, it was also called "Cantonware". European and U.S. ship museums chronicling the early China trade display shelf after shelf of these beautiful and prized objects.

Then, in 1709, an alchemist, Johann Boettger (1682-1719), working in Meissen, Germany (a suburb of Dresden), was trying to produce gold from base metals. Instead, he produced Europe's first hard-paste porcelain. The Royal Saxon Porcelain Manufactory was established in 1710. During Boettger's management, the factory produced red stoneware and the new porcelain.

His achievement was remarkable. Without any documentary information, or any previous experience of pottery manufacture, he produced a porcelain paste and glaze and he built kilns capable of producing the high temperatures necessary to fire them.

Other European companies followed the lead of the "Meissenware Revolution", one after another. Here is a partial list of some of the great European factories through history after Johann Boettger's discovery and the periods during which they made "true porcelain":

Lladró's *Little Gardener,* sculpted by J. Fernandez, 1970, 9.25".

		Began	Stopped	Years
Germany	Hoechst	1750	1798	48
	Frankenthal	1755	1799	44
	Ludwigsburg	1758	1824	66
	KPM	1761	Present	231
	Fulda	1765	1775	10
	Wuerzburg	1775	1780	5
	Amberg	1790	1910	120
	Hutschenreuther	1856	Present	136
	Rosenthal	1880	Present	112
France	Sevres	1769	1847	78
	Rue de la Roquette	1773	1784	11
	Rue Thiroux	1775	1820	45
	Bordeaux	1781	1790	9
	Limoges	1783	1886	103
	Fontainebleu	1795	1875	80
	Charles F. Haviland	1886	Present	106
	Haviland and Co.	1892	1991	99
Spain	Alcora	1774	1820	46
	Buen Retiro	1804	1808	4
	La Mancloa	1817	1850	33
	Lladró	1953	Present	39
Russia	St. Petersburg	1744	1917	173
	Popoff Factory	1806	1872	66
	Arkhangelkoie	1814	1831	17
Poland	Korzec	1790	1797	7
	Baranovka	1801	1917	127
	Tomaszov	1805	1810	5
England	Plymouth	1768	1770	2
	Bristol	1770	1781	11
Italy	Capo di Monte	1771	1821	50
	Rome	1790	1831	41
Denmark	Royal Copenhagen	1775	Present	217
	Bing & Grondahl	1853	Present	139
Sweden	Marieberg	1777	1788	11
	Roerstrand	1880	Present	112
Czechoslovakia	Schlaggenwald	1792	1840	48
	Pirkenhammer	1803	1853	50
Austria	Vienna	1719	1864	145
Switzerland	Zurich	1765	1775	10
Netherlands	Amstel	1784	1820	36
Ireland	Belleek	1857	Present	135

Frankenthal figures of ballet subjects — Oceanus and Thetis — painted in colors and gilt from models by Konrad Linck, 1765. Mark, "CT" in monogram. 10.5", Fitzwilliam Museum, Cambridge, England.

The companies listed above share several characteristics:

1. They were all located in European countries.
2. They all made hard-paste porcelain tableware or figurines.
3. They all had a serious enough impact on true porcelain history to be included in at least three of the eight histories we researched for this study.

They differ in at least two significant respects:

1. Some appeared on the scene briefly and then disappeared forever. Of the 42 porcelain houses listed:

   Only nine are still in business, producing in the "Now".
   Fourteen were in business for a shorter period of time than Lladró, a newcomer in true porcelain history.

2. More importantly, many houses (Meissen, Sevres, Vienna, St. Petersburg) have become legends, enshrined in the finest museums and in the hearts of collectors everywhere. More (Rue Thiroux, Korzec, Pirkenhammer) are not familiar to most collectors and survive only as pedantic oddities, carried in name only from book to book.

No one in 1720 could possibly have known that pieces of Meissen, Sevres, Vienna and St. Petersburg porcelain would be on display in the Louvre, the Prado, the Metropolitan Museum of Art and the Chicago Art Institute.

No one in 1992 can possibly know whether a particular Lladró figurine will appear in the same and other new museums a century from now.

We *do* know that Lladró, from 1953 to now, has planted itself firmly in the midst of the world's great porcelain houses.

We *do* know that Lladró's success up to this point has been based on the public's acceptance of its art and uninterrupted quality.

While reading this book, shopping in fine stores and studying next year's new introductions, please recall, perhaps just for a moment, that Lladró, in addition to the glitz and urgency of the "Now", is also deeply involved, like it or not, in the deep "Past" and promising "Future" of true porcelain art.

Lladró's *Romance,* sculpted by A. Ruiz, 1972, 17.75".

Lladró Personalities

The Lladró Collection is almost 3,000 porcelain figurines, vases, ornaments, bowls, plates, lamps and other shapes. It is also a community of people in Valencia, Spain and New York City; Sunland, California and Naples, Florida; Munich, Germany and Tokyo, Japan; Copenhagen, Denmark and the island of Aruba in the Netherlands Antilles; Le Havre, France and Coeur d'Alene, Idaho. The Lladró community exists wherever sculptors, painters, kiln operators, sales office secretaries, warehouse shippers, airline pilots and boat captains, dealers, sales clerks, auctioneers and collectors make, handle, ship, display and purchase Lladró figurines. It is an immense world, one we too often take for granted.

Since this is the first edition of what will probably become a long, long series of revised and updated collector guides, we have decided to headline just a few of the people who have done so much to make the guide possible.

But first, consider for a moment a performance of Carl Orff's *Carmina Burana* by the Boston Symphony Orchestra and Tanglewood Choir at Tanglewood, the BSO's summer home in the Berkshire Mountains of western Massachusetts. The performance, attended by thousands in August, 1992, demanded the following ingredients:

1. A solid Western tradition of eight-tone scale, medieval music, Gregorian chant and modern orchestral voicing.
2. Carl Orff (Munich: 1895-1982), a trained musical genius who, in 1937, not only heard the inspirational music in his head but also had the training, ability and personal discipline required to write it down on paper so that people alive ten years after his death could sense and interpret the sounds he'd heard.
3. Seiji Ozawa, the orchestra's conductor, who had learned and relearned Orff's music in his youth and who had so excelled in interpreting music that he'd been placed in charge of one of the world's great orchestras.
4. About 120 members of the Boston Symphony Orchestra, some of the finest musicians in the world; violinists and cellists and trombonists and bassoonists and a man who pounded the kettle drums before him.
5. About 100 members of the Tanglewood Chorus, men and women who had worked so hard on their voices and musical skills that they were capable of singing Orff's difficult music.
6. About 20 members of the Tanglewood Boys Choir; young men who, before their voices change, had been chosen and trained to sing the parts Carl Orff had written for them.
7. Finally, about 8,000 classical music fans who knew that this concert offered the potential of extreme excellence and pure bliss. We were not disappointed.

Questions: Is the music we heard that night an artistic creation?

Excluding Orff and Ozawa (the focuses of all the headlines) was any single person of all those above not necessary?

Which one? It certainly wasn't that kettle drummer who added such incredible force to the beautiful sound.

The audience? When an orchestra plays without an audience they're doing something called "rehearsing."

Could you have recruited *any* 8,000 people to sit there and "be" an audience?

The brothers Lladró, like Carl Orff, are the sustaining geniuses behind the Lladró collection. They receive all the headlines. But behind them (nay, *with* them) are thousands of people who are absolutely *necessary* for the successful completion of an artistic creation. Even you and I, the "audience" for all their inspiration, training and hard work, are necessary. To answer the last musical question above, the 8,000 Tanglewood listeners had to know and love classical music for the achievement to have come off. If the 8,000 were expecting Johnny Cash, Bruce Springsteen, Bob Dylan or the latest Hard Metal group, they would have been sadly disappointed. Beautiful porcelain demands beautiful porcelain lovers. Without exaggeration, we're all in this together.

Now, the headliners:

The Founders

Juan Lladró, oldest of the three Lladró brothers.

Jose Lladró, second born in the family of three brothers.

Vicente, the youngest of the three founding brothers.

Some of the Artists and Craftspersons

Vicente Lladró and Jose Puche, discussing a large and complicated "sketch" for a new Lladró figurine. All three brothers are artists and continue to play a significant role in the creation of every object that bears their name.

Jose (left) and Juan (right) discuss a finish on several new ballerina figures with Julio Ruiz, Lladró's head of decoration.

Antonio Ramos, Lladró sculptor

Jose Puche, sculptor and orna-
mentalist

Salvador Furio, featured in the
section on "How Lladró Porcelains are Made," puts finishing
touches on the clay face of one
of his Don Quixotes.

Vicente Martinez, sculptor

Lladró's hundreds of painters
cannot be named in this small
volume, but you can be certain
that your figures were hand-
painted with special, highly
trained skill.

Lladró is a combination of artistic creativity and technical virtuosity. The art
of porcelain is so perfect that, despite
the centuries since Johann Boettger
discovered it in Meissen, it still
demands the most precise mixing pro-
portions. Lladró's hard-paste remains
one of the company's great secrets,
and the people who work with it are
selected very carefully.

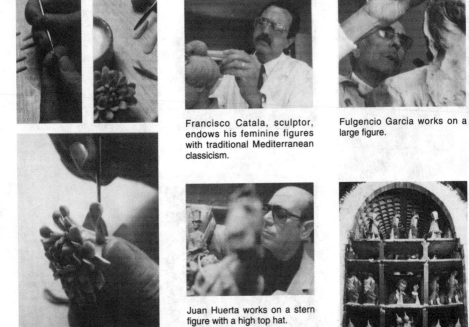

Francisco Catala, sculptor, endows his feminine figures with traditional Mediterranean classicism.

Fulgencio Garcia works on a large figure.

Juan Huerta works on a stern figure with a high top hat.

Many features create "style". Unless we've been lucky enough to tour the Lladró factories in Valencia, we would be amazed at the patience, care and skill required to create the famous Lladró flowers, still assembled, one petal at a time, by hundreds of expert hands.

Highly skilled hands, though without name or personality, assemble the fragile "biscuit" before it is painted and fired.

From conception to sculpting to molding to assembling to painting, the final product is positioned in the special hard-paste kilns, waiting for yet more people, hands and then flame to convert the colorful clay into vitrified true porcelain.

How Lladró Porcelain Figurines Are Made

To continue with last chapter's musical analogy for a moment:

Some were satisfied with the beauty alone. Without analytical dissection, the sounds that filled the Music Shed that evening were bliss enough. Others, those who knew the music well or had studied any of the instruments or voice roles involved, were, we suggest, even more blessed. Just the notion that human beings, from the 42-year-old Carl Orff to the forty-five-year-old timpanist to the eleven-year-old boy soprano to the 60-year-old listener could accomplish something this monumental, completed a circle fulfilling all expectations. It is for those latter fans, for whom knowledge of the craft increases their deep appreciation, that this section is presented.

Every Lladró figure begins with an artistic inspiration. Here Salvador Furio works on the figure of Don Quixote (1030, 14.5", 1969), Spain's *Man From La Mancha,* that will become one of Lladró's most famous figurines and the symbol on the LCS membership plaque.

Savador Furio's masterpiece is destroyed as molds of all parts and fragments are made in the Lladró mold department.

Once the clay has been sculpted, Lladró mold experts cut Furio's finished creation into castable parts.

Just as the Orff score is preserved with ink on paper, just so Florio's work is preserved in the many molds used to cast liquid porcelain "slip" into firm, white "biscuit".

Once all the different parts are cast, technicians carefully join them together again, re-creating Furio's original composition. The Don's right arm must hang straight down again with the same weariness Furio put into it in 1969, 23 years ago.

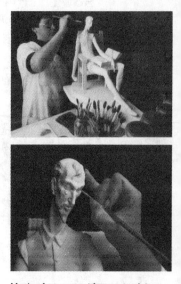

Moving from one art form — sculpture — to another, painters must apply the subtle pastel colors that have become such a vital part of the "Lladró look". First the broad areas are covered and then the final application, the details that require the steadiest hand.

A fine varnish glaze is applied to the sculpted, cast, reassembled and painted Quixote. The old boy is now ready for the kiln that will transform him into vitrified hard-paste porcelain.

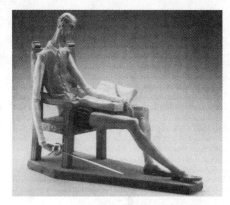

The finished product, out of the kiln, waiting only for the addition of his trusty sword and a base on which to rest his weary feet.

The Lladró corporate logo symbolizes the fusion of art and technology. Don Quixote owns not only his own base and chair, he also has his very own cardboard inserts cut for him, the traveling coach that will carry him across the Atlantic in extreme comfort. Great attention to artistic *and* technical detail has resulted in a very low breakage rate, remarkable when we consider the size, weight and fragility of the items being transported in today's fast-moving world.

Here he is! Don Quixote! The Man of La Mancha! The *hidalgo* himself! Now we're getting close to the end. Only a few steps remain. He must be photographed and added to the new catalog and price list. He must be purchased by an American dealer who has the vision to display sculpture that will catch shoppers' eyes and imaginations. Finally, to complete this 23-year-long (1969 to 1992) cycle of necessary participants, a porcelain and/or Quixote fan must

    see the Don,
        fall in love with him,
            decide he must have him,
                purchase him,
                    take him home, and
                        proudly display him for all to see!

Identification Marks

Although most Lladrós possess a "look" that the practiced eye can easily spot, it is important that collectors are secure in knowing they have an authentic Lladró, made by the people and hands illustrated in the preceding pages. Because of the protective diligence of the Lladró brothers through the years, the collection has not been endangered by copyists. However, just to make sure, the following photographs illustrate the "touchmarks" Lladró has used since the beginning of their work. In effect, these eight examples trace the development of the Lladró identification mark through time.

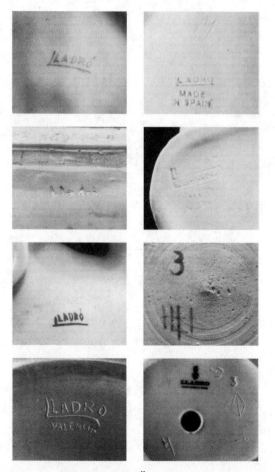

The Art and Logic of Collecting for Pleasure and Profit

Just as Lladró combines art and technology in producing their porcelains, we use art and logic in preparing this book.

Artistic and Emotional Reasons for Collecting Lladró

This is very important! If you love what you see, for whatever reason, and are bound and determined to buy it and, finally, feel you can afford it because you love it so, go ahead and buy it!

As with the pure bliss of the Boston Symphony Orchestra concert in the previous chapters, that bliss is quite enough.

Who cares why you love it and why does it even matter? You do, and that's it!

Enough said.

Logical and Intellectual Reasons for Collecting Lladró

A certain cold logic, aside from the emotional impact a figurine inspires, can be very interesting to large numbers of us and can help us decide which of the many beautiful Lladrós we decide to purchase. Thus, the remaining 500 and more pages of this book.

A hobby began in the 1960s that has continued with steady growth. More and more of us have been collecting "something".

Some collectibles go back many years before the 1960s collecting boom, collectibles such as postage stamps, rare coins and antique furniture.

Other collectibles, not as mature and developed, have attracted a great deal of media attention in recent years, such as baseball cards, Disneyana, and Coca-Cola memorabilia.

Some collectibles appear too recent to some. It's somewhat difficult for some of us born in the 1930s to view Shirley Temple and Elvis Presley artifacts and "Beatlemania" as "collectibles."

Lladró's *Eagle Owl*, the current record holder for increase in original investment. Purchased in 1971 for $15 and auctioned in 1991 for $750, a 50-times increase.

Little Pals, the Lladró Collectors Society first "Reserved for members only" annual special in 1985. Sold that year for $95 and auctioned in 1992 for $4,500.

Still others may appear somewhat bizarre to the outsider. Clubs exist for, and newsletters are sent to, collectors of:

Tom Mix (the old Western film star) artifacts,

"Abdicationware", items involving England's King Edward and American Wallis Simpson,

barbed wire (especially in the Western states, where barbed wire can be used to trace the history of the West) and

prisoners' old leg shackles, to name but a few.

For the most part, porcelains are in the first group, "Mature and Developed Collectibles". Meissen, Sevres and Hoechst porcelains have been purchased by museums and private collectors for well over a hundred years. Major auction houses and experts around the world monitor and report current prices paid for these objects.

Lladró porcelains do not fall into this category. The secondary market for soldout and retired issues is still too young to be considered mature and stable. Therefore this book is the first of what surely will be many, many books and articles in the future that report on the current state of the Lladró market. Rather than the accumulation of many facts, we must rely on logic.

What Investment Collectors Must Know

Lladró's *Skye Terrier,* purchased in 1969 for $15 and auctioned in 1992 for $700.

Collectors need to be knowledgeable when they are deciding whether or not to invest in a field.

What is this?

What is it worth if I wish to buy or sell it?

How much should I insure it for?

Postage stamp and rare coin publishers and clubs literally swamp potential collectors with information that is helpful in answering these questions. One need not invest huge amounts of money or time to become an expert in these fields. For example, it doesn't take long to determine how much a 1909 SVBD Lincoln-head penny is worth; we can look it up in hundreds of publications. Professional students, writers and publishers use reports on tens of thousands of sales transactions at stamp and coin shows, auctions and from the cash registers and computers owned by thousands of dealers within these specialties to write their informational books and weekly newspapers. These collectibles are monitored essentially the same way Dow-Jones operates when it reports the flow of New York Stock Exchange sales.

The most important function of this volume is helping past and future Lladró collectors begin the long process of identifying Lladró's thousands of porcelain objects and determining fair secondary market prices for permanently retired open issues and soldout limited editions.

Only a handful of public Lladró auctions have taken place up to this time in the company's history in the United States. Prior to these scattered sales, beginning in 1989, we have enjoyed little organized secondary market data on which to base our estimates.

Since 1969, a total of 1,516 objects issued as "open" series (that is, without preannounced limits, either in numbers or in time) have been permanently retired from production. These 1,516, along with 146 fully subscribed limited editions and 164 very rare Lladró objects created before the company began broad distribution, form Lladró's secondary market of 1,826 porcelains.

Of these 1,826, a total of 401 have been sold at auction within the past two years. Actual public sale prices for these objects give

Lladró's *Boy with Drums,* purchased in 1969 for $16.50 and auctioned in 1992 for $625, a 38-times price increase.

us the statistical anchors from which we can project "LCS Value Estimates" for all the remaining discontinued open issues.

To emphasize the tentative nature of these first-ever LCS Value Estimates, here is how we arrived at them. Five assumptions have guided us:

Assumption 1: There is a fundamental logic to the prices in a secondary market as large and old as the Lladró Collection.

Assumption 2: Through research, we can isolate patterns within that logic and we can use them to project values. Put simply, Lladró objects for which we have no secondary market sales records should be worth about as much as "like" designs for which we *do* have actual sales prices.

We have used current statistical sampling techniques to develop a complicated formula based on three factors:

Assumption 3: The shorter a Lladró design is available on the retail market, the rarer it is. If a figure has been in production and circulation for a long time, we can assume it has been popular enough to delay retiring it. Some figures (1010: *Girl with Lamb;* 4551: *Little Duck*) were introduced in 1969 and are still available on the 1992 retail market. Conversely, some figures were introduced in 1969 and permanently retired in 1970 (1079: *Boy with Lyre;* 4521: *Deer Hunt*). These last two are certainly far rarer than the first.

We can thus assume the "long runs" have been very popular. Their sales were so good that Lladró decided, after reviewing sales year after year, to keep them as production staples. Similarly, and with the same reasoning, we can also assume that very few of the "short-timers" were purchased. They did not sell well enough during their one or two years on the active market to warrant keeping them in production.

Assumption 4: The degree of rarity ought to influence secondary market prices. The fewer pieces in circulation, the more difficult they are to find and the more an ardent collector should be willing to pay for them.

Assumption 5: On the other hand, and opposed to this notion, the effect of inflation from 1969 to now (especially during the highly inflationary 1970s) plus the unspectacular but steady strengthening of the Spanish peseta against the U.S. dollar reveals that the very popular old designs still on the retail market have risen dramatically in price.

Combining these five factors, we have arrived at an LCS (Lladró Collectors Society) Value Index to calculate the LCS Value Estimates for the 1,516 permanently retired open issues. We list them in this volume for each design. In the 401 cases where the designs have been sold at auction, we also list the highest actual price paid for them.

Since Lladró's 146 soldout limited editions and 164 pre-distribution rarities are so few in number, we have listed only the highest auction prices paid for each and have let them stand on their numbers. With this method, you have an idea of how much was paid at auction and you can decide for yourself how much you would be willing to pay.

One more important word on our LCS Value Estimates. These values are based on dealer auctions and dealer sales. These professionals purchase Lladrós and sell them to make a profit. As a collector, you should not expect to receive the value listed when selling your statues to a dealer or another collector. Profit percentages

Lladró's *Hebrew Student,* introduced in 1970 at $33 and auctioned in 1991 for $1,050.

vary with specialty fields and individual dealers and there are no "standards" as such. However, since postage stamp and rare coin dealers' profits fluctuate between 35 and 40 percent, you should expect to sell your Lladró statues for between 60 to 65 percent of the LCS Estimate. If the LCS Estimate for a figure is $1,000, you can ask $600 to $650 and consider your request reasonable.

The Lladró Collectors Society

If you've read this far from the beginning, you will realize that Lladró porcelain has had the time, since the early 1950s, to gain a firm and permanent foothold in both national and international collecting markets. On the other hand, this same time has not been long enough for Lladró to be an established, mature collectible specialty.

We find ourselves straddling two periods. One is the inspired and enormous productivity represented in the 500 pages that follow. The other is the sudden appearance, since the first Lladró American auction in 1989, of an authentic and brisk secondary market now being created by collectors who are instinctively sensing they are at the dawn of what will probably become a legendary and hallowed body of work. Suffice it to say that an early Lladró vase which was originally sold for seven dollars was purchased recently for $10,000 — and few of us knew about it!

U.S. Collectors Society Formed

The Lladró Collectors Society, now headquartered in the new nine-story Lladró Museum & Galleries, 43 West 57th Street in New York City, was begun in 1985 by the three Lladró brothers.

The Lladró Society was formed to provide information, benefits and services to Lladró collectors. The need for such a society became more and more apparent as the popularity of Lladró porcelains continued to increase.

The Lladró brothers chose Hugh Robinson as the Director of the Collectors Society due to his many years of experience in the collectibles field.

The Plan

After their international search for the most experienced person to organize and execute what they envisioned as the most complete and exciting international collector organization in the world, the Lladró brothers and Robinson were quick to assess the situation in the United States, their starting point. They saw 40 years of Spanish design, production and distribution confronting a vacuum of collector information.

After several months of planning, they developed an eight-point plan.

1. Tell Lladró collectors, the good people who had purchased and displayed their cherished figurines since the late 1960s, that they were not alone. Do this by organizing a Lladró Collectors Society and advertising its existence through thousands of displays in museums, stores and antique shops and through advertisements in major art, antique and collectibles magazines.
2. Begin providing LCS members with the type of information true collectors want and need.
3. Plan, design and produce special porcelain issues from Spain that serve as "perks" for those who have chosen to join the Lladró family with their tangible membership.
4. Start the planning, design and construction of a U.S. Lladró museum and art gallery in our nation's cultural center, New York City, that will serve as a dramatic "thank you" and an obvious statement to the American people that the Lladró porcelain collection is here to stay.
5. Begin a continuing series of tours from Spain to the United States, exposing American collectors to first-hand contact with the friendly Spaniards who have brought such pleasure to their lives.

A Lladró Collectors Society membership card, identifying Mrs. Eva James as a member in good standing of the Society. The card qualifies her as the recipient of the annual subscription to *Expressions* magazine and "Don Quixote" LCS display plaque. It also serves as the "passport" to the purchase of LCS member-only figurines, admittance to the Lladró Museum in New York City and opportunities to purchase other LCS literature and tours to Porcelain City in Valencia and other entertainment spots in historic Spain.

The first issue of *Expressions* magazine, Vol. 1, No. 1, Spring, 1985, the Lladró Collectors Society magazine, now out-of-print and a collector's item in its own right.

6. Begin a continuing series of tours from the United States to Spain that expose fortunate American collectors to Spanish culture in general and the wonders of Lladró's Porcelain City in particular.
7. Develop a series of independent public auctions that furnish valid prices for secondary market figurines. Use these prices to begin the long process of organizing and validating the secondary market prices for *all* Lladró pieces that has finally resulted in the publication of this book, some eight years after the formation of the Society.
8. Once having executed all these projects in the United States, and having hired and trained adequate staff to continue their operation, turn LCS attention to some of the other countries in which Lladró is collected and cherished, countries such as Germany, France, Italy and Japan.

Information

Information is the primary reason for the Lladró Collectors Society's existence. Collectors need and want information. What's new? Who are the artists? What limited editions are selling out and what pieces are going to be retired? In general, what can we learn that improves our appreciation and enjoyment of the Lladró collection?

To give some idea of the variety of collector information appearing in *Expressions'* pages, here are just a few of the hundreds of articles that have appeared in the magazine through the years:

"Restoration: Picking Up the Pieces"

"Market Watch: Secondary Market Values"

"Insuring Collectibles: Are You Sheltered Against Loss?"

"The History of Porcelain Part II: Europe Breaks Into Production"

"Feature Figurines: Japanese Vase LL1536"

"Rostand: Pioneering Lladró's Secondary Market"

"Celebrating the Season with Lladró Gift Suggestions"

"An Ornament Encore for Collectors"

"Mastering the Masquerade: Porcelain Masks"

"Blueprint for a Figurine"

"Retired Figurines: 1991"

"The City that Lladró Built"

"Spain: Barcelona"

The second issue of *Expressions*, the issue that introduced *Little Pals*, the Society's first exclusive Society member-only figurine, issued to attract attention to and promote the new and steadily-growing collector club.

LCS Books

Two other color-filled books have been photographed, written in English and published for LCS Society members:

Lladró: The Magic World of Porcelain, 1989, Salvat Editores, S.A.

A beautifully-illustrated history of the Lladró Collection, containing photo-filled essays by, among others:

Geoffrey A. Godden, Fellow of the Royal Society of Arts, Member of the British Antique Dealers' Association and author of more than 20 books on porcelain, including *The Encyclopaedia of British Pottery and Porcelain Marks.*

Masaaki Maeda, Professor of Western Ceramic Art at the Department of Art History, Musashino Art University, Tokyo and author of such books as *The Story of European Ceramics* and *The Victoria & Albert Museum.*

This book, available for purchase by LCS members, provides an objective view of the Lladró collection and its place in the history of European porcelain art as reported by European and Asian writers.

Collectors Catalogue: Volumes I and II, published by the Lladró Collectors Society for LCS members in 1990.

These two three-ring-bound volumes, also available for purchase by LCS members, presents, in beautiful full-color photographs, the 2,764 ceramic tiles, vases, lamps and figurines produced by the Lladró brothers from 1941, when Juan Lladró painted his first ceramic tile for a Valencian factory, to 1990. The volumes represent the Lladró brothers' gigantic effort to research and assemble every porcelain object bearing their name, photographing it and identifying the original artist, issue year, the year it was retired and its height. The book you are reading would not have been possible without this germinal work.

For more information on all LCS publications, write:

**Lladró Collectors Society
43 West 57th Street
New York NY 10019**

Exclusive Member Figurines

Little Pals, the first figurine created exclusively for charter LCS members in 1985. Permanently retired a year later, the $95 figure has risen steadily in subsequent auctions until a sale price of $4,500 was achieved in 1992.

Don Quixote membership plaque and a leather binder designed to hold *Expressions* issues

The Society periodically offers figurines to its members that only they can purchase. All a member has to do is show proof of membership to an authorized Lladró dealer. The dealer will place an order for the active figure and a few weeks later the collector can pick it up at the store.

An index to all the "LCS Specials" is listed on page 521. As you skim the offerings to date, note the beauty of the figures and their value appreciation over the years.

A member joining the Society the first time automatically receives a bisque porcelain plaque with the figure of Don Quixote in *bas relief* and bearing the signatures of the three Lladró brothers. Displayed with your collection, it tells everyone of your role in the larger Lladró family.

The Lladró Museum and Galleries

After years of planning, design and construction beginning in the earliest days of the Society, the doors to the towering Lladró Museum and Galleries at 43 West 57th Street in the heart of New York City's midtown district opened to LCS members on September 18, 1988. It has served as the center of club activities ever since.

The retail gallery and mezzanine, the distinctive greeting to LCS members as they enter the museum from 57th Street's sidewalks. The slick, undecorated mahogany panels of the lobby rise from the glistening marble floor to the ceiling.

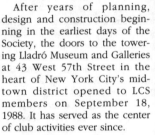

The theater on the fifth floor, where films bring the Lladró story and the production of Lladró porcelains to an American audience.

Floor upon floor of spacious galleries and comfortable lounging facilities allow the LCS member to trace Lladró's past, present and future. Every major component of the vast Lladró collection can be found in this magnificent building, an important example of the significance of the Lladró brothers' work in the history of porcelain art.

Displays of early wall plaques, vases, plates and ceramic tiles testify to the 1940s and early 1950s. This is the period when the three young Valencian brothers were learning their art in local ceramics factories before they founded their own small firm in 1953. A special display of sculpture displays Vicente's early penchant for three-dimensional art.

Spain Comes to the United States

A typical view, repeated in city after city: Lladró collectors waiting in malls and on sidewalks to see the Lladró road show and meet and chat with one of the dignitaries.

Jose Lladró signs the title page of a Lladró book during one of his many American appearances.

A group of collectors sit next to a Lladró store display and view a video describing the creation and production of a Lladró figurine.

One of the pillars of the emerging Lladró Collectors Society activities plan was an emphasis of bringing information and personalities from Valencia to the United States. Subsequently, the Lladró brothers, their heirs and employees have flown the Atlantic and toured our nation from Boston to Los Angeles and Seattle to Florida.

LCS members around the country are given plenty of advance notice of "a visit from Valencia" by mail, newsletter and the *Expressions* magazine.

Hugh Robinson, LCS executive director, signs figures and answers collector questions.

The United States Goes to Spain

Also since 1985, the LCS has been organizing charter air tours to Valencia for visits to Porcelain City and the beautiful surrounding countryside. Group fares, charming hosts and hostesses and the chance to visit the center of the Lladró universe have made these tours among the most popular of all the LCS scheduled activities.

Lladró Auctions

The 18th century Church of Santa Catalina, located in the center of the old/modern city of Valencia, located on the shores of the Mediterranean.

The first Lladró Festival and Auction was held in 1989 on the Sunday preceding Labor Day at Universal City in California. Over 1,600 collectors and members of the Lladró Collectors Society gathered at the Registry Hotel adjacent to Universal Studios. Herb Rostand, who has played a major role in the development of the secondary market for sold out and retired Lladró figurines, nodded to the auctioneer and the bidding began.

So did this book. Rare Lladrós have been bought, sold and traded for many years, but Rostand's 1989 auction marked the beginning of the Lladró secondary market's formal organization and monitoring. Now, after four Rostand auctions and one early in 1992 by Thalheimers Jewelers in

Herb Rostand, president of Rostand's Fine Jewelers in Sunland, California and acknowledged Lladró secondary market pioneer.

Naples, Florida, the LCS has accumulated enough valid price information to begin the long, careful and continuous process of informing collectors of the current fair market values of their collections. After all the researching, photographing and cataloging, these prices are the final piece in providing complete collector information.

We are informed by these independent businessmen that they will continue their successful auctions, so we can now inform you the LCS will continue to report on new headline prices and general assessments of the current state of the market as it develops.

We have classified the Lladró Collection into nine readily-recognizable basic shapes. During the last half-century (1941 to 1993), Lladró produced a total of 26 shapes that have not yet reached 25 examples. This "Miscellaneous" chapter is the catchall for those shapes.

One to four examples

Six to ten examples

More than ten examples

Miscellaneous

Chapter: 1-1   **No.:** 5613
Form: Pipe
Name: Sealore Pipe
Height: 3.50"
Current Status: Open edition,
   permanently retired
Original Issue Year: 1989
Last Year: 1993
Rarity: D
Issue Price: $ 125
Last Retail Price: $ 160

Chapter: 1-2   **No.:** 5133
Form: Trophy
Name: FIFA Trophy
Height: 9.50"
Current Status: Open edition,
   permanently retired
Year of Issue: 1982
Last Year: 1983
Rarity: B
Issue Price: $ 250
LCS Estimate: $ 650
High Auction Price: $ 500

Chapter: 1-3   **No.:** 4725
Form: Toiletry set
Name: Toiletry Set
Height: 7"
Current Status: Open edition,
   permanently retired
Year of Issue: 1970
Last Year: 1972
Rarity: B
Issue Price: $ 30
LCS Estimate: $ 350
Comments: Two pieces

Chapter: 1-4   **No.:** 6006
Form: Collonade
Name: Oriental Collonade
Height: 19.25"
Current Status: Open edition, currently
   active
Year of Issue: 1993
Issue Price: $ 1950
Current Price: $

Chapter: 1-5   **No.:** 1540
Form: Ballet Slippers
Name: Pink Ballet Slippers
Height: 3"
Current Status: Open edition,
   permanently retired
Year of Issue: 1988
Last Year: 1991
Rarity: C
Issue Price: $ 275
LCS Estimate: $ 275

Chapter: 1-5   **No.:** 1540.30
Form: Ballet Slippers
Name: White Ballet Slippers
Height: 3"
Current Status: Open edition,
   permanently retired
Year of Issue: 1988
Last Year: 1991
Rarity: C
Issue Price: $ 275
LCS Estimate: $ 275

Chapter: 1-6   **No.:** 333.13
Form: Men's boots
Name: Renaissance Boot
Height: 6.25"
Year of Issue: 1972
Last Year: N/A
Rarity: A
Issue Price: N/A

Chapter: 1-6   **No.:** 332.13
Form: Men's boots
Name: Boot
Height: 7.50"
Year of Issue: 1972
Last Year: N/A
Rarity: A
Issue Price: N/A

Chapter: 1-7   **No.:** 5263.30
Form: Drinking Chalices
Name: Chalice
Height: 3.25 "
Current Status: Open edition, permanently retired
Year of Issue: 1984
Last Year: 1988
Rarity: C
Issue Price: $ 45
LCS Estimate: $ 135

Chapter: 1-7   **No.:** 5263
Form: Drinking Chalices
Name: Chalice-Decorated
Height: 3.25"
Current Status: Open edition, permanently retired
Year of Issue: 1984
Last Year: 1990
Rarity: D
Issue Price: $ 45
LCS Estimate: $ 100

Chapter: 1-8   **No.:** 4833
Form: Chess sets
Name: Chess Set with Board
Height: 7.75"
Current Status: Open edition, permanently retired
Year of Issue: 1972
Last Year: 1985
Rarity: E
Issue Price: $ 600
Highest Auction Price: $ 2400
LCS Estimate: $ 3500

Chapter: 1-8   **No.:** 4833.30
Form: Chess sets
Name: Chess Pieces Only
Height: 7.75"
Current Status: Open edition, permanently retired
Year of Issue: 1972
Last Year: 1985
Rarity: E
Issue Price: $ 410
LCS Estimate: $ 2500
Highest Auction Price: $ 2750

Chapter: 1-9   **No.:** 1546.30
Form: Fans
Name: White Fan with Base
Height: 9.75"
Current Status: Open edition,
  permanently retired
Year of Issue: 1987
Last Year: 1987
Rarity: B
Issue Price: $ 650
LCS Estimate: $ 2500

Chapter: 1-9   **No.:** 1546
Form: Fans
Name: Violet Fan with Base
Height: 9.75"
Current Status: Open edition,
  permanently retired
Year of Issue: 1987
Last Year: 1987
Rarity: B
Issue Price: $ 650
LCS Estimate: $ 2600

Chapter: 1-10   **No.:** 4626
Form: Bookends
Name: Velazquez Bookend
Height: 12.50"
Current Status: Open edition,
  permanently retired
Year of Issue: 1969
Last Year: 1975
Rarity: D
Issue Price: $ 90
LCS Estimate: $ 1000

Chapter: 1-10   **No.:** 4627
Form: Bookends
Name: Columbus Bookend
Height: 12.25"
Current Status: Open edition,
  permanently retired
Year of Issue: 1969
Last Year: 1975
Rarity: D
Issue Price: $ 90
LCS Estimate: $ 1000

Chapter: 1-10   **No.:** 4661
Form: Bookends
Name: Horse Head Bookend
Height: 10.25"
Current Status: Open edition,
  permanently retired
Year of Issue: 1969
Last Year: 1972
Rarity: C
Issue Price: $ 16.50
LCS Estimate: $ 200

Chapter: 1-10   **No.:** 2010
Form: Bookends
Name: Horse's Head
Height: 9.50"
Current Status: Open edition,
  permanently retired
Year of Issue: 1970
Last Year: 1981
Rarity: E
Issue Price: $ 12.50
LCS Estimate: $ 85

Chapter: 1-11   **No.:** 5267.30
Form: Decorative Boxes
Name: Oval Box
Height: 1"
Current Status: Open edition,
  permanently retired
Year of Issue: 1984
Last Year: 1988
Rarity: C
Issue Price: $ 40
LCS Estimate: $ 120

Chapter: 1-11   **No.:** 5266
Form: Decorative Boxes
Name: Heart Box
Height: 1"
Current Status: Open edition,
  permanently retired
Year of Issue: 1984
Last Year: 1990
Rarity: D
Issue Price: $ 37.50
LCS Estimate: $ 75

Chapter: 1-11   **No.:** 5266.30
Form: Decorative Boxes
Name: Heart Box
Height: 1"
Current Status: Open edition,
  permanently retired
Year of Issue: 1984
Last Year: 1988
Rarity: C
Issue Price: $ 37.50
LCS Estimate: $ 115

Chapter: 1-11   **No.:** 5267
Form: Decorative Boxes
Name: Oval Box
Height: 1"
Current Status: Open edition,
  permanently retired
Year of Issue: 1984
Last Year: 1990
Rarity: D
Issue Price: $ 40
LCS Estimate: $ 80

Chapter: 1-12   **No.:** 1556
Form: Empty porcelain baskets
Name: Oval Basket with Pink Trim
Height: 2.75"
Current Status: Open edition,
  permanently retired
Year of Issue: 1987
Last Year: 1991
Rarity: C
Issue Price: $ 60
LCS Estimate: $ 60

Chapter: 1-12   **No.:** 1557
Form: Empty porcelain baskets
Name: Small Round Basket with Pink
  Trim
Height: 3.75"
Current Status: Open edition,
  permanently retired
Year of Issue: 1987
Last Year: 1991
Rarity: C
Issue Price: $ 60
LCS Estimate: $ 60

Chapter: 1-12   **No.:** 1557.30
Form: Empty porcelain baskets
Name: Small Round Basket with Blue
  Trim
Height: 3.75"
Current Status: Open edition,
  permanently retired
Year of Issue: 1987
Last Year: 1991
Rarity: C
Issue Price: $ 60
LCS Estimate: $ 60

Chapter: 1-12   **No.:** 1558
Form: Empty porcelain baskets
Name: Small Basket with Pink Lace
Height: 3"
Current Status: Open edition,
  permanently retired
Year of Issue: 1987
Last Year: 1991
Rarity: C
Issue Price: $ 60
LCS Estimate: $ 60

Chapter: 1-12   **No.:** 1558.30
Form: Empty porcelain baskets
Name: Small Basket with Blue Lace
Height: 3"
Current Status: Open edition,
  permanently retired
Year of Issue: 1987
Last Year: 1991
Rarity: C
Issue Price: $ 60
LCS Estimate: $ 60

Chapter: 1-12   **No.:** 1556.30
Form: Empty porcelain baskets
Name: Oval Basket with Blue Trim
Height: 2.75"
Current Status: Open edition,
  permanently retired
Year of Issue: 1987
Last Year: 1991
Rarity: C
Issue Price: $ 60
LCS Estimate: $ 60

Chapter: 1-13   **No.:** 5639
Form: Collector Spoons
Name: Beige Lily Spoon
Height: 6"
Current Status: Open edition,
  permanently retired
Year of Issue: 1989
Last Year: 1991
Rarity: B
Issue Price: $ 150
LCS Estimate: $ 150

Chapter: 1-13   **No.:** 5639.30
Form: Collector Spoons
Name: Blue Lily Spoon
Height: 6"
Current Status: Open edition,
  permanently retired
Year of Issue: 1989
Last Year: 1991
Rarity: B
Issue Price: $ 150
LCS Estimate: $ 150

Chapter: 1-13   **No.:** 1548.10
Form: Collector Spoons
Name: Dark Blue Lladró Spoon
Height: 6"
Current Status: Open edition,
  permanently retired
Year of Issue: 1987
Last Year: 1991
Rarity: C
Issue Price: $ 70
LCS Estimate: $ 70

Chapter: 1-13   **No.:** 1548.30
Form: Collector Spoons
Name: White Lladró Spoon
Height: 6"
Current Status: Open edition,
  permanently retired
Year of Issue: 1987
Last Year: 1991
Rarity: C
Issue Price: $ 70
LCS Estimate: $ 70

Chapter: 1-13   **No.:** 1548.40
Form: Collector Spoons
Name: Brown Lladró Spoon
Height: 6"
Current Status: Open edition,
  permanently retired
Year of Issue: 1987
Last Year: 1991
Rarity: C
Issue Price: $ 70
LCS Estimate: $ 70

Chapter: 1-13   **No.:** 1548
Form: Collector Spoons
Name: Light Blue Lladró Spoon
Height: 6"
Current Status: Open edition,
  permanently retired
Year of Issue: 1987
Last Year: 1991
Rarity: C
Issue Price: $ 70
LCS Estimate: $ 70

Chapter: 1-14   **No.:** 5626
Form: Candleholders
Name: Lladró Candleholder
Height: 7.75"
Current Status: Open edition,
  permanently retired
Year of Issue: 1989
Last Year: 1990
Rarity: B
Issue Price: $ 90
LCS Estimate: $ 180

Chapter: 1-14   **No.:** 5627
Form: Candleholders
Name: Lladró Candleholder
Height: 5.50"
Current Status: Open edition,
  permanently retired
Year of Issue: 1989
Last Year: 1990
Rarity: B
Issue Price: $ 55
LCS Estimate: $ 110

Chapter: 1-14   **No.:** 5628
Form: Candleholders
Name: Lladró Candleholder
Height: 6.50"
Current Status: Open edition,
   permanently retired
Year of Issue: 1989
Last Year: 1990
Rarity: B
Issue Price: $ 80
LCS Estimate: $ 160

Chapter: 1-14   **No.:** 5949
Form: Candleholders
Name: Angel Candleholder with Lyre
Height: 11.75"
Current Status: Open edition, currently
   active
Year of Issue: 1993
Issue Price: $ 295

Chapter: 1-14   **No.:** 5950
Form: Candleholders
Name: Angel Candleholder with
   Tambourine
Height: 11.75"
Current Status: Open edition, currently
   active
Year of Issue: 1993
Issue Price: $ 295

Chapter: 1-14   **No.:** 5225
Form: Candleholders
Name: Oriental Candelabra
Height: 17.25"
Current Status: Open edition,
   permanently retired
Year of Issue: 1984
Last Year: 1985
Rarity: B
Issue Price: $ 685
LCS Estimate: $ 3400

Chapter: 1-14   **No.:** 5227
Form: Candleholders
Name: Candelabra, Female Figures
Height: 10.50"
Current Status: Open edition,
   permanently retired
Year of Issue: 1984
Last Year: 1985
Rarity: B
Issue Price: $ 660
Highest Auction Price: $ 880
LCS Estimate: $ 800

Chapter: 1-14   **No.:** 1110
Form: Candleholders
Name: Mermaid Candleholder
Height: 9"
Current Status: Open edition,
   permanently retired
Year of Issue: 1971
Last Year: 1972
Rarity: B
Issue Price: $ 20
LCS Estimate: $ 225

Chapter: 1-14   **No.:** 5625
Form: Candleholders
Name: Lladró Candleholder
Height: 6"
Current Status: Open edition,
 permanently retired
Year of Issue: 1989
Last Year: 1990
Rarity: B
Issue Price: $ 105
LCS Estimate: $ 210

Chapter: 1-14   **No.:** 5629
Form: Candleholders
Name: Lladró Candleholder
Height: 4.75"
Current Status: Open edition,
 permanently retired
Year of Issue: 1989
Last Year: 1990
Rarity: B
Issue Price: $ 55
LCS Estimate: $ 110

Chapter: 1-14   **No.:** 5226
Form: Candleholders
Name: Candelabra, Male Figures
Height: 10.25"
Current Status: Open edition,
 permanently retired
Year of Issue: 1984
Last Year: 1985
Rarity: B
Issue Price: $ 660
Highest Auction Price: $ 800
LCS Estimate: $ 800

Chapter: 1-15   **No.:** 1268
Form: Decorative plaques
Name: Virgin Mural
Height: 33.75"
Current Status: Open edition,
 permanently retired
Year of Issue: 1974
Last Year: 1981
Rarity: D
Issue Price: $ 915
LCS Estimate: $ 6000

Chapter: 1-15   **No.:** 334.13
Form: Decorative plaques
Name: Nativity Plaque
Height: 7.50"
Current Status: Very rare early issue
Year of Issue: 1970
Last Year: Not available
Rarity: A
Issue Price: Not available

Chapter: 1-15   **No.:** 229.09
Form: Decorative plaques
Name: Nativity
Height: 6.25"
Current Status: Very rare early issue
Year of Issue: 1961
Last Year: Not available
Rarity: A
Issue Price: Not available

Chapter: 1-15   **No.:** 43.03
Form: Decorative plaques
Name: Gametime
Height: 15.75"
Current Status: Very rare early issue
Year of Issue: 1948
Last Year: Not available
Rarity: A
Issue Price: Not available
Comments: Created personally by Jose
Lladró

Chapter: 1-15   **No.:** 7601
Form: Decorative plaques
Name: Collectors Society Membership
Plaque
Height: 4"
Current Status: Limited to LCS
members
Year of Issue: 1985
Issue Price: $ 35
Current Price: $ 35

Chapter: 1-15   **No.:** 5808
Form: Decorative plaques
Name: New World Medallion
Height: 6.50"
Current Status: Limited edition,
currently active
Edition Limit: 5000
Year of Issue: 1991
Issue Price: $ 200
Current Price: $ 200

Chapter: 1-15   **No.:** 5281
Form: Decorative plaques
Name: Nativity Haute Relief
Height: 11"
Current Status: Open edition,
permanently retired
Year of Issue: 1985
Last Year: 1988
Rarity: C
Issue Price: $ 210
Highest Auction Price: $ 450
LCS Estimate: $ 450

Chapter: 1-15   **No.:** 2092
Form: Decorative plaques
Name: Holy Virgin
Height: 16"
Current Status: Open edition,
permanently retired
Year of Issue: 1978
Last Year: 1981
Rarity: C
Issue Price: $ 200
LCS Estimate: $ 1200

Chapter: 1-15   **No.:** 2054
Form: Decorative plaques
Name: Mounted Ballerina
Height: 25.25"
Current Status: Open edition,
permanently retired
Year of Issue: 1974
Last Year: 1981
Rarity: D
Issue Price: $ 350
LCS Estimate: $ 2500

Chapter: 1-15   **No.:** 2012
Form: Decorative plaques
Name: Mounted Harlequin
Height: 21.50"
Current Status: Open edition,
  permanently retired
Year of Issue: 1970
Last Year: 1981
Rarity: E
Issue Price: $ 200
LCS Estimate: $ 1400

Chapter: 1-16   **No.:** 7006
Form: Annual Christmas plates
Name: 1971 Christmas Plate
Height: 8"
Current Status: Limited edition, fully
  subscribed
Year of Issue: 1971
Last Year: 1971
Rarity: B
Issue Price: $ 35
Highest Auction Price: $ 250

Chapter: 1-16   **No.:** 7008
Form: Annual Christmas plates
Name: Christmas Plate 1972
Height: 8"
Current Status: Limited edition, fully
  subscribed
Year of Issue: 1972
Last Year: 1972
Rarity: B
Issue Price: $ 70
Highest Auction Price: $ 225

Chapter: 1-16   **No.:** 7010
Form: Annual Christmas plates
Name: 1973 Christmas Plate
Height: 8"
Current Status: Limited edition, fully
  subscribed
Year of Issue: 1973
Last Year: 1973
Rarity: B
Issue Price: $ 35
Highest Auction Price: $ 200

Chapter: 1-16   **No.:** 7012
Form: Annual Christmas plates
Name: 1974 Christmas Plate
Height: 8"
Current Status: Limited edition, fully
  subscribed
Year of Issue: 1974
Last Year: 1974
Rarity: B
Issue Price: $ 75

Chapter: 1-16   **No.:** 7014
Form: Annual Christmas plates
Name: 1975 Christmas Plate
Height: 8"
Current Status: Limited edition, fully
  subscribed
Year of Issue: 1975
Last Year: 1975
Rarity: B
Issue Price: $ 85

Chapter: 1-16   **No.:** 7016
Form: Annual Christmas plates
Name: 1976 Christmas Plate
Height: 8"
Current Status: Limited edition, fully
  subscribed
Year of Issue: 1976
Last Year: 1976
Rarity: B
Issue Price: $ 65

Chapter: 1-16   **No.:** 7022
Form: Annual Christmas plates
Name: 1977 Christmas Plate
Height: 8"
Current Status: Limited edition, fully
  subscribed
Year of Issue: 1977
Last Year: 1977
Rarity: B
Issue Price: $ 65

Chapter: 1-16   **No.:** 7106
Form: Annual Christmas plates
Name: 1978 Christmas Plate
Height: 8"
Current Status: Limited edition, fully
  subscribed
Year of Issue: 1978
Last Year: 1978
Rarity: B
Issue Price: $ 65

Chapter: 1-16   **No.:** 7108
Form: Annual Christmas plates
Name: 1979 Christmas Plate
Height: 8"
Current Status: Limited edition, fully
  subscribed
Year of Issue: 1979
Last Year: 1979
Rarity: B
Issue Price: $ 55

Chapter: 1-16   **No.:** 7024
Form: Annual Christmas plates
Name: 1980 Christmas Plate
Height: 8"
Current Status: Limited edition, fully
  subscribed
Year of Issue: 1980
Last Year: 1980
Rarity: B
Issue Price: $ 45

Chapter: 1-17   **No.:** 7025
Form: Annual Mothers Day plates
Name: 1971 Mothers Day plate
Height: 8"
Current Status: Limited edition, fully
  subscribed
Year of Issue: 1971
Last Year: 1972
Rarity: B
Issue Price: $ 50

Chapter: 1-17   **No.:** 7007
Form: Annual Mothers Day plates
Name: 1972 Mothers Day plate
Height: 8"
Current Status: Limited edition, fully
  subscribed
Year of Issue: 1972
Last Year: 1972
Rarity: B
Issue Price: $ 70
Highest Auction Price: $ 175

Chapter: 1-17   **No.:** 7009
Form: Annual Mothers Day plates
Name: 1973 Mother's Day plate
Height: 8"
Current Status: Limited edition, fully
  subscribed
Year of Issue: 1973
Last Year: 1974
Rarity: B
Issue Price: $ 70

Chapter: 1-17   **No.:** 7011
Form: Annual Mothers Day plates
Name: 1974 Mothers Day plate
Height: 8"
Current Status: Limited edition, fully
  subscribed
Year of Issue: 1974
Last Year: 1975
Rarity: B
Issue Price: $ 75

Chapter: 1-17   **No.:** 7013
Form: Annual Mothers Day plates
Name: 1975 Mothers Day plate
Height: 8"
Current Status: Limited edition, fully
  subscribed
Year of Issue: 1975
Last Year: 1976
Rarity: B
Issue Price: $ 85

Chapter: 1-17   **No.:** 7015
Form: Annual Mothers Day plates
Name: 1976 Mothers Day plate
Height: 8"
Current Status: Limited edition, fully
  subscribed
Year of Issue: 1976
Last Year: 1977
Rarity: B
Issue Price: $ 65

Chapter: 1-17   **No.:** 7021
Form: Annual Mothers Day plates
Name: 1977 Mothers Day plate
Height: 8"
Current Status: Limited edition, fully
  subscribed
Year of Issue: 1977
Last Year: 1978
Rarity: B
Issue Price: $ 65

Chapter: 1-17   **No.:** 7105
Form: Annual Mothers Day plates
Name: 1978 Mothers Day plate
Height: 8"
Current Status: Limited edition, fully
    subscribed
Year of Issue: 1978
Last Year: 1979
Rarity: B
Issue Price: $ 65

Chapter: 1-17   **No.:** 7107
Form: Annual Mothers Day plates
Name: 1979 Mothers Day plate
Height: 8"
Current Status: Limited edition, fully
    subscribed
Year of Issue: 1979
Last Year: 1980
Rarity: B
Issue Price: $ 55

Chapter: 1-17   **No.:** 7023
Form: Annual Mothers Day plates
Name: 1980 Mothers Day plate
Height: 8"
Current Status: Limited edition, fully
    subscribed
Year of Issue: 1980
Last Year: 1981
Rarity: B
Issue Price: $ 45

Chapter: 1-18   **No.:** 1635
Form: Porcelain Masks
Name: Pansy Mask No. 1
Height: 7"
Current Status: Open edition,
    permanently retired
Year of Issue: 1989
Last Year: 1991
Rarity: B
Issue Price: $ 975
LCS Estimate: $ 975

Chapter: 1-18   **No.:** 1636
Form: Porcelain Masks
Name: Flower Queen Mask No. 2
Height: 6"
Current Status: Open edition,
    permanently retired
Year of Issue: 1989
Last Year: 1991
Rarity: B
Issue Price: $ 660
LCS Estimate: $ 660

Chapter: 1-18   **No.:** 1637
Form: Porcelain Masks
Name: Princess Mask No. 3
Height: 5"
Current Status: Open edition,
    permanently retired
Year of Issue: 1989
Last Year: 1991
Rarity: B
Issue Price: $ 400
LCS Estimate: $ 400

Chapter: 1-18   **No.:** 1638
Form: Porcelain Masks
Name: Celebration Mask No. 4
Height: 5"
Current Status: Open edition,
    permanently retired
Year of Issue: 1989
Last Year: 1991
Rarity: B
Issue Price: $ 700
LCS Estimate: $ 700

Chapter: 1-18   **No.:** 1639
Form: Porcelain Masks
Name: Magician's Mask No. 5
Height: 5.50"
Current Status: Open edition,
    permanently retired
Year of Issue: 1989
Last Year: 1991
Rarity: B
Issue Price: $ 660
LCS Estimate: $ 660

Chapter: 1-18   **No.:** 1640
Form: Porcelain Masks
Name: Fire Dancer Mask No. 6
Height: 6"
Current Status: Open edition,
    permanently retired
Year of Issue: 1989
Last Year: 1991
Rarity: B
Issue Price: $ 530
LCS Estimate: $ 530

Chapter: 1-18   **No.:** 1641
Form: Porcelain Masks
Name: Kaleidoscope Mask No. 7
Height: 5"
Current Status: Open edition,
    permanently retired
Year of Issue: 1989
Last Year: 1991
Rarity: B
Issue Price: $ 725
LCS Estimate: $ 725

Chapter: 1-18   **No.:** 1642
Form: Porcelain Masks
Name: Bat Mask No. 8
Height: 4.25"
Current Status: Open edition,
    permanently retired
Year of Issue: 1989
Last Year: 1991
Rarity: B
Issue Price: $ 690
LCS Estimate: $ 690

Chapter: 1-18   **No.:** 1643
Form: Porcelain Masks
Name: Bird of Paradise No. 9
Height: 4.75"
Current Status: Open edition,
    permanently retired
Year of Issue: 1989
Last Year: 1991
Rarity: B
Issue Price: $ 490
LCS Estimate: $ 490

Chapter: 1-18   **No.:** 1644
Form: Porcelain Masks
Name: Cat Eyes Mask No. 10
Height: 4.25"
Current Status: Open edition,
   permanently retired
Year of Issue: 1989
Last Year: 1991
Rarity: B
Issue Price: $ 465
LCS Estimate: $ 465

Chapter: 1-18   **No.:** 1645
Form: Porcelain Masks
Name: Snow Queen Mask No. 11
Height: 4.25"
Current Status: Open edition,
   permanently retired
Year of Issue: 1989
Last Year: 1991
Rarity: B
Issue Price: $ 390
LCS Estimate: $ 390

Chapter: 1-19   **No.:** 2.01
Form: Other decorated plates, not
   Christmas or Mothers Day
Name: Village
Height: 9.50"
Current Status: Very rare early issue
Year of Issue: 1942
Last Year: Not available
Rarity: A
Issue Price: Not available
Comments: Created personally by Jose
   Lladró

Chapter: 1-19   **No.:** 44.03
Form: Other decorated plates, not
   Christmas or Mothers Day
Name: Man's Portrait
Height: 7.50"
Current Status: Very rare early issue
Year of Issue: 1949
Last Year: Not available
Rarity: A
Issue Price: Not available
Comments: Created personally by Jose
   Lladró

Chapter: 1-19   **No.:** 41.03
Form: Other decorated plates, not
   Christmas or Mothers Day
Name: Serenade
Height: 13.25"
Current Status: Very rare early issue
Year of Issue: 1949
Last Year: Not available
Rarity: A
Issue Price: Not available
Comments: Created personally by Jose
   Lladró

Chapter: 1-19   **No.:** 31.02
Form: Other decorated plates, not
   Christmas or Mothers Day
Name: Horse and Dogs Plate
Height: 13.75"
Current Status: Very rare early issue
Year of Issue: 1944
Last Year: Not available
Rarity: A
Issue Price: Not available
Comments: Created personally by Jose
   Lladró

Chapter: 1-19   **No.:** 27.02
Form: Other decorated plates, not
  Christmas or Mothers Day
Name: Don Quixote
Height: 15.50"
Current Status: Very rare early issue
Year of Issue: 1949
Last Year: Not available
Rarity: A
Issue Price: Not available
Comments: Created personally by Jose
  Lladró

Chapter: 1-19   **No.:** 21.02
Form: Other decorated plates, not
  Christmas or Mothers Day
Name: Boy's Portrait
Height: 13.50"
Current Status: Very rare early issue
Year of Issue: 1943
Last Year: Not available
Rarity: A
Issue Price: Not available
Comments: Created personally by Jose
  Lladró

Chapter: 1-19   **No.:** 18.02
Form: Other decorated plates, not
  Christmas or Mothers Day
Name: The Round Plate
Height: 9.50"
Current Status: Very rare early issue
Year of Issue: 1946
Last Year: Not available
Rarity: A
Issue Price: Not available
Comments: Created personally by Jose
  Lladró

Chapter: 1-19   **No.:** 15.02
Form: Other decorated plates, not
  Christmas or Mothers Day
Name: Waiting for Daddy
Height: 13.25"
Current Status: Very rare early issue
Year of Issue: 1945
Last Year: Not available
Rarity: A
Issue Price: Not available
Comments: Created personally by Jose
  Lladró

Chapter: 1-19   **No.:** 13.02
Form: Other decorated plates, not
  Christmas or Mothers Day
Name: Waiting
Height: 11.50"
Current Status: Very rare early issue
Year of Issue: 1943
Last Year: Not available
Rarity: A
Issue Price: Not available
Comments: Created personally by Jose
  Lladró

Chapter: 1-19   **No.:** 12.02
Form: Other decorated plates, not
  Christmas or Mothers Day
Name: Surprised Cat
Height: 7.50"
Current Status: Very rare early issue
Year of Issue: 1943
Last Year: Not available
Rarity: A
Issue Price: Not available
Comments: Created personally by Jose
  Lladró

Chapter: 1-19   **No.:** 11.02
Form: Other decorated plates, not Christmas or Mothers Day
Name: Old Salts
Height: 10.25"
Current Status: Very rare early issue
Year of Issue: 1944
Last Year: Not available
Rarity: A
Issue Price: Not available
Comments: Created personally by Jose Lladró

Chapter: 1-19   **No.:** 42.03
Form: Other decorated plates, not Christmas or Mothers Day
Name: Young Man's Portrait
Height: 9.50"
Current Status: Very rare early issue
Year of Issue: 1948
Last Year: Not available
Rarity: A
Issue Price: Not available
Comments: Created personally by Jose Lladró

Chapter: 1-20   **No.:** 5956
Form: Collector Bells
Name: Sounds of Spring
Height: 4.75"
Current Status: Open edition, currently active
Year of Issue: 1993
Issue Price: $ 150

Chapter: 1-20   **No.:** 5953
Form: Collector Bells
Name: Sounds of Summer
Height: 4.75"
Current Status: Open edition, currently active
Year of Issue: 1993
Issue Price: $ 150

Chapter: 1-20   **No.:** 5955
Form: Collector Bells
Name: Sounds of Fall
Height: 4.50"
Current Status: Open edition, currently active
Year of Issue: 1993
Issue Price: $ 150

Chapter: 1-20   **No.:** 5954
Form: Collector Bells
Name: Sounds of Winter
Height: 4.50"
Current Status: Open edition, currently active
Year of Issue: 1993
Issue Price: $ 150

Chapter: 1-20   **No.:** 5458
Form: Collector Bells
Name: 1987 Christmas Bell
Height: 2.75"
Current Status: Limited edition, fully
  subscribed
Year of Issue: 1987
Last Year: 1987
Rarity: B
Issue Price: $ 29.50

Chapter: 1-20   **No.:** 5525
Form: Collector Bells
Name: Christmas Bell 1988
Height: 3"
Current Status: Limited edition, fully
  subscribed
Year of Issue: 1988
Last Year: 1988
Issue Price: $ 32.50

Chapter: 1-20   **No.:** 5616
Form: Collector Bells
Name: 1989 Christmas Bell
Height: 3"
Current Status: Limited edition, fully
  subscribed
Year of Issue: 1989
Last Year: 1989
Issue Price: $ 35
Highest Auction Price: $ 150

Chapter: 1-20   **No.:** 5641
Form: Collector Bells
Name: 1990 Christmas Bell
Height: 2.75"
Current Status: Limited edition, fully
  subscribed
Year of Issue: 1990
Last Year: 1990
Issue Price: $ 35

Chapter: 1-20   **No.:** 5803
Form: Collector Bells
Name: 1991 Christmas Bell
Height: 2.75"
Current Status: Limited edition, fully
  subscribed
Year of Issue: 1991
Last Year: 1991
Issue Price: $ 37.50

Chapter: 1-20   **No.:** 5913
Form: Collector Bells
Name: 1992 Christmas Bell
Height: 2.75"
Current Status: Limited edition, fully
  subscribed
Year of Issue: 1992
Last Year: 1992
Issue Price: $37.50

Chapter: 1-20   **No.:** 6010
Form: Collector Bells
Name: 1993 Christmas Bell
Height: 3"
Current Status: Limited edition,
  currently active
Year of Issue: 1993
Last Year: 1993
Issue Price: $

Chapter: 1-20   **No.:** 5264
Form: Collector Bells
Name: Bell - Decorated
Height: 4.75"
Current Status: Open edition,
  permanently retired
Year of Issue: 1984
Last Year: 1990
Rarity: D
Issue Price: $ 50
LCS Estimate: $ 100

Chapter: 1-20   **No.:** 5264.30
Form: Collector Bells
Name: Bell
Height: 4.75"
Current Status: Open edition,
  permanently retired
Year of Issue: 1984
Last Year: 1988
Rarity: C
Issue Price: $ 50
LCS Estimate: $ 150

Chapter: 1-21   **No.:** 5992
Form: Clocks
Name: Time For Love
Height: 9.75"
Current Status: Open edition, currently
  active
Year of Issue: 1993
Issue Price: $ 800

Chapter: 1-21   **No.:** 5776
Form: Clocks
Name: Two Sisters Clock
Height: 6"
Current Status: Open edition, currently
  active
Year of Issue: 1991
Issue Price: $ 400
Current Price: $ 420

Chapter: 1-21   **No.:** 5777
Form: Clocks
Name: Swan Clock
Height: 7.25"
Current Status: Open edition, currently
  active
Year of Issue: 1991
Issue Price: $ 425
Current Price: $ 440

Chapter: 1-21   **No.:** 5778
Form: Clocks
Name: Pierrot Clock
Height: 8.50"
Current Status: Open edition, currently active
Year of Issue: 1991
Issue Price: $ 400
Current Price: $ 420

Chapter: 1-21   **No.:** 5973
Form: Clocks
Name: Angelic Time
Height: 11.50"
Current Status: Open edition, currently active
Year of Issue: 1993
Issue Price: $ 1100

Chapter: 1-21   **No.:** 5970
Form: Clocks
Name: Bow Clock
Height: 5.50"
Current Status: Open edition, currently active
Year of Issue: 1993
Issue Price: $ 270

Chapter: 1-21   **No.:** 5655.30
Form: Clocks
Name: Diamond Clock
Height: 3"
Current Status: Open edition, currently active
Year of Issue: 1990
Issue Price: $ 100
Current Price: $ 120

Chapter: 1-21   **No.:** 5652
Form: Clocks
Name: Marbella Clock
Height: 3"
Current Status: Open edition, currently active
Year of Issue: 1989
Issue Price: $ 125
Current Price: $ 140

Chapter: 1-21   **No.:** 5653
Form: Clocks
Name: Avila Clock
Height: 2.75"
Current Status: Open edition, currently active
Year of Issue: 1989
Issue Price: $ 125
Current Price: $ 140

Chapter: 1-21   **No.:** 5653.10
Form: Clocks
Name: Garland Clock (Large)
Height: 5.75"
Current Status: Open edition, currently active
Year of Issue: 1990
Issue Price: $ 160
Current Price: $ 180

Chapter: 1-21   **No.:** 5654
Form: Clocks
Name: Valencia Clock
Height: 5"
Current Status: Open edition, currently active
Year of Issue: 1989
Issue Price: $ 175
Current Price: $ 180

Chapter: 1-21   **No.:** 5654.30
Form: Clocks
Name: Floral Clock
Height: 3.25"
Current Status: Open edition, currently active
Year of Issue: 1990
Issue Price: $ 100
Current Price: $ 120

Chapter: 1-21   **No.:** 5655
Form: Clocks
Name: Segovia Clock
Height: 5.75"
Current Status: Open edition, currently active
Year of Issue: 1989
Issue Price: $ 175
Current Price: $ 195

Chapter: 1-22   **No.:** 1562.30
Form: Porcelain Women's Hats
Name: Medium Pink Broad-brimmed Hat
Height: 1.50"
Current Status: Open edition, permanently retired
Year of Issue: 1987
Last Year: 1991
Rarity: C
Issue Price: $ 80
LCS Estimate: $ 80

Chapter: 1-22   **No.:** 1564.30
Form: Porcelain Women's Hats
Name: Small Blue Hat with Ridges
Height: 1"
Current Status: Open edition, permanently retired
Year of Issue: 1987
Last Year: 1991
Rarity: C
Issue Price: $ 45
LCS Estimate: $ 45

Chapter: 1-22   **No.:** 1565
Form: Porcelain Women's Hats
Name: Feathered Pink Hat
Height: 1"
Current Status: Open edition,
  permanently retired
Year of Issue: 1987
Last Year: 1991
Rarity: C
Issue Price: $ 30
LCS Estimate: $ 30

Chapter: 1-22   **No.:** 1569
Form: Porcelain Women's Hats
Name: Lace Soft Hat
Height: 2"
Current Status: Open edition,
  permanently retired
Year of Issue: 1987
Last Year: 1991
Rarity: C
Issue Price: $ 45
LCS Estimate: $ 45

Chapter: 1-22   **No.:** 1570
Form: Porcelain Women's Hats
Name: Closed Hat with Blue Ribbon
Height: 2.25"
Current Status: Open edition,
  permanently retired
Year of Issue: 1987
Last Year: 1991
Rarity: C
Issue Price: $ 45
LCS Estimate: $ 45

Chapter: 1-22   **No.:** 1571
Form: Porcelain Women's Hats
Name: Pink and Blue Flying Hat
Height: 2.25"
Current Status: Open edition,
  permanently retired
Year of Issue: 1987
Last Year: 1991
Rarity: C
Issue Price: $ 65
LCS Estimate: $ 65

Chapter: 1-22   **No.:** 1564
Form: Porcelain Women's Hats
Name: Small Pink Hat with Ridges
Height: 1"
Current Status: Open edition,
  permanently retired
Year of Issue: 1987
Last Year: 1991
Rarity: C
Issue Price: $ 45
LCS Estimate: $ 45

Chapter: 1-22   **No.:** 1565.30
Form: Porcelain Women's Hats
Name: Feathered Blue Hat
Height: 1"
Current Status: Open edition,
  permanently retired
Year of Issue: 1987
Last Year: 1991
Rarity: C
Issue Price: $ 30
LCS Estimate: $ 30

Chapter: 1-22   **No.:** 1563
Form: Porcelain Women's Hats
Name: Small Blue Broad Brimmed Hat
Height: 1"
Current Status: Open edition,
   permanently retired
Year of Issue: 1987
Last Year: 1991
Rarity: C
Issue Price: $ 45
LCS Estimate: $ 45

Chapter: 1-22   **No.:** 1560
Form: Porcelain Women's Hats
Name: Plain Hat
Height: .75"
Current Status: Open edition,
   permanently retired
Year of Issue: 1987
Last Year: 1991
Rarity: C
Issue Price: $ 35
LCS Estimate: $ 35

Chapter: 1-22   **No.:** 1563.30
Form: Porcelain Women's Hats
Name: Small Pink Broad Brimmed Hat
Height: 1"
Current Status: Open edition,
   permanently retired
Year of Issue: 1987
Last Year: 1991
Rarity: C
Issue Price: $ 45
LCS Estimate: $ 45

Chapter: 1-22   **No.:** 1561
Form: Porcelain Women's Hats
Name: White Hat with Blue Ribbon
Height: 1"
Current Status: Open edition,
   permanently retired
Year of Issue: 1987
Last Year: 1991
Rarity: C
Issue Price: $ 40
LCS Estimate: $ 40

Chapter: 1-22   **No.:** 1561.30
Form: Porcelain Women's Hats
Name: Pink Hat with White Ribbon
Height: 1.50"
Current Status: Open edition,
   permanently retired
Year of Issue: 1987
Last Year: 1991
Rarity: C
Issue Price: $ 40
LCS Estimate: $ 40

Chapter: 1-22   **No.:** 1562
Form: Porcelain Women's Hats
Name: Medium White Broad Brimmed
   Hat
Height: 1.50"
Current Status: Open edition,
   permanently retired
Year of Issue: 1987
Last Year: 1991
Rarity: C
Issue Price: $ 80
LCS Estimate: $ 80

Chapter: 1-23   **No.:** 1673
Form: Decorated Porcelain Butterflies
Name: Lacy Butterfly No. 1
Height: 3"
Current Status: Open edition,
  permanently retired
Year of Issue: 1989
Last Year: 1991
Rarity: B
Issue Price: $ 95
LCS Estimate: $ 95

Chapter: 1-23   **No.:** 1674
Form: Decorated Porcelain Butterflies
Name: Beautiful Butterfly No. 2
Height: 3.25"
Current Status: Open edition,
  permanently retired
Year of Issue: 1989
Last Year: 1991
Rarity: B
Issue Price: $ 100
LCS Estimate: $ 100

Chapter: 1-23   **No.:** 1675
Form: Decorated Porcelain Butterflies
Name: Black Butterfly No. 3
Height: 2.25"
Current Status: Open edition,
  permanently retired
Year of Issue: 1989
Last Year: 1991
Rarity: B
Issue Price: $ 120
LCS Estimate: $ 120

Chapter: 1-23   **No.:** 1676
Form: Decorated Porcelain Butterflies
Name: Pink and White Butterfly No. 4
Height: 2"
Current Status: Open edition,
  permanently retired
Year of Issue: 1989
Last Year: 1991
Rarity: B
Issue Price: $ 100
LCS Estimate: $ 100

Chapter: 1-23   **No.:** 1677
Form: Decorated Porcelain Butterflies
Name: Black and White Butterfly No. 5
Height: 1.50"
Current Status: Open edition,
  permanently retired
Year of Issue: 1989
Last Year: 1991
Rarity: B
Issue Price: $ 100
LCS Estimate: $ 100

Chapter: 1-23   **No.:** 1678
Form: Decorated Porcelain Butterflies
Name: Large Pink Butterfly No. 6
Height: 3"
Current Status: Open edition,
  permanently retired
Year of Issue: 1989
Last Year: 1991
Rarity: B
Issue Price: $ 100
LCS Estimate: $ 100

Chapter: 1-23   **No.:** 1679
Form: Decorated Porcelain Butterflies
Name: Pink and Blue Butterfly No. 7
Height: 1.25"
Current Status: Open edition,
  permanently retired
Year of Issue: 1989
Last Year: 1991
Rarity: B
Issue Price: $ 80
LCS Estimate: $ 80

Chapter: 1-23   **No.:** 1680
Form: Decorated Porcelain Butterflies
Name: Small Pink Butterfly No. 8
Height: 1.50"
Current Status: Open edition,
  permanently retired
Year of Issue: 1989
Last Year: 1991
Rarity: B
Issue Price: $ 72.50
LCS Estimate: $ 72.50

Chapter: 1-23   **No.:** 1681
Form: Decorated Porcelain Butterflies
Name: Blue Butterfly No. 9
Height: 4"
Current Status: Open edition,
  permanently retired
Year of Issue: 1989
Last Year: 1991
Rarity: B
Issue Price: $ 185
LCS Estimate: $ 185

Chapter: 1-23   **No.:** 1682
Form: Decorated Porcelain Butterflies
Name: Pretty Butterfly No. 10
Height: 4"
Current Status: Open edition,
  permanently retired
Year of Issue: 1989
Last Year: 1991
Rarity: B
Issue Price: $ 185
LCS Estimate: $ 185

Chapter: 1-23   **No.:** 1683
Form: Decorated Porcelain Butterflies
Name: Spotted Butterfly No. 11
Height: 3"
Current Status: Open edition,
  permanently retired
Year of Issue: 1989
Last Year: 1991
Rarity: B
Issue Price: $ 175
LCS Estimate: $ 175

Chapter: 1-23   **No.:** 1684
Form: Decorated Porcelain Butterflies
Name: Leopard Butterfly No. 12
Height: 3"
Current Status: Open edition,
  permanently retired
Year of Issue: 1989
Last Year: 1991
Rarity: B
Issue Price: $ 165
LCS Estimate: $ 165

Chapter: 1-23   **No.:** 1685
Form: Decorated Porcelain Butterflies
Name: Great Butterfly No. 13
Height: 2.75"
Current Status: Open edition,
   permanently retired
Year of Issue: 1989
Last Year: 1991
Rarity: B
Issue Price: $ 150
LCS Estimate: $ 150

Chapter: 1-23   **No.:** 1686
Form: Decorated Porcelain Butterflies
Name: Queen Butterfly No. 14
Height: 2.75"
Current Status: Open edition,
   permanently retired
Year of Issue: 1989
Last Year: 1991
Rarity: B
Issue Price: $ 125
LCS Estimate: $ 125

Chapter: 1-24   **No.:** 1603
Form: Christmas Ornaments, Limited
   and Open Editions
Name: 1988 Christmas Ball
Height: 4"
Current Status: Limited edition, fully
   subscribed
Year of Issue: 1988
Last Year: 1988
Rarity: B
Issue Price: $ 60
Highest Auction Price: $ 75

Chapter: 1-24   **No.:** 5656
Form: Christmas Ornaments
Name: 1989 Christmas Ball
Height: 4"
Current Status: Limited edition, fully
   subscribed
Year of Issue: 1989
Last Year: 1989
Issue Price: $ 65
Highest Auction Price: $ 75

Chapter: 1-24   **No.:** 5730
Form: Christmas Ornaments, Limited
   and Open Editions
Name: 1990 Christmas Ball
Height: 4"
Current Status: Limited edition, fully
   subscribed
Year of Issue: 1990
Last Year: 1990
Issue Price: $ 70
Highest Auction Price: $ 75

Chapter: 1-24   **No.:** 5829
Form: Christmas Ornaments, Limited
   and Open Editions
Name: 1991 Christmas Ball
Height: 4"
Current Status: Limited edition, fully
   subscribed
Year of Issue: 1991
Last Year: 1991
Issue Price: $ 52.00

Chapter: 1-24   **No.:** 5914
Form: Christmas Ornaments, Limited and Open Editions
Name: 1992 Christmas Ball
Height: 4"
Current Status: Limited edition, fully subscribed
Year of Issue: 1992
Last Year: 1992
Issue Price: $ 52

Chapter: 1-24   **No.:** 6009
Form: Christmas Ornaments, Limited and Open Editions
Name: 1993 Christmas Ball
Height: 4"
Current Status: Limited edition, currently active
Year of Issue: 1993
Last Year: 1993
Issue Price: $

Chapter: 1-24   **No.:** 1604
Form: Christmas Ornaments, Limited and Open Editions
Name: Angels
Height: 2"
Current Status: Limited edition, fully subscribed
Year of Issue: 1988
Last Year: 1988
Issue Price: $ 75
Highest Auction Price: $ 108
Comments: Set of three

Chapter: 1-24   **No.:** 5657
Form: Christmas Ornaments, Limited and Open Editions
Name: Miniature ornaments portraying the Holy Family
Height: 4.50"
Current Status: Limited edition, fully subscribed
Year of Issue: 1989
Last Year: 1989
Issue Price: $ 79.50
Highest Auction Price: $ 109
LCS Estimate: $ 175
Comments: Set of three ornaments

Chapter: 1-24   **No.:** 5729
Form: Christmas Ornaments, Limited and Open Editions
Name: Three Kings Ornament
Height: 4.25"
Current Status: Limited edition, fully subscribed
Year of Issue: 1990
Last Year: 1990
Issue Price: $ 87.50
Highest Auction Price: $ 108
Comments: Set of three ornaments

Chapter: 1-24   **No.:** 5809
Form: Christmas Ornaments, Limited and Open Editions
Name: Holy Shepherds
Height: 3.25"
Current Status: Limited edition, fully subscribed
Year of Issue: 1991
Last Year: 1991
Issue Price: $ 97.50

Chapter: 1-24   **No.:** 5842
Form: Christmas Ornaments, Limited
    and Open Editions
Name: Santa Ornament
Height: 4.75"
Current Status: Open issue,
    permanently retired
Year of Issue: 1992
Last Year: 1993
Issue Price: $ 55
Last Retail Price: $ 57

Chapter: 1-24   **No.:** 5841
Form: Christmas Ornaments, Limited
    and Open Editions
Name: Snowman Ornament
Height: 4"
Current Status: Open issue,
    permanently retired
Year of Issue: 1992
Last Year: 1993
Issue Price: $ 50
Last Retail Price: $ 52

Chapter: 1-24   **No.:** 5922
Form: Christmas Ornaments, Limited
    and Open Editions
Name: Baby's First Christmas - 1992
Height: 5.25"
Current Status: Limited edition, fully
    subscribed
Year of Issue: 1992
Last Year: 1992
Issue Price: $ 55

Chapter: 1-24   **No.:** 5923
Form: Christmas Ornaments, Limited
    and Open Editions
Name: Our First Christmas - 1992
Height: 2"
Current Status: Limited edition, fully
    subscribed
Year of Issue: 1992
Last Year: 1992
Issue Price: $ 50

Chapter: 1-24   **No.:** 5938
Form: Christmas Ornaments, Limited
    and Open Editions
Name: Elf Ornament
Height: 3"
Current Status: Open issue,
    permanently retired
Year of Issue: 1992
Last Year: 1993
Issue Price: $ 50
Last Retail Price: $ 52

Chapter: 1-24   **No.:** 5939
Form: Christmas Ornaments, Limited
    and Open Editions
Name: Mrs. Claus Ornament
Height: 4.50"
Current Status: Open issue,
    permanently retired
Year of Issue: 1992
Last Year: 1993
Issue Price: $ 55
Last Retail Price: $ 57

Chapter: 1-24   **No.:** 5940
Form: Christmas Ornaments, Limited and Open Editions
Name: Christmas Morning
Height: 3.25"
Current Status: Open edition, currently active
Year of Issue: 1992
Issue Price: $ 97.50
Current Price: $ 97.50

Chapter: 1-24   **No.:** 5969
Form: Christmas Ornaments, Limited and Open Editions
Name: Nativity Lamb
Height: 3"
Current Status: Open issue, permanently retired
Year of Issue: 1993
Last Year: 1993
Issue Price: $ 85

Chapter: 1-25   **No.:** 1649
Form: Porcelain Crosses and Rosaries
Name: Floral Cross No. 1
Height: 2.75"
Current Status: Open edition, permanently retired
Year of Issue: 1989
Last Year: 1991
Rarity: B
Issue Price: $ 300
LCS Estimate: $ 300

Chapter: 1-25   **No.:** 1650
Form: Porcelain Crosses and Rosaries
Name: Floral Cross No. 2
Height: 2.75"
Current Status: Open edition, permanently retired
Year of Issue: 1989
Last Year: 1991
Rarity: B
Issue Price: $ 230
LCS Estimate: $ 230

Chapter: 1-25   **No.:** 1651
Form: Porcelain Crosses and Rosaries
Name: Roses Cross No. 3
Height: 2"
Current Status: Open edition, permanently retired
Year of Issue: 1989
Last Year: 1991
Rarity: B
Issue Price: $ 200
LCS Estimate: $ 200

Chapter: 1-25   **No.:** 1652
Form: Porcelain Crosses and Rosaries
Name: Medieval Cross No. 4
Height: 2.75"
Current Status: Open edition, permanently retired
Year of Issue: 1989
Last Year: 1991
Rarity: B
Issue Price: $ 250
LCS Estimate: $ 250

Chapter: 1-25   **No.:** 1653
Form: Porcelain Crosses and Rosaries
Name: Baroque Cross No. 5
Height: 2.75"
Current Status: Open edition,
   permanently retired
Year of Issue: 1989
Last Year: 1991
Rarity: B
Issue Price: $ 215
LCS Estimate: $ 215

Chapter: 1-25   **No.:** 1654
Form: Porcelain Crosses and Rosaries
Name: Cross of Hearts No. 6
Height: 2.25"
Current Status: Open edition,
   permanently retired
Year of Issue: 1989
Last Year: 1991
Rarity: B
Issue Price: $ 220
LCS Estimate: $ 220

Chapter: 1-25   **No.:** 1655
Form: Porcelain Crosses and Rosaries
Name: Romantic Cross No. 7
Height: 2"
Current Status: Open edition,
   permanently retired
Year of Issue: 1989
Last Year: 1991
Rarity: B
Issue Price: $ 115
LCS Estimate: $ 115

Chapter: 1-25   **No.:** 1656
Form: Porcelain Crosses and Rosaries
Name: Ornate Cross No. 8
Height: 2"
Current Status: Open edition,
   permanently retired
Year of Issue: 1989
Last Year: 1991
Rarity: B
Issue Price: $ 125
LCS Estimate: $ 125

Chapter: 1-25   **No.:** 1657
Form: Porcelain Crosses and Rosaries
Name: Renaissance Cross No. 9
Height: 2"
Current Status: Open edition,
   permanently retired
Year of Issue: 1989
Last Year: 1991
Rarity: B
Issue Price: $ 115
LCS Estimate: $ 115

Chapter: 1-25   **No.:** 1658
Form: Porcelain Crosses and Rosaries
Name: Simplicity Cross No. 10
Height: 2"
Current Status: Open edition,
   permanently retired
Year of Issue: 1989
Last Year: 1991
Rarity: B
Issue Price: $ 155
LCS Estimate: $ 155

Chapter: 1-25 **No.:** 1659
Form: Porcelain Crosses and Rosaries
Name: Cross of Lilies No. 11
Height: 2"
Current Status: Open edition,
 permanently retired
Year of Issue: 1989
Last Year: 1991
Rarity: B
Issue Price: $ 185
LCS Estimate: $ 185

Chapter: 1-25 **No.:** 1660
Form: Porcelain Crosses and Rosaries
Name: Cross of Diamonds No. 12
Height: 2"
Current Status: Open edition,
 permanently retired
Year of Issue: 1989
Last Year: 1991
Rarity: B
Issue Price: $ 135
LCS Estimate: $ 135

Chapter: 1-25 **No.:** 1647
Form: Porcelain Crosses and Rosaries
Name: White Rosary
Height: 2.25"
Current Status: Open edition,
 permanently retired
Year of Issue: 1989
Last Year: 1991
Rarity: B
Issue Price: $ 290
LCS Estimate: $ 290

Chapter: 1-25 **No.:** 1648
Form: Porcelain Crosses and Rosaries
Name: Gray Rosary
Height: 2.25"
Current Status: Open edition,
 permanently retired
Year of Issue: 1989
Last Year: 1991
Rarity: B
Issue Price: $ 300
LCS Estimate: $ 300

Chapter: 1-25 **No.:** 1646
Form: Porcelain Crosses and Rosaries
Name: Violet Rosary
Height: 2.25"
Current Status: Open edition,
 permanently retired
Year of Issue: 1989
Last Year: 1991
Rarity: B
Issue Price: $ 325
LCS Estimate: $ 325

Chapter: 1-26 **No.:** 3.01
Form: Decorated Ceramic Tiles
Name: Fantasy
Height: 11"
Current Status: Very rare early issue
Year of Issue: 1941
Last Year: Not available
Rarity: A
Issue Price: Not available
Comments: Created personally by Juan
 Lladró

Chapter: 1-26   **No.:** 5.01
Form: Decorated Ceramic Tiles
Name: Advice to Sancho
Height: 9.75"
Current Status: Very rare early issue
Year of Issue: 1944
Last Year: Not available
Rarity: A
Issue Price: Not available
Comments: Created personally by Juan Lladró

Chapter: 1-26   **No.:** 4.01
Form: Decorated Ceramic Tiles
Name: Acrobats
Height: 11.50"
Current Status: Very rare early issue
Year of Issue: 1944
Last Year: Not available
Rarity: A
Issue Price: Not available
Comments: Created personally by Juan Lladró

Chapter: 1-26   **No.:** 1.01
Form: Decorated Ceramic Tiles
Name: Contemplation
Height: 8.25"
Current Status: Very rare early issue
Year of Issue: 1944
Last Year: Not available
Rarity: A
Issue Price: Not available
Comments: Created personally by Jose Lladró

Chapter: 1-26   **No.:** 14.02
Form: Decorated Ceramic Tiles
Name: Returning Home
Height: 9"
Current Status: Very rare early issue
Year of Issue: 1945
Last Year: Not available
Rarity: A
Issue Price: Not available
Comments: Created personally by Juan Lladró

Chapter: 1-26   **No.:** 19.02
Form: Decorated Ceramic Tiles
Name: The Square Plate
Height: 7.50"
Current Status: Very rare early issue
Year of Issue: 1946
Last Year: Not available
Rarity: A
Issue Price: Not available
Comments: Created personally by Juan Lladró

Chapter: 1-26   **No.:** 17.02
Form: Decorated Ceramic Tiles
Name: The Portrait
Height: 7.25"
Current Status: Very rare early issue
Year of Issue: 1946
Last Year: Not available
Rarity: A
Issue Price: Not available
Comments: Created personally by Juan Lladró

Chapter: 1-26   **No.:** 16.02
Form: Decorated Ceramic Tiles
Name: The Umbrella
Height: 7.25"
Current Status: Very rare early issue
Year of Issue: 1946
Last Year: Not available
Rarity: A
Issue Price: Not available
Comments: Created personally by Juan
  Lladró

Chapter: 1-26   **No.:** 25.02
Form: Decorated Ceramic Tiles
Name: Tenderness
Height: 7.50"
Current Status: Very rare early issue
Year of Issue: 1946
Last Year: Not available
Rarity: A
Issue Price: Not available
Comments: Created personally by Juan
  Lladró

Chapter: 1-26   **No.:** 22.02
Form: Decorated Ceramic Tiles
Name: Lady's Portrait
Height: 7.50"
Current Status: Very rare early issue
Year of Issue: 1947
Last Year: Not available
Rarity: A
Issue Price: Not available
Comments: Created personally by Jose
  Lladró

Chapter: 1-26   **No.:** 20.02
Form: Decorated Ceramic Tiles
Name: Flower Vase
Height: 7.50"
Current Status: Very rare early issue
Year of Issue: 1947
Last Year: Not available
Rarity: A
Issue Price: Not available
Comments: Created personally by Jose
  Lladró

Chapter: 1-26   **No.:** 26.02
Form: Decorated Ceramic Tiles
Name: Portrait of an Artis
Height: 4.50"
Current Status: Very rare early issue
Year of Issue: 1948
Last Year: Not available
Rarity: A
Issue Price: Not available
Comments: Created personally by Juan
  Lladró

Chapter: 1-26   **No.:** 24.02
Form: Decorated Ceramic Tiles
Name: Lover
Height: 4.25"
Current Status: Very rare early issue
Year of Issue: 1948
Last Year: Not available
Rarity: A
Issue Price: Not available
Comments: Created personally by Juan
  Lladró

Chapter: 1-26   **No.:** 23.02
Form: Decorated Ceramic Tiles
Name: Jesus
Height: 5"
Current Status: Very rare early issue
Year of Issue: 1949
Last Year: Not available
Rarity: A
Issue Price: Not available
Comments: Created personally by Juan
   Lladró

Chapter: 1-26   **No.:** 29.02
Form: Decorated Ceramic Tiles
Name: Nobleman
Height: 3.75"
Current Status: Very rare early issue
Year of Issue: 1949
Last Year: Not available
Rarity: A
Issue Price: Not available
Comments: Created personally by Jose
   Lladró

Chapter: 1-26   **No.:** 28.02
Form: Decorated Ceramic Tiles
Name: Old Man
Height: 7.25"
Current Status: Very rare early issue
Year of Issue: 1949
Last Year: Not available
Rarity: A
Issue Price: Not available
Comments: Created personally by Jose
   Lladró

No. 4737—Lladró Fruit Bowl, *issued in 1970 and permanently retired in 1972.*

No. 4694—Fish Centerpiece, introduced in 1970 and permanently retired in 1974: auctioned for $425.

For purposes of this volume, we are classifying bowls, centerpieces and dishes as all those pieces that are larger at their neck than at their body. This classification separates all receptacles from vases, urns and jugs that are smaller at their necks than at their bodies. These bowls are further classified by their height, from shortest to highest, and from shortest to tallest.

Bowls, Centerpieces and Dishes

No.: 53.04
Name: Bon-bon Dish
Height: 2
Current Status: Early edition, very rare
Original Issue Year: 1952
Last Year: Not Available
Rarity: Very early, very rare
Issue Price: Not available

No.: 5268
Name: Centerpiece - Decorated
Height: 2
Current status: Open edition,
  permanently retired
Original Issue Year: 1984
Last Year: 1990
Rarity: D
Issue Price: $ 60
LCS Estimate: $ 120

No.: 5268.30
Name: Centerpiece
Height: 2
Current status: Open edition,
  permanently retired
Original Issue Year: 1984
Last Year: 1988
Rarity: C
Issue Price: $ 60
LCS Estimate: $ 180

No.: 5265.30
Name: Centerpiece
Height: 2
Current status: Open edition,
  permanently retired
Original Issue Year: 1984
Last Year: 1988
Rarity: C
Issue Price: $ 50
LCS Estimate: $ 150

No.: 5265
Name: Centerpiece - Decorated
Height: 2
Current status: Open edition,
  permanently retired
Original Issue Year: 1984
Last Year: 1990
Rarity: D
Issue Price: $ 50
LCS Estimate: $ 100

No.: 4737
Name: Fruit Bowl
Height: 4
Current status: Open edition,
  permanently retired
Original Issue Year: 1970
Last Year: 1972
Rarity: B
Issue Price: $ 15
LCS Estimate: $ 165

No.: 4737.30
Name: Fruit Bowl
Height: 4
Current status: Open edition,
    permanently retired
Original Issue Year: 1970
Last Year: 1972
Rarity: B
Issue Price: $ 12
LCS Estimate: $ 130

No.: 4797
Name: Damask Gray Centerpiece
Height: 4
Current status: Open edition,
    permanently retired
Original Issue Year: 1972
Last Year: 1973
Rarity: B
Issue Price: $ 25
LCS Estimate: $ 275

No.: 4796
Name: Damask Green Centerpiece
Height: 4
Current status: Open edition,
    permanently retired
Original Issue Year: 1972
Last Year: 1973
Rarity: B
Issue Price: $ 25
LCS Estimate: $ 275

No.: 1168.30
Name: Bowl with Flowers, White
Height: 4.75
Current status: Open edition,
    permanently retired
Original Issue Year: 1971
Last Year: 1978
Rarity: D
Issue Price: $ 12.50
LCS Estimate: $ 100

No.: 1168
Name: Bowl with Flowers
Height: 4.75
Current status: Open edition,
    permanently retired
Original Issue Year: 1971
Last Year: 1979
Rarity: E
Issue Price: $ 22.50
LCS Estimate: $ 180

No.: 4736
Name: Star Centerpiece
Height: 5
Current status: Open edition,
    permanently retired
Original Issue Year: 1970
Last Year: 1972
Rarity: B
Issue Price: $ 35
LCS Estimate: $ 400

No.: 4736.30
Name: Star Centerpiece
Height: 5
Current status: Open edition,
    permanently retired
Original Issue Year: 1970
Last Year: 1972
Rarity: B
Issue Price: $ 30
LCS Estimate: $ 350

No.: 4724.30
Name: Star Centerpiece, White
Height: 5.50
Current status: Open edition,
    permanently retired
Original Issue Year: 1970
Last Year: 1972
Rarity: B
Issue Price: $ 35
LCS Estimate: $ 400

No.: 4724
Name: Star Centerpiece
Height: 5.50
Current status: Open edition,
    permanently retired
Original Issue Year: 1970
Last Year: 1972
Rarity: B
Issue Price: $ 40
LCS Estimate: $ 450

No.: 1113
Name: Mermaid Centerpiece
Height: 6
Current status: Open edition,
    permanently retired
Original Issue Year: 1971
Last Year: 1972
Rarity: B
Issue Price: $ 135
LCS Estimate: $ 1500

No.: 1079
Name: Boy with Lyre
Height: 6.50
Current status: Open edition,
    permanently retired
Original Issue Year: 1969
Last Year: 1970
Rarity: B
Issue Price: $ 20
LCS Estimate: $ 240

No.: 1080
Name: Girl with Watering Can Bowl
Height: 6.50
Current status: Open edition,
    permanently retired
Original Issue Year: 1969
Last Year: 1970
Rarity: B
Issue Price: $ 20
LCS Estimate: $ 240

No.: 4733
Name: Butterfly Centerpiece
Height: 7
Current status: Open edition,
    permanently retired
Original Issue Year: 1970
Last Year: 1973
Rarity: C
Issue Price: $ 40
LCS Estimate: $ 450

No.: 4767
Name: Royal Peacock
Height: 7
Current status: Open edition,
    permanently retired
Original Issue Year: 1971
Last Year: 1978
Rarity: D
Issue Price: $ 13.50
LCS Estimate: $ 110

No.: 4766
Name: Decorative Peacock
Height: 7
Current status: Open edition,
    permanently retired
Original Issue Year: 1971
Last Year: 1973
Rarity: B
Issue Price: $ 27.50
LCS Estimate: $ 300

No.: 4766.30
Name: Decorative Peacock
Height: 7
Current status: Open edition,
    permanently retired
Original Issue Year: 1971
Last Year: 1973
Rarity: B
Issue Price: $ 27.50
LCS Estimate: $ 300

No.: 4692
Name: Decorative Dove
Height: 7.50
Current status: Open edition,
    permanently retired
Original Issue Year: 1970
Last Year: 1973
Rarity: C
Issue Price: $ 17.50
LCS Estimate: $ 200

No.: 4695
Name: Mandarin Duck
Height: 8.50
Current status: Open edition,
    permanently retired
Original Issue Year: 1970
Last Year: 1975
Rarity: D
Issue Price: $ 13.50
LCS Estimate: $ 350
High Auction Price: $ 350

No.: 1114
Name: Pastoral Bowl
Height: 8.50
Current status: Open edition,
  permanently retired
Original Issue Year: 1971
Last Year: 1975
Rarity: C
Issue Price: $ 85
LCS Estimate: $ 850

No.: 1114.30
Name: Pastoral Bowl White
Height: 8.50
Current status: Open edition,
  permanently retired
Original Issue Year: 1971
Last Year: 1975
Rarity: C
Issue Price: $ 60
LCS Estimate: $ 600

No.: 1111
Name: Little Mermaid Bowl
Height: 9.50
Current status: Open edition,
  permanently retired
Original Issue Year: 1971
Last Year: 1972
Rarity: B
Issue Price: $ 35
LCS Estimate: $ 400

No.: 4694
Name: Fish Centerpiece
Height: 9.75
Current status: Open edition,
  permanently retired
Original Issue Year: 1970
Last Year: 1974
Rarity: C
Issue Price: $ 35
High Auction Price: $ 425
LCS Estimate: $ 400

No.: 4694.30
Name: Fish Centerpiece
Height: 9.75
Current status: Open edition,
  permanently retired
Original Issue Year: 1970
Last Year: 1974
Rarity: C
Issue Price: $ 35
LCS Estimate: $ 400

No.: 4693
Name: Decorative Pheasant
Height: 9.75
Current status: Open edition,
  permanently retired
Original Issue Year: 1970
Last Year: 1973
Rarity: C
Issue Price: $ 20
LCS Estimate: $ 225

No.: 30.02
Name: Center Piece
Height: 11.25
Current status: Early edition, very rare
Original Issue Year: 1949
Last Year: Not Available
Rarity: Very early, very rare
Issue Price: Not available
Comments: Personally created by Jose Lladró

No.: 4734.30
Name: Star Cup: 30 centimeters
Height: 11.75
Current status: Open edition, permanently retired
Original Issue Year: 1970
Last Year: 1972
Rarity: B
Issue Price: $ 40
LCS Estimate: $ 450

No.: 4734
Name: Star Cup: 30 centimeters
Height: 11.75
Current status: Open edition, permanently retired
Original Issue Year: 1970
Last Year: 1972
Rarity: B
Issue Price: $ 50
LCS Estimate: $ 550

No.: 4735
Name: Star Cup: 26 centimeters
Height: 12.25
Current status: Open edition, permanently retired
Original Issue Year: 1970
Last Year: 1972
Rarity: B
Issue Price: $ 45
LCS Estimate: $ 500

No.: 4735.30
Name: Star Cup: 26 centimeters
Height: 12.25
Current status: Open edition, permanently retired
Original Issue Year: 1970
Last Year: 1972
Rarity: B
Issue Price: $ 35
LCS Estimate: $ 400

No.: 4738.30
Name: Star Fruit Bowl: two levels
Height: 12.50
Current status: Open edition, permanently retired
Original Issue Year: 1970
Last Year: 1972
Rarity: B
Issue Price: $ 65
LCS Estimate: $ 700

No.: 4738
Name: Star Fruit Bowl: two levels
Height: 12.50
Current status: Open edition,
 permanently retired
Original Issue Year: 1970
Last Year: 1972
Rarity: B
Issue Price: $ 85
LCS Estimate: $ 950

No.: 4739.30
Name: Star Fruit Bowl: three levels
Height: 18.50
Current status: Open edition,
 permanently retired
Original Issue Year: 1970
Last Year: 1972
Rarity: B
Issue Price: $ 85
LCS Estimate: $ 950

No.: 4739
Name: Star Fruit Bowl: three levels
Height: 18.50
Current status: Open edition,
 permanently retired
Original Issue Year: 1970
Last Year: 1972
Rarity: B
Issue Price: $ 100
LCS Estimate: $ 1100

The first part of this category includes electric lamps based on figurine motifs, from the smallest to the highest.

The second part includes lamps with a flat geometrical design, modern or traditional, again classed from the smallest to the highest.

No. 4528—Ballet Lamp, *(No. 4528), introduced in 1969, retired in 1985 and auctioned for $950.*

No. 1616—Carousel Lamp, *introduced in 1989, retired in 1991 and auctioned for $1,250.*

Lamps

No.: 88.06
Name: Young Flutist Lamp
Height: 5.25
Current Status: Early edition, very rare
Original Issue Year: 1956
Last Year: Not Available
Rarity: Very early, very rare
Issue Price: Not Available

No.: 4573
Name: Duck's Group Lamp
Height: 10.25
Current Status: Open edition,
  permanently retired
Original Issue Year: 1969
Last Year: 1972
Rarity: C
Issue Price: $ 30
LCS Estimate: $ 350

No.: 4543
Name: Angel with Flute Lamp
Height: 10.5
Current Status: Open edition,
  permanently retired
Original Issue Year: 1969
Last Year: 1975
Rarity: D
Issue Price: $ 25
LCS Estimate: $ 275

No.: 4546
Name: Thinking Angel Lamp
Height: 10.5
Current Status: Open edition,
  permanently retired
Original Issue Year: 1969
Last Year: 1976
Rarity: D
Issue Price: $ 25
LCS Estimate: $ 250

No.: 4545
Name: Black Angel Lamp
Height: 10.5
Current Status: Open edition,
  permanently retired
Original Issue Year: 1969
Last Year: 1975
Rarity: D
Issue Price: $ 25
LCS Estimate: $ 275

No.: 4547
Name: Praying Angel Lamp
Height: 10.5
Current Status: Open edition,
  permanently retired
Original Issue Year: 1969
Last Year: 1975
Rarity: D
Issue Price: $ 25
LCS Estimate: $ 275

No.: 4574
Name: Fairy Lamp
Height: 10.5
Current Status: Open edition,
  permanently retired
Original Issue Year: 1969
Last Year: 1972
Rarity: C
Issue Price: $ 30
LCS Estimate: $ 350

No.: 4544
Name: Chinese Angel Lamp
Height: 10.5
Current Status: Open edition,
  permanently retired
Original Issue Year: 1969
Last Year: 1970
Rarity: B
Issue Price: $ 25
LCS Estimate: $ 300

No.: 355.13
Name: Giraffe Lamp
Height: 11
Current Status: Early edition, very rare
Original Issue Year: 1960
Last Year: Not Available
Rarity: Very early, very rare
Issue Price: Not Available

No.: 307.13
Name: Fawns Lamp
Height: 11.25
Current Status: Early edition, very rare
Original Issue Year: 1969
Last Year: Not Available
Rarity: Very early, very rare
Issue Price: Not Available

No.: 2011
Name: Horse Head Lamp
Height: 11.5
Current Status: Open edition,
  permanently retired
Original Issue Year: 1970
Last Year: 1982
Rarity: E
Issue Price: $ 20
LCS Estimate: $ 150

No.: 4578
Name: New Shepherdess Lamp
Height: 11.5
Current Status: Open edition,
  permanently retired
Original Issue Year: 1969
Last Year: 1976
Rarity: D
Issue Price: $ 45
LCS Estimate: $ 450

No.: 4702
Name: Horse Head Lamp
Height: 11.5
Current Status: Open edition, permanently retired
Original Issue Year: 1970
Last Year: 1972
Rarity: B
Issue Price: $ 30
LCS Estimate: $ 350

No.: 4579
Name: New Shepherd Lamp
Height: 11.5
Current Status: Open edition, permanently retired
Original Issue Year: 1969
Last Year: 1976
Rarity: D
Issue Price: $ 45
LCS Estimate: $ 450

No.: 86.06
Name: The Hunter Lamp
Height: 11.75
Current Status: Early edition, very rare
Original Issue Year: 1956
Last Year: Not Available
Rarity: Very early, very rare
Issue Price: Not Available

No.: 87.06
Name: Girl with Flower Basket Lamp
Height: 11.75
Current Status: Early edition, very rare
Original Issue Year: 1956
Last Year: Not Available
Rarity: Very early, very rare
Issue Price: Not Available

No.: 4508
Name: Boy Lamp
Height: 13
Current Status: Open edition, permanently retired
Original Issue Year: 1969
Last Year: 1985
Rarity: F
Issue Price: $ 55
LCS Estimate: $ 450

No.: 4711
Name: Girl with Dove Lamp
Height: 13
Current Status: Open edition, permanently retired
Original Issue Year: 1970
Last Year: 1985
Rarity: E
Issue Price: $ 27.50
LCS Estimate: $ 165

No.: 4507
Name: Girl Lamp
Height: 13
Current Status: Open edition,
  permanently retired
Original Issue Year: 1969
Last Year: 1985
Rarity: F
Issue Price: $ 55
LCS Estimate: $ 450

No.: 4712
Name: Shepherd Lamp
Height: 13
Current Status: Open edition,
  permanently retired
Original Issue Year: 1970
Last Year: 1985
Rarity: E
Issue Price: $ 35
LCS Estimate: $ 200

No.: 350.13
Name: Gazelle Lamp
Height: 13.25
Current Status: Early edition, very rare
Original Issue Year: 1961
Last Year: Not Available
Rarity: Very early, very rare
Issue Price: Not Available

No.: 354.13
Name: Gazelle Lamp
Height: 13.75
Current Status: Early edition, very rare
Original Issue Year: 1960
Last Year: Not Available
Rarity: Very early, very rare
Issue Price: Not Available

No.: 4555
Name: Shepherd with Girl Lamp
Height: 13.75
Current Status: Open edition,
  permanently retired
Original Issue Year: 1969
Last Year: 1970
Rarity: B
Issue Price: $ 75
LCS Estimate: $ 900

No.: 4526
Name: Colombine Lamp
Height: 14.5
Current Status: Open edition,
  permanently retired
Original Issue Year: 1969
Last Year: 1985
Rarity: F
Issue Price: $ 75
LCS Estimate: $ 600

No.: 4527
Name: Violinist Lamp
Height: 14.5
Current Status: Open edition,
    permanently retired
Original Issue Year: 1969
Last Year: 1985
Rarity: F
Issue Price: $ 75
LCS Estimate: $ 600

No.: 4528
Name: Ballet Lamp
Height: 15
Current Status: Open edition,
    permanently retired
Original Issue Year: 1969
Last Year: 1985
Rarity: F
Issue Price: $ 120
High Auction Price: $ 950
LCS Estimate: $ 750

No.: 351.13
Name: Horse Lamp
Height: 15
Current Status: Early edition, very rare
Original Issue Year: 1965
Last Year: Not Available
Rarity: Very early, very rare
Issue Price: Not Available

No.: 245.10
Name: Harlequin and Ballerina Lamp
Height: 15.25
Current Status: Early edition, very rare
Original Issue Year: 1961
Last Year: Not Available
Rarity: Very early, very rare
Issue Price: Not Available

No.: 4728
Name: Shepherdess with Lamb Lamp
Height: 15.5
Current Status: Open edition,
    permanently retired
Original Issue Year: 1970
Last Year: 1975
Rarity: D
Issue Price: $ 25
LCS Estimate: $ 250

No.: 4727
Name: Shepherd with Kid Lamp
Height: 15.5
Current Status: Open edition,
    permanently retired
Original Issue Year: 1970
Last Year: 1975
Rarity: D
Issue Price: $ 25
LCS Estimate: $ 250

No.: 4820
Name: Woman from Guadalupe Lamp
Height: 15.75
Current Status: Open edition,
  permanently retired
Original Issue Year: 1972
Last Year: 1973
Rarity: B
Issue Price: $ 80
LCS Estimate: $ 900

No.: 4681
Name: Turtle Dove Lamp
Height: 16
Current Status: Open edition,
  permanently retired
Original Issue Year: 1969
Last Year: 1970
Rarity: B
Issue Price: $ 22.50
LCS Estimate: $ 270

No.: 4634
Name: Boy with Violin Lamp
Height: 17
Current Status: Open edition,
  permanently retired
Original Issue Year: 1969
Last Year: 1985
Rarity: F
Issue Price: $ 100
High Auction Price: $ 400
LCS Estimate: $ 400

No.: 1607
Name: Nymph Lamp
Height: 17
Current Status: Open edition,
  permanently retired
Original Issue Year: 1989
Last Year: 1991
Rarity: B
Issue Price: $ 1750
LCS Estimate: $ 1750

No.: 4633
Name: Girl with Mandolin Lamp
Height: 17
Current Status: Open edition,
  permanently retired
Original Issue Year: 1969
Last Year: 1985
Rarity: F
Issue Price: $ 100
High Auction Price: $ 475
LCS Estimate: $ 475

No.: 4625
Name: From the Mountains Lamp
Height: 17
Current Status: Open edition,
  permanently retired
Original Issue Year: 1969
Last Year: 1972
Rarity: C
Issue Price: $ 60
LCS Estimate: $ 700

No.: 4593
Name: Bucking Horse Lamp
Height: 17.25
Current Status: Open edition,
   permanently retired
Original Issue Year: 1969
Last Year: 1972
Rarity: C
Issue Price: $ 60
High Auction Price: $ 400
LCS Estimate: $ 400

No.: 4592
Name: Rearing Horse Lamp
Height: 17.25
Current Status: Open edition,
   permanently retired
Original Issue Year: 1969
Last Year: 1972
Rarity: C
Issue Price: $ 60
LCS Estimate: $ 700

No.: 4624
Name: Afternoon Snack Lamp
Height: 17.75
Current Status: Open edition,
   permanently retired
Original Issue Year: 1969
Last Year: 1972
Rarity: C
Issue Price: $ 60
LCS Estimate: $ 700

No.: 2111
Name: Elephant Lamp
Height: 19.75
Current Status: Open edition,
   permanently retired
Original Issue Year: 1978
Last Year: 1985
Rarity: D
Issue Price: $ 685
LCS Estimate: $ 3400

No.: 5241
Name: Ballet Theme Lamp
Height: 22
Current Status: Open edition,
   permanently retired
Original Issue Year: 1984
Last Year: 1991
Rarity: D
Issue Price: $ 565
LCS Estimate: $ 1125

No.: 5242
Name: Ballet Theme Lamp
Height: 22.5
Current Status: Open edition,
   permanently retired
Original Issue Year: 1984
Last Year: 1991
Rarity: D
Issue Price: $ 490
LCS Estimate: $ 1000

No.: 1124
Name: La Tarantela Lamp
Height: 24.5
Current Status: Open edition,
 permanently retired
Original Issue Year: 1971
Last Year: 1989
Rarity: F
Issue Price: $ 575
High Auction Price: $ 2250
LCS Estimate: $ 2000

No.: 4785
Name: Lamp with Blue Fluting
Height: 9.25
Current Status: Open edition,
 permanently retired
Original Issue Year: 1971
Last Year: 1973
Rarity: B
Issue Price: $ 35
LCS Estimate: $ 400

No.: 5575
Name: Lilac Round Cuboid Lamp
Height: 11
Current Status: Open edition,
 permanently retired
Original Issue Year: 1989
Last Year: 1990
Rarity: B
Issue Price: $ 335
LCS Estimate: $ 670

No.: 5575.10
Name: Brown Round Cuboid Lamp
Height: 11
Current Status: Open edition,
 permanently retired
Original Issue Year: 1989
Last Year: 1990
Rarity: B
Issue Price: $ 250
LCS Estimate: $ 5000

No.: 5575.30
Name: Green Round Cuboid Lamp
Height: 11
Current Status: Open edition,
 permanently retired
Original Issue Year: 1989
Last Year: 1990
Rarity: B
Issue Price: $ 265
LCS Estimate: $ 530

No.: 4794
Name: Grey Lamp
Height: 12.25
Current Status: Open edition,
 permanently retired
Original Issue Year: 1972
Last Year: 1975
Rarity: C
Issue Price: $ 30
LCS Estimate: $ 300

No.: 4793
Name: Blue Pomal Lamp
Height: 12.25
Current Status: Open edition, permanently retired
Original Issue Year: 1972
Last Year: 1979
Rarity: D
Issue Price: $ 30
LCS Estimate: $ 250

No.: 4704
Name: Minuet Florelia Lamp
Height: 12.25
Current Status: Open edition, permanently retired
Original Issue Year: 1970
Last Year: 1979
Rarity: E
Issue Price: $ 18.50
LCS Estimate: $ 150

No.: 4795
Name: White Lamp
Height: 12.25
Current Status: Open edition, permanently retired
Original Issue Year: 1972
Last Year: 1979
Rarity: D
Issue Price: $ 27.50
LCS Estimate: $ 225

No.: 5574.30
Name: Green Menphis Lamp
Height: 13.25
Current Status: Open edition, permanently retired
Original Issue Year: 1989
Last Year: 1990
Rarity: B
Issue Price: $ 285
LCS Estimate: $ 570

No.: 5574
Name: Blue Menphis Lamp
Height: 13.25
Current Status: Open edition, permanently retired
Original Issue Year: 1989
Last Year: 1990
Rarity: B
Issue Price: $ 250
LCS Estimate: $ 500

No.: 4776
Name: Opal Blue Lamp
Height: 13.25
Current Status: Open edition, permanently retired
Original Issue Year: 1971
Last Year: 1975
Rarity: C
Issue Price: $ 20
LCS Estimate: $ 200

No.: 4777
Name: Opal Green Lamp
Height: 13.25
Current Status: Open edition,
  permanently retired
Original Issue Year: 1971
Last Year: 1975
Rarity: C
Issue Price: $ 20
LCS Estimate: $ 200

No.: 4775
Name: Lantern Lamp
Height: 13.25
Current Status: Open edition,
  permanently retired
Original Issue Year: 1971
Last Year: 1973
Rarity: B
Issue Price: $ 22.50
LCS Estimate: $ 225

No.: 303.13
Name: Lamp
Height: 14.25
Current Status: Early edition, very rare
Original Issue Year: 1958
Last Year: Not Available
Rarity: Very early, very rare
Issue Price: Not Available

No.: 5576.30
Name: Green Compact Vase
Height: 15
Current Status: Open edition,
  permanently retired
Original Issue Year: 1989
Last Year: 1990
Rarity: B
Issue Price: $ 285
LCS Estimate: $ 570

No.: 5576.10
Name: Brown Compact Vase
Height: 15
Current Status: Open edition,
  permanently retired
Original Issue Year: 1989
Last Year: 1990
Rarity: B
Issue Price: $ 275
LCS Estimate: $ 550

No.: 5576.40
Name: Violet Compact Vase
Height: 15
Current Status: Open edition,
  permanently retired
Original Issue Year: 1989
Last Year: 1990
Rarity: B
Issue Price: $ 325
LCS Estimate: $ 650

No.: 5576
Name: Lilac Compact Vase
Height: 15
Current Status: Open edition,
    permanently retired
Original Issue Year: 1989
Last Year: 1990
Rarity: B
Issue Price: $ 325
LCS Estimate: $ 650

No.: 4787
Name: Beige Rialto Lamp
Height: 15
Current Status: Open edition,
    permanently retired
Original Issue Year: 1972
Last Year: 1979
Rarity: D
Issue Price: $ 50
LCS Estimate: $ 400

No.: 4788
Name: Green Rialto Lamp
Height: 15
Current Status: Open edition,
    permanently retired
Original Issue Year: 1972
Last Year: 1979
Rarity: D
Issue Price: $ 35
LCS Estimate: $ 275

No.: 4786
Name: Brown Excelsior Lamp
Height: 15
Current Status: Open edition,
    permanently retired
Original Issue Year: 1971
Last Year: 1973
Rarity: B
Issue Price: $ 45
LCS Estimate: $ 500

No.: 4789
Name: White Rialto Lamp
Height: 15
Current Status: Open edition,
    permanently retired
Original Issue Year: 1972
Last Year: 1979
Rarity: D
Issue Price: $ 30
LCS Estimate: $ 250

No.: 4703
Name: Spring Lamp
Height: 15.5
Current Status: Open edition,
    permanently retired
Original Issue Year: 1970
Last Year: 1979
Rarity: E
Issue Price: $ 30
LCS Estimate: $ 240

No.: 5632.30
Name: Lladro Vase
Height: 15.75
Current Status: Open edition,
  permanently retired
Original Issue Year: 1989
Last Year: 1990
Rarity: B
Issue Price: $ 195
LCS Estimate: $ 390

No.: 4792
Name: White Pomal Lamp
Height: 15.75
Current Status: Open edition,
  permanently retired
Original Issue Year: 1972
Last Year: 1979
Rarity: D
Issue Price: $ 30
LCS Estimate: $ 200
High Auction Price: $ 150

No.: 4791
Name: Grey Pomal Lamp
Height: 15.75
Current Status: Open edition,
  permanently retired
Original Issue Year: 1972
Last Year: 1975
Rarity: C
Issue Price: $ 30
LCS Estimate: $ 300

No.: 4790
Name: Brown Pomal Lamp
Height: 15.75
Current Status: Open edition,
  permanently retired
Original Issue Year: 1972
Last Year: 1979
Rarity: D
Issue Price: $ 45
High Auction Price: $ 325
LCS Estimate: $ 300

No.: 4705
Name: Pisa Lamp
Height: 15.75
Current Status: Open edition,
  permanently retired
Original Issue Year: 1970
Last Year: 1973
Rarity: C
Issue Price: $ 30
LCS Estimate: $ 325

No.: 5632
Name: Lladro Lamp
Height: 15.75
Current Status: Open edition,
  permanently retired
Original Issue Year: 1989
Last Year: 1990
Rarity: B
Issue Price: $ 225
LCS Estimate: $ 450

No.: 4782
Name: Blue Full Moon Lamp
Height: 16
Current Status: Open edition,
  permanently retired
Original Issue Year: 1971
Last Year: 1975
Rarity: C
Issue Price: $ 60
LCS Estimate: $ 600

No.: 4784
Name: Brown Full Moon Lamp
Height: 16
Current Status: Open edition,
  permanently retired
Original Issue Year: 1971
Last Year: 1975
Rarity: C
Issue Price: $ 40
LCS Estimate: $ 250
High Auction Price: $ 150

No.: 4783
Name: Grey Full Moon Lamp
Height: 16
Current Status: Open edition,
  permanently retired
Original Issue Year: 1971
Last Year: 1973
Rarity: B
Issue Price: $ 40
LCS Estimate: $ 450

No.: 1689
Name: Lladro Lamp
Height: 16.5
Current Status: Open edition,
  permanently retired
Original Issue Year: 1989
Last Year: 1990
Rarity: B
Issue Price: $ 210
LCS Estimate: $ 420

No.: 5579
Name: Lily Vase Lamp
Height: 16.5
Current Status: Open edition,
  permanently retired
Original Issue Year: 1989
Last Year: 1990
Rarity: B
Issue Price: $ 340
LCS Estimate: $ 680

No.: 5573
Name: Square Vase Lamp
Height: 17.25
Current Status: Open edition,
  permanently retired
Original Issue Year: 1989
Last Year: 1990
Rarity: B
Issue Price: $ 310
LCS Estimate: $ 620

No.: 4706
Name: Lamp
Height: 18
Current Status: Open edition,
  permanently retired
Original Issue Year: 1970
Last Year: 1979
Rarity: E
Issue Price: $ 35
LCS Estimate: $ 275

No.: 4751
Name: Minerva Lamp
Height: 18
Current Status: Open edition,
  permanently retired
Original Issue Year: 1971
Last Year: 1979
Rarity: E
Issue Price: $ 35
LCS Estimate: $ 350
High Auction Price: $ 350

No.: 1616
Name: Carousel Lamp
Height: 19
Current Status: Open edition,
  permanently retired
Original Issue Year: 1989
Last Year: 1991
Rarity: B
Issue Price: $ 1700
High Auction Price: $ 1250
LCS Estimate: $ 2000

No.: 4746
Name: Pink Octogonal Jar Lamp
Height: 19
Current Status: Open edition,
  permanently retired
Original Issue Year: 1971
Last Year: 1973
Rarity: B
Issue Price: $ 45
LCS Estimate: $ 500

No.: 4748
Name: Green Octogonal Jar Lamp
Height: 19
Current Status: Open edition,
  permanently retired
Original Issue Year: 1971
Last Year: 1973
Rarity: B
Issue Price: $ 45
LCS Estimate: $ 500

No.: 4747
Name: Blue Octogonal Jar Lamp
Height: 19
Current Status: Open edition,
  permanently retired
Original Issue Year: 1971
Last Year: 1972
Rarity: B
Issue Price: $ 45
LCS Estimate: $ 500

No.: 1622
Name: Birds and Peonies Lamp
Height: 19.75
Current Status: Limited edition,
  currently active
Edition Limit: 300
Original Issue Year: 1989
Issue Price: $ 3000
Current Retail Price: $ 3600

No.: 4708.30
Name: White Dragons Jug Lamp
Height: 20
Current Status: Open edition,
  permanently retired
Original Issue Year: 1970
Last Year: 1981
Rarity: E
Issue Price: $ 70
LCS Estimate: $ 500

No.: 4708
Name: Dragons Jug Lamp
Height: 20
Current Status: Open edition,
  permanently retired
Original Issue Year: 1970
Last Year: 1980
Rarity: E
Issue Price: $ 70
LCS Estimate: $ 500

No.: 4707
Name: Olympia Lamp
Height: 20.5
Current Status: Open edition,
  permanently retired
Original Issue Year: 1970
Last Year: 1979
Rarity: E
Issue Price: $ 45
LCS Estimate: $ 350

No.: 5572
Name: Vase with Handles Lamp
Height: 23.25
Current Status: Open edition,
  permanently retired
Original Issue Year: 1989
Last Year: 1990
Rarity: B
Issue Price: $ 650
LCS Estimate: $ 1300

From 1969 to 1989, Lladró has introduced a total of 98 porcelain flowers. Ninety-seven have been permanently retired and one remains active on the retail market.

No. 1572—Flowers Chest, *(L1572), was issued in 1987 at $550 and remains active in 1992 at $660.*

For ease of identification, we have classified the 98 into three groups:

42 porcelain "more-than-one-stem" flowers or floral "bouquets", in a Lladró vase, basket or chest

33 porcelain "more-than-one-stem" flowers or floral "bouquets", standing alone, *not* in a Lladró vase, basket or chest

23 single stems or flowers, with or without a vase.

The first determinant, then, is whether you have a single flower or a group of flowers. Then, if a group of flowers, whether they are in a Lladró porcelain container or not. If you own a Lladró vase *without* flowers, we have classified it in Chapter 8: Vases.

Flowers

No.: 1073
Name: Basket of Flowers
Height: 4
Current Status: Open edition,
  permanently retired
Original Issue Year: 1969
Last Year: 1981
Rarity: E
Issue Price: $ 65
LCS Estimate: $ 520

No.: 1073.30
Name: Basket of White Flowers
Height: 4
Current Status: Open edition,
  permanently retired
Original Issue Year: 1969
Last Year: 1981
Rarity: E
Issue Price: $ 55
LCS Estimate: $ 440

No.: 1184
Name: Anemonas Bunch
Height: 15
Current Status: Limited edition, fully
  subscribed
Edition Limit: 200
Original Issue Year: 1971
Issue Price: $ 400

No.: 1185
Name: Flowers
Height: 15.50
Current Status: Limited edition, fully
  subscribed
Edition Limit: 200
Original Issue Year: 1971
Issue Price: $ 475

No.: 1186
Name: Buds Branch
Height: 15.75
Current Status: Limited edition, fully
  subscribed
Edition Limit: 200
Original Issue Year: 1971
Issue Price: $ 575

No.: 1218
Name: Blue Vase with Flowers
Height: 7
Current Status: Open edition,
  permanently retired
Original Issue Year: 1972
Last Year: 1979
Rarity: D
Issue Price: $ 40
LCS Estimate: $ 300

No.: 1219
Name: Mini-vase with Flowers
Height: 6.25
Current Status: Open edition,
    permanently retired
Original Issue Year: 1972
Last Year: 1979
Rarity: D
Issue Price: $ 40
LCS Estimate: $ 300

No.: 1220
Name: Little Vase with Flowers
Height: 7.50
Current Status: Open edition,
    permanently retired
Original Issue Year: 1972
Last Year: 1979
Rarity: D
Issue Price: $ 40
LCS Estimate: $ 300

No.: 1221
Name: Little Vase with Flowers
Height: 4.25
Current Status: Open edition,
    permanently retired
Original Issue Year: 1972
Last Year: 1980
Rarity: E
Issue Price: $ 45
LCS Estimate: $ 300

No.: 1222
Name: Little Jug with Flowers
Height: 7
Current Status: Open edition,
    permanently retired
Original Issue Year: 1972
Last Year: 1979
Rarity: D
Issue Price: $ 40
LCS Estimate: $ 300

No.: 1291
Name: Flower Basket No. 1
Height: 1.5
Current Status: Open edition,
    permanently retired
Original Issue Year: 1974
Last Year: 1983
Rarity: E
Issue Price: $ 70
LCS Estimate: $ 425

No.: 1292
Name: Floral Basket No. 2
Height: 2
Current Status: Open edition,
    permanently retired
Original Issue Year: 1974
Last Year: 1983
Rarity: E
Issue Price: $ 85
LCS Estimate: $ 500

No.: 1293
Name: Floral Basket No. 3
Height: 2
Current Status: Open edition,
 permanently retired
Original Issue Year: 1974
Last Year: 1983
Rarity: E
Issue Price: $ 225
LCS Estimate: $ 1300

No.: 1294
Name: Floral Basket No. 4A
Height: 2
Current Status: Open edition,
 permanently retired
Original Issue Year: 1974
Last Year: 1983
Rarity: E
Issue Price: $ 125
LCS Estimate: $ 750

No.: 1295
Name: Floral Basket No. 4B
Height: 2
Current Status: Open edition,
 permanently retired
Original Issue Year: 1974
Last Year: 1983
Rarity: E
Issue Price: $ 110
LCS Estimate: $ 650

No.: 1296
Name: Floral Basket No. 6
Height: 1.5
Current Status: Open edition,
 permanently retired
Original Issue Year: 1974
Last Year: 1983
Rarity: E
Issue Price: $ 145
LCS Estimate: $ 850

No.: 1542
Name: Iris Arrangement
Height: 6
Current Status: Open edition,
 permanently retired
Original Issue Year: 1988
Last Year: 1990
Rarity: B
Issue Price: $ 800
LCS Estimate: $ 1600

No.: 1543
Name: Basket of Margaritas
Height: 6.25
Current Status: Open edition,
 permanently retired
Original Issue Year: 1988
Last Year: 1991
Rarity: C
Issue Price: $ 450
LCS Estimate: $ 1200

No.: 1544
Name: Basket of Roses
Height: 7
Current Status: Open edition,
  permanently retired
Original Issue Year: 1988
Last Year: 1991
Rarity: C
Issue Price: $ 400
LCS Estimate: $ 400

No.: 1545
Name: Basket of Dahlias
Height: 4
Current Status: Open edition,
  permanently retired
Original Issue Year: 1988
Last Year: 1991
Rarity: C
Issue Price: $ 375
LCS Estimate: $ 375

No.: 1549
Name: Square Handkerchief with
  Flowers
Height: 2
Current Status: Open edition,
  permanently retired
Original Issue Year: 1988
Last Year: 1991
Rarity: C
Issue Price: $ 180
LCS Estimate: $ 180

No.: 1550
Name: Round Handkerchief with
  Flowers
Height: 2
Current Status: Open edition,
  permanently retired
Original Issue Year: 1987
Last Year: 1991
Rarity: C
Issue Price: $ 170
LCS Estimate: $ 170

No.: 1552
Name: Small Brown Basket with
  Flowers
Height: 2.75
Current Status: Open edition,
  permanently retired
Original Issue Year: 1987
Last Year: 1991
Rarity: C
Issue Price: $ 115
LCS Estimate: $ 115

No.: 1552.10
Name: Small Brown Basket with
  Colored Flowers
Height: 2.75
Current Status: Open edition,
  permanently retired
Original Issue Year: 1987
Last Year: 1991
Rarity: C
Issue Price: $ 160
LCS Estimate: $ 160

No.: 1552.30
Name: Small Grey Basket with Flowers
Height: 2.75
Current Status: Open edition,
  permanently retired
Original Issue Year: 1987
Last Year: 1991
Rarity: C
Issue Price: $ 115
LCS Estimate: $ 115

No.: 1553
Name: Small Brown Basket with
  Flowers
Height: 4
Current Status: Open edition,
  permanently retired
Original Issue Year: 1987
Last Year: 1991
Rarity: C
Issue Price: $ 115
LCS Estimate: $ 115

No.: 1553.10
Name: Small Brown Basket with
  Colored Flowers
Height: 4
Current Status: Open edition,
  permanently retired
Original Issue Year: 1987
Last Year: 1991
Rarity: C
Issue Price: $ 160
LCS Estimate: $ 160

No.: 1553.30
Name: Small Grey Basket with Flowers
Height: 4
Current Status: Open edition,
  permanently retired
Original Issue Year: 1987
Last Year: 1991
Rarity: C
Issue Price: $ 115
LCS Estimate: $ 115

No.: 1554
Name: Small Brown Basket with
  Flowers
Height: 2.75
Current Status: Open edition,
  permanently retired
Original Issue Year: 1987
Last Year: 1991
Rarity: C
Issue Price: $ 110
LCS Estimate: $ 110

No.: 1554.10
Name: Small Brown Basket with
  Colored Flowers
Height: 2.75
Current Status: Open edition,
  permanently retired
Original Issue Year: 1987
Last Year: 1991
Rarity: C
Issue Price: $ 130
LCS Estimate: $ 130

No.: 1554.30
Name: Small Grey Basket with Flowers
Height: 2.75
Current Status: Open edition,
   permanently retired
Original Issue Year: 1987
Last Year: 1991
Rarity: C
Issue Price: $ 110
LCS Estimate: $ 110

No.: 1555
Name: Pink Basket with Flowers
Height: 2.75
Current Status: Open edition,
   permanently retired
Original Issue Year: 1987
Last Year: 1991
Rarity: C
Issue Price: $ 140
LCS Estimate: $ 140

No.: 1559
Name: Small Pink Basket with Flowers
Height: 2
Current Status: Open edition,
   permanently retired
Original Issue Year: 1987
Last Year: 1991
Rarity: C
Issue Price: $ 90
LCS Estimate: $ 90

No.: 1559.30
Name: Small Blue Basket with Flowers
Height: 2
Current Status: Open edition,
   permanently retired
Original Issue Year: 1987
Last Year: 1991
Rarity: C
Issue Price: $ 90
LCS Estimate: $ 90

No.: 1572
Name: Flowers Chest
Height: 4.25
Current Status: Open edition, currently
   active
Original Issue Year: 1987
Issue Price: $ 550
Current Retail Price: $ 660

No.: 1573
Name: Small Basket with Lace and
   Flowers
Height: 3
Current Status: Open edition,
   permanently retired
Original Issue Year: 1987
Last Year: 1991
Rarity: C
Issue Price: $ 115
LCS Estimate: $ 115

No.: 1573.30
Name: Small Basket with Lace and
Flowers
Height: 3
Current Status: Open edition,
permanently retired
Original Issue Year: 1987
Last Year: 1991
Rarity: C
Issue Price: $ 115
LCS Estimate: $ 115

No.: 1574
Name: Small Round Basket with
Flowers
Height: 3.75
Current Status: Open edition,
permanently retired
Original Issue Year: 1987
Last Year: 1991
Rarity: C
Issue Price: $ 140
LCS Estimate: $ 140

No.: 1574.30
Name: Small Round Basket with
Flowers
Height: 3.75
Current Status: Open edition,
permanently retired
Original Issue Year: 1987
Last Year: 1991
Rarity: C
Issue Price: $ 140
LCS Estimate: $ 140

No.: 1575
Name: Flat Basket with Flowers
Height: 6.25
Current Status: Open edition,
permanently retired
Original Issue Year: 1987
Last Year: 1991
Rarity: C
Issue Price: $ 450
LCS Estimate: $ 450

No.: 1576
Name: Flat Basket with Violets
Height: 6.25
Current Status: Open edition,
permanently retired
Original Issue Year: 1987
Last Year: 1991
Rarity: C
Issue Price: $ 375
LCS Estimate: $ 375

No.: 1577
Name: Basket with Handkerchief and
Roses
Height: 3.5
Current Status: Open edition,
permanently retired
Original Issue Year: 1987
Last Year: 1991
Rarity: C
Issue Price: $ 275
LCS Estimate: $ 275

No.: 1624
Name: Summer Basket
Height: 6.5
Current Status: Open edition, permanently retired
Original Issue Year: 1989
Last Year: 1991
Rarity: B
Issue Price: $ 675
LCS Estimate: $ 675

No.: 1625
Name: Yellow Oval Basket
Height: 4
Current Status: Open edition, permanently retired
Original Issue Year: 1989
Last Year: 1991
Rarity: B
Issue Price: $ 445
LCS Estimate: $ 445

No.: 1626
Name: Blue Oval Basket
Height: 4
Current Status: Open edition, permanently retired
Original Issue Year: 1989
Last Year: 1991
Rarity: B
Issue Price: $ 445
LCS Estimate: $ 445

No.: 1627
Name: Spring Shower Basket
Height: 4.25
Current Status: Open edition, permanently retired
Original Issue Year: 1989
Last Year: 1991
Rarity: B
Issue Price: $ 675
LCS Estimate: $ 675

No.: 1628
Name: May Flower Basket
Height: 4.25
Current Status: Open edition, permanently retired
Original Issue Year: 1989
Last Year: 1991
Rarity: B
Issue Price: $ 485
LCS Estimate: $ 485

No.: 1629
Name: Spring Basket
Height: 6
Current Status: Open edition, permanently retired
Original Issue Year: 1989
Last Year: 1991
Rarity: B
Issue Price: $ 550
LCS Estimate: $ 550

No.: 1630
Name: Fall Basket
Height: 4.5
Current Status: Open edition, permanently retired
Original Issue Year: 1989
Last Year: 1991
Rarity: B
Issue Price: $ 535
LCS Estimate: $ 535

No.: 1631
Name: Spring Blossom
Height: 7.5
Current Status: Open edition, permanently retired
Original Issue Year: 1989
Last Year: 1991
Rarity: B
Issue Price: $ 550
LCS Estimate: $ 550

No.: 1632
Name: Violet Vase
Height: 7.5
Current Status: Open edition, permanently retired
Original Issue Year: 1989
Last Year: 1991
Rarity: B
Issue Price: $ 445
LCS Estimate: $ 445

No.: 1633
Name: Rust Wild Flower Vase
Height: 4.75
Current Status: Open edition, permanently retired
Original Issue Year: 1989
Last Year: 1991
Rarity: B
Issue Price: $ 300
LCS Estimate: $ 300

No.: 1634
Name: Blue Wild Flower Vase
Height: 5
Current Status: Open edition, permanently retired
Original Issue Year: 1989
Last Year: 1991
Rarity: B
Issue Price: $ 275
LCS Estimate: $ 275

No.: 1541
Name: Orchid Arrangement
Height: 10.25
Current Status: Open edition, permanently retired
Original Issue Year: 1988
Last Year: 1990
Rarity: B
Issue Price: $ 500
High Auction Price: $ 1700
LCS Estimate: $ 1500

No.: 5179
Name: Three Pink Roses
Height: 1.5
Current Status: Open edition,
  permanently retired
Original Issue Year: 1984
Last Year: 1990
Rarity: D
Issue Price: $ 70
LCS Estimate: $ 140

No.: 5179.30
Name: Three Pink Roses
Height: 1.5
Current Status: Open edition,
  permanently retired
Original Issue Year: 1984
Last Year: 1988
Rarity: C
Issue Price: $ 67.50
LCS Estimate: $ 203

No.: 5181
Name: Japanese Camellia
Height: 1.5
Current Status: Open edition,
  permanently retired
Original Issue Year: 1984
Last Year: 1990
Rarity: D
Issue Price: $ 70
LCS Estimate: $ 140

No.: 5181.30
Name: Japanese Camellia
Height: 1.5
Current Status: Open edition,
  permanently retired
Original Issue Year: 1984
Last Year: 1988
Rarity: C
Issue Price: $ 60
LCS Estimate: $ 180

No.: 5182
Name: White Peony w Base
Height: 1.5
Current Status: Open edition,
  permanently retired
Original Issue Year: 1984
Last Year: 1990
Rarity: D
Issue Price: $ 85
LCS Estimate: $ 170

No.: 5182.30
Name: White Peony
Height: 1.5
Current Status: Open edition,
  permanently retired
Original Issue Year: 1984
Last Year: 1988
Rarity: C
Issue Price: $ 85
LCS Estimate: $ 255

No.: 5183
Name: Two Yellow Roses
Height: 1.5
Current Status: Open edition,
 permanently retired
Original Issue Year: 1984
Last Year: 1990
Rarity: D
Issue Price: $ 57.50
LCS Estimate: $ 115

No.: 5183.30
Name: Two Yellow Roses
Height: 1.5
Current Status: Open edition,
 permanently retired
Original Issue Year: 1984
Last Year: 1988
Rarity: C
Issue Price: $ 57.50
LCS Estimate: $ 173

No.: 5185
Name: Lactiflora Peony
Height: 1.5
Current Status: Open edition,
 permanently retired
Original Issue Year: 1984
Last Year: 1990
Rarity: D
Issue Price: $ 67.50
LCS Estimate: $ 135

No.: 5185.30
Name: Lactiflora Peony
Height: 1.5
Current Status: Open edition,
 permanently retired
Original Issue Year: 1984
Last Year: 1988
Rarity: C
Issue Price: $ 65
LCS Estimate: $ 195

No.: 5186
Name: Yellow Begonia
Height: 1.5
Current Status: Open edition,
 permanently retired
Original Issue Year: 1984
Last Year: 1990
Rarity: D
Issue Price: $ 67.50
LCS Estimate: $ 135

No.: 5186.30
Name: Yellow Begonia
Height: 1.5
Current Status: Open edition,
 permanently retired
Original Issue Year: 1984
Last Year: 1988
Rarity: C
Issue Price: $ 65
LCS Estimate: $ 195

No.: 5187
Name: Rhododendron
Height: 1.5
Current Status: Open edition,
  permanently retired
Original Issue Year: 1984
Last Year: 1990
Rarity: D
Issue Price: $ 67.50
LCS Estimate: $ 135

No.: 5187.30
Name: Rhododendron
Height: 1.5
Current Status: Open edition,
  permanently retired
Original Issue Year: 1984
Last Year: 1988
Rarity: C
Issue Price: $ 65
LCS Estimate: $ 195

No.: 5188
Name: Miniature Begonia
Height: 1.5
Current Status: Open edition,
  permanently retired
Original Issue Year: 1984
Last Year: 1990
Rarity: D
Issue Price: $ 85
LCS Estimate: $ 170

No.: 5188.30
Name: Miniature Begonia
Height: 1.5
Current Status: Open edition,
  permanently retired
Original Issue Year: 1984
Last Year: 1988
Rarity: C
Issue Price: $ 80
LCS Estimate: $ 240

No.: 5189
Name: Chrysanthemum
Height: 1.5
Current Status: Open edition,
  permanently retired
Original Issue Year: 1984
Last Year: 1990
Rarity: D
Issue Price: $ 105
LCS Estimate: $ 210

No.: 5189.30
Name: Chrysanthemum
Height: 1.5
Current Status: Open edition,
  permanently retired
Original Issue Year: 1984
Last Year: 1988
Rarity: C
Issue Price: $ 100
LCS Estimate: $ 300

No.: 5190
Name: California Poppy
Height: 1.5
Current Status: Open edition,
   permanently retired
Original Issue Year: 1984
Last Year: 1990
Rarity: D
Issue Price: $ 100
LCS Estimate: $ 200

No.: 5190.30
Name: California Poppy
Height: 1.5
Current Status: Open edition,
   permanently retired
Original Issue Year: 1984
Last Year: 1988
Rarity: C
Issue Price: $ 97.50
LCS Estimate: $ 293

No.: 1095
Name: Big Rose in Case
Height: 1.5
Current Status: Open edition,
   permanently retired
Original Issue Year: 1969
Last Year: 1979
Rarity: E
Issue Price: $ 22.50
LCS Estimate: $ 200

No.: 1095.30
Name: Big Rose in Case White
Height: 1.5
Current Status: Open edition,
   permanently retired
Original Issue Year: 1969
Last Year: 1979
Rarity: E
Issue Price: $ 22.50
LCS Estimate: $ 200

No.: 1096
Name: Big Rose on Plaque
Height: 1.5
Current Status: Open edition,
   permanently retired
Original Issue Year: 1969
Last Year: 1975
Rarity: D
Issue Price: $ 32.50
LCS Estimate: $ 360

No.: 1096.30
Name: Big Rose on Plaque White
Height: 1.5
Current Status: Open edition,
   permanently retired
Original Issue Year: 1969
Last Year: 1979
Rarity: E
Issue Price: $ 27.50
LCS Estimate: $ 240

No.: 1097
Name: Medium Rose in Case
Height: 1.25
Current Status: Open edition,
  permanently retired
Original Issue Year: 1969
Last Year: 1978
Rarity: E
Issue Price: $ 18
LCS Estimate: $ 160

No.: 1097.30
Name: Medium Rose in CaseWhite
Height: 1.25
Current Status: Open edition,
  permanently retired
Original Issue Year: 1969
Last Year: 1978
Rarity: E
Issue Price: $ 18
LCS Estimate: $ 160

No.: 1098
Name: Medium Rose on Plaque
Height: 1.25
Current Status: Open edition,
  permanently retired
Original Issue Year: 1969
Last Year: 1975
Rarity: D
Issue Price: $ 35
LCS Estimate: $ 400

No.: 1098.30
Name: Medm Rose on PlaqueWhite
Height: 1.25
Current Status: Open edition,
  permanently retired
Original Issue Year: 1969
Last Year: 1975
Rarity: D
Issue Price: $ 35
LCS Estimate: $ 400

No.: 1099
Name: Small Rose in Case
Height: 1
Current Status: Open edition,
  permanently retired
Original Issue Year: 1969
Last Year: 1979
Rarity: E
Issue Price: $ 17.50
LCS Estimate: $ 160

No.: 1099.30
Name: Small Rose in Case White
Height: 1
Current Status: Open edition,
  permanently retired
Original Issue Year: 1969
Last Year: 1979
Rarity: E
Issue Price: $ 17.50
LCS Estimate: $ 160

No.: 1100
Name: Small Rose on Plaque
Height: 1
Current Status: Open edition,
  permanently retired
Original Issue Year: 1969
Last Year: 1975
Rarity: D
Issue Price: $ 35
LCS Estimate: $ 400

No.: 1100.30
Name: Small Rose on Plaque White
Height: 1
Current Status: Open edition,
  permanently retired
Original Issue Year: 1969
Last Year: 1975
Rarity: D
Issue Price: $ 35
LCS Estimate: $ 400

No.: 1101
Name: Two Roses in Case
Height: 1.5
Current Status: Open edition,
  permanently retired
Original Issue Year: 1969
Last Year: 1979
Rarity: E
Issue Price: $ 30
LCS Estimate: $ 275

No.: 1101.30
Name: Two Roses in Case White
Height: 1.5
Current Status: Open edition,
  permanently retired
Original Issue Year: 1969
Last Year: 1979
Rarity: E
Issue Price: $ 30
LCS Estimate: $ 275

No.: 1102
Name: Two Roses on Plaque White
Height: 1.5
Current Status: Open edition,
  permanently retired
Original Issue Year: 1969
Last Year: 1975
Rarity: D
Issue Price: $ 42.50
LCS Estimate: $ 470

No.: 1102.30
Name: Two Roses on Plaque
Height: 1.5
Current Status: Open edition,
  permanently retired
Original Issue Year: 1969
Last Year: 1975
Rarity: D
Issue Price: $ 45
LCS Estimate: $ 500

No.: 1273
Name: Rose
Height: 2
Current Status: Open edition,
  permanently retired
Original Issue Year: 1974
Last Year: 1983
Rarity: E
Issue Price: $ 25
LCS Estimate: $ 150

No.: 1551
Name: Small Vase with Iris
Height: 5
Current Status: Open edition,
  permanently retired
Original Issue Year: 1987
Last Year: 1991
Rarity: C
Issue Price: $ 110
LCS Estimate: $ 160

No.: 4717
Name: Bellflower
Height: 13.75
Current Status: Open edition,
  permanently retired
Original Issue Year: 1970
Last Year: 1972
Rarity: B
Issue Price: $ 10
LCS Estimate: $ 120

No.: 5180
Name: Dahlia with Base
Height: 1.5
Current Status: Open edition,
  permanently retired
Original Issue Year: 1984
Last Year: 1990
Rarity: D
Issue Price: $ 65
LCS Estimate: $ 130

No.: 5180.30
Name: Dahlia
Height: 1.5
Current Status: Open edition,
  permanently retired
Original Issue Year: 1984
Last Year: 1988
Rarity: C
Issue Price: $ 62.50
LCS Estimate: $ 188

No.: 5184
Name: White Carnation
Height: 1.5
Current Status: Open edition,
  permanently retired
Original Issue Year: 1984
Last Year: 1990
Rarity: D
Issue Price: $ 67.50
LCS Estimate: $ 135

No.: 5184.30
Name: White Carnation
Height: 1.5
Current Status: Open edition,
  permanently retired
Original Issue Year: 1984
Last Year: 1988
Rarity: C
Issue Price: $ 65
LCS Estimate: $ 195

No. 82.06—Parrot *(82.06) was produced in 1956. Since then, Lladró has produced a total of 114 bird figurines.*

No. 1335—Doves Group *(1335), issued in 1977 at $475, permanently retired in 1990 and auctioned in 1992 for $1,700.*

Birds have always been a popular subject for makers of porcelain figurines. Through 1993, Lladró has issued 114 bird figurines, including the majestic *Eagles Nest* whose wing tips stand two-and-a-half feet above its base.

Of the 114:

15 are fully-subscribed limited editions,

 6 are limited editions that are still currently active,

60 are open issues that have been permanently retired,

25 are currently active open issues, and

 8 are classed as "very rare," pieces produced and discontinued before widespread distribution in the United States.

Our three classifications with this chapter are:

39 Two or more birds, from smallest to highest

36 Single birds, up to 5-1/2" in height, small to high

39 Single birds, 6" in height and more, small to high

No.: 4895
Name: Ducklings
Height: 2
Current Status: Open issue, currently active
Original Issue Year: 1974
Issue Price: $ 27.50
Current Retail Price: $ 85

No.: 1307
Name: Ducklings and Mother
Height: 4
Current Status: Open issue, currently active
Original Issue Year: 1974
Issue Price: $ 47.50
Current Retail Price: $ 145

No.: 1439
Name: How Do You Do!
Height: 4.25
Current Status: Open issue, currently active
Original Issue Year: 1983
Issue Price: $ 185
Current Retail Price: $ 295

No.: 5722
Name: Follow Me
Height: 4.5
Current Status: Open issue, currently active
Original Issue Year: 1990
Issue Price: $ 140
Current Retail Price: $ 155

No.: 1171
Name: Dove Pair
Height: 4.75
Current Status: Open issue, permanently retired
Original Issue Year: 1971
Last Year: 1978
Rarity: D
Issue Price: $ 25
LCS Estimate: $ 200

No.: 1170
Name: Kissing Doves
Height: 4.75
Current Status: Open issue, permanently retired
Original Issue Year: 1971
Last Year: 1988
Rarity: F
Issue Price: $ 25
LCS Estimate: $ 125

No.: 1169
Name: Kissing Doves
Height: 4.75
Current Status: Open issue, currently active
Original Issue Year: 1971
Issue Price: $ 32
Current Retail Price: $ 140

No.: 4525
Name: Turkeys
Height: 5
Current Status: Open issue, permanently retired
Original Issue Year: 1969
Last Year: 1972
Rarity: C
Issue Price: $ 17.50
LCS Estimate: $ 200

No.: 1228
Name: Nightingale Pair
Height: 5
Current Status: Open issue, permanently retired
Original Issue Year: 1972
Last Year: 1981
Rarity: E
Issue Price: $ 80
LCS Estimate: $ 560

No.: 4628
Name: Hen with Chicks
Height: 5.5
Current Status: Open issue, permanently retired
Original Issue Year: 1969
Last Year: 1972
Rarity: C
Issue Price: $ 20
LCS Estimate: $ 240

No.: 4549
Name: Ducks Group
Height: 6
Current Status: Open issue, currently active
Original Issue Year: 1969
Issue Price: $ 28.5
Current Retail Price: $ 200

No.: 4667
Name: Birds
Height: 6.5
Current Status: Open issue, permanently retired
Original Issue Year: 1969
Last Year: 1985
Rarity: F
Issue Price: $ 25
LCS Estimate: $ 200

No.: 1298
Name: Birds Resting
Height: 7
Current Status: Open issue,
    permanently retired
Original Issue Year: 1974
Last Year: 1985
Rarity: E
Issue Price: $ 235
LCS Estimate: $ 1400

No.: 297.13
Name: Ostriches
Height: 8.5
Current Status: Very rare early issue
Original Issue Year: 1963
Last Year: Not available
Rarity: A
Issue Price: Not available

No.: 1370
Name: Birds Singing
Height: 8.5
Current Status: Open issue,
    permanently retired
Original Issue Year: 1978
Last Year: 1985
Rarity: D
Issue Price: $ 510
High Auction Price: $ 1250
LCS Estimate: $ 1250

No.: 1368
Name: Spring Birds
Height: 9.5
Current Status: Open issue,
    permanently retired
Original Issue Year: 1978
Last Year: 1990
Rarity: E
Issue Price: $ 1600
LCS Estimate: $ 3200

No.: 1243
Name: Birds and Flowers
Height: 9.75
Current Status: Limited edition, fully
    subscribed
Edition Limit: 500
Original Issue Year: 1973
Issue Price: $ 625

No.: 330.13
Name: Group of Pelicans
Height: 10.25
Current Status: Very rare early issue
Original Issue Year: 1968
Last Year: Not available
Rarity: A
Issue Price: Not available

No.: 1611
Name: Courting Cranes
Height: 10.5
Current Status: Open issue, currently active
Original Issue Year: 1989
Issue Price: $ 565
Current Retail Price: $ 670

No.: 1462
Name: Flock of Birds
Height: 11.5
Current Status: Limited edition, currently active
Edition Limit: 1500
Original Issue Year: 1985
Issue Price: $ 1060
Current Retail Price: $ 1650

No.: 4759
Name: Ducks Flapping
Height: 11.75
Current Status: Open issue, permanently retired
Original Issue Year: 1971
Last Year: 1981
Rarity: E
Issue Price: $ 45
LCS Estimate: $ 300

No.: 2116
Name: Divers with Chicken
Height: 12.5
Current Status: Open issue, permanently retired
Original Issue Year: 1980
Last Year: 1985
Rarity: D
Issue Price: $ 1250
High Auction Price: $ 800
LCS Estimate: $ 800

No.: 2117
Name: Divers
Height: 12.75
Current Status: Open issue, permanently retired
Original Issue Year: 1980
Last Year: 1985
Rarity: D
Issue Price: $ 925
High Auction Price: $ 1000
LCS Estimate: $ 1000

No.: 1240
Name: Turtle Doves
Height: 13
Current Status: Limited edition, fully subscribed
Edition Limit: 850
Original Issue Year: 1973
Issue Price: $ 250

No.: 5691
Name: Marshland Mates
Height: 13.75
Current Status: Open issue, currently active
Original Issue Year: 1990
Issue Price: $ 950
Current Retail Price: $ 1150

No.: 1223
Name: Group of Eagle Owls
Height: 14.5
Current Status: Limited edition, fully subscribed
Edition Limit: 750
Original Issue Year: 1972
Issue Price: $ 225
High Auction Price: $ 1250

No.: 1317
Name: Ducks at the Pond
Height: 15
Current Status: Limited edition, fully subscribed
Edition Limit: 1200
Original Issue Year: 1974
Issue Price: $ 4250

No.: 1194
Name: Divers
Height: 15.5
Current Status: Limited edition, fully subscribed
Edition Limit: 500
Original Issue Year: 1972
Issue Price: $ 300

No.: 3519
Name: Turtle Dove Nest
Height: 15.75
Current Status: Limited edition, currently active
Edition Limit: 1200
Original Issue Year: 1980
Issue Price: $ 3600
Current Retail Price: $ 5750

No.: 2064
Name: Partridges Flying
Height: 15.75
Current Status: Limited edition, fully subscribed
Edition Limit: 1500
Original Issue Year: 1977
Issue Price: $ 1750

No.: 1196
Name: Turkey Group
Height: 15.75
Current Status: Limited edition, fully
  subscribed
Edition Limit: 350
Original Issue Year: 1972
Issue Price: $ 325

No.: 276.12
Name: Turtle Doves
Height: 17
Current Status: Very rare early issue
Original Issue Year: 1959
Last Year: Not available
Rarity: A
Issue Price: Not available

No.: 3520
Name: Turtle Dove Group
Height: 17.75
Current Status: Limited edition,
  currently active
Edition Limit: 750
Original Issue Year: 1980
Issue Price: $ 6800
Current Retail Price: $10900

No.: 1456
Name: Cranes
Height: 19
Current Status: Open issue, currently
  active
Original Issue Year: 1983
Issue Price: $ 1000
Current Retail Price: $ 1850

No.: 1335
Name: Doves Group
Height: 20.75
Current Status: Open issue,
  permanently retired
Original Issue Year: 1977
Last Year: 1990
Rarity: E
Issue Price: $ 475
High Auction Price: $ 1700
LCS Estimate: $ 1500

No.: 1319
Name: Herons
Height: 22.5
Current Status: Open issue, currently
  active
Original Issue Year: 1976
Issue Price: $ 1550
Current Retail Price: $ 2500

No.: 5912
Name: Swans Take Flight
Height: 22.75
Current Status: Open issue, currently active
Original Issue Year: 1992
Issue Price: $ 2850
Current Retail Price: $ 2850

No.: 1189
Name: Eagles
Height: 25.25
Current Status: Limited edition, fully subscribed
Edition Limit: 750
Original Issue Year: 1972
Issue Price: $ 450
High Auction Price: $ 3000

No.: 3523
Name: Eagles Nest
Height: 30.25
Current Status: Limited edition, currently active
Edition Limit: 300
Original Issue Year: 1981
Issue Price: $ 6900
Current Retail Price: $10900

No.: 4630
Name: Chick on the Watch
Height: 1.5
Current Status: Open issue, permanently retired
Original Issue Year: 1969
Last Year: 1972
Rarity: C
Issue Price: $ 3.50
LCS Estimate: $ 40

No.: 4631
Name: Coquettish Chick
Height: 1.5
Current Status: Open issue, permanently retired
Original Issue Year: 1969
Last Year: 1972
Rarity: C
Issue Price: $ 3.50
LCS Estimate: $ 40

No.: 4632
Name: Sleepy Chick
Height: 2
Current Status: Open issue, permanently retired
Original Issue Year: 1969
Last Year: 1972
Rarity: C
Issue Price: $ 3.50
LCS Estimate: $ 40

No.: 1053
Name: Bird
Height: 2.25
Current Status: Open issue,
  permanently retired
Original Issue Year: 1969
Last Year: 1985
Rarity: F
Issue Price: $ 13
LCS Estimate: $ 100

No.: 1599
Name: Nesting Crane
Height: 2.5
Current Status: Open issue, currently
  active
Original Issue Year: 1989
Issue Price: $ 95
Current Retail Price: $ 110

No.: 4629
Name: Guardian Chick
Height: 2.75
Current Status: Open issue,
  permanently retired
Original Issue Year: 1969
Last Year: 1972
Rarity: C
Issue Price: $ 3.50
LCS Estimate: $ 40

No.: 4551
Name: Little Duck
Height: 2.75
Current Status: Open issue, currently
  active
Original Issue Year: 1969
Issue Price: $ 45
Current Retail Price: $ 130

No.: 1264
Name: Flying Duck
Height: 2.75
Current Status: Open issue, currently
  active
Original Issue Year: 1974
Issue Price: $ 20
Current Retail Price: $ 85

No.: 1600
Name: Landing Crane
Height: 3
Current Status: Open issue, currently
  active
Original Issue Year: 1989
Issue Price: $ 115
Current Retail Price: $ 135

No.: 1598
Name: Fluttering Crane
Height: 3
Current Status: Open issue, currently active
Original Issue Year: 1989
Issue Price: $ 115
Current Retail Price: $ 135

No.: 1056
Name: Duck
Height: 4
Current Status: Open issue, permanently retired
Original Issue Year: 1969
Last Year: 1978
Rarity: E
Issue Price: $ 19
LCS Estimate: $ 170

No.: 4553
Name: Little Duck
Height: 4
Current Status: Open issue, permanently retired
Original Issue Year: 1969
Last Year: 1991
Rarity: F
Issue Price: $ 45
LCS Estimate: $ 30

No.: 1226
Name: Nightingale
Height: 4
Current Status: Open issue, permanently retired
Original Issue Year: 1972
Last Year: 1981
Rarity: E
Issue Price: $ 30
LCS Estimate: $ 210

No.: 1301
Name: Little Bird
Height: 4.25
Current Status: Open issue, permanently retired
Original Issue Year: 1974
Last Year: 1983
Rarity: E
Issue Price: $ 72.50
LCS Estimate: $ 440

No.: 1227
Name: Ladybird and Nightingale
Height: 4.25
Current Status: Open issue, permanently retired
Original Issue Year: 1973
Last Year: 1981
Rarity: E
Issue Price: $ 40
LCS Estimate: $ 280

No.: 5288
Name: Mallard Duck
Height: 4.25
Current Status: Open issue, currently active
Original Issue Year: 1985
Issue Price: $ 310
Current Retail Price: $ 495

No.: 1265
Name: Duck Jumping
Height: 4.25
Current Status: Open issue, currently active
Original Issue Year: 1974
Issue Price: $ 20
Current Retail Price: $ 85

No.: 4715
Name: Mandarin Duck
Height: 4.25
Current Status: Open issue, permanently retired
Original Issue Year: 1970
Last Year: 1972
Rarity: B
Issue Price: $ 13.50
LCS Estimate: $ 150

No.: 1041
Name: Hen
Height: 4.25
Current Status: Open issue, permanently retired
Original Issue Year: 1969
Last Year: 1975
Rarity: D
Issue Price: $ 13
LCS Estimate: $ 140

No.: 1302
Name: Blue Creeper
Height: 4.75
Current Status: Open issue, permanently retired
Original Issue Year: 1974
Last Year: 1985
Rarity: E
Issue Price: $ 110
LCS Estimate: $ 650

No.: 1244
Name: Fluttering Nightingale
Height: 4.75
Current Status: Open issue, permanently retired
Original Issue Year: 1973
Last Year: 1981
Rarity: E
Issue Price: $ 44
LCS Estimate: $ 310
Comments: Nightingale

No.: 5422
Name: Hawk Owl
Height: 4.75
Current Status: Open issue,
  permanently retired
Original Issue Year: 1987
Last Year: 1990
Rarity: C
Issue Price: $ 120
LCS Estimate: $ 240

No.: 5421
Name: Barn Owl
Height: 4.75
Current Status: Open issue,
  permanently retired
Original Issue Year: 1987
Last Year: 1990
Rarity: C
Issue Price: $ 120
LCS Estimate: $ 240

No.: 4552
Name: Little Duck
Height: 4.75
Current Status: Open issue,
  permanently retired
Original Issue Year: 1969
Last Year: 1991
Rarity: F
Issue Price: $ 45
LCS Estimate: $ 30

No.: 1042
Name: Hen
Height: 4.75
Current Status: Open issue,
  permanently retired
Original Issue Year: 1969
Last Year: 1975
Rarity: D
Issue Price: $ 13
LCS Estimate: $ 140

No.: 1054
Name: Bird
Height: 5
Current Status: Open issue,
  permanently retired
Original Issue Year: 1969
Last Year: 1985
Rarity: F
Issue Price: $ 14
LCS Estimate: $ 110

No.: 1300
Name: Bird and Butterfly
Height: 5
Current Status: Open issue,
  permanently retired
Original Issue Year: 1974
Last Year: 1985
Rarity: E
Issue Price: $ 100
LCS Estimate: $ 600

No.: 329.13
Name: Martin
Height: 5
Current Status: Very rare early issue
Original Issue Year: 1968
Last Year: Not available
Rarity: A
Issue Price: Not available

No.: 1051
Name: Tern
Height: 5
Current Status: Open issue, permanently retired
Original Issue Year: 1969
Last Year: 1978
Rarity: E
Issue Price: $ 21
LCS Estimate: $ 180

No.: 1057
Name: Duck
Height: 5
Current Status: Open issue, permanently retired
Original Issue Year: 1969
Last Year: 1978
Rarity: E
Issue Price: $ 19.50
LCS Estimate: $ 170

No.: 1015
Name: Dove
Height: 5
Current Status: Open issue, currently active
Original Issue Year: 1969
Issue Price: $ 21
Current Retail Price: $ 100

No.: 1043
Name: Cock
Height: 5
Current Status: Open issue, permanently retired
Original Issue Year: 1969
Last Year: 1975
Rarity: D
Issue Price: $ 13
LCS Estimate: $ 140

No.: 2088
Name: Small Partridge
Height: 5
Current Status: Open issue, permanently retired
Original Issue Year: 1978
Last Year: 1981
Rarity: C
Issue Price: $ 45
LCS Estimate: $ 275

No.: 1303
Name: Bird on Cactus
Height: 5.5
Current Status: Open issue,
   permanently retired
Original Issue Year: 1974
Last Year: 1983
Rarity: E
Issue Price: $ 150
LCS Estimate: $ 900

No.: 5248
Name: Penguin
Height: 5.5
Current Status: Open issue,
   permanently retired
Original Issue Year: 1984
Last Year: 1988
Rarity: C
Issue Price: $ 70
High Auction Price: $ 187.5
LCS Estimate: $ 210

No.: 1263
Name: Duck Running
Height: 5.5
Current Status: Open issue, currently
   active
Original Issue Year: 1974
Issue Price: $ 20
Current Retail Price: $ 85

No.: 4829
Name: Swan
Height: 6
Current Status: Open issue,
   permanently retired
Original Issue Year: 1972
Last Year: 1983
Rarity: E
Issue Price: $ 16
High Auction Price: $ 300
LCS Estimate: $ 300

No.: 5249
Name: Penguin
Height: 6
Current Status: Open issue,
   permanently retired
Original Issue Year: 1984
Last Year: 1988
Rarity: C
Issue Price: $ 70
High Auction Price: $ 187.50
LCS Estimate: $ 210

No.: 5420
Name: Horned Owl
Height: 6
Current Status: Open issue,
   permanently retired
Original Issue Year: 1987
Last Year: 1990
Rarity: C
Issue Price: $ 150
LCS Estimate: $ 300

No.: 2020
Name: Little Eagle Owl
Height: 6.25
Current Status: Open issue,
   permanently retired
Original Issue Year: 1971
Last Year: 1985
Rarity: E
Issue Price: $ 15
High Auction Price: $ 750
LCS Estimate: $ 600

No.: 1299
Name: Bird in Nest
Height: 6.25
Current Status: Open issue,
   permanently retired
Original Issue Year: 1974
Last Year: 1985
Rarity: E
Issue Price: $ 120
LCS Estimate: $ 700

No.: 5419
Name: Great Gray Owl
Height: 6.5
Current Status: Open issue,
   permanently retired
Original Issue Year: 1987
Last Year: 1990
Rarity: C
Issue Price: $ 190
High Auction Price: $ 175
LCS Estimate: $ 300

No.: 5247
Name: Penguin
Height: 6.5
Current Status: Open issue,
   permanently retired
Original Issue Year: 1984
Last Year: 1988
Rarity: C
Issue Price: $ 70
LCS Estimate: $ 210

No.: 1371
Name: Ready to Fly
Height: 7
Current Status: Open issue,
   permanently retired
Original Issue Year: 1978
Last Year: 1985
Rarity: D
Issue Price: $ 375
LCS Estimate: $ 1750

No.: 2036
Name: Decorative Hen
Height: 7
Current Status: Open issue,
   permanently retired
Original Issue Year: 1971
Last Year: 1973
Rarity: B
Issue Price: $ 25
LCS Estimate: $ 275

No.: 4589
Name: Rooster (reduced)
Height: 7.5
Current Status: Open issue,
  permanently retired
Original Issue Year: 1969
Last Year: 1981
Rarity: E
Issue Price: $ 15
LCS Estimate: $ 125

No.: 1612
Name: Preening Crane
Height: 7.5
Current Status: Open issue, currently
  active
Original Issue Year: 1989
Issue Price: $ 385
Current Retail Price: $ 465

No.: 1016
Name: Dove
Height: 7.5
Current Status: Open issue, currently
  active
Original Issue Year: 1969
Issue Price: $ 36
Current Retail Price: $ 170

No.: 5418
Name: Short Eared Owl
Height: 7.75
Current Status: Open issue,
  permanently retired
Original Issue Year: 1987
Last Year: 1990
Rarity: C
Issue Price: $ 200
High Auction Price: $ 225
LCS Estimate: $ 250

No.: 1613
Name: Bowing Crane
Height: 7.75
Current Status: Open issue, currently
  active
Original Issue Year: 1989
Issue Price: $ 385
Current Retail Price: $ 465

No.: 82.06
Name: Parrot
Height: 8.25
Current Status: Very rare early issue
Original Issue Year: 1956
Last Year: Not available
Rarity: A
Issue Price: Not available

No.: 1224
Name: Eagle Owl
Height: 8.25
Current Status: Open issue,
   permanently retired
Original Issue Year: 1972
Last Year: 1978
Rarity: D
Issue Price: $ 170
LCS Estimate: $ 1360

No.: 5230
Name: Graceful Swan
Height: 8.5
Current Status: Open issue,
   permanently retired
Original Issue Year: 1984
Last Year: 1991
Rarity: D
Issue Price: $ 35
LCS Estimate: $ 35

No.: 4588
Name: White Cockerel
Height: 8.5
Current Status: Open issue,
   permanently retired
Original Issue Year: 1969
Last Year: 1979
Rarity: E
Issue Price: $ 17.50
LCS Estimate: $ 160

No.: 4587
Name: Rooster
Height: 8.5
Current Status: Open issue,
   permanently retired
Original Issue Year: 1969
Last Year: 1979
Rarity: E
Issue Price: $ 25
LCS Estimate: $ 225

No.: 2087
Name: Big Partridge
Height: 9.5
Current Status: Open issue,
   permanently retired
Original Issue Year: 1978
Last Year: 1981
Rarity: C
Issue Price: $ 85
LCS Estimate: $ 500

No.: 1290
Name: Partridge
Height: 9.75
Current Status: Limited edition, fully
   subscribed
Edition Limit: 800
Original Issue Year: 1974
Issue Price: $ 700

No.: 2019
Name: Owl
Height: 10.25
Current Status: Open issue,
  permanently retired
Original Issue Year: 1971
Last Year: 1973
Rarity: B
Issue Price: $ 27.50
LCS Estimate: $ 300

No.: 338.13
Name: Pheasant
Height: 10.5
Current Status: Very rare early issue
Original Issue Year: 1968
Last Year: Not available
Rarity: A
Issue Price: Not available

No.: 4550
Name: Turtle-Dove
Height: 11
Current Status: Open issue, currently
  active
Original Issue Year: 1969
Issue Price: $ 47.50
Current Retail Price: $ 235

No.: 331.13
Name: Pheasant
Height: 11.5
Current Status: Very rare, early issue
Original Issue Year: 1973
Last Year: Not available
Rarity: A
Issue Price: Not available

No.: 1614
Name: Dancing Crane
Height: 11.5
Current Status: Open issue, currently
  active
Original Issue Year: 1989
Issue Price: $ 385
Current Retail Price: $ 465

No.: 1009
Name: Sea Gull
Height: 11.75
Current Status: Open issue,
  permanently retired
Original Issue Year: 1969
Last Year: 1970
Rarity: B
Issue Price: $ 120
LCS Estimate: $ 1440

No.: 5231
Name: Swan with Wings Spread
Height: 12.25
Current Status: Open issue, currently active
Original Issue Year: 1984
Last Year: 1991
Rarity: D
Issue Price: $ 50
LCS Estimate: $ 115

No.: 5602
Name: Freedom
Height: 12.25
Current Status: Limited edition, fully subscribed
Edition Limit: 1500
Original Issue Year: 1989
Last Year: 1989
Rarity: B
Issue Price: $ 875
High Auction Price: $ 1200

No.: 337.13
Name: Pheasant
Height: 13.5
Current Status: Very rare early issue
Original Issue Year: 1968
Last Year: Not available
Rarity: A
Issue Price: Not available

No.: 3009.10
Name: Owl
Height: 15.5
Current Status: Limited edition, fully subscribed
Edition Limit: 400
Original Issue Year: 1986
Issue Price: $ 1375

No.: 3009.60
Name: Owl
Height: 15.5
Current Status: Limited edition, fully subscribed
Edition Limit: 400
Original Issue Year: 1986
Issue Price: $ 1375

No.: 3009.90
Name: Owl
Height: 15.5
Current Status: Limited edition, fully subscribed
Edition Limit: 400
Original Issue Year: 1986
issue Price: $ 1375

No.: 3009.80
Name: Owl
Height: 15.5
Current Status: Limited edition, fully subscribed
Edition Limit: 400
Original Issue Year: 1986
Issue Price: $ 1375

No.: 2033
Name: Decorative Rooster
Height: 15.5
Current Status: Open issue, permanently retired
Original Issue Year: 1971
Last Year: 1973
Rarity: B
Issue Price: $ 55
High Auction Price: $ 375
LCS Estimate: $ 375

No.: 3009.70
Name: Owl
Height: 15.5
Current Status: Limited edition, fully subscribed
Edition Limit: 400
Original Issue Year: 1986
Issue Price: $ 1375

No.: 1738
Name: Liberty Eagle
Height: 15.75
Current Status: Limited edition, currently active
Edition Limit: 1500
Original Issue Year: 1991
Issue Price: $ 1000
Current Retail Price: $ 1050

No.: 1032
Name: Crane
Height: 17.75
Current Status: Open issue, permanently retired
Original Issue Year: 1969
Last Year: 1975
Rarity: D
Issue Price: $ 80
LCS Estimate: $ 900

No.: 5863
Name: Justice Eagle
Height: 18.75
Current Status: Limited edition, currently active
Edition Limit: 1500
Original Issue Year: 1992
Issue Price: $ 1700
Current Retail Price: $ 1700

No. 4668—Maja Head *(4668) was produced in 1969 and issued at a price of $50. It was permanently retired in 1985. It reached a price of $850 in a 1992 auction.*

Figurines of human beings have dominated the Lladró collection since its earliest days. Most are of full-figured people, but 163 are of busts, head and partial torsos. Of the 163:

76 are of solitary females
48 are of single males and
39 are of groups, including infants, or singles and groups of fantasy characters.

Of the 163:

23 are fully-subscribed limited editions,
6 are limited editions that are still currently active,
91 are open issues that have been permanently retired,
38 are currently active open issues, and
1 is classed as "very rare," produced and discontinued before widespread distribution in the United States.

The following figures are further classified by height, from the shortest to the tallest.

No. 2078—Lola *(2078) was issued in 1978 at an original price of $250. She was retired in 1981. Placed on the auction block in 1992, she was auctioned for $900.*

Busts, Heads and Torsos

No.: 5668
Name: Valencian Harvest
Height: 5.5
Current Status: Open issue,
   permanently retired
Original Issue Year: 1990
Last Year: 1993
Rarity: C
Issue Price: $ 175
Last Retail Price: $ 205

No.: 1663
Name: Mardi Gras Bust
Height: 6
Current Status: Open issue,
   permanently retired
Original Issue Year: 1989
Last Year: 1991
Rarity: B
Issue Price: $ 460
LCS Estimate: $ 460

No.: 1661
Name: Mardi Gras Bust
Height: 6
Current Status: Open issue,
   permanently retired
Original Issue Year: 1989
Last Year: 1991
Rarity: B
Issue Price: $ 500
LCS Estimate: $ 825

No.: 5669
Name: Valencian Flowers
Height: 6
Current Status: Open issue,
   permanently retired
Original Issue Year: 1990
Last Year: 1993
Rarity: C
Issue Price: $ 370
Last Retail Price: $ 420

No.: 5670
Name: Valencian Beauty
Height: 6
Current Status: Open issue,
   permanently retired
Original Issue Year: 1990
Last Year: 1993
Rarity: C
Issue Price: $ 175
Last Retail Price: $ 205

No.: 1672
Name: Kerchief's Lady
Height: 6.25
Current Status: Open issue,
   permanently retired
Original Issue Year: 1989
Last Year: 1991
Rarity: B
Issue Price: $ 240
LCS Estimate: $ 420

No.: 1662
Name: Mardi Gras Bust
Height: 6.25
Current Status: Open issue,
permanently retired
Original Issue Year: 1989
Last Year: 1991
Rarity: B
Issue Price: $ 465
LCS Estimate: $ 950

No.: 1664
Name: Mardi Gras Bust
Height: 6.25
Current Status: Open issue,
permanently retired
Original Issue Year: 1989
Last Year: 1991
Rarity: B
Issue Price: $ 465
LCS Estimate: $ 950

No.: 2041
Name: Girl's Head
Height: 6.5
Current Status: Open issue,
permanently retired
Original Issue Year: 1971
Last Year: 1975
Rarity: C
Issue Price: $ 35
LCS Estimate: $ 350

No.: 1666
Name: Romantic Lady with Veil
Height: 6.5
Current Status: Open issue,
permanently retired
Original Issue Year: 1989
Last Year: 1993
Rarity: D
Issue Price: $ 420
Last Retail Price: $ 520

No.: 1671
Name: Lady of Style
Height: 7
Current Status: Open issue,
permanently retired
Original Issue Year: 1989
Last Year: 1991
Rarity: B
Issue Price: $ 235
LCS Estimate: $ 235

No.: 1665
Name: Lady With Hat
Height: 7
Current Status: Open issue,
permanently retired
Original Issue Year: 1989
Last Year: 1991
Rarity: B
Issue Price: $ 300
LCS Estimate: $ 640

No.: 2042
Name: Girl's Head
Height: 7
Current Status: Open issue,
  permanently retired
Original Issue Year: 1971
Last Year: 1975
Rarity: C
Issue Price: $ 32.50
LCS Estimate: $ 325

No.: 2140
Name: Pepita with Sombrero
Height: 7
Current Status: Open issue, currently
  active
Original Issue Year: 1984
Issue Price: $ 97.50
Current Retail Price: $ 175

No.: 5980
Name: The Past-White
Height: 7.5
Current Status: Open issue, currently
  active
Original Issue Year: 1993
Issue Price: $ 325

No.: 5981
Name: The Past-Black
Height: 7.5
Current Status: Open issue, currently
  active
Original Issue Year: 1993
Issue Price: $ 325

No.: 5982
Name: The Past-Sand
Height: 7.5
Current Status: Open issue, currently
  active
Original Issue Year: 1993
Issue Price: $ 325

No.: 5983
Name: Deity-White
Height: 7.5
Current Status: Open issue, currently
  active
Original Issue Year: 1993
Issue Price: $ 325

No.: 5984
Name: Deity-Black
Height: 7.5
Current Status: Open issue, currently active
Original Issue Year: 1993
Issue Price: $ 325

No.: 5985
Name: Deity-Sand
Height: 7.5
Current Status: Open issue, currently active
Original Issue Year: 1993
Issue Price: $ 325

No.: 1539
Name: Small Bust with Veil
Height: 8.25
Current Status: Open issue, currently active
Original Issue Year: 1988
Issue Price: $ 225
Current Retail Price: $ 340

No.: 4649
Name: Madonna Head
Height: 8.25
Current Status: Open issue, currently active
Original Issue Year: 1969
Issue Price: $ 25
Current Retail Price: $ 140

No.: 2148
Name: Head of Congolese Woman
Height: 8.5
Current Status: Open issue, permanently retired
Original Issue Year: 1984
Last Year: 1988
Rarity: C
Issue Price: $ 55
LCS Estimate: $ 165

No.: 1109
Name: Girl's Head
Height: 8.5
Current Status: Open issue, permanently retired
Original Issue Year: 1971
Last Year: 1975
Rarity: C
Issue Price: $ 70
High Auction Price: $ 700
LCS Estimate: $ 700

No.: 5977
Name: Revelation-White
Height: 8.5
Current Status: Open issue, currently active
Original Issue Year: 1993
Issue Price: $ 325

No.: 5978
Name: Revelation-Black
Height: 8.5
Current Status: Open issue, currently active
Original Issue Year: 1993
Issue Price: $ 325

No.: 5979
Name: Revelation-Sand
Height: 8.5
Current Status: Open issue, currently active
Original Issue Year: 1993
Issue Price: $ 325

No.: 1668
Name: White Lady
Height: 9
Current Status: Open issue, permanently retired
Original Issue Year: 1989
Last Year: 1991
Rarity: B
Issue Price: $ 340
LCS Estimate: $ 340

No.: 1667
Name: Lavender Lady
Height: 9
Current Status: Open issue, permanently retired
Original Issue Year: 1989
Last Year: 1991
Rarity: B
Issue Price: $ 385
LCS Estimate: $ 385

No.: 1669
Name: Turbanned Beauty
Height: 9
Current Status: Open issue, permanently retired
Original Issue Year: 1989
Last Year: 1991
Rarity: B
Issue Price: $ 410
LCS Estimate: $ 410

No.: 1670
Name: Spring Lady
Height: 9
Current Status: Open issue,
   permanently retired
Original Issue Year: 1989
Last Year: 1991
Rarity: B
Issue Price: $ 1200
LCS Estimate: $ 1200

No.: 5090
Name: Girl's Head
Height: 9
Current Status: Open issue,
   permanently retired
Original Issue Year: 1980
Last Year: 1981
Rarity: B
Issue Price: $ 130
LCS Estimate: $ 800

No.: 4946
Name: Senorita
Height: 9.5
Current Status: Open issue,
   permanently retired
Original Issue Year: 1976
Last Year: 1985
Rarity: D
Issue Price: $ 130
LCS Estimate: $ 780

No.: 1488
Name: Lady of the East
Height: 9.75
Current Status: Open issue,
   permanently retired
Original Issue Year: 1986
Last Year: 1993
Rarity: E
Issue Price: $ 625
Last Retail Price: $ 1100

No.: 5801
Name: Charm
Height: 10
Current Status: Limited edition,
   permanently retired
Edition Limit: 500
Original Issue Year: 1991
Last Year: 1993
Rarity: C
Issue Price: $ 650
Last Retail Price: $ 725

No.: 1108
Name: Girl's Head
Height: 10.5
Current Status: Open issue,
   permanently retired
Original Issue Year: 1971
Last Year: 1973
Rarity: B
Issue Price: $ 70
LCS Estimate: $ 770

No.: 1729
Name: Mayoress
Height: 10.5
Current Status: Open issue,
  permanently retired
Original Issue Year: 1989
Last Year: 1991
Rarity: B
Issue Price: $ 600
LCS Estimate: $ 600

No.: 1003
Name: Girl's Head
Height: 10.5
Current Status: Open issue,
  permanently retired
Original Issue Year: 1969
Last Year: 1985
Rarity: F
Issue Price: $ 150
High Auction Price: $ 400
LCS Estimate: $ 700

No.: 1003.30
Name: Girl's Head (White)
Height: 10.5
Current Status: Open issue,
  permanently retired
Original Issue Year: 1984
Last Year: 1985
Rarity: B
Issue Price: $ 392.5
High Auction Price: $ 500
LCS Estimate: $ 500

No.: 1106
Name: Byzantine Head
Height: 10.5
Current Status: Open issue,
  permanently retired
Original Issue Year: 1971
Last Year: 1975
Rarity: C
Issue Price: $ 105
LCS Estimate: $ 1000

No.: 2250
Name: Autumn Glow
Height: 10.75
Current Status: Limited edition,
  currently active
Original Issue Year: 1993
Edition Limit: 1500
Issue Price: $ 775

No.: 5337
Name: La Gioconda
Height: 11
Current Status: Open issue,
  permanently retired
Original Issue Year: 1985
Last Year: 1988
Rarity: C
Issue Price: $ 350
LCS Estimate: $ 1000

No.: 2014
Name: Water Carrier Girl
Height: 11
Current Status: Open issue,
  permanently retired
Original Issue Year: 1970
Last Year: 1975
Rarity: D
Issue Price: $ 325
LCS Estimate: $ 3260

No.: 1107
Name: Girl's Head
Height: 11.5
Current Status: Open issue,
  permanently retired
Original Issue Year: 1971
Last Year: 1975
Rarity: C
Issue Price: $ 95
LCS Estimate: $ 950

No.: 1391
Name: Girl's Head with Flowers
Height: 11.5
Current Status: Open issue,
  permanently retired
Original Issue Year: 1981
Last Year: 1983
Rarity: B
Issue Price: $ 1250
LCS Estimate: $ 6000

No.: 5152
Name: Girl's Head
Height: 11.75
Current Status: Open issue,
  permanently retired
Original Issue Year: 1982
Last Year: 1983
Rarity: B
Issue Price: $ 535
LCS Estimate: $ 3000

No.: 4668
Name: Maja Head
Height: 12.25
Current Status: Open issue,
  permanently retired
Original Issue Year: 1969
Last Year: 1985
Rarity: F
Issue Price: $ 50
High Auction Price: $ 850
LCS Estimate: $ 750

No.: 2249
Name: Holiday Glow
Height: 12.25
Current Status: Open issue, currently
  active
Original Issue Year: 1993
Edition Limit: 1500
Issue Price: $ 775

No.: 5150
Name: Girl's Head
Height: 12.5
Current Status: Open issue,
  permanently retired
Original Issue Year: 1982
Last Year: 1983
Rarity: B
Issue Price: $ 435
LCS Estimate: $ 2500

No.: 5151
Name: Girl's Head
Height: 12.5
Current Status: Open issue,
  permanently retired
Original Issue Year: 1982
Last Year: 1983
Rarity: B
Issue Price: $ 380
LCS Estimate: $ 2200

No.: 1724
Name: Belle Epoque
Height: 13
Current Status: Open issue,
  permanently retired
Original Issue Year: 1989
Last Year: 1993
Rarity: D
Issue Price: $ 700
Last Retail Price: $ 775

No.: 5153
Name: Girl's Head
Height: 13
Current Status: Open issue,
  permanently retired
Original Issue Year: 1982
Last Year: 1983
Rarity: B
Issue Price: $ 475
High Auction Price: $ 575
LCS Estimate: $ 600

No.: 1538
Name: Bust With Black Veil
Height: 13.25
Current Status: Open issue, currently
  active
Original Issue Year: 1988
Issue Price: $ 650
Current Retail Price: $ 795

No.: 2078
Name: Lola
Height: 13.75
Current Status: Open issue,
  permanently retired
Original Issue Year: 1978
Last Year: 1981
Rarity: C
Issue Price: $ 250
High Auction Price: $ 900
LCS Estimate: $ 750

No.: 1538.30
Name: White Bust With Veil
Height: 13.75
Current Status: Open issue, currently
  active
Original Issue Year: 1988
Issue Price: $ 550
Current Retail Price: $ 695

No.: 1712
Name: Lady With Mantilla
Height: 14.25
Current Status: Open issue,
  permanently retired
Original Issue Year: 1989
Last Year: 1991
Rarity: B
Issue Price: $ 575
LCS Estimate: $ 575

No.: 2149
Name: Young Madonna
Height: 14.5
Current Status: Open issue,
  permanently retired
Original Issue Year: 1985
Last Year: 1988
Rarity: C
Issue Price: $ 400
LCS Estimate: $ 1200

No.: 2024
Name: Little Girl
Height: 14.5
Current Status: Open issue,
  permanently retired
Original Issue Year: 1971
Last Year: 1985
Rarity: D
Issue Price: $ 120
High Auction Price: $ 400
LCS Estimate: $ 800

No.: 2046
Name: Head Bust with Bowl
Height: 14.5
Current Status: Open issue,
  permanently retired
Original Issue Year: 1971
Last Year: 1975
Rarity: C
Issue Price: $ 105
High Auction Price: $ 625
LCS Estimate: $ 675

No.: 1711
Name: School Girl
Height: 15
Current Status: Open issue,
  permanently retired
Original Issue Year: 1988
Last Year: 1993
Rarity: D
Issue Price: $ 680
Last Retail Price: $ 865

No.: 2006
Name: Water Carrier Girl
Height: 15
Current Status: Open issue,
  permanently retired
Original Issue Year: 1970
Last Year: 1975
Rarity: D
Issue Price: $ 30
LCS Estimate: $ 300

No.: 5269
Name: Lady from Elche
Height: 15.75
Current Status: Open issue,
  permanently retired
Original Issue Year: 1985
Last Year: 1988
Rarity: C
Issue Price: $ 432.5
LCS Estimate: $ 1300

No.: 1725
Name: Young Lady with Parasol
Height: 16
Current Status: Open issue,
  permanently retired
Original Issue Year: 1989
Last Year: 1993
Rarity: D
Issue Price: $ 950
Last Retail Price: $ 1020

No.: 4768
Name: Woman from Guadalupe
Height: 16
Current Status: Open issue,
  permanently retired
Original Issue Year: 1971
Last Year: 1973
Rarity: B
Issue Price: $ 75
LCS Estimate: $ 800

No.: 4952
Name: Meditation
Height: 16
Current Status: Open issue,
  permanently retired
Original Issue Year: 1976
Last Year: 1979
Rarity: C
Issue Price: $ 200
LCS Estimate: $ 1600

No.: 2017
Name: Gardener Girl
Height: 16.5
Current Status: Open issue,
  permanently retired
Original Issue Year: 1970
Last Year: 1981
Rarity: D
Issue Price: $ 120
High Auction Price: $ 700
LCS Estimate: $ 600

No.: 1726
Name: Young Lady with Fan
Height: 17
Current Status: Open issue,
  permanently retired
Original Issue Year: 1989
Last Year: 1993
Rarity: D
Issue Price: $ 750
Last Retail Price: $ 975

No.: 2107
Name: Woman with Horn
Height: 17.25
Current Status: Open issue,
  permanently retired
Original Issue Year: 1978
Last Year: 1981
Rarity: C
Issue Price: $ 800
LCS Estimate: $ 4000

No.: 2133
Name: Autumn Shepherdess
Height: 17.75
Current Status: Open issue,
  permanently retired
Original Issue Year: 1983
Last Year: 1985
Rarity: B
Issue Price: $ 285
LCS Estimate: $ 1100

No.: 4512
Name: Nude
Height: 18.5
Current Status: Open issue,
  permanently retired
Original Issue Year: 1969
Last Year: 1985
Rarity: F
Issue Price: $ 44
High Auction Price: $ 325
LCS Estimate: $ 300

No.: 2132
Name: Spring Shepherdess
Height: 18.5
Current Status: Open issue,
  permanently retired
Original Issue Year: 1983
Last Year: 1985
Rarity: B
Issue Price: $ 450
LCS Estimate: $ 1725

No.: 4512.30
Name: Torso in White
Height: 18.5
Current Status: Open issue,
  permanently retired
Original Issue Year: 1983
Last Year: 1985
Rarity: B
Issue Price: $ 100
High Auction Price: $ 375
LCS Estimate: $ 375

No.: 2128
Name: Venus
Height: 22
Current Status: Open issue, currently active
Original Issue Year: 1983
Issue Price: $ 650
Current Retail Price: $ 1150

No.: 3551
Name: Bather
Height: 23.25
Current Status: Limited edition, fully subscribed
Edition Limit: 300
Original Issue Year: 1983
Issue Price: $ 975

No.: 3531
Name: Victory
Height: 25.25
Current Status: Limited edition, fully subscribed
Edition Limit: 90
Original Issue Year: 1983
Issue Price: $ 1500

No.: 4948
Name: "Tawny" Nude
Height: 31.5
Current Status: Open issue, permanently retired
Original Issue Year: 1976
Last Year: 1979
Rarity: C
Issue Price: $ 600
LCS Estimate: $ 4800

No.: 4716
Name: Little Maurice
Height: 4.25
Current Status: Open issue, permanently retired
Original Issue Year: 1970
Last Year: 1973
Rarity: C
Issue Price: $ 55
LCS Estimate: $ 600

No.: 5600
Name: The Blues
Height: 6.5
Current Status: Open issue, permanently retired
Original Issue Year: 1989
Last Year: 1993
Rarity: D
Issue Price: $ 265
Last Retail Price: $ 340

No.: 5586
Name: Sad Note
Height: 7
Current Status: Open issue,
  permanently retired
Original Issue Year: 1989
Last Year: 1993
Rarity: D
Issue Price: $ 185
Last Retail Price: $ 275

No.: 5585
Name: Fine Melody
Height: 7
Current Status: Open issue,
  permanently retired
Original Issue Year: 1989
Last Year: 1993
Rarity: D
Issue Price: $ 225
Last Retail Price: $ 295

No.: 1696
Name: Little Boy
Height: 7.75
Current Status: Open issue,
  permanently retired
Original Issue Year: 1988
Last Year: 1991
Rarity: C
Issue Price: $ 525
LCS Estimate: $ 525

No.: 1105
Name: Boy with Cornet
Height: 8.25
Current Status: Open issue,
  permanently retired
Original Issue Year: 1971
Last Year: 1973
Rarity: B
Issue Price: $ 30
High Auction Price: $ 400
LCS Estimate: $ 600

No.: 5611
Name: Sad Clown
Height: 8.25
Current Status: Open issue, currently
  active
Original Issue Year: 1989
Issue Price: $ 335
Current Retail Price: $ 400

No.: 5610
Name: Star Struck
Height: 8.5
Current Status: Open issue, currently
  active
Original Issue Year: 1989
Issue Price: $ 335
Current Retail Price: $ 400

No.: 5612
Name: Reflecting
Height: 9.5
Current Status: Open issue, currently active
Original Issue Year: 1989
Issue Price: $ 335
Current Retail Price: $ 400

No.: 4685
Name: Tricornered Hat
Height: 9.5
Current Status: Open issue, permanently retired
Original Issue Year: 1970
Last Year: 1984
Rarity: D
Issue Price: $ 25
LCS Estimate: $ 175

No.: 5130
Name: Clown's Head with Bowler Hat
Height: 9.75
Current Status: Open issue, currently active
Original Issue Year: 1982
Issue Price: $ 250
Current Retail Price: $ 395

No.: 1702
Name: Harlequin Bust with Hat
Height: 10.25
Current Status: Open issue, permanently retired
Original Issue Year: 1988
Last Year: 1991
Rarity: C
Issue Price: $ 765
LCS Estimate: $ 765

No.: 1703
Name: Harlequin Bust with Cornered Hat
Height: 10.5
Current Status: Open issue, permanently retired
Original Issue Year: 1988
Last Year: 1991
Rarity: C
Issue Price: $ 595
LCS Estimate: $ 595

No.: 5355
Name: Consideration
Height: 10.5
Current Status: Open issue, permanently retired
Original Issue Year: 1986
Last Year: 1988
Rarity: B
Issue Price: $ 100
High Auction Price: $ 250
LCS Estimate: $ 300

No.: 1697
Name: Country Guide
Height: 10.5
Current Status: Open issue,
   permanently retired
Original Issue Year: 1988
Last Year: 1991
Rarity: C
Issue Price: $ 725
LCS Estimate: $ 725

No.: 5800
Name: Youth
Height: 10.75
Current Status: Limited edition,
   permanently retired
Edition Limit: 500
Original Issue Year: 1991
Last Year: 1993
Rarity: C
Issue Price: $ 650
Last Retail Price: $ 725

No.: 2127
Name: Indian Chief
Height: 11
Current Status: Open issue,
   permanently retired
Original Issue Year: 1983
Last Year: 1988
Rarity: D
Issue Price: $ 525
High Auction Price: $ 500
LCS Estimate: $ 600

No.: 1708
Name: Boy at the Fair
Height: 11
Current Status: Open issue,
   permanently retired
Original Issue Year: 1988
Last Year: 1993
Rarity: D
Issue Price: $ 550
Last Retail Price: $ 685

No.: 1708.30
Name: Boy at the Fair (Bronze)
Height: 11
Current Status: Open issue,
   permanently retired
Original Issue Year: 1988
Last Year: 1991
Rarity: C
Issue Price: $ 650
LCS Estimate: $ 650

No.: 1728
Name: Mayor
Height: 11.5
Current Status: Open issue,
   permanently retired
Original Issue Year: 1989
Last Year: 1991
Rarity: D
Issue Price: $ 1100
LCS Estimate: $ 1100

No.: 5542
Name: Melancholy
Height: 11.5
Current Status: Open issue, currently active
Original Issue Year: 1989
Issue Price: $ 375
Current Retail Price: $ 420

No.: 3011.60
Name: Don Quixote
Height: 12.25
Current Status: Limited edition, fully subscribed
Edition Limit: 750
Original Issue Year: 1986
Issue Price: $ 975

No.: 3011.10
Name: Don Quixote
Height: 12.25
Current Status: Limited edition, fully subscribed
Edition Limit: 750
Original Issue Year: 1986
Issue Price: $ 975

No.: 3011.20
Name: Don Quixote
Height: 12.25
Current Status: Limited edition, fully subscribed
Edition Limit: 750
Original Issue Year: 1986
Issue Price: $ 975

No.: 3011.30
Name: Don Quixote
Height: 12.25
Current Status: Limited edition, fully subscribed
Edition Limit: 750
Original Issue Year: 1986
Issue Price: $ 975

No.: 5129
Name: Clown's Head
Height: 12.25
Current Status: Open issue, currently active
Original Issue Year: 1982
Issue Price: $ 220
Current Retail Price: $ 385

No.: 2063
Name: Violin Player
Height: 12.25
Current Status: Limited edition, fully
  subscribed
Edition Limit: 1200
Original Issue Year: 1977
Issue Price: $ 500
High Auction Price: $ 1300

No.: 1700
Name: Cellist
Height: 13
Current Status: Open issue,
  permanently retired
Original Issue Year: 1988
Last Year: 1993
Rarity: D
Issue Price: $ 950
Last Retail Price: $ 1050

No.: 2108
Name: Fisherman
Height: 13.25
Current Status: Open issue,
  permanently retired
Original Issue Year: 1978
Last Year: 1985
Rarity: D
Issue Price: $ 500
High Auction Price: $ 1200
LCS Estimate: $ 1100

No.: 1325
Name: Seaman
Height: 14.25
Current Status: Open issue,
  permanently retired
Original Issue Year: 1976
Last Year: 1988
Rarity: D
Issue Price: $ 600
High Auction Price: $ 1200
LCS Estimate: $ 1100

No.: 1701
Name: Saxophone Player
Height: 14.5
Current Status: Open issue,
  permanently retired
Original Issue Year: 1988
Last Year: 1993
Rarity: D
Issue Price: $ 835
Last Retail Price: $ 1100

No.: 1710
Name: School Boy
Height: 15.5
Current Status: Open issue,
  permanently retired
Original Issue Year: 1988
Last Year: 1993
Rarity: D
Issue Price: $ 750
Last Retail Price: $ 865

No.: 4943
Name: Troubadour
Height: 15.5
Current Status: Open issue, permanently retired
Original Issue Year: 1976
Last Year: 1981
Rarity: D
Issue Price: $ 435
High Auction Price: $ 700
LCS Estimate: $ 700

No.: 3560
Name: The Reader
Height: 16
Current Status: Limited edition, currently active
Edition Limit: 200
Original Issue Year: 1992
Issue Price: $ 2650
Current Retail Price: $ 2650

No.: 3006.10
Name: Don Quixote
Height: 17
Current Status: Limited edition, fully subscribed
Edition Limit: 200
Original Issue Year: 1986
Issue Price: $ 1375

No.: 3006.20
Name: Don Quixote
Height: 17
Current Status: Limited edition, fully subscribed
Edition Limit: 200
Original Issue Year: 1986
Issue Price: $ 1375

No.: 3006.30
Name: Don Quixote
Height: 17
Current Status: Limited edition, fully subscribed
Edition Limit: 200
Original Issue Year: 1986
Issue Price: $ 1375

No.: 3006.40
Name: Don Quixote
Height: 17
Current Status: Limited edition, fully subscribed
Edition Limit: 200
Original Issue Year: 1986
Issue Price: $ 1375

No.: 3007.50
Name: Miguel de Cervantes
Height: 17.25
Current Status: Limited edition, fully
 subscribed
Edition Limit: 200
Original Issue Year: 1986
Issue Price: $ 1375

No.: 3007.60
Name: Miguel de Cervantes
Height: 17.25
Current Status: Limited edition, fully
 subscribed
Edition Limit: 200
Original Issue Year: 1986
Issue Price: $ 1375

No.: 3007.20
Name: Miguel de Cervantes
Height: 17.25
Current Status: Limited edition, fully
 subscribed
Edition Limit: 200
Original Issue Year: 1986
Issue Price: $ 1350

No.: 3007.10
Name: Miguel de Cervantes
Height: 17.25
Current Status: Limited edition, fully
 subscribed
Edition Limit: 200
Original Issue Year: 1986
Issue Price: $ 1375

No.: 2004
Name: Torero
Height: 18
Current Status: Open issue,
 permanently retired
Original Issue Year: 1970
Last Year: 1975
Rarity: D
Issue Price: $ 100
LCS Estimate: $ 1000

No.: 2004.30
Name: Torero
Height: 18
Current Status: Open issue,
 permanently retired
Original Issue Year: 1970
Last Year: 1975
Rarity: D
Issue Price: $ 92.50
LCS Estimate: $ 920

No.: 2176
Name: Christopher Columbus
Height: 19.25
Current Status: Open issue, currently active
Original Issue Year: 1987
Issue Price: $ 950
Current Retail Price: $ 1250

No.: 3550
Name: Boxer
Height: 19.5
Current Status: Limited edition, permanently retired
Edition Limit: 300
Original Issue Year: 1983
Last Year: 1993
Rarity: E
Issue Price: $ 850
Last Retail Price: $ 1450

No.: 1520
Name: Listen to Don Quixote
Height: 20
Current Status: Limited edition, currently active
Edition Limit: 750
Original Issue Year: 1987
Issue Price: $ 1800
Current Retail Price: $ 2750

No.: 2055
Name: Harlequin
Height: 22
Current Status: Open issue, permanently retired
Original Issue Year: 1974
Last Year: 1978
Rarity: C
Issue Price: $ 350
LCS Estimate: $ 3150

No.: 4884
Name: Angel's Head No. 1
Height: 2
Current Status: Open issue, permanently retired
Original Issue Year: 1974
Last Year: 1985
Rarity: D
Issue Price: $ 10
LCS Estimate: $ 60

No.: 4885
Name: Angels's Head No. 2
Height: 2
Current Status: Open issue, permanently retired
Original Issue Year: 1974
Last Year: 1985
Rarity: D
Issue Price: $ 10
LCS Estimate: $ 60

No.: 4886
Name: Angel's Head No. 3
Height: 2
Current Status: Open issue,
  permanently retired
Original Issue Year: 1974
Last Year: 1985
Rarity: D
Issue Price: $ 10
LCS Estimate: $ 60

No.: 1744
Name: My Only Friend
Height: 7
Current Status: Limited edition, fully
  subscribed
Edition Limit: 200
Original Issue Year: 1990
Last Year: 1991
Rarity: B
Issue Price: $ 1474
High Auction Price: $ 1900

No.: 5820
Name: Dance of Love
Height: 11.5
Current Status: Open issue,
  permanently retired
Original Issue Year: 1991
Last Year: 1993
Rarity: C '
Issue Price: $ 575
Last Retail Price: $ 625

No.: 2109
Name: Laundress and Water Carrier
Height: 12.25
Current Status: Open issue,
  permanently retired
Original Issue Year: 1978
Last Year: 1983
Rarity: D
Issue Price: $ 325
High Auction Price: $ 550
LCS Estimate: $ 500

No.: 1714
Name: Nanny
Height: 12.25
Current Status: Open issue,
  permanently retired
Original Issue Year: 1988
Last Year: 1993
Rarity: D
Issue Price: $ 575
Last Retail Price: $ 700

No.: 2199
Name: Devoted Friends
Height: 12.25
Current Status: Open issue, currently
  active
Original Issue Year: 1990
Issue Price: $ 700
Current Retail Price: $ 785

No.: 2134
Name: Nautical Watch
Height: 12.5
Current Status: Open issue,
  permanently retired
Original Issue Year: 1984
Last Year: 1988
Rarity: C
Issue Price: $ 450
LCS Estimate: $ 1350

No.: 3024
Name: Discoveries
Height: 13
Current Status: Limited edition,
  currently active
Edition Limit: 100
Original Issue Year: 1990
Issue Price: $ 1500
Current Retail Price: $ 1650

No.: 1331
Name: My Baby
Height: 13.25
Current Status: Limited edition, fully
  subscribed
Edition Limit: 1000
Original Issue Year: 1976
Issue Price: $ 275
High Auction Price: $ 1000

No.: 2009.30
Name: Boy with Goat (White)
Height: 13.75
Current Status: Open issue,
  permanently retired
Original Issue Year: 1970
Last Year: 1975
Rarity: D
Issue Price: $ 92.50
LCS Estimate: $ 920

No.: 2009
Name: Boy With Goat
Height: 13.75
Current Status: Open issue,
  permanently retired
Original Issue Year: 1970
Last Year: 1981
Rarity: D
Issue Price: $ 100
LCS Estimate: $ 700

No.: 1709
Name: Exodus
Height: 13.75
Current Status: Open issue,
  permanently retired
Original Issue Year: 1988
Last Year: 1993
Rarity: D
Issue Price: $ 785
Last Retail Price: $ 865

No.: 1718
Name: Dress Rehearsal
Height: 13.75
Current Status: Open issue,
  permanently retired
Original Issue Year: 1988
Last Year: 1993
Rarity: D
Issue Price: $ 1150
Last Retail Price: $ 1200

No.: 3008.20
Name: Quixote and Sancho
Height: 14.25
Current Status: Limited edition, fully
  subscribed
Edition Limit: 400
Original Issue Year: 1986
Issue Price: $ 1375

No.: 3008.60
Name: Quixote and Sancho
Height: 14.25
Current Status: Limited edition, fully
  subscribed
Edition Limit: 400
Original Issue Year: 1986
Issue Price: $ 1375

No.: 3008.10
Name: Quixote and Sancho
Height: 14.25
Current Status: Limited edition, fully
  subscribed
Edition Limit: 400
Original Issue Year: 1986
Issue Price: $ 1375

No.: 3008.30
Name: Quixote and Sancho
Height: 14.25
Current Status: Limited edition, fully
  subscribed
Edition Limit: 400
Original Issue Year: 1986
Issue Price: $ 1375

No.: 1719
Name: Back From The Fair
Height: 14.25
Current Status: Open issue,
  permanently retired
Original Issue Year: 1989
Last Year: 1993
Rarity: D
Issue Price: $ 1650
Last Retail Price: $ 1785

No.: 2082
Name: Nuns Singing
Height: 15
Current Status: Open issue,
 permanently retired
Original Issue Year: 1978
Last Year: 1981
Rarity: C
Issue Price: $ 800
LCS Estimate: $ 4000

No.: 2131
Name: Mother Typical Dress
Height: 15
Current Status: Open issue, currently
 active
Original Issue Year: 1983
Issue Price: $ 850
Current Retail Price: $ 1350

No.: 3521
Name: Mother Love
Height: 15.5
Current Status: Open issue,
 permanently retired
Original Issue Year: 1980
Last Year: 1990
Rarity: D
Issue Price: $ 1000
High Auction Price: $ 1150
LCS Estimate: $ 1200

No.: 1329
Name: Mother Kissing Child
Height: 15.5
Current Status: Limited edition, fully
 subscribed
Edition Limit: 750
Original Issue Year: 1976
Issue Price: $ 350

No.: 1723
Name: Hopeful Group
Height: 15.75
Current Status: Limited edition,
 permanently retired
Edition Limit: 1000
Original Issue Year: 1989
Last Year: 1993
Rarity: D
Issue Price: $ 1825
Last Retail Price: $ 1970

No.: 2013
Name: Girl with Little Dog
Height: 15.75
Current Status: Open issue,
 permanently retired
Original Issue Year: 1970
Last Year: 1975
Rarity: D
Issue Price: $ 300
LCS Estimate: $ 3000

No.: 1727
Name: Pose
Height: 16
Current Status: Open issue, permanently retired
Original Issue Year: 1989
Last Year: 1993
Rarity: D
Issue Price: $ 725
Last Retail Price: $ 875

No.: 1716
Name: Harlequin with Puppy
Height: 16
Current Status: Open issue, permanently retired
Original Issue Year: 1988
Last Year: 1993
Rarity: D
Issue Price: $ 825
Last Retail Price: $ 940

No.: 2224
Name: Cherish
Height: 16
Current Status: Open issue, currently active
Original Issue Year: 1992
Issue Price: $ 1750
Current Retail Price: $ 1750

No.: 1722
Name: Group Discussion
Height: 16.5
Current Status: Open issue, permanently retired
Original Issue Year: 1989
Last Year: 1993
Rarity: D
Issue Price: $ 1500
Last Retail Price: $ 1550

No.: 2005.30
Name: Shepherdess Sleeping
Height: 17.25
Current Status: Open issue, permanently retired
Original Issue Year: 1970
Last Year: 1975
Rarity: D
Issue Price: $ 92.5
High Auction Price: $ 600
LCS Estimate: $ 600

No.: 2005
Name: Shepherdess Sleeping
Height: 17.25
Current Status: Open issue, permanently retired
Original Issue Year: 1970
Last Year: 1981
Rarity: D
Issue Price: $ 100
High Auction Price: $ 750
LCS Estimate: $ 700

No.: 2150
Name: A Tribute to Peace
Height: 17.25
Current Status: Open issue, currently active
Original Issue Year: 1985
Issue Price: $ 470
Current Retail Price: $ 825

No.: 1717
Name: Harlequin with Dove
Height: 17.25
Current Status: Open issue, permanently retired
Original Issue Year: 1988
Last Year: 1993
Rarity: D
Issue Price: $ 900
Last Retail Price: $ 940

No.: 1715
Name: On Our Way Home
Height: 17.25
Current Status: Open issue, permanently retired
Original Issue Year: 1988
Last Year: 1993
Rarity: D
Issue Price: $ 1900
Last Retail Price: $ 2100

No.: 2051
Name: Passionate Dance
Height: 18.5
Current Status: Limited edition, fully subscribed
Edition Limit: 500
Original Issue Year: 1973
Issue Price: $ 375

No.: 981.14
Name: Allegory to Peace
Height: 19
Current Status: Very rare early issue
Original Issue Year: 1969
Last Year: Not available
Rarity: A
Issue Price: Not available

No.: 2180
Name: Dreams of Peace
Height: 20.5
Current Status: Open issue, currently active
Original Issue Year: 1988
Issue Price: $ 880
Current Retail Price: $ 995

No.: 2072
Name: Woman Bust and Child
Height: 23.25
Current Status: Open issue,
  permanently retired
Original Issue Year: 1977
Last Year: 1981
Rarity: C
Issue Price: $ 1325
High Auction Price: $ 1800
LCS Estimate: $ 1800

No. 4643—Skye Terrier *was produced in 1969, one of 215 animal figurines through 1993. Issued in 1969 for $15 and retired in 1985, he was auctioned in 1992 for $700, the Lladró record-to-date for value increase.*

Animals have been a more popular subject for makers of porcelain figurines than birds. So many Lladró animal figurines have been produced (215 in all) that we have had to classify them by popularity of species. Rather than ask you to define a Beagle hound from a Basset, the following animal figurines are divided into nine groups, from smallest to highest:

64 dogs and puppies
22 deer, elk, gazelles and
  antelopes
21 horses
16 rabbits
14 bears (with an emphasis on
  white polar bears)
14 bulls, cows, calves, oxen and
  bison
13 cats and kittens
51 "other" animals, sorted by
  species and by height

The 51 "Others" are classified into:

2 camels

8 donkeys and burros (some from
  Natvity groups)
1 little dormouse
7 elephants
1 ermine
1 fish
1 fox
4 giraffes
1 tiny hedgehog
2 hippos
2 kangaroos
2 lions
2 llamas
5 monkeys
1 pig grouping
2 rhinos
2 seals
4 sheep (also included in Nativity
  groups)
3 unicorns (they're not really
  animals, but they're certainly
  not humans either.

The animals are classified in order. If a number of deer are being chased by a number of dogs, the dogs come first. Therefore, the sculpture can be found under "Dogs" rather than "Deer".

No. 2040—Fawn Head *(2040), issued in 1977 at $70, permanently retired in 1985 and auctioned in 1992 for $600.*

Animal Figurines

129

No.: 5310
Name: Mini Cocker Spaniel
Height: 1
Current Status: Open issue, permanently retired
Original Issue Year: 1985
Last Year: 1993
Rarity: E
Issue Price: $ 35
Last Retail Price: $ 70

No.: 5309
Name: Mini Cocker Spaniel Pup
Height: 1
Current Status: Open issue, permanently retired
Original Issue Year: 1985
Last Year: 1993
Rarity: E
Issue Price: $ 35
Last Retail Price: $ 70

No.: 105.06
Name: Dog and Dice
Height: 1.5
Current Status: Very rare early issue
Original Issue Year: 1956
Last Year: Not available
Rarity: A
Issue Price: Not available

No.: 5394
Name: Poor Puppy
Height: 1.75
Current Status: Open issue, permanently retired
Original Issue Year: 1986
Last Year: 1990
Rarity: C
Issue Price: $ 25
LCS Estimate: $ 50

No.: 324.13
Name: Sleepy Dog
Height: 2
Current Status: Very rare early issue
Original Issue Year: 1976
Last Year: Not available
Rarity: A
Issue Price: Not available

No.: 5393
Name: Curiosity
Height: 2
Current Status: Open issue, permanently retired
Original Issue Year: 1986
Last Year: 1990
Rarity: C
Issue Price: $ 25
LCS Estimate: $ 50

No.: 5311
Name: Mini-Puppies (Three of them)
Height: 2
Current Status: Open issue,
   permanently retired
Original Issue Year: 1985
Last Year: 1990
Rarity: D
Issue Price: $ 65
LCS Estimate: $ 130

No.: 1072
Name: Beagle Puppy
Height: 2.25
Current Status: Open issue,
   permanently retired
Original Issue Year: 1969
Last Year: 1991
Rarity: F
Issue Price: $ 16.5
LCS Estimate: $ 175

No.: 1261
Name: Dalmation
Height: 2.25
Current Status: Open issue,
   permanently retired
Original Issue Year: 1974
Last Year: 1981
Rarity: D
Issue Price: $ 25
LCS Estimate: $ 170

No.: 1260
Name: Dalmation
Height: 2.25
Current Status: Open issue,
   permanently retired
Original Issue Year: 1974
Last Year: 1981
Rarity: D
Issue Price: $ 25
LCS Estimate: $ 170

No.: 5349
Name: Relaxing
Height: 2.5
Current Status: Open issue,
   permanently retired
Original Issue Year: 1986
Last Year: 1990
Rarity: C
Issue Price: $ 47.5
LCS Estimate: $ 145

No.: 1067
Name: Old Dog
Height: 2.75
Current Status: Open issue,
   permanently retired
Original Issue Year: 1969
Last Year: 1978
Rarity: D
Issue Price: $ 40
LCS Estimate: $ 360

No.: 4901
Name: Vagabond Dog
Height: 2.75
Current Status: Open issue,
  permanently retired
Original Issue Year: 1974
Last Year: 1979
Rarity: D
Issue Price: $ 25
LCS Estimate: $ 200

No.: 106.06
Name: Collie
Height: 3
Current Status: Very rare early issue
Original Issue Year: 1956
Last Year: Not available
Rarity: A
Issue Price: Not available

No.: 1289
Name: Good Puppy
Height: 3
Current Status: Open issue,
  permanently retired
Original Issue Year: 1974
Last Year: 1985
Rarity: D
Issue Price: $ 16.60
LCS Estimate: $ 100

No.: 4917
Name: Dog and Butterfly
Height: 3
Current Status: Open issue,
  permanently retired
Original Issue Year: 1974
Last Year: 1981
Rarity: D
Issue Price: $ 50
LCS Estimate: $ 350

No.: 4749
Name: Small Dog
Height: 3
Current Status: Open issue,
  permanently retired
Original Issue Year: 1971
Last Year: 1985
Rarity: D
Issue Price: $ 5.50
LCS Estimate: $ 35

No.: 1071
Name: Beagle Puppy
Height: 3
Current Status: Open issue,
  permanently retired
Original Issue Year: 1969
Last Year: 1992
Rarity: F
Issue Price: $ 16.5
Last Retail Price: $ 135

No.: 5350
Name: On Guard
Height: 3.5
Current Status: Open issue,
  permanently retired
Original Issue Year: 1986
Last Year: 1990
Rarity: C
Issue Price: $ 50
LCS Estimate: $ 150

No.: 5348
Name: On the Scent
Height: 3.5
Current Status: Open issue,
  permanently retired
Original Issue Year: 1986
Last Year: 1990
Rarity: C
Issue Price: $ 47.5
LCS Estimate: $ 145

No.: 5351
Name: Woe is Me
Height: 3.5
Current Status: Open issue,
  permanently retired
Original Issue Year: 1986
Last Year: 1990
Rarity: C
Issue Price: $ 45
LCS Estimate: $ 135

No.: 1262
Name: Dalmation
Height: 3.5
Current Status: Open issue,
  permanently retired
Original Issue Year: 1974
Last Year: 1981
Rarity: D
Issue Price: $ 25
LCS Estimate: $ 170

No.: 4902
Name: Moping Dog
Height: 3.5
Current Status: Open issue,
  permanently retired
Original Issue Year: 1974
Last Year: 1979
Rarity: D
Issue Price: $ 35
LCS Estimate: $ 275

No.: 308.13
Name: Hunting Dog
Height: 4
Current Status: Very rare early issue
Original Issue Year: 1963
Last Year: Not available
Rarity: A
Issue Price: Not available

No.: 5110
Name: Dog Sniffing
Height: 4
Current Status: Open issue,
    permanently retired
Original Issue Year: 1982
Last Year: 1985
Rarity: C
Issue Price: $ 50
LCS Estimate: $ 200

No.: 1367
Name: Playful Dogs
Height: 4
Current Status: Open issue,
    permanently retired
Original Issue Year: 1978
Last Year: 1982
Rarity: C
Issue Price: $ 160
LCS Estimate: $ 800

No.: 5356
Name: Wolf Hound
Height: 4
Current Status: Open issue,
    permanently retired
Original Issue Year: 1986
Last Year: 1990
Rarity: C
Issue Price: $ 45
LCS Estimate: $ 90

No.: 1070
Name: Beagle Puppy
Height: 4.25
Current Status: Open issue,
    permanently retired
Original Issue Year: 1969
Last Year: 1991
Rarity: F
Issue Price: $ 16.5
LCS Estimate: $ 70

No.: 1066
Name: Basset
Height: 4.25
Current Status: Open issue,
    permanently retired
Original Issue Year: 1969
Last Year: 1981
Rarity: D
Issue Price: $ 23.50
High Auction Price: $ 600
LCS Estimate: $ 500

No.: 5111
Name: Timid Dog
Height: 4.75
Current Status: Open issue,
    permanently retired
Original Issue Year: 1982
Last Year: 1985
Rarity: C
Issue Price: $ 44
LCS Estimate: $ 175

No.: 321.13
Name: Bulldog
Height: 5
Current Status: Very rare early issue
Original Issue Year: 1968
Last Year: Not available
Rarity: A
Issue Price: Not available

No.: 1316
Name: Dog
Height: 5
Current Status: Open issue,
  permanently retired
Original Issue Year: 1974
Last Year: 1981
Rarity: D
Issue Price: $ 45
LCS Estimate: $ 300

No.: 1282
Name: Afghan Hound
Height: 5
Current Status: Open issue,
  permanently retired
Original Issue Year: 1974
Last Year: 1985
Rarity: D
Issue Price: $ 45
High Auction Price: $ 450
LCS Estimate: $ 450

No.: 1441
Name: A Litter of Love
Height: 5
Current Status: Open issue, currently
  active
Original Issue Year: 1983
Issue Price: $ 385
Current Retail Price: $ 625

No.: 1259
Name: Poodle
Height: 5.5
Current Status: Open issue,
  permanently retired
Original Issue Year: 1974
Last Year: 1985
Rarity: D
Issue Price: $ 27.5
High Auction Price: $ 475
LCS Estimate: $ 400

No.: 4642
Name: Dog
Height: 5.5
Current Status: Open issue,
  permanently retired
Original Issue Year: 1969
Last Year: 1981
Rarity: D
Issue Price: $ 22.50
LCS Estimate: $ 175

No.: 323.13
Name: Flirt
Height: 6
Current Status: Very rare early issue
Original Issue Year: 1971
Last Year: Not available
Rarity: A
Issue Price: Not available

No.: 1139
Name: Dog and Snail
Height: 6
Current Status: Open issue,
  permanently retired
Original Issue Year: 1971
Last Year: 1981
Rarity: D
Issue Price: $ 40
LCS Estimate: $ 280

No.: 4643
Name: Skye Terrier
Height: 6
Current Status: Open issue,
  permanently retired
Original Issue Year: 1969
Last Year: 1985
Rarity: F
Issue Price: $ 15
High Auction Price: $ 700
LCS Estimate: $ 500

No.: 4641
Name: Pekingese Sitting
Height: 6
Current Status: Open issue,
  permanently retired
Original Issue Year: 1969
Last Year: 1985
Rarity: F
Issue Price: $ 20
High Auction Price: $ 475
LCS Estimate: $ 450

No.: 1149
Name: Dog's Head
Height: 6
Current Status: Open issue,
  permanently retired
Original Issue Year: 1971
Last Year: 1981
Rarity: D
Issue Price: $ 27.5
LCS Estimate: $ 190

No.: 1258
Name: Playing Dogs
Height: 6
Current Status: Open issue,
  permanently retired
Original Issue Year: 1974
Last Year: 1981
Rarity: D
Issue Price: $ 47.5
LCS Estimate: $ 330

No.: 1153
Name: Dog Playing Guitar
Height: 6
Current Status: Open issue,
  permanently retired
Original Issue Year: 1971
Last Year: 1978
Rarity: D
Issue Price: $ 32.5
LCS Estimate: $ 260

No.: 1257
Name: Mother with Pups
Height: 6
Current Status: Open issue,
  permanently retired
Original Issue Year: 1974
Last Year: 1981
Rarity: D
Issue Price: $ 50
LCS Estimate: $ 350

No.: 322.13
Name: Sad Dog
Height: 6.5
Current Status: Very rare early issue
Original Issue Year: 1971
Last Year: Not available
Rarity: A
Issue Price: Not available

No.: 1068
Name: Great Dane
Height: 6.5
Current Status: Open issue,
  permanently retired
Original Issue Year: 1969
Last Year: 1989
Rarity: F
Issue Price: $ 55
LCS Estimate: $ 280

No.: 2067
Name: Dogs - Bust
Height: 7
Current Status: Open issue,
  permanently retired
Original Issue Year: 1977
Last Year: 1979
Rarity: B
Issue Price: $ 280
LCS Estimate: $ 1900

No.: 4583
Name: Dog
Height: 7
Current Status: Open issue,
  permanently retired
Original Issue Year: 1969
Last Year: 1981
Rarity: D
Issue Price: $ 21
High Auction Price: $ 650
LCS Estimate: $ 650

No.: 1128
Name: Dog in the Basket
Height: 7.5
Current Status: Open issue,
  permanently retired
Original Issue Year: 1971
Last Year: 1985
Rarity: D
Issue Price: $ 17.50
High Auction Price: $ 425
LCS Estimate: $ 350

No.: 1156
Name: Dog Playing Bongos
Height: 7.5
Current Status: Open issue,
  permanently retired
Original Issue Year: 1971
Last Year: 1978
Rarity: D
Issue Price: $ 32.50
High Auction Price: $ 750
LCS Estimate: $ 400

No.: 4857
Name: Papillon Dog
Height: 7.5
Current Statu s: Open issue,
  permanently retired
Original Issue Year: 1974
Last Year: 1979
Rarity: D
Issue Price: $ 40
LCS Estimate: $ 320

No.: 2045
Name: Setter's Head
Height: 7.75
Current Status: Open issue,
  permanently retired
Original Issue Year: 1971
Last Year: 1981
Rarity: D
Issue Price: $ 42.5
High Auction Price: $ 550
LCS Estimate: $ 450

No.: 4731
Name: German Shepherd with Pup
Height: 7.75
Current Status: Open issue,
  permanently retired
Original Issue Year: 1970
Last Year: 1975
Rarity: D
Issue Price: $ 40
LCS Estimate: $ 400

No.: 1155
Name: Dog Singer
Height: 7.75
Current Status: Open issue,
  permanently retired
Original Issue Year: 1971
Last Year: 1978
Rarity: D
Issue Price: $ 32.50
High Auction Price: $ 375
LCS Estimate: $ 400

No.: 1121
Name: Pups in Box
Height: 8.5
Current Status: Open issue,
  permanently retired
Original Issue Year: 1971
Last Year: 1978
Rarity: D
Issue Price: $ 33
LCS Estimate: $ 260

No.: 1152
Name: Dog Playing Guitar
Height: 8.5
Current Status: Open issue,
  permanently retired
Original Issue Year: 1971
Last Year: 1978
Rarity: D
Issue Price: $ 32.5
LCS Estimate: $ 260

No.: 1154
Name: Dog Playing Bass Fiddle
Height: 8.5
Current Status: Open issue,
  permanently retired
Original Issue Year: 1971
Last Year: 1978
Rarity: D
Issue Price: $ 36.5
LCS Estimate: $ 290

No.: 325.13
Name: Poodle
Height: 8.75
Current Status: Very rare early issue
Original Issue Year: 1966
Last Year: Not available
Rarity: A
Issue Price: Not available

No.: 4957
Name: Attentive Dogs
Height: 9.75
Current Status: Open issue,
  permanently retired
Original Issue Year: 1977
Last Year: 1981
Rarity: C
Issue Price: $ 350
LCS Estimate: $ 2000

No.: 4521
Name: Deer Hunt
Height: 10.5
Current Status: Open issue,
  permanently retired
Original Issue Year: 1969
Last Year: 1970
Rarity: B
Issue Price: $ 110
LCS Estimate: $ 1300

No.: 4880
Name: Pursuit
Height: 11
Current Status: Open issue,
   permanently retired
Original Issue Year: 1974
Last Year: 1983
Rarity: D
Issue Price: $ 425
LCS Estimate: $ 2500

No.: 1069
Name: Afghan
Height: 11.5
Current Status: Open issue,
   permanently retired
Original Issue Year: 1969
Last Year: 1985
Rarity: F
Issue Price: $ 36
High Auction Price: $ 525
LCS Estimate: $ 500

No.: 1238
Name: Buck Hunters
Height: 17.75
Current Status: Limited edition, fully
   subscribed
Edition Limit: 800
Original Issue Year: 1973
Issue Price: $ 400

No.: 1377
Name: Fearful Flight
Height: 22
Current Status: Limited edition,
   currently active
Edition Limit: 750
Original Issue Year: 1978
Issue Price: $ 7000
Current Retail Price: $13500

No.: 5314
Name: Mini Deer
Height: 2
Current Status: Open issue,
   permanently retired
Original Issue Year: 1985
Last Year: 1990
Rarity: D
Issue Price: $ 40
LCS Estimate: $ 80

No.: 5673
Name: A Quiet Moment
Height: 4.25
Current Status: Open issue, currently
   active
Original Issue Year: 1990
Issue Price: $ 450
Current Retail Price: $ 495

No.: 327.13
Name: Gazelle
Height: 5
Current Status: Very rare early issue
Original Issue Year: 1963
Last Year: Not available
Rarity: A
Issue Price: Not available

No.: 2048
Name: Gazelle Resting
Height: 5
Current Status: Open issue, permanently retired
Original Issue Year: 1971
Last Year: 1979
Rarity: D
Issue Price: $ 65
LCS Estimate: $ 520

No.: 5672
Name: Hi There!
Height: 5.75
Current Status: Open issue, currently active
Original Issue Year: 1990
Issue Price: $ 450
Current Retail Price: $ 495

No.: 56.04
Name: Baby Deer and Bunny
Height: 6
Current Status: Very rare early issue
Original Issue Year: 1955
Last Year: Not available
Rarity: A
Issue Price: Not available

No.: 5674
Name: A Fawn and a Friend
Height: 6
Current Status: Open issue, currently active
Original Issue Year: 1990
Issue Price: $ 450
Current Retail Price: $ 495

No.: 1064
Name: Deer
Height: 6.5
Current Status: Open issue, permanently retired
Original Issue Year: 1969
Last Year: 1986
Rarity: F
Issue Price: $ 27.5
High Auction Price: $ 450
LCS Estimate: $ 400

No.: 5302
Name: Antelope Drinking
Height: 7
Current Status: Open issue,
   permanently retired
Original Issue Year: 1985
Last Year: 1988
Rarity: C
Issue Price: $ 215
High Auction Price: $ 375
LCS Estimate: $ 375

No.: 2191
Name: Forest Born
Height: 7.75
Current Status: Open issue,
   permanently retired
Original Issue Year: 1990
Last Year: 1991
Rarity: B
Issue Price: $ 230
LCS Estimate: $ 420

No.: 4532
Name: Watchful Gazelle
Height: 8.5
Current Status: Open issue,
   permanently retired
Original Issue Year: 1969
Last Year: 1970
Rarity: B
Issue Price: $ 30
LCS Estimate: $ 360

No.: 5001
Name: Elk Family
Height: 9
Current Status: Open issue,
   permanently retired
Original Issue Year: 1978
Last Year: 1981
Rarity: C
Issue Price: $ 550
LCS Estimate: $ 2800

No.: 4529
Name: Gazelle Jumping
Height: 10.5
Current Status: Open issue,
   permanently retired
Original Issue Year: 1969
Last Year: 1970
Rarity: B
Issue Price: $ 45
LCS Estimate: $ 560

No.: 4531
Name: Gazelle Group
Height: 10.5
Current Status: Open issue,
   permanently retired
Original Issue Year: 1969
Last Year: 1971
Rarity: B
Issue Price: $ 85
LCS Estimate: $ 1000

No.: 4530
Name: Gazelle Landing
Height: 11.5
Current Status: Open issue,
  permanently retired
Original Issue Year: 1969
Last Year: 1970
Rarity: B
Issue Price: $ 45
LCS Estimate: $ 540

No.: 5271
Name: Gazelle
Height: 13
Current Status: Open issue,
  permanently retired
Original Issue Year: 1985
Last Year: 1988
Rarity: C
Issue Price: $ 205
High Auction Price: $ 400
LCS Estimate: $ 400

No.: 4964
Name: Bucks
Height: 13.75
Current Status: Open issue,
  permanently retired
Original Issue Year: 1977
Last Year: 1981
Rarity: C
Issue Price: $ 725
LCS Estimate: $ 4000

No.: 5043
Name: Hind and Baby Deer
Height: 14.5
Current Status: Open issue,
  permanently retired
Original Issue Year: 1980
Last Year: 1981
Rarity: B
Issue Price: $ 650
LCS Estimate: $ 3500

No.: 2040
Name: Fawn Head
Height: 17
Current Status: Open issue,
  permanently retired
Original Issue Year: 1971
Last Year: 1985
Rarity: D
Issue Price: $ 70
High Auction Price: $ 600
LCS Estimate: $ 550

No.: 1352
Name: Gazelles
Height: 17
Current Status: Limited edition, fully
  subscribed
Edition Limit: 1500
Original Issue Year: 1978
Issue Price: $ 1225

No.: 3501
Name: Elk
Height: 17.75
Current Status: Limited edition, fully subscribed
Edition Limit: 500
Original Issue Year: 1982
Issue Price: $ 950

No.: 5131
Name: Deer's Fight
Height: 18
Current Status: Open issue, permanently retired
Original Issue Year: 1982
Last Year: 1985
Rarity: C
Issue Price: $ 1250
LCS Estimate: $ 4800

No.: 1203
Name: Little Horse Resting
Height: 4.75
Current Status: Open issue, permanently retired
Original Issue Year: 1972
Last Year: 1981
Rarity: D
Issue Price: $ 40
LCS Estimate: $ 320

No.: 4639
Name: Naughty Pony
Height: 4.75
Current Status: Open issue, permanently retired
Original Issue Year: 1969
Last Year: 1972
Rarity: C
Issue Price: $ 15
LCS Estimate: $ 180

No.: 4863
Name: Horse
Height: 5
Current Status: Open issue, permanently retired
Original Issue Year: 1974
Last Year: 1978
Rarity: C
Issue Price: $ 55
LCS Estimate: $ 500

No.: 4861
Name: Horse
Height: 5
Current Status: Open issue, permanently retired
Original Issue Year: 1974
Last Year: 1978
Rarity: C
Issue Price: $ 55
LCS Estimate: $ 500

No.: 4862
Name: Horse
Height: 7
Current Status: Open issue,
  permanently retired
Original Issue Year: 1974
Last Year: 1978
Rarity: C
Issue Price: $ 55
LCS Estimate: $ 500

No.: 5544
Name: Derby Winner
Height: 8.25
Current Status: Open issue,
  permanently retired
Original Issue Year: 1989
Last Year: 1991
Rarity: B
Issue Price: $ 225
LCS Estimate: $ 225

No.: 277.12
Name: Horse
Height: 9.5
Current Status: Very rare early issue
Original Issue Year: 1958
Last Year: Not available
Rarity: A
Issue Price: Not available

No.: 356.13
Name: Horse and Squirrel
Height: 9.5
Current Status: Very rare early issue
Original Issue Year: 1965
Last Year: Not available
Rarity: A
Issue Price: Not available

No.: 1133
Name: Horse
Height: 10.5
Current Status: Open issue,
  permanently retired
Original Issue Year: 1971
Last Year: 1972
Rarity: B
Issue Price: $ 115
LCS Estimate: $ 1250

No.: 3511
Name: Horse Heads
Height: 11.5
Current Status: Open issue,
  permanently retired
Original Issue Year: 1978
Last Year: 1990
Rarity: D
Issue Price: $ 260
High Auction Price: $ 700
LCS Estimate: $ 550

No.: 4655
Name: Horses Galloping
Height: 11.5
Current Status: Open issue, currently active
Original Issue Year: 1969
Issue Price: $ 110
Current Retail Price: $ 725

No.: 4597
Name: Two Horses
Height: 14.5
Current Status: Open issue, permanently retired
Original Issue Year: 1969
Last Year: 1990
Rarity: F
Issue Price: $ 240
High Auction Price: $ 1000
LCS Estimate: $ 950

No.: 1420
Name: Born Free
Height: 15
Current Status: Open issue, currently active
Original Issue Year: 1982
Issue Price: $ 1520
Current Retail Price: $ 2785

No.: 5340
Name: Thoroughbred Horse
Height: 15.5
Current Status: Limited edition, currently active
Edition Limit: 1000
Original Issue Year: 1985
Issue Price: $ 590
Current Retail Price: $ 985

No.: 4781
Name: Horse
Height: 16.5
Current Status: Open issue, permanently retired
Original Issue Year: 1971
Last Year: 1979
Rarity: D
Issue Price: $ 150
LCS Estimate: $ 1200

No.: 1021
Name: Horse's Group
Height: 17.25
Current Status: Open issue, permanently retired
Original Issue Year: 1969
Last Year: 1975
Rarity: D
Issue Price: $ 465
LCS Estimate: $ 2500

No.: 1022
Name: Horse's Group White
Height: 17.25
Current Status: Open issue, currently active
Original Issue Year: 1969
Issue Price: $ 465
Current Retail Price: $ 2000

No.: 2044
Name: Horse Head
Height: 18
Current Status: Open issue, permanently retired
Original Issue Year: 1971
Last Year: 1975
Rarity: C
Issue Price: $ 115
LCS Estimate: $ 1100

No.: 1567
Name: Running Free
Height: 19
Current Status: Open issue, currently active
Original Issue Year: 1987
Issue Price: $ 1150
Current Retail Price: $ 1450

No.: 1566
Name: Wild Stallions
Height: 20.5
Current Status: Open issue, permanently retired
Original Issue Year: 1987
Last Year: 1993
Rarity: D
Issue Price: $ 1100
Last Retail Price: $ 1465

No.: 2030
Name: Oriental Horse
Height: 26
Current Status: Limited edition, fully subscribed
Edition Limit: 350
Original Issue Year: 1971
Issue Price: $ 1100

No.: 279.12
Name: Rabbit Couple
Height: 2
Current Status: Very rare early issue
Original Issue Year: 1962
Last Year: Not available
Rarity: A
Issue Price: Not available

No.:   352.13
Name: Long Rabbit
Height: 2
Current Status: Very rare early issue
Original Issue Year: 1965
Last Year: Not available
Rarity: A
Issue Price: Not available

No.:   55.04
Name: Bunny
Height: 2.25
Current Status: Very rare early issue
Original Issue Year: 1954
Last Year: Not available
Rarity: A
Issue Price: Not available

No.: 5904
Name: Sleeping Bunny
Height: 2.25
Current Status: Open issue, currently active
Original Issue Year: 1992
Issue Price: $ 75
Current Retail Price: $ 75

No.: 278.12
Name: Rabbit Scratching
Height: 2.75
Current Status: Very rare early issue
Original Issue Year: 1962
Last Year: Not available
Rarity: A
Issue Price: Not available

No.: 4773
Name: Rabbit Eating (Grey)
Height: 3
Current Status: Open issue, currently active
Original Issue Year: 1971
Issue Price: $ 16
Current Retail Price: $ 120

No.: 4772
Name: Rabbit Eating
Height: 3
Current Status: Open issue, currently active
Original Issue Year: 1971
Issue Price: $ 16
Current Retail Price: $ 120

No.: 5888
Name: That Tickles!
Height: 3.5
Current Status: Open issue, currently active
Original Issue Year: 1992
Issue Price: $ 95
Current Retail Price: $ 95

No.: 5906
Name: Preening Bunny
Height: 3.75
Current Status: Open issue, currently active
Original Issue Year: 1992
Issue Price: $ 75
Current Retail Price: $ 75

No.: 5905
Name: Attentive Bunny
Height: 4.5
Current Status: Open issue, currently active
Original Issue Year: 1992
Issue Price: $ 75
Current Retail Price: $ 75

No.: 5887
Name: Washing Up
Height: 5
Current Status: Open issue, currently active
Original Issue Year: 1992
Issue Price: $ 95
Current Retail Price: $ 95

No.: 5886
Name: Hippity Hop
Height: 5.5
Current Status: Open issue. currently active
Original Issue Year: 1992
Issue Price: $ 95
Current Retail Price: $ 95

No.: 5907
Name: Sitting Bunny
Height: 5.5
Current Status: Open issue, currently active
Original Issue Year: 1992
Issue Price: $ 75
Current Retail Price: $ 75

No.: 309.13
Name: Rabbit Standing
Height: 6
Current Status: Very rare early issue
Original Issue Year: 1965
Last Year: Not available
Rarity: A
Issue Price: Not available

No.: 5902
Name: Easter Bunnies
Height: 6.25
Current Status: Open issue, currently active
Original Issue Year: 1992
Issue Price: $ 240
Current Retail Price: $ 240

No.: 5889
Name: Snack Time
Height: 6.75
Current Status: Open issue, currently active
Original Issue Year: 1992
Issue Price: $ 95
Current Retail Price: $ 95

No.: 1206
Name: Bear Seated
Height: 3
Current Status: Open issue, permanently retired
Original Issue Year: 1972
Last Year: 1989
Rarity: F
Issue Price: $ 16
LCS Estimate: $ 100

No.: 1209
Name: Seated Polar Bear
Height: 3
Current Status: Open issue, currently active
Original Issue Year: 1972
Issue Price: $ 16
Current Retail Price: $ 70

No.: 5434
Name: Polar Bear Miniature
Height: 3.5
Current Status: Open issue, currently active
Original Issue Year: 1987
Issue Price: $ 65
Current Retail Price: $ 95

No.: 1443
Name: Bearly Love
Height: 3.5
Current Status: Open issue, currently active
Original Issue Year: 1983
Issue Price: $ 55
Current Retail Price: $ 98

No.: 301.13
Name: Polar Bear
Height: 4
Current Status: Very rare early issue
Original Issue Year: 1965
Last Year: Not available
Rarity: A
Issue Price: Not available

No.: 1204
Name: Attentive Bear
Height: 4
Current Status: Open issue, permanently retired
Original Issue Year: 1972
Last Year: 1989
Rarity: F
Issue Price: $ 16
LCS Estimate: $ 80

No.: 1207
Name: Attentive Polar Bear
Height: 4
Current Status: Open issue, currently active
Original Issue Year: 1972
Issue Price: $ 16
Current Retail Price: $ 70

No.: 300.13
Name: Polar Bear
Height: 4.5
Current Status: Very rare early issue
Original Issue Year: 1965
Last Year: Not available
Rarity: A
Issue Price: Not available

No.: 328.13
Name: Polar Bear
Height: 4.5
Current Status: Very rare early issue
Original Issue Year: 1965
Last Year: Not available
Rarity: A
Issue Price: Not available

No.: 1205
Name: Good Bear
Height: 4.75
Current Status: Open issue,
    permanently retired
Original Issue Year: 1972
Last Year: 1989
Rarity: F
Issue Price: $ 16
LCS Estimate: $ 80

No.: 1208
Name: Polar Bear
Height: 4.75
Current Status: Open issue, currently
    active
Original Issue Year: 1972
Issue Price: $ 16
Current Retail Price: $ 70

No.: 299.13
Name: Polar Bear
Height: 7
Current Status: Very rare early issue
Original Issue Year: 1965
Last Year: Not available
Rarity: A
Issue Price: Not available

No.: 5021
Name: Painful Bear
Height: 7.25
Current Status: Open issue,
    permanently retired
Original Issue Year: 1978
Last Year: 1981
Rarity: C
Issue Price: $ 75
LCS Estimate: $ 450

No.: 5461
Name: Koala Love
Height: 8.25
Current Status: Open issue,
    permanently retired
Original Issue Year: 1988
Last Year: 1993
Rarity: D
Issue Price: $ 115
Last Retail Price: $ 150

No.: 5312
Name: Mini Bison Resting
Height: 1.5
Current Status: Open issue,
    permanently retired
Original Issue Year: 1985
Last Year: 1990
Rarity: D
Issue Price: $ 50
LCS Estimate: $ 100

No.: 5313
Name: Mini Bison Attacking
Height: 2.25
Current Status: Open issue,
    permanently retired
Original Issue Year: 1985
Last Year: 1990
Rarity: D
Issue Price: $ 57.5
LCS Estimate: $ 115

No.: 4680
Name: Manger Cow
Height: 2.25
Current Status: Open issue, currently
    active
Original Issue Year: 1969
Issue Price: $ 12
Current Retail Price: $ 85

No.: 5482
Name: Ox
Height: 2.75
Current Status: Open issue, currently
    active
Original Issue Year: 1988
Issue Price: $ 125
Current Retail Price: $ 155

No.: 5744
Name: Bull and Donkey
Height: 4.5
Current Status: Open issue, currently
    active
Original Issue Year: 1991
Issue Price: $ 250
Current Retail Price: $ 260

No.: 1390.30
Name: Ox (White)
Height: 5.25
Current Status: Open issue,
    permanently retired
Original Issue Year: 1983
Last Year: 1985
Rarity: B
Issue Price: $ 72
High Auction Price: $ 135
LCS Estimate: $ 300

No.: 1390
Name: Cow
Height: 5.25
Current Status: Open issue, currently
    active
Original Issue Year: 1981
Issue Price: $ 95
Current Retail Price: $ 175

No.: 5545
Name: El Toro
Height: 6.5
Current Status: Open issue,
  permanently retired
Original Issue Year: 1989
Last Year: 1991
Rarity: B
Issue Price: $ 225
LCS Estimate: $ 225

No.: 1062
Name: Bull with Head Down
Height: 6.5
Current Status: Open issue,
  permanently retired
Original Issue Year: 1969
Last Year: 1975
Rarity: D
Issue Price: $ 90
LCS Estimate: $ 1000

No.: 4683
Name: Calf
Height: 6.5
Current Status: Open issue,
  permanently retired
Original Issue Year: 1970
Last Year: 1972
Rarity: B
Issue Price: $ 17.50
LCS Estimate: $ 200

No.: 1063
Name: Bull with Head Up
Height: 7
Current Status: Open issue,
  permanently retired
Original Issue Year: 1969
Last Year: 1975
Rarity: D
Issue Price: $ 90
LCS Estimate: $ 1000

No.: 4945
Name: Bison
Height: 7.5
Current Status: Open issue,
  permanently retired
Original Issue Year: 1976
Last Year: 1978
Rarity: B
Issue Price: $ 100
High Auction Price: $ 3000
LCS Estimate: $ 3000

No.: 1134
Name: Bull
Height: 9
Current Status: Open issue,
  permanently retired
Original Issue Year: 1971
Last Year: 1972
Rarity: B
Issue Price: $ 130
LCS Estimate: $ 1400

No.: 4640
Name: Cow with Pig
Height: 10.25
Current Status: Open issue,
  permanently retired
Original Issue Year: 1969
Last Year: 1981
Rarity: D
Issue Price: $ 42.5
LCS Estimate: $ 340

No.: 5307
Name: Mini Kitten
Height: 1.75
Current Status: Open issue,
  permanently retired
Original Issue Year: 1985
Last Year: 1993
Rarity: E
Issue Price: $ 35
Last Retail Price: $ 70

No.: 5435
Name: Cougar
Height: 2
Current Status: Open issue,
  permanently retired
Original Issue Year: 1987
Last Year: 1990
Rarity: C
Issue Price: $ 65
LCS Estimate: $ 130

No.: 5308
Name: Mini Cat
Height: 2.25
Current Status: Open issue,
  permanently retired
Original Issue Year: 1985
Last Year: 1993
Rarity: E
Issue Price: $ 35
Last Retail Price: $ 70

No.: 5236
Name: Cat and Mouse
Height: 3
Current Status: Open issue, currently
  active
Original Issue Year: 1984
Issue Price: $ 55
Current Retail Price: $ 98

No.: 1442
Name: Kitty Confrontation
Height: 3.5
Current Status: Open issue, currently
  active
Original Issue Year: 1983
Issue Price: $ 155
Current Retail Price: $ 275

No.: 5114
Name: Surprised Cat
Height: 3.5
Current Status: Open issue, currently active
Original Issue Year: 1982
Issue Price: $ 40
Current Retail Price: $ 75

No.: 5112
Name: Attentive Cat
Height: 4
Current Status: Open issue, currently active
Original Issue Year: 1982
Issue Price: $ 40
Current Retail Price: $ 75

No.: 5091
Name: Scaredy Cat
Height: 4.25
Current Status: Open issue, currently active
Original Issue Year: 1980
Issue Price: $ 60
Current Retail Price: $ 95

No.: 1444
Name: Purr-Fect
Height: 5
Current Status: Open issue, currently active
Original Issue Year: 1983
Issue Price: $ 350
Current Retail Price: $ 595

No.: 5113
Name: Cat
Height: 5.25
Current Status: Open issue, currently active
Original Issue Year: 1982
Issue Price: $ 40
Current Retail Price: $ 75

No.: 2001
Name: Cat
Height: 6.25
Current Status: Open issue, permanently retired
Original Issue Year: 1970
Last Year: 1975
Rarity: D
Issue Price: $ 27.5
LCS Estimate: $ 280

No.: 5154
Name: Egyptian Cat (White)
Height: 13
Current Status: Open issue,
 permanently retired
Original Issue Year: 1982
Last Year: 1985
Rarity: C
Issue Price: $ 90
LCS Estimate: $ 350

No.: 2130
Name: Egyptian Cat
Height: 13
Current Status: Open issue,
 permanently retired
Original Issue Year: 1983
Last Year: 1985
Rarity: B
Issue Price: $ 75
LCS Estimate: $ 300

No.: 5315
Name: Mini Dromedary
Height: 2.75
Current Status: Open issue,
 permanently retired
Original Issue Year: 1985
Last Year: 1990
Rarity: D
Issue Price: $ 45
LCS Estimate: $ 100

No.: 2027
Name: Camel
Height: 18
Current Status: Open issue,
 permanently retired
Original Issue Year: 1971
Last Year: 1975
Rarity: C
Issue Price: $ 135
LCS Estimate: $ 2600

No.: 4679
Name: Manger Donkey
Height: 4.25
Current Status: Open issue, currently
 active
Original Issue Year: 1969
Issue Price: $ 11.5
Current Retail Price: $ 95

No.: 4821
Name: Burro
Height: 4.25
Current Status: Open issue,
 permanently retired
Original Issue Year: 1972
Last Year: 1979
Rarity: D
Issue Price: $ 24
High Auction Price: $ 450
LCS Estimate: $ 400

No.: 5483
Name: Donkey
Height: 4.75
Current Status: Open issue, currently active
Original Issue Year: 1988
Issue Price: $ 125
Current Retail Price: $ 155

No.: 4524
Name: Donkey in Love
Height: 5
Current Status: Open issue, permanently retired
Original Issue Year: 1969
Last Year: 1985
Rarity: F
Issue Price: $ 15
High Auction Price: $ 450
LCS Estimate: $ 400

No.: 5683
Name: Beautiful Burro
Height: 5.5
Current Status: Open issue, permanently retired
Original Issue Year: 1990
Last Year: 1993
Rarity: C
Issue Price: $ 280
Last Retail Price: $ 325

No.: 1389
Name: Donkey
Height: 6
Current Status: Open issue, currently active
Original Issue Year: 1981
Issue Price: $ 95
Current Retail Price: $ 175

No.: 1389.30
Name: Donkey (White)
Height: 6
Current Status: Open issue, permanently retired
Original Issue Year: 1983
Last Year: 1985
Rarity: B
Issue Price: $ 72
High Auction Price: $ 135
LCS Estimate: $ 300

No.: 2124
Name: Donkey with Pack Saddle
Height: 9.75
Current Status: Open issue, permanently retired
Original Issue Year: 1980
Last Year: 1983
Rarity: C
Issue Price: $ 325
LCS Estimate: $ 1500

No.: 4774
Name: Dormouse
Height: 9
Current Status: Open issue,
  permanently retired
Original Issue Year: 1971
Last Year: 1983
Rarity: D
Issue Price: $ 30
High Auction Price: $ 350
LCS Estimate: $ 350

No.: 5438
Name: Elephant
Height: 2
Current Status: Open issue,
  permanently retired
Original Issue Year: 1987
Last Year: 1990
Rarity: C
Issue Price: $ 50
LCS Estimate: $ 100

No.: 5020
Name: Painful Elephant
Height: 5.5
Current Status: Open issue,
  permanently retired
Original Issue Year: 1978
Last Year: 1981
Rarity: C
Issue Price: $ 85
LCS Estimate: $ 500

No.: 4765
Name: Maternal Elephant
Height: 7
Current Status: Open issue,
  permanently retired
Original Issue Year: 1971
Last Year: 1975
Rarity: C
Issue Price: $ 50
LCS Estimate: $ 500

No.: 1151
Name: Two Elephants
Height: 11.75
Current Status: Open issue, currently
  active
Original Issue Year: 1971
Issue Price: $ 45
Current Retail Price: $ 375

No.: 1150
Name: Elephants Walking
Height: 14.5
Current Status: Open issue, currently
  active
Original Issue Year: 1971
Issue Price: $ 100
Current Retail Price: $ 775

No.: 4764
Name: Elephant Family
Height: 14.5
Current Status: Open issue,
  permanently retired
Original Issue Year: 1971
Last Year: 1975
Rarity: C
Issue Price: $ 90
LCS Estimate: $ 900

No.: 2110
Name: Elephant
Height: 16.75
Current Status: Open issue,
  permanently retired
Original Issue Year: 1978
Last Year: 1983
Rarity: D
Issue Price: $ 750
LCS Estimate: $ 3800

No.: 4769
Name: Ermine
Height: 9.5
Current Status: Open issue,
  permanently retired
Original Issue Year: 1971
Last Year: 1975
Rarity: C
Issue Price: $ 25
LCS Estimate: $ 250

No.: 1210
Name: Round Fish
Height: 4
Current Status: Open issue,
  permanently retired
Original Issue Year: 1972
Last Year: 1981
Rarity: D
Issue Price: $ 35
LCS Estimate: $ 250

No.: 1065
Name: Fox and Cub
Height: 3
Current Status: Open issue,
  permanently retired
Original Issue Year: 1969
Last Year: 1985
Rarity: F
Issue Price: $ 17.5
High Auction Price: $ 250
LCS Estimate: $ 140

No.: 5316
Name: Mini Giraffe
Height: 3.5
Current Status: Open issue,
  permanently retired
Original Issue Year: 1985
Last Year: 1990
Rarity: D
Issue Price: $ 50
LCS Estimate: $ 100

No.: 1005
Name: Giraffe Group
Height: 6.25
Current Status: Open issue,
  permanently retired
Original Issue Year: 1969
Last Year: 1970
Rarity: B
Issue Price: $ 60
LCS Estimate: $ 720

No.: 5019
Name: Painful Giraffe
Height: 6.5
Current Status: Open issue,
  permanently retired
Original Issue Year: 1978
Last Year: 1981
Rarity: C
Issue Price: $ 115
LCS Estimate: $ 700

No.: 113.06
Name: Giraffe With Baby
Height: 7
Current Status: Very rare early issue
Original Issue Year: 1958
Last Year: Not available
Rarity: A
Issue Price: Not available

No.: 2037
Name: Hedgehog
Height: 3.5
Current Status: Open issue,
  permanently retired
Original Issue Year: 1971
Last Year: 1973
Rarity: B
Issue Price: $ 12.50
LCS Estimate: $ 135

No.: 1045
Name: Small Hippopotamus
Height: 1.5
Current Status: Open issue,
  permanently retired
Original Issue Year: 1969
Last Year: 1970
Rarity: B
Issue Price: $ 9.50
LCS Estimate: $ 115

No.: 1044
Name: Large Hippopotamus
Height: 2.25
Current Status: Open issue,
  permanently retired
Original Issue Year: 1969
Last Year: 1970
Rarity: B
Issue Price: $ 16.50
LCS Estimate: $ 200

No.: 5433
Name: Kangaroo
Height: 4.25
Current Status: Open issue,
  permanently retired
Original Issue Year: 1987
Last Year: 1990
Rarity: C
Issue Price: $ 65
LCS Estimate: $ 130

No.: 5023
Name: Painful Kangaroo
Height: 6.75
Current Status: Open issue,
  permanently retired
Original Issue Year: 1978
Last Year: 1981
Rarity: C
Issue Price: $ 150
LCS Estimate: $ 900

No.: 5436
Name: Lion
Height: 2.25
Current Status: Open issue,
  permanently retired
Original Issue Year: 1987
Last Year: 1990
Rarity: C
Issue Price: $ 50
LCS Estimate: $ 100

No.: 5022
Name: Painful Lion
Height: 3
Current Status: Open issue,
  permanently retired
Original Issue Year: 1978
Last Year: 1981
Rarity: C
Issue Price: $ 95
LCS Estimate: $ 550

No.: 4562
Name: Llama Resting
Height: 9
Current Status: Open issue,
  permanently retired
Original Issue Year: 1969
Last Year: 1972
Rarity: C
Issue Price: $ 25
LCS Estimate: $ 300

No.: 4561
Name: Llama Group
Height: 14.25
Current Status: Open issue,
  permanently retired
Original Issue Year: 1969
Last Year: 1970
Rarity: B
Issue Price: $ 55
LCS Estimate: $ 660

No.: 5432
Name: Monkey
Height: 3
Current Status: Open issue,
  permanently retired
Original Issue Year: 1987
Last Year: 1990
Rarity: C
Issue Price: $ 60
High Auction Price: $ 150
LCS Estimate: $ 120

No.: 5018
Name: Painful Monkey
Height: 5.5
Current Status: Open issue,
  permanently retired
Original Issue Year: 1978
Last Year: 1981
Rarity: C
Issue Price: $ 135
LCS Estimate: $ 800

No.: 6034
Name: Monkey Business
Height: 7.75
Current Status: Open issue, currently
  active
Original Issue Year: 1993
Issue Price: $ 785

No.: 2066
Name: Monkey Love
Height: 8.5
Current Status: Open issue,
  permanently retired
Original Issue Year: 1977
Last Year: 1979
Rarity: B
Issue Price: $ 160
LCS Estimate: $ 1120

No.: 2000
Name: Monkey
Height: 11.5
Current Status: Open issue,
  permanently retired
Original Issue Year: 1970
Last Year: 1975
Rarity: D
Issue Price: $ 35
LCS Estimate: $ 400

No.: 5228
Name: Playful Piglets
Height: 3
Current Status: Open issue, currently
  active
Original Issue Year: 1984
Issue Price: $ 80
Current Retail Price: $ 130

No.: 5437
Name: Rhino
Height: 2
Current Status: Open issue,
permanently retired
Original Issue Year: 1987
Last Year: 1990
Rarity: C
Issue Price: $ 50
LCS Estimate: $ 100

No.: 4944
Name: Rhinoceros
Height: 6.5
Current Status: Open issue,
permanently retired
Original Issue Year: 1976
Last Year: 1978
Rarity: B
Issue Price: $ 95
LCS Estimate: $ 850

No.: 5392
Name: Balancing Act
Height: 3.5
Current Status: Open issue,
permanently retired
Original Issue Year: 1986
Last Year: 1990
Rarity: C
Issue Price: $ 35
LCS Estimate: $ 75

No.: 5318
Name: Mini Seal Family
Height: 5.5
Current Status: Open issue,
permanently retired
Original Issue Year: 1985
Last Year: 1990
Rarity: D
Issue Price: $ 77.5
LCS Estimate: $ 155

No.: 5750
Name: Little Lamb
Height: 1.25
Current Status: Open issue, currently
active
Original Issue Year: 1991
Issue Price: $ 40
Current Retail Price: $ 40

No.: 5317
Name: Mini Lamb
Height: 1.25
Current Status: Open issue,
permanently retired
Original Issue Year: 1985
Last Year: 1990
Rarity: D
Issue Price: $ 30
LCS Estimate: $ 60

No.: 1047
Name: Sheep
Height: 2.75
Current Status: Open issue,
  permanently retired
Original Issue Year: 1969
Last Year: 1970
Rarity: B
Issue Price: $ 9
LCS Estimate: $ 110

No.: 1046
Name: Lamb
Height: 4
Current Status: Open issue,
  permanently retired
Original Issue Year: 1969
Last Year: 1970
Rarity: B
Issue Price: $ 10.50
LCS Estimate: $ 125

No.: 5826
Name: Little Unicorn
Height: 6.5
Current Status: Open issue, currently
  active
Original Issue Year: 1991
Issue Price: $ 275
Current Retail Price: $ 285

No.: 5880
Name: Playful Unicorn
Height: 8.5
Current Status: Open issue, currently
  active
Original Issue Year: 1992
Issue Price: $ 295
Current Retail Price: $ 295

No.: 5993
Name: Unicorn and Friend
Height: 9.25
Current Status: Open issue, currently
  active
Original Issue Year: 1993
Issue Price: $ 355
Current Retail Price: $ 355

No. 4690—Yellow Dragon Vase (4690) was issued in 1970 for $35, retired in 1981 and auctioned in 1992 for $550.

No. 1536—Japanese Vase, issued in 1988, closed in 1989 and auctioned for $3,750 in 1991.

Porcelain vases have been a favorite porcelain art form since China's earliest manufacture around 1000 A.D. Since then, European and Japanese porcelain makers have produced thousands of these tall, thin shapes. Lladró has continued the tradition with beautifully shaped and decorated vessels.

Up to this moment, Lladró has designed, decorated and issued a total of 232 vases and urns. As opposed to bowls and centerpieces (Chapter 3), vases are narrower at their neck than at their body.

To eliminate confusing descriptions, we are classifying vases by height only. They are:

Group 1   3" to 6-1/2"
      2   7" to 9-3/4"
      3   10" to 11-3/4"
      4   12" to 18-1/2"
      5   19" and taller

Vases

No.: 5636
Name: Lladro Vase
Height: 3
Current Status: Open issue,
  permanently retired
Original Issue Year: 1989
Last Year: 1990
Rarity: B
Issue Price: $ 110
LCS Estimate: $ 220

No.: 1692
Name: Small Vase
Height: 3.25
Current Status: Open issue,
  permanently retired
Original Issue Year: 1989
Last Year: 1991
Rarity: B
Issue Price: $ 65
LCS Estimate: $ 65

No.: 5260
Name: Vase - Decorated
Height: 3.5
Current Status: Open issue,
  permanently retired
Original Issue Year: 1984
Last Year: 1990
Rarity: D
Issue Price: $ 45
LCS Estimate: $ 100

No.: 5527.40
Name: Silver Vase No. 16
Height: 3.5
Current Status: Open issue,
  permanently retired
Original Issue Year: 1988
Last Year: 1991
Rarity: C
Issue Price: $ 55
LCS Estimate: $ 55

No.: 5527.50
Name: Topaz Vase No. 16
Height: 3.5
Current Status: Open issue,
  permanently retired
Original Issue Year: 1988
Last Year: 1991
Rarity: C
Issue Price: $ 55
LCS Estimate: $ 55

No.: 5260.30
Name: Vase
Height: 3.5
Current Status: Open issue,
  permanently retired
Original Issue Year: 1984
Last Year: 1988
Rarity: C
Issue Price: $ 45
LCS Estimate: $ 135

No.: 319.13
Name: Vase No. 6
Height: 4
Current Status: Very rare early issue
Original Issue Year: 1958
Last Year: Not available
Rarity: A
Issue Price: Not available
Comments: Personally handcrafted by Jose Lladro

No.: 5257
Name: Vase - Decorated
Height: 4
Current Status: Open issue, permanently retired
Original Issue Year: 1984
Last Year: 1990
Rarity: D
Issue Price: $ 55
LCS Estimate: $ 120

No.: 5258.30
Name: Vase
Height: 4
Current Status: Open issue, permanently retired
Original Issue Year: 1984
Last Year: 1988
Rarity: C
Issue Price: $ 55
LCS Estimate: $ 165

No.: 5258
Name: Vase - Decorated
Height: 4
Current Status: Open issue, permanently retired
Original Issue Year: 1984
Last Year: 1990
Rarity: D
Issue Price: $ 55
LCS Estimate: $ 120

No.: 5568
Name: Conical Snail
Height: 4
Current Status: Open issue, permanently retired
Original Issue Year: 1989
Last Year: 1990
Rarity: B
Issue Price: $ 75
LCS Estimate: $ 150

No.: 5257.30
Name: Vase
Height: 4
Current Status: Open issue, permanently retired
Original Issue Year: 1984
Last Year: 1988
Rarity: C
Issue Price: $ 55
LCS Estimate: $ 165

No.: 1221.30
Name: Little Vase
Height: 4
Current Status: Open issue,
    permanently retired
Original Issue Year: 1972
Last Year: 1980
Rarity: D
Issue Price: $ 40
LCS Estimate: $ 275

No.: 1693
Name: Round Vase
Height: 4.25
Current Status: Open issue,
    permanently retired
Original Issue Year: 1989
Last Year: 1991
Rarity: B
Issue Price: $ 75
LCS Estimate: $ 75

No.: 5262
Name: Vase - Decorated
Height: 4.25
Current Status: Open issue,
    permanently retired
Original Issue Year: 1984
Last Year: 1990
Rarity: D
Issue Price: $ 70
LCS Estimate: $ 150

No.: 5526.50
Name: Topaz Vase No. 15
Height: 4.25
Current Status: Open issue,
    permanently retired
Original Issue Year: 1988
Last Year: 1991
Rarity: C
Issue Price: $ 75
LCS Estimate: $ 75

No.: 5526.40
Name: Silver Vase No. 14
Height: 4.25
Current Status: Open issue,
    permanently retired
Original Issue Year: 1988
Last Year: 1991
Rarity: C
Issue Price: $ 75
LCS Estimate: $ 75

No.: 5259
Name: Vase - Decorated
Height: 4.25
Current Status: Open issue,
    permanently retired
Original Issue Year: 1984
Last Year: 1990
Rarity: D
Issue Price: $ 65
LCS Estimate: $ 145

No.: 5259.30
Name: Vase
Height: 4.25
Current Status: Open issue,
   permanently retired
Original Issue Year: 1984
Last Year: 1988
Rarity: C
Issue Price: $ 65
LCS Estimate: $ 195

No.: 5635
Name: Lladro Vase
Height: 4.25
Current Status: Open issue,
   permanently retired
Original Issue Year: 1989
Last Year: 1990
Rarity: B
Issue Price: $ 115
LCS Estimate: $ 230

No.: 5262.30
Name: Vase
Height: 4.25
Current Status: Open issue,
   permanently retired
Original Issue Year: 1984
Last Year: 1988
Rarity: C
Issue Price: $ 70
LCS Estimate: $ 210

No.: 1222.30
Name: Little Vase
Height: 4.25
Current Status: Open issue,
   permanently retired
Original Issue Year: 1972
Last Year: 1979
Rarity: D
Issue Price: $ 35
LCS Estimate: $ 275

No.: 5582
Name: Small Lily Vase
Height: 4.5
Current Status: Open issue,
   permanently retired
Original Issue Year: 1989
Last Year: 1990
Rarity: B
Issue Price: $ 100
LCS Estimate: $ 200

No.: 5570
Name: Octagonal Chinese Vase
Height: 4.75
Current Status: Open issue,
   permanently retired
Original Issue Year: 1989
Last Year: 1990
Rarity: B
Issue Price: $ 70
LCS Estimate: $ 140

No.: 1219.30
Name: Little Vase
Height: 4.75
Current Status: Open issue,
  permanently retired
Original Issue Year: 1972
Last Year: 1979
Rarity: D
Issue Price: $ 35
LCS Estimate: $ 275

No.: 1220.30
Name: Little Rose Vase
Height: 4.75
Current Status: Open issue,
  permanently retired
Original Issue Year: 1972
Last Year: 1979
Rarity: D
Issue Price: $ 35
LCS Estimate: $ 275

No.: 1691
Name: Large Vase
Height: 5
Current Status: Open issue,
  permanently retired
Original Issue Year: 1989
Last Year: 1991
Rarity: B
Issue Price: $ 65
LCS Estimate: $ 65

No.: 5521.40
Name: Silver Oriental Vase No. 13
Height: 5
Current Status: Open issue,
  permanently retired
Original Issue Year: 1988
Last Year: 1991
Rarity: C
Issue Price: $ 65
LCS Estimate: $ 65

No.: 5521.50
Name: Topaz Vase No. 13
Height: 5
Current Status: Open issue,
  permanently retired
Original Issue Year: 1988
Last Year: 1991
Rarity: C
Issue Price: $ 65
LCS Estimate: $ 65

No.: 5261.30
Name: Covered Jug
Height: 5
Current Status: Open issue,
  permanently retired
Original Issue Year: 1984
Last Year: 1988
Rarity: C
Issue Price: $ 70
LCS Estimate: $ 210

No.: 5567
Name: Double Nautilus Vase
Height: 5
Current Status: Open issue,
 permanently retired
Original Issue Year: 1989
Last Year: 1990
Rarity: B
Issue Price: $ 200
LCS Estimate: $ 400

No.: 5566
Name: Nautilus Vase
Height: 5
Current Status: Open issue,
 permanently retired
Original Issue Year: 1989
Last Year: 1990
Rarity: B
Issue Price: $ 110
LCS Estimate: $ 220

No.: 5261
Name: Decorated Covered Jug
Height: 5
Current Status: Open issue,
 permanently retired
Original Issue Year: 1984
Last Year: 1990
Rarity: D
Issue Price: $ 70
LCS Estimate: $ 145

No.: 5519.50
Name: Red Topaz Vase No. 12
Height: 5.25
Current Status: Open issue,
 permanently retired
Original Issue Year: 1988
Last Year: 1991
Rarity: C
Issue Price: $ 70
LCS Estimate: $ 70

No.: 5519.40
Name: Spring Red-Silver Vase No. 12
Height: 5.5
Current Status: Open issue,
 permanently retired
Original Issue Year: 1988
Last Year: 1991
Rarity: C
Issue Price: $ 70
LCS Estimate: $ 70

No.: 5528.40
Name: Silver Vase No. 17
Height: 5.5
Current Status: Open issue,
 permanently retired
Original Issue Year: 1988
Last Year: 1991
Rarity: C
Issue Price: $ 70
LCS Estimate: $ 70

No.: 5528.5
Name: Silver Vase No. 17
Height: 5.5
Current Status: Open issue,
  permanently retired
Original Issue Year: 1988
Last Year: 1991
Rarity: C
Issue Price: $ 70
LCS Estimate: $ 70

No.: 5536.40
Name: Silver Vase No. 25
Height: 6
Current Status: Open issue,
  permanently retired
Original Issue Year: 1988
Last Year: 1991
Rarity: C
Issue Price: $ 135
LCS Estimate: $ 135

No.: 5536.5
Name: Topaz Vase No. 25
Height: 6
Current Status: Open issue,
  permanently retired
Original Issue Year: 1988
Last Year: 1991
Rarity: C
Issue Price: $ 135
LCS Estimate: $ 135

No.: 5557
Name: Wide Octagonal Vase
Height: 6.25
Current Status: Open issue,
  permanently retired
Original Issue Year: 1989
Last Year: 1990
Rarity: B
Issue Price: $ 240
LCS Estimate: $ 480

No.: 4710
Name: Small Floral Vase
Height: 6.25
Current Status: Open issue,
  permanently retired
Original Issue Year: 1970
Last Year: 1975
Rarity: D
Issue Price: $ 10
LCS Estimate: $ 100

No.: 5581
Name: Medium Lily Vase
Height: 6.5
Current Status: Open issue,
  permanently retired
Original Issue Year: 1989
Last Year: 1990
Rarity: B
Issue Price: $ 135
LCS Estimate: $ 270

No.: 5631
Name: Lladro Vase
Height: 6.5
Current Status: Open issue,
  permanently retired
Original Issue Year: 1989
Last Year: 1990
Rarity: B
Issue Price: $ 150
LCS Estimate: $ 300

No.: 5633
Name: Water Dreamer Vase
Height: 6.5
Current Status: Open issue,
  permanently retired
Original Issue Year: 1989
Last Year: 1990
Rarity: B
Issue Price: $ 150
LCS Estimate: $ 300

No.: 5634
Name: Water Baby Vase
Height: 6.5
Current Status: Open issue,
  permanently retired
Original Issue Year: 1989
Last Year: 1990
Rarity: B
Issue Price: $ 175
LCS Estimate: $ 350

No.: 5562
Name: Striped Clover Vase
Height: 6.5
Current Status: Open issue,
  permanently retired
Original Issue Year: 1989
Last Year: 1990
Rarity: B
Issue Price: $ 75
LCS Estimate: $ 150

No.: 5504.40
Name: Silver Vase No. 1
Height: 7
Current Status: Open issue,
  permanently retired
Original Issue Year: 1988
Last Year: 1991
Rarity: C
Issue Price: $ 200
LCS Estimate: $ 200

No.: 5504.50
Name: Topaz Vase No. 1
Height: 7
Current Status: Open issue,
  permanently retired
Original Issue Year: 1988
Last Year: 1991
Rarity: C
Issue Price: $ 200
LCS Estimate: $ 200

No.: 1593
Name: Chrysanthemum Vase
Height: 7
Current Status: Open issue,
  permanently retired
Original Issue Year: 1988
Last Year: 1991
Rarity: C
Issue Price: $ 425
LCS Estimate: $ 425

No.: 5510.50
Name: Topaz 7 Vase No. 24
Height: 7
Current Status: Open issue,
  permanently retired
Original Issue Year: 1988
Last Year: 1991
Rarity: C
Issue Price: $ 85
LCS Estimate: $ 85

No.: 5510.40
Name: Silver 7 Vase No. 24
Height: 7
Current Status: Open issue,
  permanently retired
Original Issue Year: 1988
Last Year: 1991
Rarity: C
Issue Price: $ 85
LCS Estimate: $ 85

No.: 5630
Name: Lladro Vase
Height: 7
Current Status: Open issue,
  permanently retired
Original Issue Year: 1989
Last Year: 1990
Rarity: B
Issue Price: $ 95
LCS Estimate: $ 190

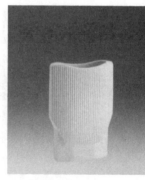

No.: 5630.30
Name: Lladro Vase
Height: 7
Current Status: Open issue,
  permanently retired
Original Issue Year: 1989
Last Year: 1990
Rarity: B
Issue Price: $ 60
LCS Estimate: $ 120

No.: 5630.10
Name: Lladro Vase
Height: 7
Current Status: Open issue,
  permanently retired
Original Issue Year: 1989
Last Year: 1990
Rarity: B
Issue Price: $ 95
LCS Estimate: $ 190

No.: 1218.30
Name: Mini-vase
Height: 7
Current Status: Open issue, permanently retired
Original Issue Year: 1972
Last Year: 1979
Rarity: D
Issue Price: $ 35
LCS Estimate: $ 275

No.: 1589
Name: Ricinus Palm Vase
Height: 7
Current Status: Open issue, permanently retired
Original Issue Year: 1988
Last Year: 1993
Rarity: D
Issue Price: $ 475
Last Retail Price: $ 630

No.: 57.04
Name: Florals Urn
Height: 7.5
Current Status: Very rare early issue
Original Issue Year: 1953
Last Year: Not available
Rarity: A
Issue Price: Not available
Comments: Personally handcrafted by Jose Lladro

No.: 58.04
Name: Landscape
Height: 7.5
Current Status: Very rare early issue
Original Issue Year: 1953
Last Year: Not available
Rarity: A
Issue Price: Not available
Comments: Personally handcrafted by Jose Lladro

No.: 5577
Name: Lilac Cuboid Vase
Height: 7.5
Current Status: Open issue, permanently retired
Original Issue Year: 1989
Last Year: 1990
Rarity: B
Issue Price: $ 175
LCS Estimate: $ 350

No.: 5577.30
Name: Green Cuboid Vase
Height: 7.5
Current Status: Open issue, permanently retired
Original Issue Year: 1989
Last Year: 1990
Rarity: B
Issue Price: $ 130
LCS Estimate: $ 260

No.: 5577.40
Name: Violet Cuboid Vase
Height: 7.5
Current Status: Open issue,
  permanently retired
Original Issue Year: 1989
Last Year: 1990
Rarity: B
Issue Price: $ 145
LCS Estimate: $ 290

No.: 5577.10
Name: Brown Cuboid Vase
Height: 7.5
Current Status: Open issue,
  permanently retired
Original Issue Year: 1989
Last Year: 1990
Rarity: B
Issue Price: $ 125
LCS Estimate: $ 250

No.: 4696
Name: Dragon Tibor Jar
Height: 7.5
Current Status: Open issue,
  permanently retired
Original Issue Year: 1970
Last Year: 1975
Rarity: D
Issue Price: $ 27.50
LCS Estimate: $ 275

No.: 5561
Name: Green Clover Vase
Height: 7.75
Current Status: Open issue,
  permanently retired
Original Issue Year: 1989
Last Year: 1991
Rarity: B
Issue Price: $ 130
LCS Estimate: $ 130

No.: 5561.30
Name: Lilac Clover Vase
Height: 7.75
Current Status: Open issue,
  permanently retired
Original Issue Year: 1989
Last Year: 1991
Rarity: B
Issue Price: $ 135
LCS Estimate: $ 135

No.: 5623.30
Name: Lladro Vase
Height: 7.75
Current Status: Open issue,
  permanently retired
Original Issue Year: 1989
Last Year: 1990
Rarity: B
Issue Price: $ 325
LCS Estimate: $ 650

No.: 5623
Name: Lladro Vase
Height: 7.75
Current Status: Open issue,
  permanently retired
Original Issue Year: 1989
Last Year: 1990
Rarity: B
Issue Price: $ 360
LCS Estimate: $ 720

No.: 5516.40
Name: Slender Silver Vase No. 10
Height: 8.25
Current Status: Open issue,
  permanently retired
Original Issue Year: 1988
Last Year: 1991
Rarity: C
Issue Price: $ 160
LCS Estimate: $ 160

No.: 5516.5
Name: Topaz Vase No. 10
Height: 8.25
Current Status: Open issue,
  permanently retired
Original Issue Year: 1988
Last Year: 1991
Rarity: C
Issue Price: $ 160
LCS Estimate: $ 160

No.: 5622.30
Name: Lladro Vase
Height: 8.25
Current Status: Open issue,
  permanently retired
Original Issue Year: 1989
Last Year: 1990
Rarity: B
Issue Price: $ 400
LCS Estimate: $ 800

No.: 5622
Name: Lladro Vase
Height: 8.25
Current Status: Open issue,
  permanently retired
Original Issue Year: 1989
Last Year: 1990
Rarity: B
Issue Price: $ 430
LCS Estimate: $ 860

No.: 5560
Name: Wide Tulip Vase
Height: 8.25
Current Status: Open issue,
  permanently retired
Original Issue Year: 1989
Last Year: 1990
Rarity: B
Issue Price: $ 110
LCS Estimate: $ 220

No.: 4723
Name: Spring Vase
Height: 8.25
Current Status: Open issue,
  permanently retired
Original Issue Year: 1970
Last Year: 1975
Rarity: D
Issue Price: $ 18
LCS Estimate: $ 180

No.: 5509.40
Name: Red-Silver Vase No. 6
Height: 8.5
Current Status: Open issue,
  permanently retired
Original Issue Year: 1988
Last Year: 1991
Rarity: C
Issue Price: $ 200
High Auction Price: $ 125
LCS Estimate: $ 150

No.: 5509.50
Name: Red-Topaz Vase No. 6
Height: 8.5
Current Status: Open issue,
  permanently retired
Original Issue Year: 1988
Last Year: 1991
Rarity: C
Issue Price: $ 200
LCS Estimate: $ 200

No.: 5559
Name: Square Vase
Height: 8.5
Current Status: Open issue,
  permanently retired
Original Issue Year: 1989
Last Year: 1990
Rarity: B
Issue Price: $ 115
LCS Estimate: $ 230

No.: 4709
Name: Spring Vase
Height: 8.5
Current Status: Open issue,
  permanently retired
Original Issue Year: 1970
Last Year: 1975
Rarity: D
Issue Price: $ 16.50
LCS Estimate: $ 175

No.: 4722
Name: Vase
Height: 8.5
Current Status: Open issue,
  permanently retired
Original Issue Year: 1970
Last Year: 1972
Rarity: B
Issue Price: $ 20
LCS Estimate: $ 225

No.: 4771
Name: Spring Vase
Height: 8.5
Current Status: Open issue,
  permanently retired
Original Issue Year: 1971
Last Year: 1975
Rarity: C
Issue Price: $ 20
LCS Estimate: $ 200

No.: 4778
Name: Deep Floral Vase
Height: 8.5
Current Status: Open issue,
  permanently retired
Original Issue Year: 1971
Last Year: 1975
Rarity: C
Issue Price: $ 20
LCS Estimate: $ 200

No.: 5511.5
Name: Topaz 8 Vase No. 14
Height: 9
Current Status: Open issue,
  permanently retired
Original Issue Year: 1988
Last Year: 1991
Rarity: C
Issue Price: $ 125
High Auction Price: $ 150
LCS Estimate: $ 150

No.: 5511.40
Name: Silver 8 Vase No. 14
Height: 9
Current Status: Open issue,
  permanently retired
Original Issue Year: 1988
Last Year: 1991
Rarity: C
Issue Price: $ 125
LCS Estimate: $ 125

No.: 1122.30
Name: White Poral Vase
Height: 9
Current Status: Open issue,
  permanently retired
Original Issue Year: 1971
Last Year: 1975
Rarity: C
Issue Price: $ 35
LCS Estimate: $ 350

No.: 1122
Name: Poral Vase
Height: 9
Current Status: Open issue,
  permanently retired
Original Issue Year: 1971
Last Year: 1975
Rarity: C
Issue Price: $ 55
LCS Estimate: $ 550

No.: 5507.40
Name: Topaz Vase No. 4
Height: 9.5
Current Status: Open issue,
  permanently retired
Original Issue Year: 1988
Last Year: 1991
Rarity: C
Issue Price: $ 155
LCS Estimate: $ 155

No.: 5531.40
Name: Silver Vase No. 20
Height: 9.5
Current Status: Open issue,
  permanently retired
Original Issue Year: 1988
Last Year: 1991
Rarity: C
Issue Price: $ 135
LCS Estimate: $ 135

No.: 5531.50
Name: Topaz Vase No. 20
Height: 9.5
Current Status: Open issue,
  permanently retired
Original Issue Year: 1988
Last Year: 1991
Rarity: C
Issue Price: $ 135
LCS Estimate: $ 135

No.: 5507.50
Name: Topaz Vase No. 4
Height: 9.5
Current Status: Open issue,
  permanently retired
Original Issue Year: 1988
Last Year: 1991
Rarity: C
Issue Price: $ 155
LCS Estimate: $ 155

No.: 5563.30
Name: White Basket Vase
Height: 9.5
Current Status: Open issue,
  permanently retired
Original Issue Year: 1989
Last Year: 1990
Rarity: B
Issue Price: $ 190
LCS Estimate: $ 380

No.: 5563
Name: Blue Basket Vase
Height: 9.5
Current Status: Open issue,
  permanently retired
Original Issue Year: 1989
Last Year: 1990
Rarity: B
Issue Price: $ 190
LCS Estimate: $ 380

No.: 1115.30
Name: White Floral Jug
Height: 9.5
Current Status: Open issue,
  permanently retired
Original Issue Year: 1971
Last Year: 1978
Rarity: D
Issue Price: $ 20
LCS Estimate: $ 160

No.: 1115
Name: Floral Jug
Height: 9.5
Current Status: Open issue,
  permanently retired
Original Issue Year: 1971
Last Year: 1979
Rarity: D
Issue Price: $ 35
LCS Estimate: $ 280

No.: 4697
Name: White Vase
Height: 9.75
Current Status: Open issue,
  permanently retired
Original Issue Year: 1970
Last Year: 1975
Rarity: D
Issue Price: $ 13.50
LCS Estimate: $ 135

No.: 4691.30
Name: White Flower Vase
Height: 9.75
Current Status: Open issue,
  permanently retired
Original Issue Year: 1970
Last Year: 1981
Rarity: D
Issue Price: $ 40
LCS Estimate: $ 280

No.: 4691
Name: Flower Vase
Height: 9.75
Current Status: Open issue,
  permanently retired
Original Issue Year: 1970
Last Year: 1981
Rarity: D
Issue Price: $ 36.50
LCS Estimate: $ 250

No.: 4690
Name: Yellow Dragon Vase
Height: 9.75
Current Status: Open issue,
  permanently retired
Original Issue Year: 1970
Last Year: 1981
Rarity: D
Issue Price: $ 35
High Auction Price: $ 550
LCS Estimate: $ 550

No.: 4690.30
Name: Decorated Jug
Height: 9.75
Current Status: Open issue,
    permanently retired
Original Issue Year: 1970
Last Year: 1981
Rarity: D
Issue Price: $ 350
High Auction Price: $ 700
LCS Estimate: $ 500

No.: 5556.30
Name: Red Octagonal Flower Vase
Height: 10
Current Status: Open issue,
    permanently retired
Original Issue Year: 1989
Last Year: 1990
Rarity: B
Issue Price: $ 225
LCS Estimate: $ 450

No.: 5533.40
Name: Silver Vase No. 22
Height: 10.25
Current Status: Open issue,
    permanently retired
Original Issue Year: 1988
Last Year: 1991
Rarity: C
Issue Price: $ 140
LCS Estimate: $ 140

No.: 5564
Name: Sparrow Vase
Height: 10.25
Current Status: Open issue,
    permanently retired
Original Issue Year: 1989
Last Year: 1991
Rarity: B
Issue Price: $ 190
LCS Estimate: $ 190

No.: 5565
Name: Fantasy Dragon Vase
Height: 10.25
Current Status: Open issue,
    permanently retired
Original Issue Year: 1989
Last Year: 1991
Rarity: B
Issue Price: $ 185
LCS Estimate: $ 185

No.: 5533.5
Name: Topaz Vase No. 22
Height: 10.25
Current Status: Open issue,
    permanently retired
Original Issue Year: 1988
Last Year: 1991
Rarity: C
Issue Price: $ 140
LCS Estimate: $ 140

No.: 1596
Name: Chrysanthemum Vase
Height: 10.25
Current Status: Open issue,
  permanently retired
Original Issue Year: 1988
Last Year: 1991
Rarity: C
Issue Price: $ 395
LCS Estimate: $ 400

No.: 1623.30
Name: Lladro Vase
Height: 10.25
Current Status: Open issue,
  permanently retired
Original Issue Year: 1989
Last Year: 1990
Rarity: B
Issue Price: $ 100
LCS Estimate: $ 200

No.: 5558
Name: Slender Octagonal Vase
Height: 10.25
Current Status: Open issue,
  permanently retired
Original Issue Year: 1989
Last Year: 1990
Rarity: B
Issue Price: $ 260
LCS Estimate: $ 520

No.: 5580
Name: Large Lily Vase
Height: 10.25
Current Status: Open issue,
  permanently retired
Original Issue Year: 1989
Last Year: 1990
Rarity: B
Issue Price: $ 165
LCS Estimate: $ 330

No.: 1623
Name: Lladro Vase
Height: 10.25
Current Status: Open issue,
  permanently retired
Original Issue Year: 1989
Last Year: 1990
Rarity: B
Issue Price: $ 360
LCS Estimate: $ 720

No.: 5569
Name: Lily Vase
Height: 10.25
Current Status: Open issue,
  permanently retired
Original Issue Year: 1989
Last Year: 1990
Rarity: B
Issue Price: $ 215
LCS Estimate: $ 430

No.: 1623.10
Name: Lladro Vase
Height: 10.25
Current Status: Open issue,
  permanently retired
Original Issue Year: 1989
Last Year: 1990
Rarity: B
Issue Price: $ 215
LCS Estimate: $ 430

No.: 1119
Name: Mermaid Vase
Height: 10.25
Current Status: Open issue,
  permanently retired
Original Issue Year: 1971
Last Year: 1972
Rarity: B
Issue Price: $ 60
LCS Estimate: $ 650

No.: 1592
Name: Ricinus Palm Vase
Height: 10.25
Current Status: Open issue,
  permanently retired
Original Issue Year: 1988
Last Year: 1993
Rarity: D
Issue Price: $ 395
Last Retail Price: $ 550

No.: 5508.5
Name: Topaz Vase No. 5
Height: 10.5
Current Status: Open issue,
  permanently retired
Original Issue Year: 1988
Last Year: 1991
Rarity: C
Issue Price: $ 150
High Auction Price: $ 150
LCS Estimate: $ 150

No.: 51.04
Name: The Bouquet Urn
Height: 10.5
Current Status: Very rare early issue
Original Issue Year: 1953
Last Year: Not available
Rarity: A
Issue Price: Not available
Comments: Personally handcrafted by
  Juan Lladro

No.: 316.13
Name: Vase No. 3
Height: 10.5
Current Status: Very rare early issue
Original Issue Year: 1958
Last Year: Not available
Rarity: A
Issue Price: Not available
Comments: Personally handcrafted by
  Jose Lladro

No.: 5508.40
Name: Topaz Vase No. 5
Height: 10.5
Current Status: Open issue,
  permanently retired
Original Issue Year: 1988
Last Year: 1991
Rarity: C
Issue Price: $ 150
High Auction Price: $ 125
LCS Estimate: $ 150

No.: 45.03
Name: Landscape Urn
Height: 10.75
Current Status: Very rare early issue
Original Issue Year: 1953
Last Year: Not available
Rarity: A
Issue Price: Not available
Comments: Personally handcrafted by
  Juan Lladro

No.: 1687
Name: Small Poppy Vase
Height: 11
Current Status: Open issue,
  permanently retired
Original Issue Year: 1989
Last Year: 1991
Rarity: B
Issue Price: $ 250
LCS Estimate: $ 250

No.: 5534.40
Name: Silver Vase No. 23
Height: 11
Current Status: Open issue,
  permanently retired
Original Issue Year: 1988
Last Year: 1991
Rarity: C
Issue Price: $ 170
LCS Estimate: $ 170

No.: 5534.5
Name: Topaz Vase No. 23
Height: 11
Current Status: Open issue,
  permanently retired
Original Issue Year: 1988
Last Year: 1991
Rarity: C
Issue Price: $ 170
LCS Estimate: $ 170

No.: 5575.40
Name: Violet Round Cuboid Lamp
Height: 11
Current Status: Open issue,
  permanently retired
Original Issue Year: 1989
Last Year: 1990
Rarity: B
Issue Price: $ 300
LCS Estimate: $ 600

No.: 5624
Name: Lladro Vase
Height: 11
Current Status: Open issue, permanently retired
Original Issue Year: 1989
Last Year: 1990
Rarity: B
Issue Price: $ 575
LCS Estimate: $ 1150

No.: 4770
Name: Don Quixote Vase
Height: 11
Current Status: Open issue, permanently retired
Original Issue Year: 1971
Last Year: 1975
Rarity: C
Issue Price: $ 25
LCS Estimate: $ 250

No.: 315.13
Name: Vase No. 2
Height: 11.25
Current Status: Very rare early issue
Original Issue Year: 1958
Last Year: Not available
Rarity: A
Issue Price: Not available
Comments: Personally handcrafted by Jose Lladro

No.: 1112
Name: Mermaid Vase
Height: 11.25
Current Status: Open issue, permanently retired
Original Issue Year: 1971
Last Year: 1972
Rarity: B
Issue Price: $ 55
LCS Estimate: $ 600

No.: 1594
Name: Chrysanthemum Vase
Height: 11.5
Current Status: Open issue, permanently retired
Original Issue Year: 1988
Last Year: 1991
Rarity: C
Issue Price: $ 495
LCS Estimate: $ 500

No.: 5621.30
Name: Lladro Vase
Height: 11.5
Current Status: Open issue, permanently retired
Original Issue Year: 1989
Last Year: 1990
Rarity: B
Issue Price: $ 250
LCS Estimate: $ 500

No.: 5578.40
Name: Violet Compact Vase
Height: 11.5
Current Status: Open issue,
   permanently retired
Original Issue Year: 1989
Last Year: 1990
Rarity: B
Issue Price: $ 150
LCS Estimate: $ 300

No.: 5621
Name: Lladro Vase
Height: 11.5
Current Status: Open issue,
   permanently retired
Original Issue Year: 1989
Last Year: 1990
Rarity: B
Issue Price: $ 270
LCS Estimate: $ 540

No.: 5578.10
Name: Brown Compact Vase
Height: 11.5
Current Status: Open issue,
   permanently retired
Original Issue Year: 1989
Last Year: 1990
Rarity: B
Issue Price: $ 130
LCS Estimate: $ 260

No.: 5578.30
Name: Green Compact Vase
Height: 11.5
Current Status: Open issue,
   permanently retired
Original Issue Year: 1989
Last Year: 1990
Rarity: B
Issue Price: $ 135
LCS Estimate: $ 270

No.: 5578
Name: Brown Compact Vase
Height: 11.5
Current Status: Open issue,
   permanently retired
Original Issue Year: 1989
Last Year: 1990
Rarity: B
Issue Price: $ 175
LCS Estimate: $ 350

No.: 5571.30
Name: Red Vase with Handles
Height: 11.5
Current Status: Open issue,
   permanently retired
Original Issue Year: 1989
Last Year: 1990
Rarity: B
Issue Price: $ 215
LCS Estimate: $ 430

No.: 4721
Name: Vase
Height: 11.5
Current Status: Open issue,
   permanently retired
Original Issue Year: 1970
Last Year: 1975
Rarity: D
Issue Price: $ 27.50
LCS Estimate: $ 275

No.: 1590
Name: Ricinus Palm Vase
Height: 11.5
Current Status: Open issue,
   permanently retired
Original Issue Year: 1988
Last Year: 1993
Rarity: D
Issue Price: $ 650
Last Retail Price: $ 865

No.: 1588
Name: Fantasy Vase
Height: 11.5
Current Status: Open issue,
   permanently retired
Original Issue Year: 1988
Last Year: 1993
Rarity: D
Issue Price: $ 695
Last Retail Price: $ 945

No.: 59.04
Name: The Lovers
Height: 11.75
Current Status: Very rare early issue
Original Issue Year: 1955
Last Year: Not available
Rarity: A
Issue Price: Not available
Comments: Personally handcrafted by
   Jose Lladro

No.: 5620.30
Name: Lladro Vase
Height: 11.75
Current Status: Open issue,
   permanently retired
Original Issue Year: 1989
Last Year: 1990
Rarity: B
Issue Price: $ 225
LCS Estimate: $ 450

No.: 5620
Name: Lladro Vase
Height: 11.75
Current Status: Open issue,
   permanently retired
Original Issue Year: 1989
Last Year: 1990
Rarity: B
Issue Price: $ 240
LCS Estimate: $ 480

No.: 5512.5
Name: Topaz Vase No. 9
Height: 11.75
Current Status: Open issue,
 permanently retired
Original Issue Year: 1988
Last Year: 1991
Rarity: C
Issue Price: $ 265
High Auction Price: $ 150
LCS Estimate: $ 150

No.: 5512.40
Name: Spring Silver Vase No. 9
Height: 11.75
Current Status: Open issue,
 permanently retired
Original Issue Year: 1988
Last Year: 1991
Rarity: C
Issue Price: $ 265
LCS Estimate: $ 265

No.: 1584
Name: Poppys Vase
Height: 11.75
Current Status: Open issue,
 permanently retired
Original Issue Year: 1988
Last Year: 1993
Rarity: D
Issue Price: $ 575
Last Retail Price: $ 785

No.: 1583
Name: Crocus Vase
Height: 11.75
Current Status: Open issue,
 permanently retired
Original Issue Year: 1988
Last Year: 1993
Rarity: D
Issue Price: $ 475
Last Retail Price: $ 630

No.: 1586
Name: Trumpet Flower Vase
Height: 11.75
Current Status: Open issue,
 permanently retired
Original Issue Year: 1988
Last Year: 1993
Rarity: D
Issue Price: $ 525
Last Retail Price: $ 735

No.: 5506.5
Name: Topaz Vase No. 3
Height: 12.25
Current Status: Open issue,
 permanently retired
Original Issue Year: 1988
Last Year: 1991
Rarity: C
Issue Price: $ 155
LCS Estimate: $ 155

No.: 5505.40
Name: Silver Vase No. 2
Height: 12.25
Current Status: Open issue, permanently retired
Original Issue Year: 1988
Last Year: 1991
Rarity: C
Issue Price: $ 150
High Auction Price: $ 125
LCS Estimate: $ 125

No.: 5505.5
Name: Topaz Vase No. 2
Height: 12.25
Current Status: Open issue, permanently retired
Original Issue Year: 1988
Last Year: 1991
Rarity: C
Issue Price: $ 150
LCS Estimate: $ 150

No.: 5506.40
Name: Turia Silver Vase No. 3
Height: 12.25
Current Status: Open issue, permanently retired
Original Issue Year: 1988
Last Year: 1991
Rarity: C
Issue Price: $ 155
High Auction Price: $ 175
LCS Estimate: $ 200

No.: 63.04
Name: Urn
Height: 12.5
Current Status: Very rare early issue
Original Issue Year: 1955
Last Year: Not available
Rarity: A
Issue Price: Not available
Comments: Personally handcrafted by Jose Lladro

No.: 314.13
Name: Vase No. 1
Height: 12.5
Current Status: Very rare early issue
Original Issue Year: 1958
Last Year: Not available
Rarity: A
Issue Price: Not available
Comments: Personally handcrafted by Jose Lladro

No.: 1585
Name: Lilly Candy Vase
Height: 12.5
Current Status: Open issue, permanently retired
Original Issue Year: 1988
Last Year: 1991
Rarity: C
Issue Price: $ 295
LCS Estimate: $ 300

No.: 5556
Name: Octagonal Flower Vase
Height: 12.5
Current Status: Open issue,
  permanently retired
Original Issue Year: 1989
Last Year: 1990
Rarity: B
Issue Price: $ 275
LCS Estimate: $ 550

No.: 62.04
Name: Urn
Height: 12.75
Current Status: Very rare early issue
Original Issue Year: 1955
Last Year: Not available
Rarity: A
Issue Price: Not available
Comments: Personally handcrafted by
  Juan Lladro

No.: 2047
Name: Jug
Height: 13
Current Status: Open issue,
  permanently retired
Original Issue Year: 1971
Last Year: 1975
Rarity: C
Issue Price: $ 40
LCS Estimate: $ 400

No.: 1688
Name: Large Poppy Vase
Height: 13.25
Current Status: Open issue,
  permanently retired
Original Issue Year: 1989
Last Year: 1991
Rarity: B
Issue Price: $ 265
LCS Estimate: $ 265

No.: 52.04
Name: Flowers Urn
Height: 13.25
Current Status: Very rare early issue
Original Issue Year: 1953
Last Year: Not available
Rarity: A
Issue Price: Not available
Comments: Personally handcrafted by
  Juan Lladro

No.: 2050
Name: Coral Vase
Height: 13.25
Current Status: Open issue,
  permanently retired
Original Issue Year: 1973
Last Year: 1979
Rarity: D
Issue Price: $ 180
High Auction Price: $ 600
LCS Estimate: $ 750

No.: 1587
Name: Gladiolus Vase
Height: 13.25
Current Status: Open issue, currently
  active
Original Issue Year: 1988
Issue Price: $ 350
Current Retail Price: $ 450

No.: 1595
Name: Chrysanthemum Vase
Height: 13.5
Current Status: Open issue,
  permanently retired
Original Issue Year: 1988
Last Year: 1991
Rarity: C
Issue Price: $ 495
LCS Estimate: $ 500

No.: 1591
Name: Ricinus Palm Vase
Height: 13.5
Current Status: Open issue,
  permanently retired
Original Issue Year: 1988
Last Year: 1993
Rarity: D
Issue Price: $ 575
Last Retail Price: $ 785

No.: 5529.5
Name: Topaz Vase No. 18
Height: 14.25
Current Status: Open issue,
  permanently retired
Original Issue Year: 1988
Last Year: 1991
Rarity: C
Issue Price: $ 235
LCS Estimate: $ 235

No.: 5529.40
Name: Silver Vase No. 18
Height: 14.25
Current Status: Open issue,
  permanently retired
Original Issue Year: 1988
Last Year: 1991
Rarity: C
Issue Price: $ 235
LCS Estimate: $ 235

No.: 61.04
Name: Urn
Height: 14.5
Current Status: Very rare early issue
Original Issue Year: 1953
Last Year: Not available
Rarity: A
Issue Price: Not available
Comments: Personally handcrafted by
  Juan Lladro

No.: 5532.40
Name: Silver Vase No. 21
Height: 15.5
Current Status: Open issue,
  permanently retired
Original Issue Year: 1988
Last Year: 1991
Rarity: C
Issue Price: $ 165
LCS Estimate: $ 165

No.: 5532.5
Name: Topaz No. 21
Height: 15.5
Current Status: Open issue,
  permanently retired
Original Issue Year: 1988
Last Year: 1991
Rarity: C
Issue Price: $ 165
LCS Estimate: $ 165

No.: 60.04
Name: Urn
Height: 15.75
Current Status: Very rare early issue
Original Issue Year: 1950
Last Year: Not available
Rarity: A
Issue Price: Not available
Comments: Personally handcrafted by
  Vicente Lladro

No.: 5572.30
Name: Red Vase with Handles Lamp
Height: 15.75
Current Status: Open issue,
  permanently retired
Original Issue Year: 1989
Last Year: 1990
Rarity: B
Issue Price: $ 325
LCS Estimate: $ 650

No.: 1690
Name: Chinese Vase
Height: 16
Current Status: Open issue,
  permanently retired
Original Issue Year: 1989
Last Year: 1991
Rarity: B
Issue Price: $ 345
LCS Estimate: $ 345

No.: 4818
Name: Red Sunflower Jar
Height: 16
Current Status: Open issue,
  permanently retired
Original Issue Year: 1972
Last Year: 1975
Rarity: C
Issue Price: $ 45
LCS Estimate: $ 450

No.: 4819
Name: Brown Sunflower Jar
Height: 16
Current Status: Open issue,
    permanently retired
Original Issue Year: 1972
Last Year: 1975
Rarity: C
Issue Price: $ 45
LCS Estimate: $ 450

No.: 1619
Name: Bird Vase
Height: 16
Current Status: Limited edition,
    currently active
Edition Limit: 300
Original Issue Year: 1989
Issue Price: $ 3125
Current Retail Price: $ 3800

No.: 4846
Name: Mandarin Vase
Height: 16.5
Current Status: Open issue,
    permanently retired
Original Issue Year: 1973
Last Year: 1981
Rarity: D
Issue Price: $ 215
LCS Estimate: $ 1500

No.: 5016
Name: Mandarin Vase
Height: 16.5
Current Status: Open issue,
    permanently retired
Original Issue Year: 1978
Last Year: 1981
Rarity: C
Issue Price: $ 450
LCS Estimate: $ 2200

No.: 4742
Name: Octogonal Jar
Height: 16.5
Current Status: Open issue,
    permanently retired
Original Issue Year: 1971
Last Year: 1973
Rarity: B
Issue Price: $ 120
LCS Estimate: $ 1300

No.: 5524.5
Name: Topaz 47 Vase No. 14
Height: 17
Current Status: Open issue,
    permanently retired
Original Issue Year: 1988
Last Year: 1991
Rarity: C
Issue Price: $ 400
LCS Estimate: $ 400

No.: 5530.40
Name: Silver Vase No. 19
Height: 17
Current Status: Open issue,
  permanently retired
Original Issue Year: 1988
Last Year: 1991
Rarity: C
Issue Price: $ 235
LCS Estimate: $ 235

No.: 5530.5
Name: Topaz Vase No. 19
Height: 17
Current Status: Open issue,
  permanently retired
Original Issue Year: 1988
Last Year: 1991
Rarity: C
Issue Price: $ 235
LCS Estimate: $ 235

No.: 5524.40
Name: Topaz 47 Vase No. 14
Height: 17
Current Status: Open issue,
  permanently retired
Original Issue Year: 1988
Last Year: 1991
Rarity: C
Issue Price: $ 400
LCS Estimate: $ 400

No.: 4743
Name: Pink Octagonal Jar
Height: 17
Current Status: Open issue,
  permanently retired
Original Issue Year: 1971
Last Year: 1973
Rarity: B
Issue Price: $ 45
LCS Estimate: $ 500

No.: 4745
Name: Green Octagonal Jar
Height: 17
Current Status: Open issue,
  permanently retired
Original Issue Year: 1971
Last Year: 1973
Rarity: B
Issue Price: $ 45
LCS Estimate: $ 500

No.: 4744
Name: Blue Octagonal Jar
Height: 17
Current Status: Open issue,
  permanently retired
Original Issue Year: 1971
Last Year: 1972
Rarity: B
Issue Price: $ 45
LCS Estimate: $ 500

No.: 1120.30
Name: Dragon Vase
Height: 17.25
Current Status: Open issue,
permanently retired
Original Issue Year: 1971
Last Year: 1974
Rarity: C
Issue Price: $ 65
LCS Estimate: $ 700

No.: 1581
Name: Lilys Vase
Height: 17.75
Current Status: Open issue,
permanently retired
Original Issue Year: 1988
Last Year: 1991
Rarity: C
Issue Price: $ 525
LCS Estimate: $ 525

No.: 317.13
Name: Vase No. 4
Height: 17.75
Current Status: Very rare early issue
Original Issue Year: 1958
Last Year: Not available
Rarity: A
Issue Price: Not available
Comments: Personally handcrafted by
Jose Lladro

No.: 1536
Name: Japanese Vase
Height: 17.75
Current Status: Limited edition,
permanently retired
Edition Limit: 750
Original Issue Year: 1988
Last Year: 1989
Rarity: B
Issue Price: $ 2600
High Auction Price: $ 3750
LCS Estimate: $ 5800

No.: 5571
Name: Vase with Handles
Height: 18.5
Current Status: Open issue,
permanently retired
Original Issue Year: 1989
Last Year: 1990
Rarity: B
Issue Price: $ 550
LCS Estimate: $ 1100

No.: 1217
Name: Pekinese Vase
Height: 18.5
Current Status: Open issue,
permanently retired
Original Issue Year: 1972
Last Year: 1981
Rarity: D
Issue Price: $ 450
LCS Estimate: $ 3150

No.: 6030
Name: Maidenhead Vase
Height: 18.5
Current Status: Open issue, currently active
Original Issue Year: 1993
Issue Price: $ 1400

No.: 1363
Name: Peking Vase
Height: 19
Current Status: Open issue, permanently retired
Original Issue Year: 1978
Last Year: 1991
Rarity: D
Issue Price: $ 540
High Auction Price: $ 550
LCS Estimate: $ 550

No.: 1364
Name: Peking Vase
Height: 19
Current Status: Open issue, permanently retired
Original Issue Year: 1978
Last Year: 1991
Rarity: D
Issue Price: $ 900
LCS Estimate: $ 900

No.: 1365
Name: Peking Vase (Birds and Flowers)
Height: 19
Current Status: Open issue, permanently retired
Original Issue Year: 1978
Last Year: 1991
Rarity: D
Issue Price: $ 900
LCS Estimate: $ 900

No.: 4754
Name: Pink Peach Cylinder Vase
Height: 19
Current Status: Open issue, permanently retired
Original Issue Year: 1971
Last Year: 1979
Rarity: D
Issue Price: $ 55
LCS Estimate: $ 450

No.: 4752
Name: Blue Peonys Cylinder Vase
Height: 19
Current Status: Open issue, permanently retired
Original Issue Year: 1971
Last Year: 1979
Rarity: D
Issue Price: $ 50
LCS Estimate: $ 400

No.: 4741
Name: Classic Flora Vase
Height: 19
Current Status: Open issue,
  permanently retired
Original Issue Year: 1971
Last Year: 1979
Rarity: D
Issue Price: $ 100
LCS Estimate: $ 800

No.: 4753
Name: Green Peonys Cylinder Vase
Height: 19
Current Status: Open issue,
  permanently retired
Original Issue Year: 1971
Last Year: 1979
Rarity: D
Issue Price: $ 50
LCS Estimate: $ 400

No.: 4845
Name: Peking Vase with Butterfly
Height: 19
Current Status: Open issue,
  permanently retired
Original Issue Year: 1973
Last Year: 1981
Rarity: D
Issue Price: $ 150
LCS Estimate: $ 1050

No.: 4832
Name: Vase
Height: 19
Current Status: Open issue,
  permanently retired
Original Issue Year: 1972
Last Year: 1981
Rarity: D
Issue Price: $ 85
High Auction Price: $ 600
LCS Estimate: $ 600

No.: 1618
Name: Rose Garden Vase
Height: 19
Current Status: Limited edition,
  currently active
Edition Limit: 300
Original Issue Year: 1989
Issue Price: $ 2750
Current Retail Price: $ 3400

No.: 5535.40
Name: Silver Vase No. 24
Height: 19.25
Current Status: Open issue,
  permanently retired
Original Issue Year: 1988
Last Year: 1991
Rarity: C
Issue Price: $ 345
LCS Estimate: $ 345

No.: 5535.5
Name: Topaz Vase No. 24
Height: 19.25
Current Status: Open issue,
permanently retired
Original Issue Year: 1988
Last Year: 1991
Rarity: C
Issue Price: $ 345
LCS Estimate: $ 345

No.: 1192
Name: Magno Red Vase
Height: 19.25
Current Status: Limited edition, fully
subscribed
Edition Limit: 150
Original Issue Year: 1972
Issue Price: $ 535

No.: 1191
Name: Floral Vase
Height: 19.25
Current Status: Limited edition, fully
subscribed
Edition Limit: 150
Original Issue Year: 1972
Issue Price: $ 465

No.: 1582
Name: Pansy Vase
Height: 19.25
Current Status: Open issue, currently
active
Original Issue Year: 1988
Issue Price: $ 775
Current Retail Price: $ 1000

No.: 5918
Name: Fanciful Flight Vase
Height: 19.25
Current Status: Limited edition,
currently active
Edition Limit: 300
Original Issue Year: 1992
Issue Price: $ 4000
Current Retail Price: $ 4000

No.: 1198
Name: Blue Empire Vase
Height: 19.25
Current Status: Open issue,
permanently retired
Original Issue Year: 1972
Last Year: 1975
Rarity: C
Issue Price: $ 300
LCS Estimate: $ 3000

No.: 1199
Name: Blue Empire Vase
Height: 19.25
Current Status: Limited edition, fully subscribed
Edition Limit: 300
Original Issue Year: 1972
Issue Price: $ 610

No.: 1137
Name: Paradise Vase
Height: 19.25
Current Status: Limited edition, fully subscribed
Original Issue Year: 1971
Issue Price: $ 335

No.: 1138
Name: Rooster Vase
Height: 19.25
Current Status: Limited edition, fully subscribed
Original Issue Year: 1971
Issue Price: $ 335

No.: 1193
Name: Empire Vase
Height: 19.75
Current Status: Open issue, permanently retired
Original Issue Year: 1972
Last Year: 1975
Rarity: C
Issue Price: $ 300
LCS Estimate: $ 3000

No.: 1197
Name: Floral Jug
Height: 19.75
Current Status: Limited edition, fully subscribed
Edition Limit: 150
Original Issue Year: 1972
Issue Price: $ 445

No.: 1142
Name: Yellow Imperial Jug
Height: 20
Current Status: Open issue, permanently retired
Original Issue Year: 1971
Last Year: 1972
Rarity: B
Issue Price: $ 60
LCS Estimate: $ 650

No.: 1143
Name: Red Imperial Jug
Height: 20
Current Status: Open issue,
   permanently retired
Original Issue Year: 1971
Last Year: 1972
Rarity: B
Issue Price: $ 70
LCS Estimate: $ 750

No.: 1141
Name: Green Imperial Vase
Height: 20
Current Status: Open issue,
   permanently retired
Original Issue Year: 1971
Last Year: 1972
Rarity: B
Issue Price: $ 60
LCS Estimate: $ 650

No.: 1190
Name: Paradise Bird Vase
Height: 20
Current Status: Open issue,
   permanently retired
Original Issue Year: 1972
Last Year: 1975
Rarity: C
Issue Price: $ 340
LCS Estimate: $ 3500

No.: 1116.30
Name: Blue-White Dragon Vase
Height: 20
Current Status: Open issue,
   permanently retired
Original Issue Year: 1971
Last Year: 1973
Rarity: B
Issue Price: $ 90
LCS Estimate: $ 1000

No.: 1116
Name: Green Dragon Vase
Height: 20
Current Status: Open issue,
   permanently retired
Original Issue Year: 1971
Last Year: 1973
Rarity: B
Issue Price: $ 90
LCS Estimate: $ 1000

No.: 1118
Name: Floral Vase
Height: 20.5
Current Status: Open issue,
   permanently retired
Original Issue Year: 1971
Last Year: 1972
Rarity: B
Issue Price: $ 160
LCS Estimate: $ 1750

No.: 4740
Name: Flora Cylindrical Vase
Height: 20.5
Current Status: Open issue,
  permanently retired
Original Issue Year: 1971
Last Year: 1979
Rarity: D
Issue Price: $ 130
LCS Estimate: $ 1000

No.: 1620
Name: Peacock Vase
Height: 20.5
Current Status: Limited edition,
  currently active
Edition Limit: 300
Original Issue Year: 1989
Issue Price: $ 2450
Current Retail Price: $ 3000

No.: 1617
Name: Swallow Vase
Height: 20.5
Current Status: Limited edition,
  currently active
Edition Limit: 300
Original Issue Year: 1989
Issue Price: $ 2300
Current Retail Price: $ 2800

No.: 1621
Name: Pheasants and Mums Vase
Height: 20.5
Current Status: Limited edition,
  currently active
Edition Limit: 300
Original Issue Year: 1989
Issue Price: $ 2575
Current Retail Price: $ 3000

No.: 5517.5
Name: Topaz Vase No. 11
Height: 20.75
Current Status: Open issue,
  permanently retired
Original Issue Year: 1988
Last Year: 1991
Rarity: C
Issue Price: $ 425
LCS Estimate: $ 425

No.: 5517.40
Name: Silver Vase No. 11
Height: 20.75
Current Status: Open issue,
  permanently retired
Original Issue Year: 1988
Last Year: 1991
Rarity: C
Issue Price: $ 425
LCS Estimate: $ 425

No.: 1760
Name: Oriental Bird Vase No. 1
Height: 20.75
Current Status: Limited edition,
   currently active
Edition Limit: 300
Original Issue Year: 1992
Issue Price: $ 6700
Current Retail Price: $ 6700

No.: 1761
Name: Oriental Bird Vase No. 2
Height: 20.75
Current Status: Limited edition,
   currently active
Edition Limit: 300
Original Issue Year: 1992
Issue Price: $ 6700
Current Retail Price: $ 6700

No.: 5916
Name: Oriental Peonies Vase No. 1
Height: 20.75
Current Status: Limited edition,
   currently active
Edition Limit: 300
Original Issue Year: 1992
Issue Price: $ 6700
Current Retail Price: $ 6700

No.: 5917
Name: Oriental Peonies Vase No. 2
Height: 20.75
Current Status: Limited edition,
   currently active
Edition Limit: 300
Original Issue Year: 1992
Issue Price: $ 6700
Current Retail Price: $ 6700

No.: 318.13
Name: Vase No. 5
Height: 21.25
Current Status: Very rare early issue
Original Issue Year: 1958
Last Year: Not available
Rarity: A
Issue Price: Not available
Comments: Personally handcrafted by
   Jose Lladro

No.: 1117
Name: Floral Vase
Height: 24.5
Current Status: Open issue,
   permanently retired
Original Issue Year: 1971
Last Year: 1972
Rarity: B
Issue Price: $ 210
LCS Estimate: $ 2300

No.: 1200
Name: Peacocks Floral Vase
Height: 28.75
Current Status: Limited edition, fully subscribed
Edition Limit: 150
Original Issue Year: 1972
Issue Price: $ 1285

No.: 1362
Name: Pheasant Vase
Height: 29.25
Current Status: Limited edition, fully subscribed
Edition Limit: 750
Original Issue Year: 1978
Issue Price: $ 4100

No.: 320.13
Name: Vase No. 7
Height: 39
Current Status: Very rare early issue
Original Issue Year: 1958
Last Year: Not available
Rarity: A
Issue Price: Not available
Comments: Personally handcrafted by Jose Lladro

No. 7600—Little Pals, *the first For-Lladró-Collectors-Society-Members-Only redemption special was issued in 1985 at $95, was closed in 1986 and was auctioned in 1992 for $4,500.*

Here we are at the great body of the Lladró porcelain collection, the 1,761 figurines portraying women, girls, men, boys, infants and fantasy figures, along with other decorative elements such as dogs, horses and vehicles that enhance the sculptures. To keep the classifications as simple as possible, we have divided these figures into nine separate groups:

A. *Solitary infants* — tiny babies. Once these 27 figures grow a little older, they will become girls and boys or, as we call them, females and males.

B. *Solitary "fantasy" figures,* where fantasy is defined as people who do not exist in nature. Lladró's 86 fantasy characters include angels, cupids, centaurs, mermaids and other figures that are half human/half animal, fish or butterfly.

This category is further divided into two classes by size, from shortest to tallest.

It is with the last seven classes, involving females and males, that we invent the term "Major Support Elements." We classify these as:

> Infants
> Fantasy figures
> Dogs
> Horses
> Cats
> Vehicles
> Birds

C. *Two females and all other major support elements except males.* This group includes:

> a mother and daughter
> two little girls playing
> two ballerinas

and any of the above with dogs, horses, and so on.

If a boy or man is present, the figurine falls into other large categories.

Full-figured Humans

This category is further divided into two classes by size, from shortest to tallest.

D. *Three or more females, males, infants or fantasy figures.* This classification of 78 figures includes all the large scenes for which Lladró has become so famous.

This category is further divided into two classes by size, from shortest to tallest.

E. *One or two males and other major support elements except females.* This group of 162 figures includes:

a father and son
two athletes
two little boys

and any number of horses, dogs, and so on. If a female is present, however, your figurine is in another category.

This category is further divided into three classes by size, from shortest to tallest.

F. *Single females and single males together and all other major support elements.* This grouping of 190 figures contains all the "couples":

a boy and girl
a mother and son
a young lady and her beau
an older man and woman out walking, and so on.

This category is further divided into three classes by size, from shortest to tallest.

G. *Single females and other major support elements except males.* This is a large group of 258 figures, so large that we've further divided it into five classes by size, from shortest to tallest.

H. *Solitary males only, without any major support elements.* These are Lladró's 337 men and boys, divided further into six size categories.

I. *Solitary females only, without any major support elements.* This grouping of 545 beauties comprises the largest single theme in the Lladró collection, their diminutive single girls and women. This grouping is so large we've divided it further for your convenience into nine size categories, from the shortest to the tallest.

No. 4616—Boy with Drum, *issued in 1969 at $16.50, retired permanently in 1979 and auctioned in 1992 for $625.*

No.: 4535.30
Name: Baby Jesus
Height: 1
Current Status: Open issue,
  permanently retired
Original Issue Year: 1969
Last Year: 1991
Rarity: F
Issue Price: $ 6
LCS Estimate: $ 30

No.: 5638
Name: Bundle of Joy
Height: 1.25
Current Status: Open issue,
  permanently retired
Original Issue Year: 1989
Last Year: 1991
Rarity: B
Issue Price: $ 170
LCS Estimate: $ 170

No.: 5478
Name: Baby Jesus
Height: 2
Current Status: Open issue, currently
  active
Original Issue Year: 1988
Issue Price: $ 55
Current Retail Price: $ 70

No.: 4670
Name: Jesus
Height: 2
Current Status: Open issue, currently
  active
Original Issue Year: 1969
Issue Price: Part of 8-piece set
Current Retail Price: $ 50

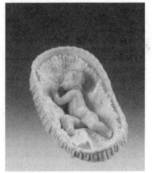

No.: 5637
Name: Bundle of Love
Height: 2
Current Status: Open issue,
  permanently retired
Original Issue Year: 1989
Last Year: 1991
Rarity: B
Issue Price: $ 275
LCS Estimate: $ 275

No.: 4535
Name: Little Jesus (figurine in box)
Height: 2.25
Current Status: Open issue, currently
  active
Original Issue Year: 1969
Issue Price: $ 6
Current Retail Price: $ 60

No.: 5805
Name: Tumbling
Height: 2.25
Current Status: Open issue,
   permanently retired
Original Issue Year: 1991
Last Year: 1993
Rarity: C
Issue Price: $ 130
Last Retail Price: $ 140

No.: 5617
Name: Little Joy
Height: 2.25
Current Status: Open issue,
   permanently retired
Original Issue Year: 1989
Last Year: 1991
Rarity: B
Issue Price: $ 400
LCS Estimate: $ 675

No.: 5619
Name: Ruffles and Lace
Height: 2.5
Current Status: Open issue,
   permanently retired
Original Issue Year: 1989
Last Year: 1991
Rarity: B
Issue Price: $ 425
LCS Estimate: $ 710

No.: 5806
Name: Tickling
Height: 2.75
Current Status: Open issue,
   permanently retired
Original Issue Year: 1991
Last Year: 1993
Rarity: C
Issue Price: $ 130
Last Retail Price: $ 145

No.: 5618
Name: Christening
Height: 2.75
Current Status: Open issue,
   permanently retired
Original Issue Year: 1989
Last Year: 1991
Rarity: B
Issue Price: $ 365
LCS Estimate: $ 620

No.: 1388
Name: Baby Jesus
Height: 3.25
Current Status: Open issue, currently
   active
Original Issue Year: 1981
Issue Price: $ 85
Current Retail Price: $ 135

No.: 5745
Name: Baby Jesus
Height: 3.25
Current Status: Open issue, currently active
Original Issue Year: 1991
Issue Price: $ 170
Current Retail Price: $ 175

No.: 1388.30
Name: Baby Jesus (White)
Height: 3.25
Current Status: Open issue, permanently retired
Original Issue Year: 1983
Last Year: 1985
Rarity: B
Issue Price: $ 50
High Auction Price: $ 135
LCS Estimate: $ 200

No.: 5772
Name: Little Dreamers
Height: 3.5
Current Status: Open issue, currently active
Original Issue Year: 1991
Issue Price: $ 230
Current Retail Price: $ 235

No.: 5804
Name: Playing Tag
Height: 3.5
Current Status: Open issue, permanently retired
Original Issue Year: 1991
Last Year: 1993
Rarity: C
Issue Price: $ 170
Last Retail Price: $ 190

No.: 216.08
Name: Toddler
Height: 3.5
Current Status: Very rare early issue
Original Issue Year: 1956
Last Year: Not available
Rarity: A
Issue Price: Not available

No.: 5102
Name: Baby with Pacifier
Height: 4.5
Current Status: Open issue, permanently retired
Original Issue Year: 1982
Last Year: 1985
Rarity: C
Issue Price: $ 57.5
LCS Estimate: $ 235

No.: 5101
Name: Baby on Floor
Height: 4.5
Current Status: Open issue,
  permanently retired
Original Issue Year: 1982
Last Year: 1985
Rarity: C
Issue Price: $ 57.5
LCS Estimate: $ 235

No.: 5717
Name: Rock a Bye Baby
Height: 4.75
Current Status: Open issue, currently
  active
Original Issue Year: 1990
Issue Price: $ 300
Current Retail Price: $ 340

No.: 5103
Name: Baby Holding Bottle
Height: 5
Current Status: Open issue,
  permanently retired
Original Issue Year: 1982
Last Year: 1985
Rarity: C
Issue Price: $ 57.5
LCS Estimate: $ 235

No.: 5099
Name: Baby with Pacifier
Height: 5
Current Status: Open issue,
  permanently retired
Original Issue Year: 1982
Last Year: 1985
Rarity: C
Issue Price: $ 57.5
High Auction Price: $ 300
LCS Estimate: $ 275

No.: 5100
Name: Baby with Pacifier, Yawning
Height: 5
Current Status: Open issue,
  permanently retired
Original Issue Year: 1982
Last Year: 1985
Rarity: C
Issue Price: $ 57.5
High Auction Price: $ 275
LCS Estimate: $ 275

No.: 1234
Name: Little Jesus of Prague
Height: 11.5
Current Status: Open issue,
  permanently retired
Original Issue Year: 1972
Last Year: 1978
Rarity: D
Issue Price: $ 70
LCS Estimate: $ 560

No.: 1129.30
Name: Boys Playing with Goat (White)
Height: 12.25
Current Status: Open issue,
permanently retired
Original Issue Year: 1971
Last Year: 1975
Rarity: C
Issue Price: $ 75
LCS Estimate: $ 750

No.: 1129
Name: Boys Playing with Goat
Height: 12.25
Current Status: Open issue,
permanently retired
Original Issue Year: 1971
Last Year: 1975
Rarity: C
Issue Price: $ 100
LCS Estimate: $ 1000

No.: 5937
Name: Infant of Cebu
Height: 12.5
Current Status: Open issue, currently
active
Original Issue Year: 1993
Issue Price: N/A

No.: 4541
Name: Angel, Lying Down
Height: 2.25
Current Status: Open issue, currently
active
Original Issue Year: 1969
Issue Price: $ 13
Current Retail Price: $ 85

No.: 5728
Name: Heavenly Dreamer
Height: 2.5
Current Status: Open issue, currently
active
Original Issue Year: 1990
Issue Price: $ 100
Current Retail Price: $ 115

No.: 5723
Name: Heavenly Chimes
Height: 3
Current Status: Open issue, currently
active
Original Issue Year: 1990
Issue Price: $ 100
Current Retail Price: $ 115

No.: 5725
Name: Making a Wish
Height: 3
Current Status: Open issue, currently active
Original Issue Year: 1990
Issue Price: $ 125
Current Retail Price: $ 140

No.: 1502
Name: Forgotten
Height: 3.5
Current Status: Open issue, permanently retired
Original Issue Year: 1986
Last Year: 1991
Rarity: D
Issue Price: $ 125
LCS Estimate: $ 375

No.: 2185
Name: Devoted Reader
Height: 3.5
Current Status: Open issue, currently active
Original Issue Year: 1989
Issue Price: $ 125
Current Retail Price: $ 150

No.: 1500
Name: Ragamuffin
Height: 4
Current Status: Open issue, permanently retired
Original Issue Year: 1986
Last Year: 1991
Rarity: D
Issue Price: $ 125
LCS Estimate: $ 375

No.: 4539
Name: Thinking Angel
Height: 4
Current Status: Open issue, currently active
Original Issue Year: 1969
Issue Price: $ 13
Current Retail Price: $ 85

No.: 1501
Name: Rag Doll
Height: 4
Current Status: Open issue, permanently retired
Original Issue Year: 1986
Last Year: 1991
Rarity: D
Issue Price: $ 125
LCS Estimate: $ 375

No.: 4537
Name: Black Angel
Height: 4.25
Current Status: Open issue, currently active
Original Issue Year: 1969
Issue Price: $ 13
Current Retail Price: $ 85

No.: 5320
Name: Demure Centaur Girl
Height: 5
Current Status: Open issue, permanently retired
Original Issue Year: 1985
Last Year: 1990
Rarity: D
Issue Price: $ 157.5
High Auction Price: $ 300
LCS Estimate: $ 315

No.: 4538
Name: Praying Angel
Height: 5
Current Status: Open issue, currently active
Original Issue Year: 1969
Issue Price: $ 13
Current Retail Price: $ 85

No.: 5727
Name: Angel Care
Height: 5
Current Status: Open issue, currently active
Original Issue Year: 1990
Issue Price: $ 185
Current Retail Price: $ 200

No.: 5853
Name: Floral Admiration
Height: 5.25
Current Status: Open issue, currently active
Original Issue Year: 1992
Issue Price: $ 690
Current Retail Price: $ 690

No.: 5319
Name: Wistful Centaur Girl
Height: 5.5
Current Status: Open issue, permanently retired
Original Issue Year: 1985
Last Year: 1990
Rarity: D
Issue Price: $ 157.5
High Auction Price: $ 300
LCS Estimate: $ 315

No.: 4536
Name: Chinese Angel
Height: 5.5
Current Status: Open issue, currently active
Original Issue Year: 1969
Issue Price: $ 45
Current Retail Price: $ 85

No.: 2184
Name: Angel and Friend
Height: 5.75
Current Status: Open issue, currently active
Original Issue Year: 1989
Issue Price: $ 150
Current Retail Price: $ 175

No.: 2214
Name: Seaside Angel
Height: 6
Current Status: Open issue, currently active
Original Issue Year: 1991
Issue Price: $ 150
Current Retail Price: $ 155

No.: 1415
Name: Mirage
Height: 6
Current Status: Open issue, currently active
Original Issue Year: 1982
Issue Price: $ 115
Current Retail Price: $ 235

No.: 4962
Name: Wondering Angel
Height: 6.25
Current Status: Open issue, currently active
Original Issue Year: 1977
Issue Price: $ 40
Current Retail Price: $ 98

No.: 5724
Name: Angelic Voice
Height: 6.25
Current Status: Open issue, currently active
Original Issue Year: 1990
Issue Price: $ 125
Current Retail Price: $ 140

No.: 1414
Name: Fantasy
Height: 6.25
Current Status: Open issue, currently active
Original Issue Year: 1982
Issue Price: $ 115
Current Retail Price: $ 235

No.: 4540
Name: Angel with Flute
Height: 6.25
Current Status: Open issue, currently active
Original Issue Year: 1969
Issue Price: $ 13
Current Retail Price: $ 85

No.: 1413
Name: Illusion
Height: 6.25
Current Status: Open issue, currently active
Original Issue Year: 1982
Issue Price: $ 115
Current Retail Price: $ 235

No.: 4542
Name: Angels Group
Height: 6.5
Current Status: Open issue, currently active
Original Issue Year: 1969
Issue Price: $ 31
Current Retail Price: $ 180

No.: 5726
Name: Sweep Away the Clouds
Height: 6.5
Current Status: Open issue, currently active
Original Issue Year: 1990
Issue Price: $ 125
Current Retail Price: $ 140

No.: 4961
Name: Dreaming Angel
Height: 6.5
Current Status: Open issue, currently active
Original Issue Year: 1977
Issue Price: $ 40
Current Retail Price: $ 98

No.: 1475
Name: Wishing on a Star
Height: 6.5
Current Status: Open issue,
 permanently retired
Original Issue Year: 1985
Last Year: 1988
Rarity: C
Issue Price: $ 130
High Auction Price: $ 425
LCS Estimate: $ 400

No.: 1437
Name: Moonlight
Height: 7
Current Status: Open issue,
 permanently retired
Original Issue Year: 1983
Last Year: 1988
Rarity: D
Issue Price: $ 97.5
High Auction Price: $ 450
LCS Estimate: $ 400

No.: 1476
Name: Star Light, Star Bright
Height: 7
Current Status: Open issue,
 permanently retired
Original Issue Year: 1985
Last Year: 1988
Rarity: C
Issue Price: $ 130
High Auction Price: $ 375
LCS Estimate: $ 350

No.: 1436
Name: Moon Glow
Height: 7
Current Status: Open issue,
 permanently retired
Original Issue Year: 1983
Last Year: 1988
Rarity: D
Issue Price: $ 97.5
High Auction Price: $ 450
LCS Estimate: $ 400

No.: 5719
Name: Angel Tree Topper
Height: 7
Current Status: Limited edition, fully
 subscribed
Original Issue Year: 1990
Last Year: 1990
Issue Price: $ 100

No.: 5831
Name: Angel Tree Topper
Height: 7.25
Current Status: Limited edition, fully
 subscribed
Original Issue Year: 1991
Last Year: 1991
Issue Price: $ 115

No.: 5830
Name: Heavenly Harpist
Height: 7.25
Current Status: Limited edition, fully
subscribed
Original Issue Year: 1991
Last Year: 1991
Issue Price: $ 135

No.: 5876
Name: Angelic Cymbalist
Height: 7.25
Current Status: Limited edition, fully
subscribed
Original Issue Year: 1992
Last Year: 1992
Issue Price: $ 140

No.: 5962
Name: 1993 Angel Tree Topper
Height: 7.25
Current Status: Limited edition,
permanently retired
Original Issue Year: 1993
Last Year: 1993
Issue Price: $ 125

No.: 5875
Name: Angel Tree Topper Green
Height: 7.25
Current Status: Limited edition, fully
subscribed
Original Issue Year: 1992
Last Year: 1992
Issue Price: $ 120

No.: 5854
Name: Floral Fantasy
Height: 7.25
Current Status: Open issue, currently
active
Original Issue Year: 1992
Issue Price: $ 690
Current Retail Price: $ 690

No.: 5963
Name: Angelic Melody
Height: 7.25
Current Status: Open issue,
permanently retired
Original Issue Year: 1993
Last Year: 1993
Issue Price: $ 145

No.: 2195
Name: Heavenly Sounds
Height: 7.25
Current Status: Open issue,
  permanently retired
Original Issue Year: 1990
Last Year: 1993
Rarity: C
Issue Price: $ 170
Last Retail Price: $ 195

No.: 2194
Name: Heavenly Strings
Height: 7.5
Current Status: Open issue,
  permanently retired
Original Issue Year: 1990
Last Year: 1993
Rarity: C
Issue Price: $ 170
Last Retail Price: $ 195

No.: 1477
Name: Star Gazing
Height: 7.5
Current Status: Open issue,
  permanently retired
Original Issue Year: 1985
Last Year: 1988
Rarity: C
Issue Price: $ 130
High Auction Price: $ 450
LCS Estimate: $ 400

No.: 1438
Name: Full Moon
Height: 7.5
Current Status: Open issue,
  permanently retired
Original Issue Year: 1983
Last Year: 1988
Rarity: D
Issue Price: $ 115
High Auction Price: $ 600
LCS Estimate: $ 575

No.: 2196
Name: Heavenly Solo
Height: 7.75
Current Status: Open issue,
  permanently retired
Original Issue Year: 1990
Last Year: 1993
Rarity: C
Issue Price: $ 170
Last Retail Price: $ 195

No.: 1092
Name: Satyr with Snail
Height: 7.75
Current Status: Open issue,
  permanently retired
Original Issue Year: 1971
Last Year: 1975
Rarity: C
Issue Price: $ 30
LCS Estimate: $ 300

No.: 5491
Name: Heavenly Strings
Height: 7.75
Current Status: Open issue,
  permanently retired
Original Issue Year: 1988
Last Year: 1993
Rarity: D
Issue Price: $ 140
Last Retail Price: $ 185

No.: 5861
Name: Fairy Flowers
Height: 8
Current Status: Open issue, currently
  active
Original Issue Year: 1992
Issue Price: $ 630
Current Retail Price: $ 630

No.: 5493
Name: Angel with Lute
Height: 8.25
Current Status: Open issue,
  permanently retired
Original Issue Year: 1988
Last Year: 1993
Rarity: D
Issue Price: $ 140
Last Retail Price: $ 185

No.: 5492
Name: Heavenly Cellist
Height: 8.25
Current Status: Open issue,
  permanently retired
Original Issue Year: 1988
Last Year: 1993
Rarity: D
Issue Price: $ 240
Last Retail Price: $ 315

No.: 5494
Name: Angel with Clarinet
Height: 8.25
Current Status: Open issue,
  permanently retired
Original Issue Year: 1988
Last Year: 1993
Rarity: D
Issue Price: $ 140
Last Retail Price: $ 185

No.: 1013
Name: Centaur Boy
Height: 8.25
Current Status: Open issue,
  permanently retired
Original Issue Year: 1969
Last Year: 1989
Rarity: F
Issue Price: $ 45
High Auction Price: $ 375
LCS Estimate: $ 350

No.: 4959
Name: Mime Angel
Height: 8.5
Current Status: Open issue, currently active
Original Issue Year: 1977
Issue Price: $ 40
Current Retail Price: $ 98

No.: 1435
Name: Blue Moon
Height: 8.5
Current Status: Open issue, permanently retired
Original Issue Year: 1983
Last Year: 1988
Rarity: D
Issue Price: $ 97.50
High Auction Price: $ 375
LCS Estimate: $ 325

No.: 1233
Name: Angel with Flute
Height: 8.5
Current Status: Open issue, permanently retired
Original Issue Year: 1972
Last Year: 1988
Rarity: F
Issue Price: $ 60
High Auction Price: $ 375
LCS Estimate: $ 400

No.: 1231
Name: Angel with Lute
Height: 8.5
Current Status: Open issue, permanently retired
Original Issue Year: 1972
Last Year: 1988
Rarity: F
Issue Price: $ 60
High Auction Price: $ 425
LCS Estimate: $ 400

No.: 2197
Name: Heavenly Song
Height: 8.5
Current Status: Open issue, permanently retired
Original Issue Year: 1990
Last Year: 1993
Rarity: D
Issue Price: $ 170
Last Retail Price: $ 185

No.: 5860
Name: Fairy Garland
Height: 8.5
Current Status: Open issue, currently active
Original Issue Year: 1992
Issue Price: $ 630
Current Retail Price: $ 630

No.: 2215
Name: Friends in Flight
Height: 8.75
Current Status: Open issue, currently
active
Original Issue Year: 1991
Issue Price: $ 165
Current Retail Price: $ 170

No.: 1739
Name: Heavenly Swing
Height: 8.75
Current Status: Limited edition,
currently active
Edition Limit: 1000
Original Issue Year: 1991
Issue Price: $ 1900
Current Retail Price: $ 1975

No.: 4607
Name: Cupid
Height: 9
Current Status: Open issue,
permanently retired
Original Issue Year: 1969
Last Year: 1980
Rarity: E
Issue Price: $ 15
LCS Estimate: $ 125

No.: 1093
Name: Satyr with Frog
Height: 9
Current Status: Open issue,
permanently retired
Original Issue Year: 1971
Last Year: 1975
Rarity: C
Issue Price: $ 50
LCS Estimate: $ 500

No.: 312.13
Name: Snowman
Height: 9
Current Status: Very rare early issue
Original Issue Year: 1970
Last Year: Not available
Rarity: A
Issue Price: Not available

No.: 4960
Name: Curious Angel
Height: 9.5
Current Status: Open issue, currently
active
Original Issue Year: 1977
Issue Price: $ 40
Current Retail Price: $ 98

No.: 1012
Name: Centaur Girl
Height: 9.5
Current Status: Open issue,
  permanently retired
Original Issue Year: 1969
Last Year: 1989
Rarity: F
Issue Price: $ 45
High Auction Price: $ 250
LCS Estimate: $ 225

No.: 5495
Name: Angelic Choir
Height: 9.5
Current Status: Open issue,
  permanently retired
Original Issue Year: 1988
Last Year: 1993
Rarity: D
Issue Price: $ 300
Last Retail Price: $ 395

No.: 1464
Name: Carefree Angel with Lyre
Height: 9.75
Current Status: Open issue,
  permanently retired
Original Issue Year: 1985
Last Year: 1988
Rarity: C
Issue Price: $ 220
High Auction Price: $ 575
LCS Estimate: $ 550

No.: 1232
Name: Angel with Clarinet
Height: 9.75
Current Status: Open issue,
  permanently retired
Original Issue Year: 1972
Last Year: 1978
Rarity: D
Issue Price: $ 60
High Auction Price: $ 400
LCS Estimate: $ 400

No.: 5785
Name: Ocean Beauty
Height: 10
Current Status: Open issue, currently
  active
Original Issue Year: 1991
Issue Price: $ 625
Current Retail Price: $ 650

No.: 1322
Name: Angel Recital
Height: 10.5
Current Status: Open issue,
  permanently retired
Original Issue Year: 1976
Last Year: 1985
Rarity: E
Issue Price: $ 125
LCS Estimate: $ 750

No.: 1320
Name: Angel with Tambourine
Height: 10.5
Current Status: Open issue,
 permanently retired
Original Issue Year: 1976
Last Year: 1985
Rarity: E
Issue Price: $ 125
High Auction Price: $ 350
LCS Estimate: $ 350

No.: 1007
Name: Pan with Pipes
Height: 10.5
Current Status: Open issue,
 permanently retired
Original Issue Year: 1969
Last Year: 1975
Rarity: D
Issue Price: $ 45
High Auction Price: $ 450
LCS Estimate: $ 500

No.: 1006
Name: Pan with Cymbals
Height: 10.5
Current Status: Open issue,
 permanently retired
Original Issue Year: 1969
Last Year: 1975
Rarity: D
Issue Price: $ 45
High Auction Price: $ 500
LCS Estimate: $ 500

No.: 5791
Name: Fairy Godmother
Height: 11
Current Status: Open issue, currently
 active
Original Issue Year: 1991
Issue Price: $ 375
Current Retail Price: $ 390

No.: 4595
Name: Fairy
Height: 11
Current Status: Open issue, currently
 active
Original Issue Year: 1969
Issue Price: $ 27.5
Current Retail Price: $ 130

No.: 1131
Name: Faun
Height: 11.5
Current Status: Open issue,
 permanently retired
Original Issue Year: 1971
Last Year: 1972
Rarity: B
Issue Price: $ 155
LCS Estimate: $ 1700

No.: 1463
Name: Carefree Angel with Flute
Height: 11.5
Current Status: Open issue,
   permanently retired
Original Issue Year: 1985
Last Year: 1988
Rarity: C
Issue Price: $ 220
High Auction Price: $ 650
LCS Estimate: $ 550

No.: 1321
Name: Angel with Lyre
Height: 11.75
Current Status: Open issue,
   permanently retired
Original Issue Year: 1976
Last Year: 1985
Rarity: E
Issue Price: $ 125
LCS Estimate: $ 750

No.: 1348
Name: Pearl Mermaid
Height: 11.75
Current Status: Open issue,
   permanently retired
Original Issue Year: 1978
Last Year: 1983
Rarity: D
Issue Price: $ 225
High Auction Price: $ 2750
LCS Estimate: $ 2500

No.: 1323
Name: Angel with Accordion
Height: 12.25
Current Status: Open issue,
   permanently retired
Original Issue Year: 1976
Last Year: 1985
Rarity: E
Issue Price: $ 125
High Auction Price: $ 400
LCS Estimate: $ 350

No.: 1324
Name: Angel with Violin
Height: 12.25
Current Status: Open issue,
   permanently retired
Original Issue Year: 1976
Last Year: 1985
Rarity: E
Issue Price: $ 125
LCS Estimate: $ 750

No.: 2240
Name: Winged Love
Height: 13.5
Current Status: Open issue, currently
   active
Original Issue Year: 1993
Issue Price: $ 300

No.: 242.10
Name: Nativity Chorus
Height: 14.25
Current Status: Very rare early issue
Original Issue Year: 1962
Last Year: Not available
Rarity: A
Issue Price: Not available

No.: 2241
Name: Winged Harmony
Height: 14.5
Current Status: Open issue, currently active
Original Issue Year: 1993
Issue Price: $ 300

No.: 1349
Name: Mermaids Playing
Height: 16
Current Status: Open issue, permanently retired
Original Issue Year: 1978
Last Year: 1983
Rarity: D
Issue Price: $ 425
High Auction Price: $ 3250
LCS Estimate: $ 3250

No.: 1347
Name: Mermaid on Wave
Height: 16.5
Current Status: Open issue, permanently retired
Original Issue Year: 1978
Last Year: 1983
Rarity: D
Issue Price: $ 260
High Auction Price: $ 2250
LCS Estimate: $ 2500

No.: 4635
Name: Angel with Baby
Height: 7
Current Status: Open issue, currently active
Original Issue Year: 1969
Issue Price: $ 15
Current Retail Price: $ 95

No.: 5384
Name: Petite Pair
Height: 4.75
Current Status: Open issue, permanently retired
Original Issue Year: 1986
Last Year: 1990
Rarity: C
Issue Price: $ 225
High Auction Price: $ 375
LCS Estimate: $ 450

No.: 1606
Name: Latest Addition
Height: 6.25
Current Status: Open issue, currently active
Original Issue Year: 1989
Issue Price: $ 385
Current Retail Price: $ 475

No.: 5735
Name: Big Sister
Height: 6.75
Current Status: Open issue, currently active
Original Issue Year: 1991
Issue Price: $ 650
Current Retail Price: $ 675

No.: 1534
Name: Little Sister
Height: 7
Current Status: Open issue, currently active
Original Issue Year: 1988
Issue Price: $ 180
Current Retail Price: $ 235

No.: 5720
Name: Sharing Secrets
Height: 7
Current Status: Open issue, currently active
Original Issue Year: 1990
Issue Price: $ 290
Current Retail Price: $ 320

No.: 5497
Name: Dress Rehearsal
Height: 7.5
Current Status: Open issue, currently active
Original Issue Year: 1988
Issue Price: $ 290
Current Retail Price: $ 365

No.: 5537
Name: Flowers For Sale
Height: 7.5
Current Status: Open issue, currently active
Original Issue Year: 1989
Issue Price: $ 1200
Current Retail Price: $ 1470

No.: 5675
Name: Tee Time
Height: 7.5
Current Status: Open issue,
  permanently retired
Original Issue Year: 1990
Last Year: 1993
Rarity: C
Issue Price: $ 270
Last Retail Price: $ 315

No.: 5715
Name: Mommy, It's Cold!
Height: 7.75
Current Status: Open issue, currently
  active
Original Issue Year: 1990
Issue Price: $ 360
Current Retail Price: $ 395

No.: 5714
Name: First Ballet
Height: 7.75
Current Status: Open issue, currently
  active
Original Issue Year: 1990
Issue Price: $ 370
Current Retail Price: $ 400

No.: 5486
Name: Debutantes
Height: 8.25
Current Status: Open issue, currently
  active
Original Issue Year: 1988
Issue Price: $ 490
Current Retail Price: $ 660

No.: 5449
Name: Good Night
Height: 8.25
Current Status: Open issue, currently
  active
Original Issue Year: 1987
Issue Price: $ 225
Current Retail Price: $ 340

No.: 1014
Name: Two Women with Water Jugs
Height: 18.5
Current Status: Open issue,
  permanently retired
Original Issue Year: 1969
Last Year: 1985
Rarity: F
Issue Price: $ 85
High Auction Price: $ 700
LCS Estimate: $ 650

No.: 1527
Name: Tenderness
Height: 8.5
Current Status: Open issue, currently active
Original Issue Year: 1987
Issue Price: $ 260
Current Retail Price: $ 395

No.: 5305
Name: Visit with Granny
Height: 9
Current Status: Open issue, permanently retired
Original Issue Year: 1985
Last Year: 1993
Rarity: E
Issue Price: $ 275
Last Retail Price: $ 515

No.: 2206
Name: Sisterly Love
Height: 9
Current Status: Open issue, currently active
Original Issue Year: 1990
Issue Price: $ 300
Current Retail Price: $ 330

No.: 5344
Name: A Stitch in Time
Height: 9
Current Status: Open issue, currently active
Original Issue Year: 1986
Issue Price: $ 425
Current Retail Price: $ 715

No.: 5995
Name: Soft Meow
Height: 9
Current Status: Open issue, currently active
Original Issue Year: 1993
Issue Price: $ 550

No.: 5601
Name: "Ole"
Height: 9.25
Current Status: Open issue, currently active
Original Issue Year: 1989
Issue Price: $ 365
Current Retail Price: $ 430

No.: 5994
Name: Meet My Friend
Height: 9.25
Current Status: Open issue, currently
   active
Original Issue Year: 1993
Issue Price: $ 785

No.: 5700
Name: Southern Charm
Height: 9.5
Current Status: Open issue, currently
   active
Original Issue Year: 1990
Issue Price: $ 775
Current Retail Price: $ 995

No.: 5989
Name: A Mother's Touch
Height: 9.5
Current Status: Open issue, currently
   active
Original Issue Year: 1993
Issue Price: $ 495

No.: 5299
Name: Mother with Child and Lamb
Height: 9.5
Current Status: Open issue,
   permanently retired
Original Issue Year: 1985
Last Year: 1988
Rarity: C
Issue Price: $ 180
High Auction Price: $ 425
LCS Estimate: $ 400

No.: 4890
Name: Bathing the Girl
Height: 9.5
Current Status: Open issue,
   permanently retired
Original Issue Year: 1974
Last Year: 1978
Rarity: C
Issue Price: $ 165
LCS Estimate: $ 1500

No.: 5650
Name: Anticipation
Height: 9.5
Current Status: Open issue,
   permanently retired
Original Issue Year: 1990
Last Year: 1993
Rarity: C
Issue Price: $ 300
Last Retail Price: $ 340

No.: 2098
Name: Girls Collecting Wheat
Height: 9.5
Current Status: Open issue, permanently retired
Original Issue Year: 1978
Last Year: 1981
Rarity: C
Issue Price: $ 250
High Auction Price: $ 650
LCS Estimate: $ 650

No.: 5721
Name: Once Upon A Time
Height: 10.25
Current Status: Open issue, currently active
Original Issue Year: 1990
Issue Price: $ 550
Current Retail Price: $ 595

No.: 5793
Name: Precocious Ballerina
Height: 10.25
Current Status: Open issue, currently active
Original Issue Year: 1991
Issue Price: $ 575
Current Retail Price: $ 595

No.: 5786
Name: Story Hour
Height: 10.25
Current Status: Open issue, currently active
Original Issue Year: 1991
Issue Price: $ 550
Current Retail Price: $ 570

No.: 5766
Name: Charming Duet
Height: 10.25
Current Status: Open issue, currently active
Original Issue Year: 1991
Issue Price: $ 575
Current Retail Price: $ 595

No.: 5893
Name: Friendship In Bloom
Height: 10.25
Current Status: Open issue, currently active
Original Issue Year: 1992
Issue Price: $ 650
Current Retail Price: $ 650

No.: 5142
Name: Comforting Daughter
Height: 10.5
Current Status: Open issue,
  permanently retired
Original Issue Year: 1982
Last Year: 1991
Rarity: E
Issue Price: $ 195
LCS Estimate: $ 390

No.: 5408
Name: Sunday Stroll
Height: 10.5
Current Status: Open issue,
  permanently retired
Original Issue Year: 1987
Last Year: 1990
Rarity: C
Issue Price: $ 250
High Auction Price: $ 500
LCS Estimate: $ 500

No.: 5067
Name: Snow White with Apple
Height: 10.5
Current Status: Open issue,
  permanently retired
Original Issue Year: 1980
Last Year: 1983
Rarity: C
Issue Price: $ 375
High Auction Price: $ 1250
LCS Estimate: $ 1200

No.: 5457
Name: Bedtime Story
Height: 10.5
Current Status: Open issue, currently
  active
Original Issue Year: 1988
Issue Price: $ 275
Current Retail Price: $ 345

No.: 5085
Name: Woman and Sleeping Girl
Height: 10.75
Current Status: Open issue,
  permanently retired
Original Issue Year: 1980
Last Year: 1985
Rarity: D
Issue Price: $ 530
High Auction Price: $ 800
LCS Estimate: $ 800

No.: 1326
Name: Comforting Her Friend
Height: 11
Current Status: Open issue,
  permanently retired
Original Issue Year: 1976
Last Year: 1981
Rarity: D
Issue Price: $ 195
LCS Estimate: $ 1375

No.: 5946
Name: A Mother's Way
Height: 11.25
Current Status: Open issue, currently active
Original Issue Year: 1993
Issue Price: $ 1400

No.: 5757
Name: Beautiful Tresses
Height: 11.5
Current Status: Open issue, permanently retired
Original Issue Year: 1991
Last Year: 1993
Rarity: C
Issue Price: $ 725
Last Retail Price: $ 785

No.: 5360
Name: Sewing Circle
Height: 11.5
Current Status: Open issue, permanently retired
Original Issue Year: 1986
Last Year: 1990
Rarity: C
Issue Price: $ 600
LCS Estimate: $ 1200

No.: 4930
Name: Sisters
Height: 11.5
Current Status: Open issue, permanently retired
Original Issue Year: 1974
Last Year: 1981
Rarity: D
Issue Price: $ 250
High Auction Price: $ 675
LCS Estimate: $ 650

No.: 1774
Name: A Treasured Moment
Height: 11.75
Current Status: Open issue, currently active
Original Issue Year: 1993
Issue Price: $ 950

No.: 1498
Name: Tahitian Dancing Girls
Height: 11.75
Current Status: Open issue, currently active
Original Issue Year: 1986
Issue Price: $ 750
Current Retail Price: $ 1250

No.: 4984
Name: The Gossips
Height: 11.75
Current Status: Open issue,
  permanently retired
Original Issue Year: 1978
Last Year: 1985
Rarity: D
Issue Price: $ 215
High Auction Price: $ 1000
LCS Estimate: $ 1000

No.: 1445
Name: Springtime in Japan
Height: 11.75
Current Status: Open issue, currently
  active
Original Issue Year: 1983
Issue Price: $ 965
Current Retail Price: $ 1750

No.: 5767
Name: First Sampler
Height: 12
Current Status: Open issue, currently
  active
Original Issue Year: 1991
Issue Price: $ 625
Current Retail Price: $ 650

No.: 5013
Name: Daughters
Height: 12.5
Current Status: Open issue,
  permanently retired
Original Issue Year: 1978
Last Year: 1991
Rarity: E
Issue Price: $ 250
High Auction Price: $ 950
LCS Estimate: $ 900

No.: 347.13
Name: Spain-USA
Height: 12.75
Current Status: Very rare early issue
Original Issue Year: 1973
Last Year: Not available
Rarity: A
Issue Price: Not available

No.: 5370
Name: Can Can
Height: 13
Current Status: Open issue,
  permanently retired
Original Issue Year: 1986
Last Year: 1990
Rarity: C
Issue Price: $ 700
High Auction Price: $ 1600
LCS Estimate: $ 1400

No.: 4611
Name: Nuns
Height: 13
Current Status: Open issue, currently active
Original Issue Year: 1969
Issue Price: $ 36.5
Current Retail Price: $ 145

No.: 1511
Name: Cafe De Paris
Height: 13.25
Current Status: Open issue, currently active
Original Issue Year: 1987
Issue Price: $ 1900
Current Retail Price: $ 2800

No.: 4666
Name: Woman with Girl and Donkey
Height: 13.25
Current Status: Open issue, permanently retired
Original Issue Year: 1969
Last Year: 1979
Rarity: E
Issue Price: $ 130
LCS Estimate: $ 1070

No.: 4604
Name: Bread and Water
Height: 13.25
Current Status: Open issue, permanently retired
Original Issue Year: 1969
Last Year: 1972
Rarity: C
Issue Price: $ 55
LCS Estimate: $ 660

No.: 5966
Name: Flowers Forever
Height: 13.5
Current Status: Open issue, currently active
Original Issue Year: 1993
Issue Price: $ 4250

No.: 2075
Name: Nuns
Height: 13.75
Current Status: Open issue, currently active
Original Issue Year: 1977
Issue Price: $ 90
Current Retail Price: $ 220

No.: 1353
Name: Lady with Girl
Height: 14.25
Current Status: Open issue,
  permanently retired
Original Issue Year: 1978
Last Year: 1985
Rarity: D
Issue Price: $ 175
High Auction Price: $ 600
LCS Estimate: $ 875

No.: 5042
Name: Ladies Talking
Height: 14.25
Current Status: Open issue,
  permanently retired
Original Issue Year: 1980
Last Year: 1983
Rarity: C
Issue Price: $ 385
LCS Estimate: $ 1625

No.: 1490
Name: Floral Offering
Height: 14.5
Current Status: Limited edition,
  currently active
Edition Limit: 3000
Original Issue Year: 1986
Issue Price: $ 2500
Current Retail Price: $ 4250

No.: 2119
Name: Dressing Up
Height: 15
Current Status: Open issue,
  permanently retired
Original Issue Year: 1980
Last Year: 1985
Rarity: D
Issue Price: $ 700
High Auction Price: $ 900
LCS Estimate: $ 700

No.: 2142
Name: Sea Harvest
Height: 15.5
Current Status: Open issue,
  permanently retired
Original Issue Year: 1984
Last Year: 1990
Rarity: D
Issue Price: $ 535
High Auction Price: $ 700
LCS Estimate: $ 675

No.: 2252
Name: Waiting for Father
Height: 15.5
Current Status: Open issue, currently
  active
Original Issue Year: 1993
Issue Price: $ 690

No.: 1366
Name: Girls in the Swing
Height: 15.5
Current Status: Open issue,
  permanently retired
Original Issue Year: 1978
Last Year: 1988
Rarity: E
Issue Price: $ 825
LCS Estimate: $ 2300

No.: 5069
Name: Girls Arch with Flowers
Height: 15.5
Current Status: Open issue,
  permanently retired
Original Issue Year: 1980
Last Year: 1981
Rarity: B
Issue Price: $ 555
LCS Estimate: $ 2575

No.: 1494
Name: My Wedding Day
Height: 15.5
Current Status: Open issue, currently
  active
Original Issue Year: 1986
Issue Price: $ 800
Current Retail Price: $ 1395

No.: 2112
Name: Charity
Height: 15.75
Current Status: Open issue,
  permanently retired
Original Issue Year: 1978
Last Year: 1981
Rarity: C
Issue Price: $ 360
LCS Estimate: $ 2200

No.: 4556
Name: Profound Contemplation
Height: 15.75
Current Status: Open issue,
  permanently retired
Original Issue Year: 1969
Last Year: 1974
Rarity: D
Issue Price: $ 195
LCS Estimate: $ 2100

No.: 4557
Name: Musical Contemplation
Height: 15.75
Current Status: Open issue,
  permanently retired
Original Issue Year: 1969
Last Year: 1970
Rarity: B
Issue Price: $ 170
LCS Estimate: $ 2000

No.: 1770
Name: Gypsy Dancers
Height: 16.25
Current Status: Open issue, currently active
Original Issue Year: 1993
Issue Price: $ 2250

No.: 5754
Name: Singapore Dancers
Height: 16.75
Current Status: Open issue, permanently retired
Original Issue Year: 1991
Last Year: 1993
Rarity: C
Issue Price: $ 950
Last Retail Price: $ 1025

No.: 1440
Name: Pleasantries
Height: 17
Current Status: Open issue, permanently retired
Original Issue Year: 1983
Last Year: 1991
Rarity: E
Issue Price: $ 960
High Auction Price: $ 1900
LCS Estimate: $ 1900

No.: 1346
Name: Under the Willow
Height: 18.5
Current Status: Open issue, permanently retired
Original Issue Year: 1978
Last Year: 1990
Rarity: E
Issue Price: $ 1600
High Auction Price: $ 2000
LCS Estimate: $ 2000

No.: 4804
Name: Harmony Group
Height: 19.25
Current Status: Open issue, permanently retired
Original Issue Year: 1972
Last Year: 1981
Rarity: E
Issue Price: $ 165
LCS Estimate: $ 1200

No.: 5819
Name: Allegory of Liberty
Height: 20.5
Current Status: Open issue, currently active
Original Issue Year: 1991
Issue Price: $ 1950
Current Retail Price: $ 2000

No.: 2070
Name: A New Hairdo
Height: 21.5
Current Status: Open issue, permanently retired
Original Issue Year: 1977
Last Year: 1991
Rarity: E
Issue Price: $ 530
High Auction Price: $ 800
LCS Estimate: $ 1000

No.: 5035
Name: Allegre Ballet
Height: 21.5
Current Status: Open issue, currently active
Original Issue Year: 1979
Issue Price: $ 700
Current Retail Price: $ 1350

No.: 2073
Name: Graceful Duo
Height: 22
Current Status: Open issue, currently active
Original Issue Year: 1977
Issue Price: $ 775
Current Retail Price: $ 1575

No.: 1766
Name: Ties That Bind
Height: 22
Current Status: Open issue, currently active
Original Issue Year: 1993
Issue Price: $ 1700

No.: 3522
Name: Philippine Girls
Height: 26.25
Current Status: Limited edition, currently active
Edition Limit: 1500
Original Issue Year: 1981
Issue Price: $ 1450
Current Retail Price: $ 2300

No.: 4980
Name: Three On a Bench
Height: 7
Current Status: Open issue, permanently retired
Original Issue Year: 1977
Last Year: 1979
Rarity: B
Issue Price: $ 145
LCS Estimate: $ 1020

No.: 5343
Name: Love Boat
Height: 7.75
Current Status: Limited edition,
 currently active
Edition Limit: 3000
Original Issue Year: 1985
Issue Price: $ 775
Current Retail Price: $ 1300

No.: 5380
Name: Sweet Harvest
Height: 8.5
Current Status: Open issue,
 permanently retired
Original Issue Year: 1986
Last Year: 1990
Rarity: C
Issue Price: $ 450
High Auction Price: $ 700
LCS Estimate: $ 900

No.: 4585
Name: Nativity
Height: 8.5
Current Status: Open issue, currently
 active
Original Issue Year: 1969
Issue Price: $ 18
Current Retail Price: $ 130

No.: 3513
Name: A Wintry Day
Height: 8.75
Current Status: Open issue,
 permanently retired
Original Issue Year: 1978
Last Year: 1988
Rarity: E
Issue Price: $ 525
High Auction Price: $ 850
LCS Estimate: $ 850

No.: 1239
Name: Christmas Carols
Height: 9
Current Status: Open issue,
 permanently retired
Original Issue Year: 1973
Last Year: 1981
Rarity: E
Issue Price: $ 125
High Auction Price: $ 950
LCS Estimate: $ 880

No.: 5847
Name: The Voyage of Columbus
Height: 9
Current Status: Limited edition,
 currently active
Edition Limit: 7500
Original Issue Year: 1992
Issue Price: $ 1450
Current Retail Price: $ 1450

No.: 1742
Name: Onward!
Height: 9
Current Status: Limited edition, currently active
Edition Limit: 1000
Original Issue Year: 1991
Issue Price: $ 2500
Current Retail Price: $ 2600

No.: 5910
Name: Making a Wish
Height: 9.25
Current Status: Open issue, currently active
Original Issue Year: 1992
Issue Price: $ 790
Current Retail Price: $ 790

No.: 5596
Name: Mother's Day
Height: 9.5
Current Status: Open issue, currently active
Original Issue Year: 1989
Issue Price: $ 400
Current Retail Price: $ 495

No.: 5306
Name: Young Street Musicians
Height: 9.5
Current Status: Open issue, permanently retired
Original Issue Year: 1985
Last Year: 1988
Rarity: C
Issue Price: $ 300
High Auction Price: $ 1150
LCS Estimate: $ 1000

No.: 5702
Name: Back to School
Height: 9.75
Current Status: Open issue, permanently retired
Original Issue Year: 1990
Last Year: 1993
Rarity: C
Issue Price: $ 350
Last Retail Price: $ 405

No.: 1517
Name: At The Fair
Height: 9.75
Current Status: Open issue, currently active
Original Issue Year: 1987
Issue Price: $ 2900
Current Retail Price: $ 4200

No.: 1731
Name: Valencian Cruise
Height: 9.75
Current Status: Limited edition,
  currently active
Edition Limit: 1000
Original Issue Year: 1991
Issue Price: $ 2700
Current Retail Price: $ 2800

No.: 5423
Name: Carnival Time
Height: 10
Current Status: Limited edition,
  permanently retired
Edition Limit: 1000
Original Issue Year: 1987
Last Year: 1993
Rarity: D
Issue Price: $ 2400
Last Retail Price: $ 3900

No.: 1597
Name: Southern Tea
Height: 10.25
Current Status: Limited edition,
  currently active
Edition Limit: 1000
Original Issue Year: 1989
Issue Price: $ 1775
Current Retail Price: $ 2200

No.: 1499
Name: Blessed Family
Height: 10.25
Current Status: Open issue, currently
  active
Original Issue Year: 1986
Issue Price: $ 200
Current Retail Price: $ 340

No.: 1732
Name: Venice Vows
Height: 10.25
Current Status: Limited edition,
  currently active
Edition Limit: 1500
Original Issue Year: 1991
Issue Price: $ 3755
Current Retail Price: $ 3900

No.: 5771
Name: The Magic of Laughter
Height: 10.5
Current Status: Open issue, currently
  active
Original Issue Year: 1991
Issue Price: $ 950
Current Retail Price: $ 980

No.: 5848
Name: The Loving Family
Height: 10.75
Current Status: Open issue, currently
active
Original Issue Year: 1992
Issue Price: $ 950
Current Retail Price: $ 950

No.: 5371
Name: Family Roots
Height: 11
Current Status: Open issue, currently
active
Original Issue Year: 1986
Issue Price: $ 575
Current Retail Price: $ 895

No.: 1493
Name: At the Stroke of Twelve
Height: 11
Current Status: Limited edition,
currently active
Edition Limit: 1500
Original Issue Year: 1986
Issue Price: $ 4250
Current Retail Price: $ 7100

No.: 1610
Name: Flight to Egypt
Height: 11.5
Current Status: Open issue, currently
active
Original Issue Year: 1989
Issue Price: $ 885
Current Retail Price: $ 1100

No.: 5402
Name: Desert Tour
Height: 11.75
Current Status: Open issue,
permanently retired
Original Issue Year: 1987
Last Year: 1990
Rarity: C
Issue Price: $ 950
High Auction Price: $ 1050
LCS Estimate: $ 1000

No.: 1580
Name: Return to La Mancha
Height: 11.75
Current Status: Limited edition,
currently active
Edition Limit: 500
Original Issue Year: 1988
Issue Price: $ 6400
Current Retail Price: $ 7950

No.: 5692
Name: Street Harmonies
Height: 11.75
Current Status: Open issue,
  permanently retired
Original Issue Year: 1990
Last Year: 1993
Rarity: C
Issue Price: $ 3200
Last Retail Price: $ 3750

No.: 5878
Name: Sister's Pride
Height: 11.75
Current Status: Open issue, currently
  active
Original Issue Year: 1992
Issue Price: $ 595
Current Retail Price: $ 595

No.: 1492
Name: Three Sisters
Height: 11.75
Current Status: Limited edition,
  currently active
Edition Limit: 3000
Original Issue Year: 1986
Issue Price: $ 1850
Current Retail Price: $ 3100

No.: 1491
Name: Oriental Music
Height: 11.75
Current Status: Limited edition,
  currently active
Edition Limit: 5000
Original Issue Year: 1986
Issue Price: $ 1350
Current Retail Price: $ 2300

No.: 1521
Name: The Landau Carriage
Height: 11.75
Current Status: Open issue, currently
  active
Original Issue Year: 1987
Issue Price: $ 2500
Current Retail Price: $ 3750

No.: 2198
Name: A King is Born
Height: 12.25
Current Status: Open issue, currently
  active
Original Issue Year: 1990
Issue Price: $ 750
Current Retail Price: $ 840

No.: 5388
Name: Sidewalk Serenade
Height: 12.5
Current Status: Open issue,
  permanently retired
Original Issue Year: 1986
Last Year: 1988
Rarity: B
Issue Price: $ 750
High Auction Price: $ 1300
LCS Estimate: $ 1300

No.: 5974
Name: Family Outing
Height: 12.75
Current Status: Open issue, currently
  active
Original Issue Year: 1993
Issue Price: $ 4500

No.: 5068
Name: Fairy Queen
Height: 12.75
Current Status: Open issue,
  permanently retired
Original Issue Year: 1980
Last Year: 1983
Rarity: C
Issue Price: $ 625
High Auction Price: $ 900
LCS Estimate: $ 900

No.: 1762
Name: Paella Valenciano
Height: 13
Current Status: Limited edition,
  currently active
Edition Limit: 500
Original Issue Year: 1993
Issue Price: $ 10000

No.: 1146
Name: Antique Auto
Height: 13
Current Status: Limited edition, fully
  subscribed
Edition Limit: 750
Original Issue Year: 1971
Rarity: A
Issue Price: $ 1000
High Auction Price: $ 10500

No.: 1609
Name: Circus Parade
Height: 13
Current Status: Limited edition,
  currently active
Edition Limit: 1000
Original Issue Year: 1989
Issue Price: $ 5200
Current Retail Price: $ 6250

No.: 1225
Name: Hansom Carriage
Height: 13.25
Current Status: Limited edition, fully subscribed
Edition Limit: 750
Original Issue Year: 1972
Rarity: A
Issue Price: $ 1450
High Auction Price: $10000

No.: 4973
Name: Song Lesson
Height: 13.25
Current Status: Open issue, permanently retired
Original Issue Year: 1977
Last Year: 1981
Rarity: C
Issue Price: $ 350
LCS Estimate: $ 2000

No.: 1496
Name: Hawaian Festival
Height: 13.25
Current Status: Limited edition, currently active
Edition Limit: 4000
Original Issue Year: 1986
Issue Price: $ 1850
Current Retail Price: $ 3000

No.: 5341
Name: I've Found Thee, Dulcinea
Height: 13.25
Current Status: Limited edition, fully subscribed
Edition Limit: 750
Original Issue Year: 1985
Issue Price: $ 1460
High Auction Price: $ 3000

No.: 1756
Name: Outing in Seville
Height: 13.5
Current Status: Limited edition, currently active
Edition Limit: 500
Original Issue Year: 1991
Issue Price: $23000
Current Retail Price: $23750

No.: 4974
Name: Dutch Children
Height: 13.75
Current Status: Open issue, permanently retired
Original Issue Year: 1977
Last Year: 1981
Rarity: C
Issue Price: $ 375
LCS Estimate: $ 2200

No.: 1446
Name: Here Comes the Bride
Height: 13.75
Current Status: Open issue, currently active
Original Issue Year: 1983
Issue Price: $ 517.5
Current Retail Price: $ 945

No.: 5216
Name: On the Lake
Height: 13.75
Current Status: Open issue, permanently retired
Original Issue Year: 1984
Last Year: 1988
Rarity: C
Issue Price: $ 660
High Auction Price: $ 1050
LCS Estimate: $ 1000

No.: 1355
Name: Astronomy Lesson
Height: 14.5
Current Status: Open issue, permanently retired
Original Issue Year: 1978
Last Year: 1979
Rarity: B
Issue Price: $ 550
LCS Estimate: $ 4000

No.: 1433
Name: Venetian Serenade
Height: 14.5
Current Status: Limited edition, fully subscribed
Edition Limit: 750
Original Issue Year: 1983
Last Year: 1989
Rarity: D
Issue Price: $ 2600
High Auction Price: $ 3750
LCS Estimate: $ 4000

No.: 3528
Name: Wrestling
Height: 14.5
Current Status: Limited edition, fully subscribed
Edition Limit: 50
Original Issue Year: 1983
Issue Price: $ 950

No.: 4956
Name: Tavern Drinkers
Height: 14.5
Current Status: Open issue, permanently retired
Original Issue Year: 1977
Last Year: 1985
Rarity: E
Issue Price: $ 1125
High Auction Price: $ 3500
LCS Estimate: $ 3500

No.: 5539
Name: Puppy Dog Tails
Height: 15
Current Status: Open issue, currently active
Original Issue Year: 1989
Issue Price: $ 1200
Current Retail Price: $ 1470

No.: 1519
Name: Stroll in the Park
Height: 15
Current Status: Open issue, currently active
Original Issue Year: 1987
Issue Price: $ 1600
Current Retail Price: $ 2500

No.: 5362
Name: Fox Hunt
Height: 15
Current Status: Limited edition, currently active
Edition Limit: 1000
Original Issue Year: 1986
Issue Price: $ 5200
Current Retail Price: $ 8500

No.: 4864
Name: Mother
Height: 15
Current Status: Open issue, permanently retired
Original Issue Year: 1974
Last Year: 1979
Rarity: D
Issue Price: $ 190
LCS Estimate: $ 1500

No.: 346.13
Name: Allegory
Height: 15.25
Current Status: Very rare early issue
Original Issue Year: 1965
Last Year: Not available
Rarity: A
Issue Price: Not available

No.: 5972
Name: Before the Dance
Height: 15.5
Current Status: Open issue, currently active
Original Issue Year: 1993
Issue Price: $ 3550

No.: 1457
Name: Festival in Valencia
Height: 15.5
Current Status: Limited edition,
    currently active
Edition Limit: 3000
Original Issue Year: 1985
Issue Price: $ 1400
Current Retail Price: $ 2250

No.: 1123
Name: La Tarantela
Height: 16
Current Status: Open issue,
    permanently retired
Original Issue Year: 1971
Last Year: 1975
Rarity: C
Issue Price: $ 550
High Auction Price: $ 2400
LCS Estimate: $ 2000

No.: 1485
Name: Eighteenth Century Coach
Height: 16.5
Current Status: Limited edition,
    currently active
Edition Limit: 500
Original Issue Year: 1985
Issue Price: $14000
Current Retail Price: $24000

No.: 5911
Name: Presenting Credentials
Height: 16.75
Current Status: Limited edition,
    currently active
Edition Limit: 1500
Original Issue Year: 1992
Issue Price: $19500
Current Retail Price: $19500

No.: 5235
Name: Ballet Trio
Height: 17
Current Status: Open issue, currently
    active
Original Issue Year: 1984
Issue Price: $ 785
Current Retail Price: $ 1475

No.: 1085
Name: Musical Nineteenth Century
Height: 17
Current Status: Open issue,
    permanently retired
Original Issue Year: 1969
Last Year: 1973
Rarity: C
Issue Price: $ 180
LCS Estimate: $ 2000

No.: 3504
Name: Rescue
Height: 17
Current Status: Limited edition, fully subscribed
Edition Limit: 1500
Original Issue Year: 1978
Issue Price: $ 2900
High Auction Price: $ 3250

No.: 1757
Name: Hawaiian Ceremony
Height: 17
Current Status: Limited edition, currently active
Edition Limit: 1000
Original Issue Year: 1992
Issue Price: $ 9800
Current Retail Price: $ 9800

No.: 1350
Name: In the Gondola
Height: 17.75
Current Status: Open issue, currently active
Original Issue Year: 1978
Issue Price: $ 1350
Current Retail Price: $ 3100

No.: 5097
Name: Sedan Chair Group
Height: 17.75
Current Status: Open issue, permanently retired
Original Issue Year: 1980
Last Year: 1991
Rarity: E
Issue Price: $ 2950
LCS Estimate: $ 5700

No.: 5098
Name: A Successful Hunt
Height: 18
Current Status: Limited edition, permanently retired
Edition Limit: 1000
Original Issue Year: 1980
Last Year: 1993
Rarity: E
Issue Price: $ 5200
Last Retail Price: $ 8150

No.: 1579
Name: Blessed Lady
Height: 20
Current Status: Limited edition, fully subscribed
Edition Limit: 1000
Original Issue Year: 1988
Issue Price: $ 1150

No.: 1327
Name: Playing Cards
Height: 20.5
Current Status: Open issue, currently active
Original Issue Year: 1976
Issue Price: $ 3800
Current Retail Price: $ 6400

No.: 3556
Name: Road to Mandalay
Height: 20.75
Current Status: Limited edition, fully subscribed
Edition Limit: 750
Original Issue Year: 1982
Issue Price: $ 1390
High Auction Price: $ 2500

No.: 1201
Name: The Family
Height: 21.5
Current Status: Open issue, permanently retired
Original Issue Year: 1971
Last Year: 1979
Rarity: E
Issue Price: $ 245
LCS Estimate: $ 1960

No.: 1758
Name: Circus Time
Height: 22
Current Status: Limited edition, currently active
Edition Limit: 2500
Original Issue Year: 1992
Issue Price: $ 9200
Current Retail Price: $ 9200

No.: 1759
Name: Tea In the Garden
Height: 22.5
Current Status: Limited edition, currently active
Edition Limit: 2000
Original Issue Year: 1992
Issue Price: $ 9500
Current Retail Price: $ 9500

No.: 1578
Name: Garden Party
Height: 22.75
Current Status: Limited edition, currently active
Edition Limit: 500
Original Issue Year: 1988
Issue Price: $ 5500
Current Retail Price: $ 6900

No.: 1266
Name: Soccer Players
Height: 27.5
Current Status: Limited edition, fully subscribed
Edition Limit: 500
Original Issue Year: 1974
Issue Price: $ 1000
High Auction Price: $ 7500
LCS Estimate: $ 7000

No.: 3557
Name: Jesus in the Tiber
Height: 28.75
Current Status: Limited edition, currently active
Edition Limit: 1200
Original Issue Year: 1984
Issue Price: $ 2600
Current Retail Price: $ 4300

No.: 2245
Name: Inspired Voyage
Height: 28.75
Current Status: Open issue, currently active
Edition Limit: 1000
Original Issue Year: 1993
Issue Price: $ 4800

No.: 2028
Name: Three Girls
Height: 29.5
Current Status: Limited edition, fully subscribed
Edition Limit: 500
Original Issue Year: 1971
Issue Price: $ 950

No.: 1605
Name: Kitakami Cruise
Height: 42
Current Status: Limited edition, currently active
Edition Limit: 500
Original Issue Year: 1989
Issue Price: $ 6350
Current Retail Price: $ 7000

No.: 5988
Name: Taking Time
Height: 3.5
Current Status: Open issue, currently active
Original Issue Year: 1993
Issue Price: $ 190

No.: 2168
Name: Julio
Height: 3.5
Current Status: Open issue,
  permanently retired
Original Issue Year: 1987
Last Year: 1993
Rarity: D
Issue Price: $ 120
Last Retail Price: $ 170

No.: 5451
Name: Study Buddies
Height: 4
Current Status: Open issue, currently
  active
Original Issue Year: 1988
Issue Price: $ 225
Current Retail Price: $ 285

No.: 1535
Name: Sweet Dreams
Height: 4
Current Status: Open issue, currently
  active
Original Issue Year: 1988
Issue Price: $ 150
Current Retail Price: $ 195

No.: 6027
Name: Hanukah Lights
Height: 4.25
Current Status: Open issue, currently
  active
Original Issue Year: 1993
Issue Price: $ 395

No.: 5278
Name: Pierrot with Puppy and Ball
Height: 4.25
Current Status: Open issue, currently
  active
Original Issue Year: 1985
Issue Price: $ 95
Current Retail Price: $ 155

No.: 5277
Name: Pierrot with Puppy
Height: 4.25
Current Status: Open issue, currently
  active
Original Issue Year: 1985
Issue Price: $ 95
Current Retail Price: $ 155

No.: 5456
Name: New Playmates
Height: 4.75
Current Status: Open issue, currently active
Original Issue Year: 1988
Issue Price: $ 160
Current Retail Price: $ 200

No.: 1195
Name: Eskimo Playing with Bear
Height: 4.75
Current Status: Open issue, currently active
Original Issue Year: 1972
Issue Price: $ 30
Current Retail Price: $ 125

No.: 99.06
Name: Boys with Grapes
Height: 4.75
Current Status: Very rare early issue
Original Issue Year: 1958
Last Year: Not available
Rarity: A
Issue Price: Not available

No.: 5697
Name: Over the Clouds
Height: 5
Current Status: Open issue, currently active
Original Issue Year: 1990
Issue Price: $ 275
Current Retail Price: $ 300

No.: 5450
Name: I Hope She Does . . .
Height: 5
Current Status: Open issue, currently active
Original Issue Year: 1987
Issue Price: $ 190
Current Retail Price: $ 300

No.: 5178
Name: Stubborn Mule
Height: 5
Current Status: Open issue, permanently retired
Original Issue Year: 1982
Last Year: 1993
Rarity: E
Issue Price: $ 250
Last Retail Price: $ 420

No.: 4858
Name: Pleasant Encounter
Height: 5.5
Current Status: Open issue, permanently retired
Original Issue Year: 1974
Last Year: 1981
Rarity: D
Issue Price: $ 60
LCS Estimate: $ 420

No.: 6011
Name: Monday's Child - Boy
Height: 5.5
Current Status: Open issue, currently active
Original Issue Year: 1993
Issue Price: $ 280

No.: 5238
Name: Eskimo Boy with Pet
Height: 5.5
Current Status: Open issue, currently active
Original Issue Year: 1984
Issue Price: $ 55
Current Retail Price: $ 98

No.: 5279
Name: Pierrot with Concertina
Height: 5.5
Current Status: Open issue, currently active
Original Issue Year: 1985
Issue Price: $ 95
Current Retail Price: $ 155

No.: 5936
Name: Little Skipper
Height: 5.5
Current Status: Open issue, currently active
Original Issue Year: 1993
Issue Price: $ 320

No.: 5987
Name: Talk To Me
Height: 5.5
Current Status: Open issue, currently active
Original Issue Year: 1993
Issue Price: $ 180

No.: 2166
Name: Paco
Height: 5.5
Current Status: Open issue,
  permanently retired
Original Issue Year: 1987
Last Year: 1993
Rarity: D
Issue Price: $ 120
Last Retail Price: $ 170

No.: 311.13
Name: Boy with Bull
Height: 6
Current Status: Very rare early issue
Original Issue Year: 1963
Last Year: Not available
Rarity: A
Issue Price: Not available

No.: 5736
Name: Puppet Show
Height: 6
Current Status: Open issue, currently
  active
Original Issue Year: 1991
Issue Price: $ 280
Current Retail Price: $ 295

No.: 4676
Name: Shepherd with Lamb
Height: 6
Current Status: Open issue, currently
  active
Original Issue Year: 1969
Issue Price: $ 14
Current Retail Price: $ 90

No.: 335.13
Name: Merry Christmas
Height: 6
Current Status: Very rare early issue
Original Issue Year: 1966
Last Year: Not available
Rarity: A
Issue Price: Not available

No.: 5703
Name: Behave
Height: 6
Current Status: Open issue, currently
  active
Original Issue Year: 1990
Issue Price: $ 230
Current Retail Price: $ 255

No.: 4730
Name: Bird Watcher
Height: 6.25
Current Status: Open issue, permanently retired
Original Issue Year: 1970
Last Year: 1985
Rarity: E
Issue Price: $ 35
High Auction Price: $ 475
LCS Estimate: $ 450

No.: 2167
Name: Fernando
Height: 6.25
Current Status: Open issue, permanently retired
Original Issue Year: 1987
Last Year: 1993
Rarity: D
Issue Price: $ 120
Last Retail Price: $ 170

No.: 5376
Name: This One's Mine
Height: 6.5
Current Status: Open issue, currently active
Original Issue Year: 1986
Issue Price: $ 300
Current Retail Price: $ 495

No.: 5401
Name: My Best Friend
Height: 6.5
Current Status: Open issue, currently active
Original Issue Year: 1987
Issue Price: $ 150
Current Retail Price: $ 235

No.: 5770
Name: Out For a Spin
Height: 6.75
Current Status: Open issue, currently active
Original Issue Year: 1991
Issue Price: $ 390
Current Retail Price: $ 400

No.: 2205
Name: Prayerful Stitch
Height: 7
Current Status: Open issue, currently active
Original Issue Year: 1990
Issue Price: $ 160
Current Retail Price: $ 180

No.: 2238
Name: Learning Together
Height: 7.25
Current Status: Open issue, currently active
Original Issue Year: 1993
Issue Price: $ 500

No.: 4522
Name: Boy with Dog
Height: 7.5
Current Status: Open issue, currently active
Original Issue Year: 1970
Issue Price: $ 25
Current Retail Price: $ 150

No.: 5797
Name: Come Out and Play
Height: 7.5
Current Status: Open issue, currently active
Original Issue Year: 1991
Issue Price: $ 275
Current Retail Price: $ 285

No.: 6019
Name: Friday's Child - Boy
Height: 7.5
Current Status: Open issue, currently active
Original Issue Year: 1993
Issue Price: $ 260

No.: 5711
Name: A Christmas Wish
Height: 7.5
Current Status: Open issue, currently active
Original Issue Year: 1990
Issue Price: $ 350
Current Retail Price: $ 390

No.: 5794
Name: Precious Cargo
Height: 7.5
Current Status: Open issue, currently active
Original Issue Year: 1991
Issue Price: $ 460
Current Retail Price: $ 480

No.: 5684
Name: Barnyard Reflections
Height: 7.5
Current Status: Open issue,
  permanently retired
Original Issue Year: 1990
Last Year: 1993
Rarity: C
Issue Price: $ 460
Last Retail Price: $ 525

No.: 4659
Name: Shepherd
Height: 7.5
Current Status: Open issue,
  permanently retired
Original Issue Year: 1969
Last Year: 1985
Rarity: F
Issue Price: $ 25.5
High Auction Price: $ 200
LCS Estimate: $ 200

No.: 4971
Name: Hunter Puppet
Height: 7.5
Current Status: Open issue,
  permanently retired
Original Issue Year: 1977
Last Year: 1985
Rarity: E
Issue Price: $ 95
LCS Estimate: $ 475

No.: 6013
Name: Tuesday's Child - Boy
Height: 7.5
Current Status: Open issue, currently
  active
Original Issue Year: 1993
Issue Price: $ 260

No.: 6017
Name: Thursday's Child - Boy
Height: 7.5
Current Status: Open issue, currently
  active
Original Issue Year: 1993
Issue Price: $ 260

No.: 1181
Name: Platero an Marcelino
Height: 7.75
Current Status: Open issue,
  permanently retired
Original Issue Year: 1971
Last Year: 1981
Rarity: E
Issue Price: $ 40
LCS Estimate: $ 280

No.: 6015
Name: Wednesday's Child - Boy
Height: 7.75
Current Status: Open issue, currently active
Original Issue Year: 1993
Issue Price: $ 280

No.: 5250
Name: Exam Day
Height: 7.75
Current Status: Open issue, currently active
Original Issue Year: 1984
Issue Price: $ 115
Current Retail Price: $ 200

No.: 5220
Name: Winter
Height: 7.75
Current Status: Open issue, currently active
Original Issue Year: 1984
Issue Price: $ 90
Current Retail Price: $ 165

No.: 2226
Name: Boy's Best Friend
Height: 7.75
Current Status: Open issue, currently active
Original Issue Year: 1992
Issue Price: $ 390
Current Retail Price: $ 390

No.: 7609
Name: My Buddy
Height: 8
Current Status: Limited edition, fully subscribed
Original Issue Year: 1989
Last Year: 1989
Rarity: B
Issue Price: $ 145
High Auction Price: $ 800
Comments: LCS Special

No.: 5738
Name: Best Foot Forward
Height: 8.25
Current Status: Open issue, currently active
Original Issue Year: 1991
Issue Price: $ 280
Current Retail Price: $ 290

No.: 5358
Name: Little Sculptor
Height: 8.25
Current Status: Open issue, permanently retired
Original Issue Year: 1986
Last Year: 1990
Rarity: C
Issue Price: $ 160
High Auction Price: $ 300
LCS Estimate: $ 325

No.: 4837
Name: Student Flute Player
Height: 8.25
Current Status: Open issue, permanently retired
Original Issue Year: 1973
Last Year: 1983
Rarity: E
Issue Price: $ 66
High Auction Price: $ 375
LCS Estimate: $ 400

No.: 2203
Name: Afternoon Chores
Height: 8.25
Current Status: Open issue, currently active
Original Issue Year: 1990
Issue Price: $ 150
Current Retail Price: $ 175

No.: 2232
Name: Poor Little Bear
Height: 8.25
Current Status: Open issue, currently active
Original Issue Year: 1992
Issue Price: $ 250
Current Retail Price: $ 250

No.: 5485
Name: Shepherd Boy
Height: 8.25
Current Status: Open issue, currently active
Original Issue Year: 1988
Issue Price: $ 140
Current Retail Price: $ 175

No.: 6023
Name: Sunday's Child - Boy
Height: 8.25
Current Status: Open issue, currently active
Original Issue Year: 1993
Issue Price: $ 260

No.: 5763
Name: Musical Partners
Height: 8.25
Current Status: Open issue, currently active
Original Issue Year: 1991
Issue Price: $ 625
Current Retail Price: $ 650

No.: 1487
Name: Fantasia
Height: 8.5
Current Status: Limited edition, currently active
Edition Limit: 5000
Original Issue Year: 1986
Issue Price: $ 1500
Current Retail Price: $ 2550

No.: 2201
Name: Our Daily Bread
Height: 8.5
Current Status: Open issue, currently active
Original Issue Year: 1990
Issue Price: $ 150
Current Retail Price: $ 175

No.: 5237
Name: School Chums
Height: 8.5
Current Status: Open issue, currently active
Original Issue Year: 1984
Issue Price: $ 225
Current Retail Price: $ 420

No.: 4852
Name: Gardener in Trouble
Height: 8.5
Current Status: Open issue, permanently retired
Original Issue Year: 1973
Last Year: 1981
Rarity: E
Issue Price: $ 65
High Auction Price: $ 400
LCS Estimate: $ 450

No.: 4617
Name: Group of Musicians
Height: 8.5
Current Status: Open issue, permanently retired
Original Issue Year: 1969
Last Year: 1979
Rarity: E
Issue Price: $ 33
High Auction Price: $ 550
LCS Estimate: $ 550

No.: 5379
Name: Children's Games
Height: 8.5
Current Status: Open issue,
   permanently retired
Original Issue Year: 1986
Last Year: 1991
Rarity: D
Issue Price: $ 325
LCS Estimate: $ 800

No.: 5737
Name: Little Prince
Height: 8.75
Current Status: Open issue,
   permanently retired
Original Issue Year: 1991
Last Year: 1993
Rarity: C
Issue Price: $ 295
Current Retail Price: $ 315

No.: 2204
Name: Farmyard Grace
Height: 8.75
Current Status: Open issue,
   permanently retired
Original Issue Year: 1990
Last Year: 1993
Rarity: C
Issue Price: $ 180
Last Retail Price: $ 210

No.: 7600
Name: Little Pals
Height: 8.75
Current Status: Limited edition, fully
   subscribed
Original Issue Year: 1985
Last Year: 1985
Rarity: B
Issue Price: $ 95
High Auction Price: $ 4500
Comments: LCS Special

No.: 2097
Name: Eskimo Playing (Big)
Height: 9
Current Status: Open issue,
   permanently retired
Original Issue Year: 1978
Last Year: 1991
Rarity: E
Issue Price: $ 225
LCS Estimate: $ 250

No.: 2207
Name: What a Day
Height: 9
Current Status: Open issue, currently
   active
Original Issue Year: 1990
Issue Price: $ 550
Current Retail Price: $ 600

No.: 1283
Name: Little Gardener
Height: 9
Current Status: Open issue, currently active
Original Issue Year: 1974
Issue Price: $ 250
Current Retail Price: $ 765

No.: 5166
Name: Sea Fever
Height: 9
Current Status: Open issue, permanently retired
Original Issue Year: 1982
Last Year: 1993
Rarity: E
Issue Price: $ 130
Last Retail Price: $ 255

No.: 2202
Name: A Helping Hand
Height: 9
Current Status: Open issue, permanently retired
Original Issue Year: 1990
Last Year: 1993
Rarity: C
Issue Price: $ 150
Last Retail Price: $ 185

No.: 1460
Name: A Boy and His Pony
Height: 9.5
Current Status: Open issue, permanently retired
Original Issue Year: 1985
Last Year: 1988
Rarity: C
Issue Price: $ 285
High Auction Price: $ 750
LCS Estimate: $ 750

No.: 4608
Name: Cook in Trouble
Height: 9.5
Current Status: Open issue, permanently retired
Original Issue Year: 1969
Last Year: 1985
Rarity: F
Issue Price: $ 27.5
High Auction Price: $ 750
LCS Estimate: $ 650

No.: 2163
Name: Mountain Shepherd
Height: 9.5
Current Status: Open issue, currently active
Original Issue Year: 1987
Issue Price: $ 135
Current Retail Price: $ 180

No.: 5396
Name: The Puppet Painter
Height: 9.5
Current Status: Open issue, currently active
Original Issue Year: 1986
Issue Price: $ 500
Current Retail Price: $ 825

No.: 4817
Name: Little Shepherd with Goat
Height: 9.75
Current Status: Open issue, permanently retired
Original Issue Year: 1972
Last Year: 1981
Rarity: E
Issue Price: $ 50
LCS Estimate: $ 350

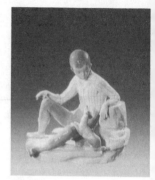

No.: 4755
Name: Boy with Dog
Height: 9.75
Current Status: Open issue, permanently retired
Original Issue Year: 1971
Last Year: 1978
Rarity: D
Issue Price: $ 50
High Auction Price: $ 600
LCS Estimate: $ 500

No.: 1229
Name: Young Harlequin
Height: 9.75
Current Status: Open issue, currently active
Original Issue Year: 1972
Issue Price: $ 70
Current Retail Price: $ 495

No.: 2237
Name: The Old Fishing Hole
Height: 9.75
Current Status: Open issue, currently active
Original Issue Year: 1993
Issue Price: $ 625

No.: 5901
Name: Surprise
Height: 9.75
Current Status: Open issue, currently active
Original Issue Year: 1992
Issue Price: $ 325
Current Retail Price: $ 325

No.: 2222
Name: Tender Moment
Height: 10
Current Status: Open issue, currently
  active
Original Issue Year: 1992
Issue Price: $ 400
Current Retail Price: $ 400

No.: 5961
Name: The Great Teacher
Height: 10
Current Status: Open issue, currently
  active
Original Issue Year: 1993
Issue Price: $ 850

No.: 5270
Name: Racing Motorcyclist
Height: 10.25
Current Status: Open issue,
  permanently retired
Original Issue Year: 1985
Last Year: 1988
Rarity: C
Issue Price: $ 360
High Auction Price: $ 850
LCS Estimate: $ 800

No.: 5059
Name: Clown with Saxophone
Height: 10.25
Current Status: Open issue,
  permanently retired
Original Issue Year: 1980
Last Year: 1985
Rarity: D
Issue Price: $ 320
High Auction Price: $ 475
LCS Estimate: $ 475

No.: 4859
Name: Peddler
Height: 10.25
Current Status: Open issue,
  permanently retired
Original Issue Year: 1974
Last Year: 1985
Rarity: E
Issue Price: $ 180
High Auction Price: $ 1200
LCS Estimate: $ 1100

No.: 1276
Name: Christmas Seller
Height: 10.25
Current Status: Open issue,
  permanently retired
Original Issue Year: 1974
Last Year: 1981
Rarity: D
Issue Price: $ 120
LCS Estimate: $ 840

No.: 4571
Name: Shepherd Resting
Height: 10.25
Current Status: Open issue, permanently retired
Original Issue Year: 1969
Last Year: 1981
Rarity: E
Issue Price: $ 60
LCS Estimate: $ 480

No.: 4911
Name: Shepherd
Height: 10.25
Current Status: Open issue, permanently retired
Original Issue Year: 1974
Last Year: 1979
Rarity: D
Issue Price: $ 175
LCS Estimate: $ 1400

No.: 5856
Name: Circus Concert
Height: 10.25
Current Status: Open issue, currently active
Original Issue Year: 1992
Issue Price: $ 570
Current Retail Price: $ 570

No.: 4506
Name: Boy with Goat
Height: 10.5
Current Status: Open issue, permanently retired
Original Issue Year: 1969
Last Year: 1985
Rarity: F
Issue Price: $ 22.5
High Auction Price: $ 375
LCS Estimate: $ 350

No.: 4509
Name: Boy with Lambs
Height: 10.5
Current Status: Open issue, permanently retired
Original Issue Year: 1969
Last Year: 1981
Rarity: E
Issue Price: $ 37.5
High Auction Price: $ 325
LCS Estimate: $ 300

No.: 1094
Name: Beggar
Height: 10.5
Current Status: Open issue, permanently retired
Original Issue Year: 1969
Last Year: 1981
Rarity: E
Issue Price: $ 65
LCS Estimate: $ 520

No.: 1183
Name: Oriental Man on Horse
Height: 10.5
Current Status: Open issue,
  permanently retired
Original Issue Year: 1971
Last Year: 1973
Rarity: B
Issue Price: $ 60
LCS Estimate: $ 650

No.: 5892
Name: Circus Magic
Height: 10.5
Current Status: Open issue, currently
  active
Original Issue Year: 1992
Issue Price: $ 470
Current Retail Price: $ 470

No.: 5971
Name: A Special Toy
Height: 10.5
Current Status: Open issue, currently
  active
Original Issue Year: 1993
Issue Price: $ 815

No.: 5879
Name: Shot On Goal
Height: 10.75
Current Status: Open issue, currently
  active
Original Issue Year: 1992
Issue Price: $ 1100
Current Retail Price: $ 1100

No.: 5838
Name: On the Move
Height: 11
Current Status: Open issue, currently
  active
Original Issue Year: 1991
Issue Price: $ 340
Current Retail Price: $ 350

No.: 5207
Name: A Tall Yarn
Height: 11
Current Status: Open issue, currently
  active
Original Issue Year: 1984
Issue Price: $ 260
Current Retail Price: $ 490

No.: 4638
Name: Honey Peddler
Height: 11
Current Status: Open issue,
  permanently retired
Original Issue Year: 1969
Last Year: 1978
Rarity: E
Issue Price: $ 60
LCS Estimate: $ 540

No.: 5850
Name: Inspiring Muse
Height: 11
Current Status: Open issue, currently
  active
Original Issue Year: 1992
Issue Price: $ 1200
Current Retail Price: $ 1200

No.: 4834
Name: Baby Lamb
Height: 11.5
Current Status: Open issue,
  permanently retired
Original Issue Year: 1972
Last Year: 1981
Rarity: E
Issue Price: $ 40
LCS Estimate: $ 280

No.: 2052
Name: Magistrates
Height: 11.5
Current Status: Open issue,
  permanently retired
Original Issue Year: 1974
Last Year: 1981
Rarity: D
Issue Price: $ 135
LCS Estimate: $ 950

No.: 1252
Name: Shepherd's Rest
Height: 11.75
Current Status: Open issue,
  permanently retired
Original Issue Year: 1974
Last Year: 1981
Rarity: D
Issue Price: $ 100
LCS Estimate: $ 700

No.: 1132
Name: Carriage of Bacchus
Height: 11.75
Current Status: Open issue,
  permanently retired
Original Issue Year: 1971
Last Year: 1972
Rarity: B
Issue Price: $ 160
LCS Estimate: $ 1750

No.: 2246
Name: Lion Tamer
Height: 12.25
Current Status: Open issue, currently active
Original Issue Year: 1993
Issue Price: $ 375

No.: 1771
Name: Country Doctor
Height: 12.5
Current Status: Open issue, currently active
Original Issue Year: 1993
Issue Price: $ 1475

No.: 2208
Name: Let's Rest
Height: 12.5
Current Status: Open issue, currently active
Original Issue Year: 1990
Issue Price: $ 550
Current Retail Price: $ 600

No.: 5342
Name: Pack of Hunting Dogs
Height: 12.5
Current Status: Limited edition, currently active
Edition Limit: 3000
Original Issue Year: 1985
Issue Price: $ 875
Current Retail Price: $ 1575
High Auction Price: $ 1350

No.: 1249
Name: The Race
Height: 13
Current Status: Open issue, permanently retired
Original Issue Year: 1974
Last Year: 1988
Rarity: E
Issue Price: $ 410
High Auction Price: $ 3200
LCS Estimate: $ 2700

No.: 5089
Name: Jockey Mounted
Height: 13.25
Current Status: Open issue, permanently retired
Original Issue Year: 1980
Last Year: 1985
Rarity: D
Issue Price: $ 660
High Auction Price: $ 1150
LCS Estimate: $ 1100

No.: 1763
Name: Trusting Friend
Height: 13.25
Current Status: Open issue, currently active
Original Issue Year: 1993
Issue Price: $ 1200

No.: 4825
Name: Veterinarian
Height: 13.25
Current Status: Open issue, permanently retired
Original Issue Year: 1972
Last Year: 1985
Rarity: E
Issue Price: $ 35
High Auction Price: $ 525
LCS Estimate: $ 500

No.: 5975
Name: Up and Away
Height: 13.25
Current Status: Open issue, currently active
Original Issue Year: 1993
Issue Price: $ 2850

No.: 5046
Name: Organ Grinder
Height: 13.5
Current Status: Open issue, permanently retired
Original Issue Year: 1980
Last Year: 1981
Rarity: B
Issue Price: $ 327.5
High Auction Price: $ 1600
LCS Estimate: $ 1600

No.: 5751
Name: Walk with Father
Height: 13.5
Current Status: Open issue, currently active
Original Issue Year: 1991
Issue Price: $ 375
Current Retail Price: $ 390

No.: 4654
Name: The Grandfather
Height: 13.75
Current Status: Open issue, permanently retired
Original Issue Year: 1969
Last Year: 1979
Rarity: E
Issue Price: $ 75
LCS Estimate: $ 670

No.: 4892
Name: Watching the Pigs
Height: 13.75
Current Status: Open issue,
  permanently retired
Original Issue Year: 1974
Last Year: 1978
Rarity: C
Issue Price: $ 160
LCS Estimate: $ 1400

No.: 4763.30
Name: Obstetrician (Reduced)
Height: 13.75
Current Status: Open issue, currently
  active
Original Issue Year: 1971
Issue Price: $ 40
Current Retail Price: $ 225

No.: 1104
Name: Shepherd Sleeping
Height: 14
Current Status: Open issue,
  permanently retired
Original Issue Year: 1971
Last Year: 1978
Rarity: D
Issue Price: $ 225
LCS Estimate: $ 1800

No.: 4652
Name: Happy Travelers
Height: 14.25
Current Status: Open issue,
  permanently retired
Original Issue Year: 1969
Last Year: 1978
Rarity: E
Issue Price: $ 115
High Auction Price: $ 650
LCS Estimate: $ 650

No.: 5642
Name: The King's Guard
Height: 14.25
Current Status: Open issue,
  permanently retired
Original Issue Year: 1990
Last Year: 1993
Rarity: C
Issue Price: $ 950
Last Retail Price: $ 1100

No.: 1310
Name: Arabian Knight
Height: 14.25
Current Status: Open issue,
  permanently retired
Original Issue Year: 1974
Last Year: 1979
Rarity: D
Issue Price: $ 285
LCS Estimate: $ 2300

No.: 5002
Name: Hunter with Dog
Height: 14.25
Current Status: Open issue,
   permanently retired
Original Issue Year: 1978
Last Year: 1979
Rarity: B
Issue Price: $ 325
LCS Estimate: $ 2300

No.: 1136
Name: Orpheus
Height: 14.5
Current Status: Open issue,
   permanently retired
Original Issue Year: 1971
Last Year: 1972
Rarity: B
Issue Price: $ 135
LCS Estimate: $ 1500

No.: 5155
Name: Monks
Height: 14.5
Current Status: Open issue, currently
   active
Original Issue Year: 1982
Issue Price: $ 130
Current Retail Price: $ 240

No.: 5942
Name: The Blessing
Height: 14.75
Current Status: Open issue, currently
   active
Original Issue Year: 1993
Edition Limit: 2000
Issue Price: $ 1345

No.: 1086
Name: Pregonero
Height: 15
Current Status: Open issue,
   permanently retired
Original Issue Year: 1969
Last Year: 1975
Rarity: D
Issue Price: $ 120
High Auction Price: $ 750
LCS Estimate: $ 1000

No.: 1470
Name: Boy On Carousel Horse
Height: 15
Current Status: Open issue, currently
   active
Original Issue Year: 1985
Issue Price: $ 470
Current Retail Price: $ 825

No.: 4780
Name: Boy with Goat
Height: 15
Current Status: Open issue,
  permanently retired
Original Issue Year: 1971
Last Year: 1978
Rarity: D
Issue Price: $ 60
LCS Estimate: $ 400

No.: 1344
Name: Derby
Height: 15.5
Current Status: Open issue,
  permanently retired
Original Issue Year: 1977
Last Year: 1985
Rarity: E
Issue Price: $ 1125
High Auction Price: $ 2300
LCS Estimate: $ 2500

No.: 4998
Name: Don Quixote and Sancho Panza
Height: 15.5
Current Status: Open issue,
  permanently retired
Original Issue Year: 1978
Last Year: 1983
Rarity: D
Issue Price: $ 875
High Auction Price: $ 2625
LCS Estimate: $ 3400

No.: 5780
Name: Walking the Fields
Height: 15.5
Current Status: Open issue,
  permanently retired
Original Issue Year: 1991
Last Year: 1993
Rarity: C
Issue Price: $ 725
Last Retail Price: $ 795

No.: 1061
Name: Campero
Height: 15.75
Current Status: Open issue,
  permanently retired
Original Issue Year: 1969
Last Year: 1975
Rarity: D
Issue Price: $ 180
LCS Estimate: $ 2000

No.: 4803
Name: Sorian Shepherd with Flock
Height: 15.75
Current Status: Open issue,
  permanently retired
Original Issue Year: 1972
Last Year: 1975
Rarity: C
Issue Price: $ 195
LCS Estimate: $ 2000

No.: 1018
Name: King Gaspar
Height: 15.75
Current Status: Open issue, currently active
Original Issue Year: 1969
Issue Price: $ 345
Current Retail Price: $ 1795

No.: 1019
Name: Melchior
Height: 15.75
Current Status: Open issue, currently active
Original Issue Year: 1969
Issue Price: $ 345
Current Retail Price: $ 1795

No.: 1020
Name: Balthazar
Height: 15.75
Current Status: Open issue, currently active
Original Issue Year: 1969
Issue Price: $ 345
Current Retail Price: $ 1795

No.: 2090
Name: Saint Francis
Height: 16
Current Status: Open issue, permanently retired
Original Issue Year: 1978
Last Year: 1981
Rarity: C
Issue Price: $ 565
LCS Estimate: $ 3400

No.: 1037
Name: Horseman
Height: 16
Current Status: Open issue, permanently retired
Original Issue Year: 1969
Last Year: 1970
Rarity: B
Issue Price: $ 170
LCS Estimate: $ 2000

No.: 4763
Name: Obstetrician
Height: 16.5
Current Status: Open issue, permanently retired
Original Issue Year: 1971
Last Year: 1973
Rarity: B
Issue Price: $ 47.5
LCS Estimate: $ 530

No.: 5732
Name: Carousel Canter
Height: 16.5
Current Status: Open issue, currently active
Original Issue Year: 1991
Issue Price: $ 1700
Current Retail Price: $ 1785

No.: 5246
Name: St. Cristobal
Height: 16.5
Current Status: Open issue, permanently retired
Original Issue Year: 1984
Last Year: 1988
Rarity: C
Issue Price: $ 265
High Auction Price: $ 500
LCS Estimate: $ 500

No.: 1253
Name: Sad Chimney-Sweep
Height: 17
Current Status: Open issue, permanently retired
Original Issue Year: 1974
Last Year: 1983
Rarity: E
Issue Price: $ 180
LCS Estimate: $ 1100

No.: 349.13
Name: Tempting the Bull
Height: 17.25
Current Status: Very rare early issue
Original Issue Year: 1965
Last Year: Not available
Rarity: A
Issue Price: Not available
High Auction Price: $ 5000

No.: 5087
Name: The Watchman
Height: 17.25
Current Status: Open issue, permanently retired
Original Issue Year: 1980
Last Year: 1983
Rarity: C
Issue Price: $ 225
High Auction Price: $ 1350
LCS Estimate: $ 1200

No.: 1075
Name: Knight
Height: 17.25
Current Status: Open issue, permanently retired
Original Issue Year: 1969
Last Year: 1970
Rarity: B
Issue Price: $ 170
LCS Estimate: $ 2000

No.: 1764
Name: He's My Brother
Height: 17.75
Current Status: Open issue, currently active
Original Issue Year: 1993
Issue Price: $ 1500

No.: 1048
Name: Hunters
Height: 18
Current Status: Open issue, permanently retired
Original Issue Year: 1969
Last Year: 1986
Rarity: F
Issue Price: $ 115
High Auction Price: $ 1875
LCS Estimate: $ 1700

No.: 5215
Name: Fishing with Grandpa
Height: 18
Current Status: Open issue, currently active
Original Issue Year: 1984
Issue Price: $ 410
Current Retail Price: $ 760

No.: 4623
Name: Shepherd
Height: 18.5
Current Status: Open issue, permanently retired
Original Issue Year: 1969
Last Year: 1975
Rarity: D
Issue Price: $ 80
LCS Estimate: $ 870

No.: 1773
Name: Michevious Musician
Height: 18.75
Current Status: Open issue, currently active
Original Issue Year: 1993
Issue Price: $ 975

No.: 4515
Name: Man on Horse
Height: 19
Current Status: Open issue, permanently retired
Original Issue Year: 1969
Last Year: 1985
Rarity: F
Issue Price: $ 180
High Auction Price: $ 1300
LCS Estimate: $ 1300

No.: 1318
Name: Don Quixote and Sancho
Height: 19
Current Status: Limited edition, fully
   subscribed
Edition Limit: 1000
Original Issue Year: 1976
High Auction Price: $ 5000
Issue Price: $ 1200

No.: 1237
Name: The Wisdom of Buddha
Height: 20
Current Status: Open issue,
   permanently retired
Original Issue Year: 1972
Last Year: 1975
Rarity: C
Issue Price: $ 350
LCS Estimate: $ 2800

No.: 3529
Name: Companionship
Height: 20.5
Current Status: Limited edition, fully
   subscribed
Edition Limit: 65
Original Issue Year: 1983
Issue Price: $ 1000

No.: 3555
Name: Desert People
Height: 20.75
Current Status: Limited edition, fully
   subscribed
Edition Limit: 750
Original Issue Year: 1982
Issue Price: $ 1680
Current Retail Price: $ 2975

No.: 2248
Name: Days of Yore
Height: 21.25
Current Status: Open issue, currently
   active
Edition Limit: 1000
Original Issue Year: 1993
Issue Price: $ 2050

No.: 1497
Name: Quixote and Windmill
Height: 21.25
Current Status: Open issue, currently
   active
Original Issue Year: 1986
Issue Price: $ 1100
Current Retail Price: $ 1950

No.: 1608
Name: Mounted Warriors
Height: 22
Current Status: Limited edition, currently active
Edition Limit: 500
Original Issue Year: 1989
Issue Price: $ 2850
Current Retail Price: $ 3300

No.: 1765
Name: Course of Adventure
Height: 22.5
Current Status: Open issue, currently active
Original Issue Year: 1993
Issue Price: $ 1625

No.: 3001
Name: Monks
Height: 27.25
Current Status: Limited edition, permanently retired
Edition Limit: 300
Original Issue Year: 1982
Last Year: 1993
Rarity: E
Issue Price: $ 1675
Last Retail Price: $ 2550

No.: 1328
Name: Man with Lamb on Shoulders
Height: 27.5
Current Status: Open issue, permanently retired
Original Issue Year: 1976
Last Year: 1981
Rarity: D
Issue Price: $ 1100
LCS Estimate: $ 7500

No.: 3515
Name: Saint Michael
Height: 37.5
Current Status: Limited edition, currently active
Edition Limit: 1500
Original Issue Year: 1978
Issue Price: $ 2200
Current Retail Price: $ 4100

No.: 5415
Name: Mexican Dancers
Height: 1.5
Current Status: Open issue, currently active
Original Issue Year: 1987
Issue Price: $ 800
Current Retail Price: $ 1100

No.: 107.06
Name: Dancers
Height: 5.5
Current Status: Very rare early issue
Original Issue Year: 1958
Last Year: Not available
Rarity: A
Issue Price: Not available

No.: 304.13
Name: Romantic Serenade
Height: 5.5
Current Status: Very rare early issue
Original Issue Year: 1960
Last Year: Not available
Rarity: A
Issue Price: Not available

No.: 5941
Name: Riding the Waves
Height: 5.5
Current Status: Open issue, currently active
Original Issue Year: 1993
Issue Price: $ 405

No.: 1230
Name: Friendship
Height: 6
Current Status: Open issue, permanently retired
Original Issue Year: 1972
Last Year: 1991
Rarity: D
Issue Price: $ 68
LCS Estimate: $ 540

No.: 5361
Name: Try This One
Height: 6
Current Status: Open issue, currently active
Original Issue Year: 1986
Issue Price: $ 225
Current Retail Price: $ 365

No.: 5454
Name: For Me?
Height: 6
Current Status: Open issue, currently active
Original Issue Year: 1988
Issue Price: $ 290
Current Retail Price: $ 360

No.: 5072
Name: Precocious Courtship
Height: 6
Current Status: Open issue,
  permanently retired
Original Issue Year: 1980
Last Year: 1990
Rarity: E
Issue Price: $ 410
LCS Estimate: $ 825

No.: 5072.30
Name: Courtship (White)
Height: 6
Current Status: Open issue,
  permanently retired
Original Issue Year: 1983
Last Year: 1987
Rarity: C
Issue Price: $ 242.50
High Auction Price: $ 375
LCS Estimate: $ 400

No.: 5779
Name: Lover's Paradise
Height: 6
Current Status: Open issue, currently
  active
Original Issue Year: 1991
Issue Price: $ 2250
Current Retail Price: $ 2350

No.: 5665
Name: Hang On!
Height: 6
Current Status: Open issue, currently
  active
Original Issue Year: 1990
Issue Price: $ 225
Current Retail Price: $ 250

No.: 5698
Name: Don't Look Down
Height: 6.25
Current Status: Open issue, currently
  active
Original Issue Year: 1990
Issue Price: $ 330
Current Retail Price: $ 370

No.: 243.10
Name: Jumping the Hoop
Height: 6.5
Current Status: Very rare early issue
Original Issue Year: 1958
Last Year: Not available
Rarity: A
Issue Price: Not available

No.: 5353
Name: Eskimo Riders
Height: 6.5
Current Status: Open issue, currently active
Original Issue Year: 1986
Issue Price: $ 150
Current Retail Price: $ 240

No.: 5701
Name: Just a Little Kiss
Height: 6.5
Current Status: Open issue, currently active
Original Issue Year: 1990
Issue Price: $ 320
Current Retail Price: $ 355

No.: 5741
Name: Dancing Class
Height: 6.75
Current Status: Open issue, currently active
Original Issue Year: 1991
Issue Price: $ 340
Current Retail Price: $ 350

No.: 5139
Name: A New Doll House
Height: 7
Current Status: Open issue, permanently retired
Original Issue Year: 1982
Last Year: 1985
Rarity: C
Issue Price: $ 185
High Auction Price: $ 850
LCS Estimate: $ 750

No.: 5835
Name: "I Do"
Height: 7.25
Current Status: Open issue, currently active
Original Issue Year: 1991
Issue Price: $ 165
Current Retail Price: $ 170

No.: 5354
Name: Ride in the Country
Height: 7.5
Current Status: Open issue, permanently retired
Original Issue Year: 1986
Last Year: 1993
Rarity: E
Issue Price: $ 225
Last Retail Price: $ 415

No.: 5430
Name: Music Time
Height: 7.5
Current Status: Open issue,
  permanently retired
Original Issue Year: 1987
Last Year: 1990
Rarity: C
Issue Price: $ 500
High Auction Price: $ 700
LCS Estimate: $ 700

No.: 2035.30
Name: Virgin of the Orange (Reduced)
Height: 7.5
Current Status: Open issue,
  permanently retired
Original Issue Year: 1971
Last Year: 1973
Rarity: B
Issue Price: $ 115
LCS Estimate: $ 1250

No.: 4874
Name: Children in Nightskirts
Height: 7.75
Current Status: Open issue, currently
  active
Original Issue Year: 1974
Issue Price: $ 25
Current Retail Price: $ 140

No.: 5555
Name: Let's Make Up
Height: 7.75
Current Status: Open issue, currently
  active
Original Issue Year: 1989
Issue Price: $ 215
Current Retail Price: $ 260

No.: 4867
Name: See Saw
Height: 7.75
Current Status: Open issue, currently
  active
Original Issue Year: 1974
Issue Price: $ 80
Current Retail Price: $ 335

No.: 4808
Name: Wedding
Height: 7.75
Current Status: Open issue, currently
  active
Original Issue Year: 1972
Issue Price: $ 50
Current Retail Price: $ 170

No.: 5884
Name: Motoring In Style
Height: 7.75
Current Status: Limited edition,
  currently active
Edition Limit: 1500
Original Issue Year: 1992
Issue Price: $ 3700
Current Retail Price: $ 3700

No.: 5885
Name: From This Day Forwad
Height: 7.75
Current Status: Open issue, currently
  active
Original Issue Year: 1992
Issue Price: $ 265
Current Retail Price: $ 265

No.: 5753
Name: Hold Her Still
Height: 8
Current Status: Open issue,
  permanently retired
Original Issue Year: 1991
Last Year: 1993
Rarity: C
Issue Price: $ 650
LasJ288
t Retail Price: $ 695

No.: 5900
Name: Sleep Tight
Height: 8
Current Status: Open issue, currently
  active
Original Issue Year: 1992
Issue Price: $ 450
Current Retail Price: $ 450

No.: 2228
Name: Snowy Sunday
Height: 8
Current Status: Open issue, currently
  active
Original Issue Year: 1992
Issue Price: $ 550
Current Retail Price: $ 550

No.: 5968
Name: Honeymoon Ride
Height: 8
Current Status: Open issue, currently
  active
Original Issue Year: 1993
Issue Price: $ 2750

No.: 4929
Name: Children Reading
Height: 8.25
Current Status: Open issue, permanently retired
Original Issue Year: 1974
Last Year: 1983
Rarity: E
Issue Price: $ 180
LCS Estimate: $ 1080

No.: 5713
Name: The Snow Man
Height: 8.25
Current Status: Open issue, currently active
Original Issue Year: 1990
Issue Price: $ 300
Current Retail Price: $ 340

No.: 5442
Name: Poetry of Love
Height: 8.5
Current Status: Open issue, currently active
Original Issue Year: 1987
Issue Price: $ 500
Current Retail Price: $ 785

No.: 5930
Name: Jazz Duo
Height: 8.5
Current Status: Open issue, currently active
Original Issue Year: 1992
Issue Price: $ 795
Current Retail Price: $ 795

No.: 5292
Name: Love in Bloom
Height: 8.5
Current Status: Open issue, currently active
Original Issue Year: 1985
Rarity:
Issue Price: $ 225.0
Current Retail Price: $ 395.0

No.: 5409
Name: Courting Time
Height: 8.5
Current Status: Open issue, permanently retired
Original Issue Year: 1987
Last Year: 1990
Rarity: C
Issue Price: $ 425
High Auction Price: $ 625
LCS Estimate: $ 600

No.: 1188
Name: Boy Meets Girl
Height: 8.5
Current Status: Open issue,
   permanently retired
Original Issue Year: 1972
Last Year: 1989
Rarity: F
Issue Price: $ 60
High Auction Price: $ 400
LCS Estimate: $ 300

No.: 4883
Name: Lady with Young Harlequin
Height: 8.5
Current Status: Open issue,
   permanently retired
Original Issue Year: 1974
Last Year: 1975
Rarity: B
Issue Price: $ 100
LCS Estimate: $ 1000

No.: 5899
Name: Just One More
Height: 8.5
Current Status: Open issue, currently
   active
Original Issue Year: 1992
Issue Price: $ 450
Current Retail Price: $ 450

No.: 5584
Name: Father's Day
Height: 8.5
Current Status: Open issue, currently
   active
Original Issue Year: 1989
Issue Price: $ 315
Current Retail Price: $ 390

No.: 4779
Name: Teaching to Pray
Height: 8.5
Current Status: Open issue, currently
   active
Original Issue Year: 1971
Issue Price: $ 32
Current Retail Price: $ 175

No.: 5453
Name: For You
Height: 9
Current Status: Open issue, currently
   active
Original Issue Year: 1988
Issue Price: $ 450
Current Retail Price: $ 585

No.: 5718
Name: A Ride in the Park
Height: 9
Current Status: Limited edition,
currently active
Edition Limit: 1000
Original Issue Year: 1990
Issue Price: $ 3200
Last Retail Price: $ 3675

No.: 5452
Name: Masquerade Ball
Height: 9
Current Status: Open issue,
permanently retired
Original Issue Year: 1988
Last Year: 1993
Rarity: D
Issue Price: $ 220
Last Retail Price: $ 290

No.: 5352
Name: Hindu Children
Height: 9
Current Status: Open issue, currently
active
Original Issue Year: 1986
Issue Price: $ 250
Current Retail Price: $ 390

No.: 5303
Name: Playing with Ducks
Height: 9
Current Status: Open issue,
permanently retired
Original Issue Year: 1985
Last Year: 1990
Rarity: D
Issue Price: $ 310
High Auction Price: $ 900
LCS Estimate: $ 850

No.: 6028
Name: Mazel Tov!
Height: 9.25
Current Status: Open issue, currently
active
Original Issue Year: 1993
Issue Price: $ 425

No.: 4935
Name: Closing Scene
Height: 9.5
Current Status: Open issue, currently
active
Original Issue Year: 1974
Issue Price: $ 180
Current Retail Price: $ 495

No.: 4935.30
Name: Closing Scene (White)
Height: 9.5
Current Status: Open issue,
  permanently retired
Original Issue Year: 1983
Last Year: 1987
Rarity: C
Issue Price: $ 212.5
LCS Estimate: $ 600

No.: 1255
Name: See Saw
Height: 9.5
Current Status: Open issue,
  permanently retired
Original Issue Year: 1974
Last Year: 1993
Rarity: F
Issue Price: $ 110
Last Retail Price: $ 550

No.: 2077
Name: The Rain in Spain
Height: 9.5
Current Status: Open issue,
  permanently retired
Original Issue Year: 1978
Last Year: 1990
Rarity: E
Issue Price: $ 195
High Auction Price: $ 550
LCS Estimate: $ 500

No.: 4993
Name: Gypsy Vendors
Height: 9.5
Current Status: Open issue,
  permanently retired
Original Issue Year: 1978
Last Year: 1985
Rarity: D
Issue Price: $ 165
High Auction Price: $ 550
LCS Estimate: $ 550

No.: 4856
Name: Waltz Time
Height: 9.5
Current Status: Open issue,
  permanently retired
Original Issue Year: 1974
Last Year: 1985
Rarity: E
Issue Price: $ 65
High Auction Price: $ 550
LCS Estimate: $ 500

No.: 5996
Name: Bless the Child
Height: 9.5
Current Status: Open issue, currently
  active
Original Issue Year: 1993
Issue Price: $ 490

No.: 4925
Name: Laziness
Height: 9.75
Current Status: Open issue,
  permanently retired
Original Issue Year: 1974
Last Year: 1980
Rarity: D
Issue Price: $ 140
High Auction Price: $ 650
LCS Estimate: $ 700

No.: 4878
Name: Adolescence
Height: 9.75
Current Status: Open issue,
  permanently retired
Original Issue Year: 1974
Last Year: 1979
Rarity: D
Issue Price: $ 65
LCS Estimate: $ 500

No.: 5033
Name: Avoiding the Goose
Height: 9.75
Current Status: Open issue,
  permanently retired
Original Issue Year: 1979
Last Year: 1993
Rarity: E
Issue Price: $ 160
Last Retail Price: $ 350

No.: 5997
Name: One More Try
Height: 10
Current Status: Open issue, currently
  active
Original Issue Year: 1993
Issue Price: $ 715

No.: 5047
Name: Couple
Height: 10.25
Current Status: Open issue,
  permanently retired
Original Issue Year: 1980
Last Year: 1981
Rarity: B
Issue Price: $ 425
LCS Estimate: $ 2500

No.: 1127
Name: Puppy Love
Height: 10.25
Current Status: Open issue, currently
  active
Original Issue Year: 1971
Issue Price: $ 50
Current Retail Price: $ 270

No.: 5282
Name: Over the Threshold
Height: 10.25
Current Status: Open issue, currently active
Original Issue Year: 1985
Issue Price: $ 150
Current Retail Price: $ 265

No.: 4882
Name: Carnival Couple
Height: 10.25
Current Status: Open issue, currently active
Original Issue Year: 1974
Issue Price: $ 60
Current Retail Price: $ 285

No.: 2173
Name: Ahoy There
Height: 10.25
Current Status: Open issue, currently active
Original Issue Year: 1987
Issue Price: $ 225
Current Retail Price: $ 285

No.: 5382
Name: Lovers' Serenade
Height: 10.5
Current Status: Open issue, permanently retired
Original Issue Year: 1986
Last Year: 1990
Rarity: C
Issue Price: $ 350
High Auction Price: $ 600
LCS Estimate: $ 700

No.: 2118
Name: Schoolmates
Height: 10.5
Current Status: Open issue, permanently retired
Original Issue Year: 1980
Last Year: 1981
Rarity: B
Issue Price: $ 525
High Auction Price: $ 650
LCS Estimate: $ 600

No.: 4926
Name: Milk for the Lamb
Height: 10.5
Current Status: Open issue, permanently retired
Original Issue Year: 1974
Last Year: 1980
Rarity: D
Issue Price: $ 185
LCS Estimate: $ 1300

No.: 5799
Name: Shall We Dance?
Height: 10.5
Current Status: Open issue,
permanently retired
Original Issue Year: 1991
Last Year: 1993
Rarity: C
Issue Price: $ 600
Last Retail Price: $ 650

No.: 1241
Name: Country Flirt
Height: 10.5
Current Status: Open issue,
permanently retired
Original Issue Year: 1973
Last Year: 1980
Rarity: D
Issue Price: $ 110
High Auction Price: $ 500
LCS Estimate: $ 600

No.: 4830
Name: You and Me
Height: 10.5
Current Status: Open issue,
permanently retired
Original Issue Year: 1972
Last Year: 1979
Rarity: D
Issue Price: $ 112.5
High Auction Price: $ 750
LCS Estimate: $ 700

No.: 5958
Name: Country Ride
Height: 10.5
Current Status: Open issue, currently
active
Original Issue Year: 1993
Issue Price: $ 2850

No.: 5658
Name: Venetian Carnival
Height: 10.5
Current Status: Open issue,
permanently retired
Original Issue Year: 1990
Last Year: 1993
Rarity: C
Issue Price: $ 500
Last Retail Price: $ 575

No.: 5844
Name: Flirtatious Jester
Height: 10.5
Current Status: Open issue, currently
active
Original Issue Year: 1992
Issue Price: $ 890
Current Retail Price: $ 890

No.: 5426
Name: One, Two, Three
Height: 10.5
Current Status: Open issue, currently active
Original Issue Year: 1987
Issue Price: $ 240
Current Retail Price: $ 350

No.: 1518
Name: Valencian Garden
Height: 10.5
Current Status: Open issue, permanently retired
Original Issue Year: 1987
Last Year: 1991
Rarity: C
Issue Price: $ 1100
LCS Estimate: $ 1100

No.: 5082
Name: Little Flower Seller
Height: 10.75
Current Status: Open issue, permanently retired
Original Issue Year: 1980
Last Year: 1985
Rarity: D
Issue Price: $ 750
LCS Estimate: $ 3000

No.: 5677
Name: Twilight Years
Height: 10.75
Current Status: Open issue, currently active
Original Issue Year: 1990
Issue Price: $ 370
Current Retail Price: $ 400

No.: 5381
Name: Serenade
Height: 11
Current Status: Open issue, permanently retired
Original Issue Year: 1986
Last Year: 1990
Rarity: C
Issue Price: $ 450
High Auction Price: $ 625
LCS Estimate: $ 600

No.: 5124
Name: Dutch Couple and Tulips
Height: 11
Current Status: Open issue, permanently retired
Original Issue Year: 1982
Last Year: 1985
Rarity: C
Issue Price: $ 310
LCS Estimate: $ 1200

No.: 2086
Name: The Little Kiss
Height: 11
Current Status: Open issue,
  permanently retired
Original Issue Year: 1978
Last Year: 1985
Rarity: D
Issue Price: $ 180
LCS Estimate: $ 875

No.: 4931
Name: Children with Fruit
Height: 11
Current Status: Open issue,
  permanently retired
Original Issue Year: 1974
Last Year: 1981
Rarity: D
Issue Price: $ 210
High Auction Price: $ 450
LCS Estimate: $ 500

No.: 4963
Name: Infantile Candor
Height: 11
Current Status: Open issue,
  permanently retired
Original Issue Year: 1977
Last Year: 1979
Rarity: B
Issue Price: $ 285
LCS Estimate: $ 1900

No.: 2242
Name: Away to School
Height: 11
Current Status: Open issue, currently
  active
Original Issue Year: 1993
Issue Price: $ 465

No.: 1472
Name: Valencian Couple
Height: 11
Current Status: Limited edition,
  currently active
Edition Limit: 3000
Original Issue Year: 1985
Issue Price: $ 885
Current Retail Price: $ 1450

No.: 1489
Name: Valencian Children
Height: 11
Current Status: Open issue, currently
  active
Original Issue Year: 1986
Issue Price: $ 700
Current Retail Price: $ 1150

No.: 1383
Name: A Rickshaw Ride
Height: 11
Current Status: Open issue, currently active
Original Issue Year: 1978
Issue Price: $ 1500
Current Retail Price: $ 2100

No.: 5037
Name: Sleigh Ride
Height: 11
Current Status: Open issue, currently active
Original Issue Year: 1980
Issue Price: $ 585
Current Retail Price: $ 995

No.: 5447
Name: Will You Marry Me?
Height: 11
Current Status: Open issue, currently active
Original Issue Year: 1987
Issue Price: $ 750
Current Retail Price: $ 1200

No.: 5304
Name: Children at Play
Height: 11
Current Status: Open issue, permanently retired
Original Issue Year: 1985
Last Year: 1990
Rarity: D
Issue Price: $ 220
High Auction Price: $ 550
LCS Estimate: $ 440

No.: 5274
Name: Wedding Day
Height: 11
Current Status: Open issue, currently active
Original Issue Year: 1985
Issue Price: $ 240
Current Retail Price: $ 395

No.: 4662
Name: Romantic Group
Height: 11.5
Current Status: Open issue, permanently retired
Original Issue Year: 1969
Last Year: 1981
Rarity: E
Issue Price: $ 100
LCS Estimate: $ 800

No.: 4669
Name: Pastoral Couple
Height: 11.5
Current Status: Open issue,
   permanently retired
Original Issue Year: 1969
Last Year: 1978
Rarity: E
Issue Price: $ 100
LCS Estimate: $ 900

No.: 1305
Name: Vivandiere and Soldier
Height: 11.5
Current Status: Open issue,
   permanently retired
Original Issue Year: 1974
Last Year: 1979
Rarity: D
Issue Price: $ 550
High Auction Price: $ 775
LCS Estimate: $ 850

No.: 1251
Name: Pony Ride
Height: 11.5
Current Status: Open issue,
   permanently retired
Original Issue Year: 1974
Last Year: 1979
Rarity: D
Issue Price: $ 220
LCS Estimate: $ 1750

No.: 4891
Name: Looking for Refuge
Height: 11.5
Current Status: Open issue,
   permanently retired
Original Issue Year: 1974
Last Year: 1979
Rarity: D
Issue Price: $ 400
LCS Estimate: $ 3000

No.: 4913
Name: Lesson in the Country
Height: 11.5
Current Status: Open issue,
   permanently retired
Original Issue Year: 1974
Last Year: 1978
Rarity: C
Issue Price: $ 240
LCS Estimate: $ 2200

No.: 1256
Name: Napping
Height: 11.5
Current Status: Open issue,
   permanently retired
Original Issue Year: 1974
Last Year: 1981
Rarity: D
Issue Price: $ 140
High Auction Price: $ 600
LCS Estimate: $ 600

No.: 5541
Name: Pious
Height: 11.75
Current Status: Limited edition, fully
  subscribed
Original Issue Year: 1989
Last Year: 1991
Rarity: B
Issue Price: $ 1075
High Auction Price: $ 1100

No.: 5256
Name: Folk Dancing
Height: 11.75
Current Status: Open issue,
  permanently retired
Original Issue Year: 1984
Last Year: 1990
Rarity: D
Issue Price: $ 205
High Auction Price: $ 550
LCS Estimate: $ 500

No.: 4760
Name: Rest in the Country
Height: 11.75
Current Status: Open issue,
  permanently retired
Original Issue Year: 1971
Last Year: 1981
Rarity: E
Issue Price: $ 70
LCS Estimate: $ 500

No.: 4554
Name: Shepherd with Girl and Lamb
Height: 11.75
Current Status: Open issue,
  permanently retired
Original Issue Year: 1969
Last Year: 1972
Rarity: C
Issue Price: $ 65
LCS Estimate: $ 800

No.: 5734
Name: Pilgrim Couple
Height: 11.75
Current Status: Open issue,
  permanently retired
Original Issue Year: 1991
Last Year: 1993
Rarity: C
Issue Price: $ 490
Last Retail Price: $ 525

No.: 5935
Name: Nutcracker Suite
Height: 11.75
Current Status: Open issue, currently
  active
Original Issue Year: 1993
Issue Price: $ 620

No.: 5325
Name: Ice Cream Vendor
Height: 11.75
Current Status: Open issue, currently active
Original Issue Year: 1985
Issue Price: $ 380
Current Retail Price: $ 625

No.: 1274
Name: Lovers in the Park
Height: 11.75
Current Status: Open issue, permanently retired
Original Issue Year: 1974
Last Year: 1993
Rarity: F
Issue Price: $ 450
Last Retail Price: $ 1365

No.: 2227
Name: Arctic Allies
Height: 12
Current Status: Open issue, currently active
Original Issue Year: 1992
Issue Price: $ 585
Current Retail Price: $ 585

No.: 2239
Name: Valencian Courtship
Height: 12
Current Status: Open issue, currently active
Original Issue Year: 1993
Issue Price: $ 880

No.: 4992
Name: Dancers Resting
Height: 12.25
Current Status: Open issue, permanently retired
Original Issue Year: 1978
Last Year: 1983
Rarity: D
Issue Price: $ 350
High Auction Price: $ 800
LCS Estimate: $ 750

No.: 2115
Name: Mother's Kiss
Height: 12.25
Current Status: Open issue, permanently retired
Original Issue Year: 1980
Last Year: 1981
Rarity: B
Issue Price: $ 575
High Auction Price: $ 650
LCS Estimate: $ 650

No.: 5252
Name: Dancing the Polka
Height: 12.25
Current Status: Open issue, currently active
Original Issue Year: 1984
Issue Price: $ 205
Current Retail Price: $ 385

No.: 1372
Name: Anniversary Waltz
Height: 12.25
Current Status: Open issue, currently active
Original Issue Year: 1978
Issue Price: $ 260
Current Retail Price: $ 530

No.: 1404
Name: Wedding
Height: 12.25
Current Status: Open issue, currently active
Original Issue Year: 1982
Issue Price: $ 320
Current Retail Price: $ 560

No.: 5821
Name: Minstrel's Love
Height: 12.25
Current Status: Open issue, permanently retired
Original Issue Year: 1991
Last Year: 1993
Rarity: C
Issue Price: $ 525
Last Retail Price: $ 575

No.: 6003
Name: Ready to Learn
Height: 12.25
Current Status: Open issue, currently active
Original Issue Year: 1993
Issue Price: $ 650

No.: 5425
Name: Studying in the Park
Height: 12.5
Current Status: Open issue, permanently retired
Original Issue Year: 1987
Last Year: 1991
Rarity: C
Issue Price: $ 675
High Auction Price: $ 850
LCS Estimate: $ 800

No.: 5540
Name: An Evening Out
Height: 12.5
Current Status: Open issue,
   permanently retired
Original Issue Year: 1989
Last Year: 1991
Rarity: B
Issue Price: $ 350
LCS Estimate: $ 350

No.: 5276
Name: A Sailor's Serenade
Height: 12.5
Current Status: Open issue,
   permanently retired
Original Issue Year: 1985
Last Year: 1988
Rarity: C
Issue Price: $ 315
High Auction Price: $ 450
LCS Estimate: $ 950

No.: 5843
Name: A Quiet Afternoon
Height: 12.5
Current Status: Open issue, currently
   active
Original Issue Year: 1992
Issue Price: $ 1050
Current Retail Price: $ 1050

No.: 2230
Name: Mary's Child
Height: 12.5
Current Status: Open issue, currently
   active
Original Issue Year: 1992
Issue Price: $ 525
Current Retail Price: $ 525

No.: 5897
Name: Trimming the Tree
Height: 12.75
Current Status: Open issue, currently
   active
Original Issue Year: 1992
Issue Price: $ 900
Current Retail Price: $ 900

No.: 5849
Name: Sorrowful Mother
Height: 12.75
Current Status: Limited edition,
   currently active
Edition Limit: 1500
Original Issue Year: 1992
Issue Price: $ 1750
Current Retail Price: $ 1750

No.: 5049
Name: At the Pond
Height: 12.75
Current Status: Open issue,
   permanently retired
Original Issue Year: 1980
Last Year: 1981
Rarity: B
Issue Price: $ 525
LCS Estimate: $ 3000

No.: 2114
Name: Kissing Father
Height: 12.75
Current Status: Open issue,
   permanently retired
Original Issue Year: 1980
Last Year: 1981
Rarity: B
Issue Price: $ 575
High Auction Price: $ 550
LCS Estimate: $ 550

No.: 5952
Name: Where to, Sir?
Height: 12.75
Current Status: Open issue, currently
   active
Original Issue Year: 1993
Edition Limit: 1500
Issue Price: $ 5250

No.: 2038.30
Name: Eskimo Boy and Girl (Reduced)
Height: 13
Current Status: Open issue, currently
   active
Original Issue Year: 1971
Issue Price: $ 70
Current Retail Price: $ 435

No.: 1145
Name: Othello and Desdemona
Height: 13
Current Status: Limited edition, fully
   subscribed
Edition Limit: 750
Original Issue Year: 1971
Rarity: A
Issue Price: $ 275
High Auction Price: $ 3000

No.: 5583
Name: Sad Parting
Height: 13
Current Status: Open issue,
   permanently retired
Original Issue Year: 1989
Last Year: 1991
Rarity: B
Issue Price: $ 375
LCS Estimate: $ 375

No.: 5052
Name: At the Circus
Height: 13
Current Status: Open issue,
  permanently retired
Original Issue Year: 1979
Last Year: 1985
Rarity: D
Issue Price: $ 525
High Auction Price: $ 1250
LCS Estimate: $ 1500

No.: 4888
Name: The Kiss
Height: 13
Current Status: Open issue,
  permanently retired
Original Issue Year: 1974
Last Year: 1983
Rarity: E
Issue Price: $ 150
High Auction Price: $ 700
LCS Estimate: $ 650

No.: 1523
Name: A Happy Encounter
Height: 13
Current Status: Limited edition,
  currently active
Edition Limit: 1500
Original Issue Year: 1987
Issue Price: $ 2900
Current Retail Price: $ 4700

No.: 1504
Name: The Reception
Height: 13.25
Current Status: Open issue,
  permanently retired
Original Issue Year: 1986
Last Year: 1990
Rarity: C
Issue Price: $ 625
High Auction Price: $ 1050
LCS Estimate: $ 1250

No.: 1513
Name: Flower For My Lady
Height: 13.25
Current Status: Open issue,
  permanently retired
Original Issue Year: 1987
Last Year: 1990
Rarity: C
Issue Price: $ 1150
High Auction Price: $ 1600
LCS Estimate: $ 1500

No.: 5161
Name: Old Fashion Motorist
Height: 13.25
Current Status: Open issue,
  permanently retired
Original Issue Year: 1982
Last Year: 1985
Rarity: C
Issue Price: $ 2000
High Auction Price: $ 3750
LCS Estimate: $ 4500

No.: 1453
Name: Golfing Couple
Height: 13.25
Current Status: Open issue, currently active
Original Issue Year: 1983
Issue Price: $ 248
Current Retail Price: $ 480

No.: 5587
Name: Wedding Cake
Height: 13.25
Current Status: Open issue, currently active
Original Issue Year: 1989
Issue Price: $ 595
Current Retail Price: $ 725

No.: 1772
Name: Back to Back
Height: 13.5
Current Status: Open issue, currently active
Original Issue Year: 1993
Issue Price: $ 1450

No.: 2218
Name: Costumed Couple
Height: 13.5
Current Status: Open issue, permanently retired
Original Issue Year: 1991
Last Year: 1993
Rarity: C
Issue Price: $ 680
Last Retail Price: $ 750

No.: 5300
Name: Medieval Courtship
Height: 13.75
Current Status: Open issue, permanently retired
Original Issue Year: 1985
Last Year: 1990
Rarity: D
Issue Price: $ 735
High Auction Price: $ 900
LCS Estimate: $ 900

No.: 2129
Name: Waiting for Sailor
Height: 13.75
Current Status: Open issue, permanently retired
Original Issue Year: 1983
Last Year: 1985
Rarity: B
Issue Price: $ 325
High Auction Price: $ 700
LCS Estimate: $ 700

No.: 5051
Name: Samson and Delilah
Height: 13.75
Current Status: Open issue,
  permanently retired
Original Issue Year: 1980
Last Year: 1981
Rarity: B
Issue Price: $ 350
LCS Estimate: $ 2000

No.: 1279
Name: The Wind
Height: 13.75
Current Status: Open issue, currently
  active
Original Issue Year: 1974
Issue Price: $ 250
Current Retail Price: $ 765

No.: 5398
Name: At the Ball
Height: 13.75
Current Status: Open issue,
  permanently retired
Original Issue Year: 1986
Last Year: 1991
Rarity: D
Issue Price: $ 375
LCS Estimate: $ 1050

No.: 1434
Name: Vows
Height: 13.75
Current Status: Open issue,
  permanently retired
Original Issue Year: 1983
Last Year: 1991
Rarity: E
Issue Price: $ 300
High Auction Price: $ 925
LCS Estimate: $ 800

No.: 1017
Name: Idyl
Height: 14.25
Current Status: Open issue,
  permanently retired
Original Issue Year: 1969
Last Year: 1991
Rarity: F
Issue Price: $ 115
LCS Estimate: $ 460

No.: 5459
Name: Graduation Dance
Height: 14.25
Current Status: Open issue,
  permanently retired
Original Issue Year: 1988
Last Year: 1990
Rarity: B
Issue Price: $ 350
High Auction Price: $ 450
LCS Estimate: $ 450

No.: 4937
Name: Golden Wedding
Height: 14.25
Current Status: Open issue,
  permanently retired
Original Issue Year: 1976
Last Year: 1981
Rarity: D
Issue Price: $ 285
High Auction Price: $ 650
LCS Estimate: $ 650

No.: 4610
Name: Peruvian Group
Height: 14.25
Current Status: Open issue,
  permanently retired
Original Issue Year: 1969
Last Year: 1970
Rarity: B
Issue Price: $ 180
LCS Estimate: $ 220

No.: 1430
Name: High Society
Height: 14.25
Current Status: Open issue,
  permanently retired
Original Issue Year: 1982
Last Year: 1993
Rarity: E
Issue Price: $ 305
Last Retail Price: $ 595

No.: 5991
Name: Love Story
Height: 14.25
Current Status: Open issue, currently
  active
Original Issue Year: 1993
Issue Price: $ 2800

No.: 6005
Name: Christening Day
Height: 14.25
Current Status: Open issue, currently
  active
Original Issue Year: 1993
Issue Price: $ 1425

No.: 1452
Name: On The Town
Height: 14.5
Current Status: Open issue,
  permanently retired
Original Issue Year: 1983
Last Year: 1993
Rarity: E
Issue Price: $ 220
Last Retail Price: $ 440

No.: 1528
Name: I Love You Truly
Height: 14.5
Current Status: Open issue, currently active
Original Issue Year: 1987
Issue Price: $ 375
Current Retail Price: $ 565

No.: 4903
Name: Serenity
Height: 14.5
Current Status: Open issue, permanently retired
Original Issue Year: 1974
Last Year: 1979
Rarity: D
Issue Price: $ 285
High Auction Price: $ 750
LCS Estimate: $ 800

No.: 5932
Name: Jester's Serenade
Height: 14.5
Current Status: Limited edition, currently active
Edition Limit: 3000
Original Issue Year: 1993
Issue Price: $ 1995

No.: 1510
Name: A Sunday Drive
Height: 14.5
Current Status: Limited edition, currently active
Edition Limit: 1000
Original Issue Year: 1987
Issue Price: $ 3400
Current Retail Price: $ 4950

No.: 6008
Name: Joyful Event
Height: 14.5
Current Status: Open issue, currently active
Original Issue Year: 1993
Issue Price: $ 825

No.: 339.13
Name: Nativity Cone
Height: 15
Current Status: Very rare early issue
Original Issue Year: 1964
Last Year: Not available
Rarity: A
Issue Price: Not available

No.: 5229
Name: Story Time
Height: 15
Current Status: Open issue,
  permanently retired
Original Issue Year: 1984
Last Year: 1990
Rarity: D
Issue Price: $ 245
High Auction Price: $ 1000
LCS Estimate: $ 900

No.: 1458
Name: Camelot
Height: 15
Current Status: Limited edition,
  currently active
Edition Limit: 3000
Original Issue Year: 1985
Issue Price: $ 950
Current Retail Price: $ 1550

No.: 4881
Name: Typical Group
Height: 15.5
Current Status: Open issue,
  permanently retired
Original Issue Year: 1974
Last Year: 1979
Rarity: D
Issue Price: $ 560
LCS Estimate: $ 4500

No.: 1250
Name: Lovers from Verona
Height: 15.5
Current Status: Open issue,
  permanently retired
Original Issue Year: 1974
Last Year: 1990
Rarity: F
Issue Price: $ 330
High Auction Price: $ 1450
LCS Estimate: $ 1300

No.: 4605
Name: Magic
Height: 15.5
Current Status: Open issue,
  permanently retired
Original Issue Year: 1969
Last Year: 1985
Rarity: F
Issue Price: $ 160
High Auction Price: $ 1050
LCS Estimate: $ 1000

No.: 4996
Name: Ready To Go
Height: 15.5
Current Status: Open issue,
  permanently retired
Original Issue Year: 1978
Last Year: 1981
Rarity: C
Issue Price: $ 425
LCS Estimate: $ 2500

No.: 2038
Name: Eskimo Boy and Girl
Height: 15.75
Current Status: Open issue,
  permanently retired
Original Issue Year: 1971
Last Year: 1982
Rarity: E
Issue Price: $ 70
LCS Estimate: $ 490

No.: 5004
Name: Walk in Versailles
Height: 15.75
Current Status: Open issue,
  permanently retired
Original Issue Year: 1978
Last Year: 1981
Rarity: C
Issue Price: $ 375
High Auction Price: $ 875
LCS Estimate: $ 900

No.: 5014
Name: Genteel
Height: 15.75
Current Status: Open issue,
  permanently retired
Original Issue Year: 1978
Last Year: 1981
Rarity: C
Issue Price: $ 725
LCS Estimate: $ 3500

No.: 4560
Name: Pensive Pierrot
Height: 15.75
Current Status: Open issue,
  permanently retired
Original Issue Year: 1969
Last Year: 1975
Rarity: D
Issue Price: $ 160
LCS Estimate: $ 1750

No.: 313.13
Name: Reposing
Height: 16
Current Status: Very rare early issue
Original Issue Year: 1970
Last Year: Not available
Rarity: A
Issue Price: Not available

No.: 1393
Name: First Date
Height: 16.25
Current Status: Limited edition,
  currently active
Edition Limit: 1500
Original Issue Year: 1982
Issue Price: $ 3800
Current Retail Price: $ 5600

No.: 5036
Name: Jockey and Lady
Height: 16.5
Current Status: Open issue, currently active
Original Issue Year: 1979
Issue Price: $ 950
Current Retail Price: $ 1950

No.: 1375
Name: Car In Trouble
Height: 16.75
Current Status: Limited edition, fully subscribed
Edition Limit: 1500
Original Issue Year: 1978
Issue Price: $ 3000
High Auction Price: $ 8500

No.: 4648
Name: Valencians Group
Height: 17
Current Status: Open issue, permanently retired
Original Issue Year: 1969
Last Year: 1990
Rarity: F
Issue Price: $ 250
High Auction Price: $ 1050
LCS Estimate: $ 1000

No.: 4647
Name: Andalucians Group
Height: 17
Current Status: Open issue, permanently retired
Original Issue Year: 1969
Last Year: 1990
Rarity: F
Issue Price: $ 250
High Auction Price: $ 1100
LCS Estimate: $ 1000

No.: 5012
Name: Re-encounter
Height: 17
Current Status: Open issue, permanently retired
Original Issue Year: 1978
Last Year: 1981
Rarity: C
Issue Price: $ 600
LCS Estimate: $ 3000

No.: 4564
Name: The Flirt
Height: 17.25
Current Status: Open issue, permanently retired
Original Issue Year: 1969
Last Year: 1978
Rarity: E
Issue Price: $ 115
LCS Estimate: $ 700

N o.: 1039
Name: Violinist with Girl
Height: 17.75
Current Status: Open issue,
   permanently retired
Original Issue Year: 1969
Last Year: 1991
Rarity: F
Issue Price: $ 120
High Auction Price: $ 1000
LCS Estimate: $ 900

No.: 5096
Name: A Summer Afternoon
Height: 17.75
Current Status: Open issue,
   permanently retired
Original Issue Year: 1980
Last Year: 1985
Rarity: D
Issue Price: $ 2150
High Auction Price: $ 2775
LCS Estimate: $ 3000

No.: 4831
Name: Romance
Height: 17.75
Current Status: Open issue,
   permanently retired
Original Issue Year: 1972
Last Year: 1981
Rarity: E
Issue Price: $ 175
LCS Estimate: $ 1200

No.: 1308
Name: The Hunt
Height: 17.75
Current Status: Limited edition, fully
   subscribed
Edition Limit: 750
Original Issue Year: 1974
Issue Price: $ 4750
High Auction Price: $ 6750

No.: 4750
Name: Romeo and Juliet
Height: 17.75
Current Status: Open issue, currently
   active
Original Issue Year: 1971
Issue Price: $ 150
Current Retail Price: $ 1200

No.: 2035
Name: Virgin of the Orange
Height: 18
Current Status: Open issue,
   permanently retired
Original Issue Year: 1971
Last Year: 1973
Rarity: B
Issue Price: $ 85
LCS Estimate: $ 950

No.: 1033
Name: Old Folks
Height: 19
Current Status: Open issue,
  permanently retired
Original Issue Year: 1969
Last Year: 1985
Rarity: F
Issue Price: $ 140
High Auction Price: $ 1600
LCS Estimate: $ 1600

No.: 4598
Name: Sweethearts
Height: 19.5
Current Status: Open issue,
  permanently retired
Original Issue Year: 1969
Last Year: 1978
Rarity: E
Issue Price: $ 85
LCS Estimate: $ 760

No.: 4563
Name: Couple with Parasol
Height: 19.75
Current Status: Open issue,
  permanently retired
Original Issue Year: 1969
Last Year: 1985
Rarity: F
Issue Price: $ 180
High Auction Price: $ 800
LCS Estimate: $ 800

No.: 4519
Name: Flamenco Dancers
Height: 19.75
Current Status: Open issue,
  permanently retired
Original Issue Year: 1969
Last Year: 1993
Rarity: F
Issue Price: $ 150
Last Retail Price: $ 1100

No.: 2058
Name: Thai Couple
Height: 20
Current Status: Open issue, currently
  active
Original Issue Year: 1974
Issue Price: $ 650
Current Retail Price: $ 1650

No.: 3016
Name: Passion
Height: 20.5
Current Status: Limited edition,
  currently active
Edition Limit: 750
Original Issue Year: 1988
Issue Price: $ 865
Current Retail Price: $ 1050

No.: 5017
Name: Horsewoman and Jockey
Height: 20.5
Current Status: Open issue,
  permanently retired
Original Issue Year: 1978
Last Year: 1981
Rarity: C
Issue Price: $ 3150
LCS Estimate: $ 9000

No.: 3527
Name: Togetherness
Height: 20.5
Current Status: Limited edition, fully
  subscribed
Edition Limit: 75
Original Issue Year: 1982
Issue Price: $ 375

No.: 3524
Name: Watusi Queen
Height: 23.25
Current Status: Limited edition,
  currently active
Edition Limit: 1500
Original Issue Year: 1981
Issue Price: $ 1875
Current Retail Price: $ 2900

No.: 5609
Name: Playful Friends
Height: 3.5
Current Status: Open issue, currently
  active
Original Issue Year: 1989
Issue Price: $ 135
Current Retail Price: $ 160

No.: 1720
Name: Sprite
Height: 3.75
Current Status: Open issue, currently
  active
Original Issue Year: 1990
Issue Price: $ 1200
Current Retail Price: $ 1325

No.: 5837
Name: Sing With Me
Height: 4
Current Status: Open issue, currently
  active
Original Issue Year: 1991
Issue Price: $ 240
Current Retail Price: $ 240

No.: 5594
Name: Playful Romp
Height: 4
Current Status: Open issue, currently active
Original Issue Year: 1989
Issue Price: $ 215
Current Retail Price: $ 260

No.: 5760
Name: Interupted Nap
Height: 4.5
Current Status: Open issue, currently active
Original Issue Year: 1991
Issue Price: $ 325
Current Retail Price: $ 340

No.: 92.06
Name: Ballerina with Squirrel
Height: 4.75
Current Status: Very rare early issue
Original Issue Year: 1957
Last Year: Not available
Rarity: A
Issue Price: Not available

No.: 6012
Name: Monday's Child - Girl
Height: 4.75
Current Status: Open issue, currently active
Original Issue Year: 1993
Issue Price: $ 295

No.: 5455
Name: Bashful Bather
Height: 5
Current Status: Open issue, currently active
Original Issue Year: 1988
Issue Price: $ 150
Current Retail Price: $ 185

No.: 5484
Name: Lost Lamb
Height: 5.25
Current Status: Open issue, currently active
Original Issue Year: 1988
Issue Price: $ 100
Current Retail Price: $ 130

No.: 5781
Name: Not Too Close!
Height: 5.5
Current Status: Open issue, currently active
Original Issue Year: 1991
Issue Price: $ 365
Current Retail Price: $ 380

No.: 5640
Name: Cat Nap
Height: 5.5
Current Status: Open issue, currently active
Original Issue Year: 1990
Issue Price: $ 125
Current Retail Price: $ 140

No.: 5595
Name: Joy in a Basket
Height: 5.5
Current Status: Open issue, currently active
Original Issue Year: 1989
Issue Price: $ 215
Current Retail Price: $ 260

No.: 4569
Name: Girl with Turkey
Height: 5.5
Current Status: Open issue, permanently retired
Original Issue Year: 1969
Last Year: 1981
Rarity: E
Issue Price: $ 28.5
LCS Estimate: $ 230

No.: 5468
Name: Who's the Fairest?
Height: 5.5
Current Status: Open issue, currently active
Original Issue Year: 1988
Issue Price: $ 150
Current Retail Price: $ 195

No.: 5410
Name: Pilar
Height: 6
Current Status: Open issue, permanently retired
Original Issue Year: 1987
Last Year: 1990
Rarity: C
Issue Price: $ 200
High Auction Price: $ 325
LCS Estimate: $ 400

No.: 5706
Name: We Can't Play
Height: 6
Current Status: Open issue, currently active
Original Issue Year: 1990
Issue Price: $ 200
Current Retail Price: $ 225

No.: 5688
Name: Dog's Best Friend
Height: 6
Current Status: Open issue, currently active
Original Issue Year: 1990
Issue Price: $ 250
Current Retail Price: $ 280

No.: 5475
Name: A Lesson Shared
Height: 6
Current Status: Open issue, currently active
Original Issue Year: 1988
Issue Price: $ 150
Current Retail Price: $ 175

No.: 5679
Name: In No Hurry
Height: 6
Current Status: Open issue, currently active
Original Issue Year: 1990
Issue Price: $ 550
Current Retail Price: $ 615

No.: 5469
Name: Lambkins
Height: 6
Current Status: Open issue, permanently retired
Original Issue Year: 1988
Last Year: 1993
Rarity: D
Issue Price: $ 150
Last Retail Price: $ 210

No.: 5881
Name: Mischievous Mouse
Height: 6
Current Status: Open issue, currently active
Original Issue Year: 1992
Issue Price: $ 285
Current Retail Price: $ 285

No.: 5784
Name: A Cradle of Kittens
Height: 6
Current Status: Open issue, currently active
Original Issue Year: 1991
Issue Price: $ 360
Current Retail Price: $ 375

No.: 5553
Name: Wild Goose Chase
Height: 6
Current Status: Open issue, currently active
Original Issue Year: 1989
Issue Price: $ 175
Current Retail Price: $ 220

No.: 6024
Name: Sunday's Child - Girl
Height: 6.25
Current Status: Open issue, currently active
Original Issue Year: 1993
Issue Price: $ 260

No.: 5474
Name: How You've Grown!
Height: 6.25
Current Status: Open issue, currently active
Original Issue Year: 1988
Issue Price: $ 180
Current Retail Price: $ 225

No.: 1312
Name: Little Bo Peep
Height: 6.5
Current Status: Open issue, permanently retired
Original Issue Year: 1974
Last Year: 1985
Rarity: E
Issue Price: $ 72.5
High Auction Price: $ 425
LCS Estimate: $ 440

No.: 5921
Name: Take Your Medicine
Height: 6.5
Current Status: Open issue, currently active
Original Issue Year: 1992
Issue Price: $ 360
Current Retail Price: $ 360

No.: 5074
Name: Girl, Pan and Ducks
Height: 6.5
Current Status: Open issue, currently
active
Original Issue Year: 1980
Issue Price: $ 295
Current Retail Price: $ 395

No.: 5712
Name: Sleepy Kitten
Height: 6.5
Current Status: Open issue, currently
active
Original Issue Year: 1990
Issue Price: $ 110
Current Retail Price: $ 125

No.: 6014
Name: Tuesday's Child - Girl
Height: 6.5
Current Status: Open issue, currently
active
Original Issue Year: 1993
Issue Price: $ 280

No.: 2165
Name: Chiquita
Height: 6.5
Current Status: Open issue,
permanently retired
Original Issue Year: 1987
Last Year: 1993
Rarity: D
Issue Price: $ 120
Last Retail Price: $ 170

No.: 1312.30
Name: Little Bo Peep (White)
Height: 6.5
Current Status: Open issue,
permanently retired
Original Issue Year: 1984
Last Year: 1985
Rarity: B
Issue Price: $ 92.5
High Auction Price: $ 425
LCS Estimate: $ 400

No.: 5680
Name: Traveling in Style
Height: 6.5
Current Status: Open issue, currently
active
Original Issue Year: 1990
Issue Price: $ 425
Current Retail Price: $ 480

No.: 2183
Name: Wakeup Kitty
Height: 6.5
Current Status: Open issue,
  permanently retired
Original Issue Year: 1989
Last Year: 1993
Rarity: E
Issue Price: $ 225
Last Retail Price: $ 285

No.: 4849
Name: Feeding the Ducks
Height: 6.5
Current Status: Open issue, currently
  active
Original Issue Year: 1973
Issue Price: $ 60
Current Retail Price: $ 240

No.: 4660
Name: Shepherdess with Dove
Height: 6.5
Current Status: Open issue,
  permanently retired
Original Issue Year: 1969
Last Year: 1993
Rarity: F
Issue Price: $ 21
Last Retail Price: $ 175

No.: 5769
Name: Faithful Steed
Height: 6.75
Current Status: Open issue, currently
  active
Original Issue Year: 1991
Issue Price: $ 370
Current Retail Price: $ 385

No.: 5032
Name: Dog and Cat
Height: 6.75
Current Status: Open issue, currently
  active
Original Issue Year: 1979
Issue Price: $ 107.5
Current Retail Price: $ 210

No.: 5704
Name: Swan Song
Height: 6.75
Current Status: Open issue, currently
  active
Original Issue Year: 1990
Issue Price: $ 350
Current Retail Price: $ 390

No.: 6020
Name: Friday's Child - Girl
Height: 5.75
Current Status: Open issue, currently active
Original Issue Year: 1993
Issue Price: $ 260

No.: 6025
Name: Barnyard See Saw
Height: 6
Current Status: Open issue, currently active
Original Issue Year: 1993
Issue Price: $ 500

No.: 5959
Name: It's Your Turn
Height: 6.5
Current Status: Open issue, currently active
Original Issue Year: 1993
Issue Price: $ 365

No.: 1483
Name: Free As a Butterfly
Height: 7
Current Status: Open issue, permanently retired
Original Issue Year: 1985
Last Year: 1988
Rarity: C
Issue Price: $ 145
High Auction Price: $ 450
LCS Estimate: $ 425

No.: 1334
Name: "Chow Time"
Height: 7
Current Status: Open issue, permanently retired
Original Issue Year: 1977
Last Year: 1981
Rarity: C
Issue Price: $ 135
High Auction Price: $ 700
LCS Estimate: $ 600

No.: 5710
Name: Fantasy Friend
Height: 7
Current Status: Open issue, permanently retired
Original Issue Year: 1990
Last Year: 1993
Rarity: C
Issue Price: $ 420
Last Retail Price: $ 495

No.: 5503
Name: Hurry Now
Height: 7
Current Status: Open issue, currently active
Original Issue Year: 1988
Issue Price: $ 180
Current Retail Price: $ 235

No.: 1011
Name: Girl with Pig
Height: 7
Current Status: Open issue, currently active
Original Issue Year: 1969
Issue Price: $ 13
Current Retail Price: $ 82

No.: 5689
Name: Can I Help?
Height: 7
Current Status: Open issue, currently active
Original Issue Year: 1990
Issue Price: $ 250
Current Retail Price: $ 280

No.: 5836
Name: Sharing Sweets
Height: 7
Current Status: Open issue, currently active
Original Issue Year: 1991
Issue Price: $ 220
Current Retail Price: $ 235

No.: 6018
Name: Thursday's Child - Girl
Height: 7.25
Current Status: Open issue, currently active
Original Issue Year: 1993
Issue Price: $ 280

No.: 5883
Name: Loving Mouse
Height: 7.5
Current Status: Open issue, currently active
Original Issue Year: 1992
Issue Price: $ 285
Current Retail Price: $ 285

No.: 5845
Name: Dressing the Baby
Height: 7.5
Current Status: Open issue, currently active
Original Issue Year: 1992
Issue Price: $ 295
Current Retail Price: $ 295

No.: 5217
Name: Spring
Height: 7.5
Current Status: Open issue, currently active
Original Issue Year: 1984
Issue Price: $ 90
Current Retail Price: $ 165

No.: 5465
Name: Look At Me!
Height: 7.5
Current Status: Open issue, currently active
Original Issue Year: 1988
Issue Price: $ 375
Current Retail Price: $ 450

No.: 1248
Name: Sweety
Height: 7.5
Current Status: Open issue, permanently retired
Original Issue Year: 1974
Last Year: 1990
Rarity: F
Issue Price: $ 100
High Auction Price: $ 600
LCS Estimate: $ 500

No.: 1280
Name: Child's Play
Height: 7.5
Current Status: Open issue, permanently retired
Original Issue Year: 1974
Last Year: 1983
Rarity: E
Issue Price: $ 110
High Auction Price: $ 650
LCS Estimate: $ 650

No.: 4827
Name: Caressing Little Calf
Height: 7.5
Current Status: Open issue, permanently retired
Original Issue Year: 1972
Last Year: 1981
Rarity: E
Issue Price: $ 55
LCS Estimate: $ 390

No.: 2200
Name: A Big Hug
Height: 7.5
Current Status: Open issue, currently active
Original Issue Year: 1990
Issue Price: $ 250
Current Retail Price: $ 275

No.: 5795
Name: Floral Getaway
Height: 7.5
Current Status: Open issue, permanently retired
Original Issue Year: 1991
Last Year: 1993
Rarity: C
Issue Price: $ 625
Last Retail Price: $ 685

No.: 6022
Name: Saturday's Child - Girl
Height: 7.5
Current Status: Open issue, currently active
Original Issue Year: 1993
Issue Price: $ 280

No.: 5645
Name: Elizabeth
Height: 7.75
Current Status: Open issue, currently active
Original Issue Year: 1990
Issue Price: $ 190
Current Retail Price: $ 210

No.: 1212
Name: Woman Carrying Water
Height: 7.75
Current Status: Open issue, permanently retired
Original Issue Year: 1972
Last Year: 1983
Rarity: E
Issue Price: $ 100
LCS Estimate: $ 600

No.: 4909
Name: Girl with Dove
Height: 7.75
Current Status: Open issue, permanently retired
Original Issue Year: 1974
Last Year: 1982
Rarity: E
Issue Price: $ 70
High Auction Price: $ 400
LCS Estimate: $ 450

No.: 6016
Name: Wednesday's Child - Girl
Height: 7.75
Current Status: Open issue, currently active
Original Issue Year: 1993
Issue Price: $ 280

No.: 1180
Name: Little Girl with Turkeys
Height: 7.75
Current Status: Open issue, permanently retired
Original Issue Year: 1971
Last Year: 1981
Rarity: E
Issue Price: $ 55
High Auction Price: $ 475
LCS Estimate: $ 400

No.: 1267
Name: Girl with Ducks
Height: 7.75
Current Status: Open issue, permanently retired
Original Issue Year: 1974
Last Year: 1993
Rarity: F
Issue Price: $ 55
Last Retail Price: $ 260

No.: 5882
Name: Restful Mouse
Height: 7.75
Current Status: Open issue, currently active
Original Issue Year: 1992
Issue Price: $ 285
Current Retail Price: $ 285

No.: 4677
Name: Shepherdess with Rooster
Height: 7.75
Current Status: Open issue, currently active
Original Issue Year: 1969
Issue Price: $ 14
Current Retail Price: $ 85

No.: 4982
Name: Naughty Dog
Height: 7.75
Current Status: Open issue, currently active
Original Issue Year: 1978
Issue Price: $ 130
Current Retail Price: $ 240

No.: 5466
Name: "Chit-Chat"
Height: 7.75
Current Status: Open issue, currently active
Original Issue Year: 1988
Issue Price: $ 150
Current Retail Price: $ 185

No.: 1288
Name: Aggressive Goose
Height: 8.25
Current Status: Open issue, currently active
Original Issue Year: 1974
Issue Price: $ 170
Current Retail Price: $ 450

No.: 5739
Name: Lap Full of Love
Height: 8.25
Current Status: Open issue, currently active
Original Issue Year: 1991
Issue Price: $ 275
Current Retail Price: $ 285

No.: 2094
Name: Tenderness
Height: 8.25
Current Status: Open issue, currently active
Original Issue Year: 1978
Issue Price: $ 100
Current Retail Price: $ 195

No.: 1533
Name: Not So Fast
Height: 8.25
Current Status: Open issue, currently active
Original Issue Year: 1987
Issue Price: $ 175
Current Retail Price: $ 235

No.: 2169
Name: Repose
Height: 8.25
Current Status: Open issue, currently active
Original Issue Year: 1987
Issue Price: $ 135
Current Retail Price: $ 165

No.: 5549
Name: My New Pet
Height: 8.25
Current Status: Open issue, currently active
Original Issue Year: 1989
Issue Price: $ 150
Current Retail Price: $ 175

No.: 5232
Name: Playful Kittens
Height: 8.25
Current Status: Open issue, currently active
Original Issue Year: 1983
Issue Price: $ 130
Current Retail Price: $ 245

No.: 1088
Name: Girl with Flowers
Height: 8.25
Current Status: Open issue, permanently retired
Original Issue Year: 1969
Last Year: 1989
Rarity: F
Issue Price: $ 42.5
High Auction Price: $ 725
LCS Estimate: $ 700

No.: 1187
Name: Little Girl with Cat
Height: 8.25
Current Status: Open issue, permanently retired
Original Issue Year: 1972
Last Year: 1989
Rarity: F
Issue Price: $ 37
LCS Estimate: $ 190

No.: 5460
Name: A Barrow of Fun
Height: 8.25
Current Status: Open issue, currently active
Original Issue Year: 1988
Issue Price: $ 370
Current Retail Price: $ 470

No.: 5743
Name: Don't Forget Me!
Height: 8.25
Current Status: Open issue, currently active
Original Issue Year: 1991
Issue Price: $ 150
Current Retail Price: $ 155

No.: 1246
Name: Caress and Rest
Height: 8.25
Current Status: Open issue, permanently retired
Original Issue Year: 1972
Last Year: 1990
Rarity: F
Issue Price: $ 50
LCS Estimate: $ 200

No.: 7612
Name: Picture Perfect
Height: 8.5
Current Status: Limited edition, fully subscribed
Original Issue Year: 1991
Last Year: 1991
Rarity: B
Issue Price: $ 350
High Auction Price: $ 500
Comments: LCS Special

No.: 4910
Name: Girl with Lantern
Height: 8.5
Current Status: Open issue, permanently retired
Original Issue Year: 1974
Last Year: 1990
Rarity: F
Issue Price: $ 85
LCS Estimate: $ 340

No.: 4915
Name: Girl with Pigeons
Height: 8.5
Current Status: Open issue, permanently retired
Original Issue Year: 1974
Last Year: 1990
Rarity: F
Issue Price: $ 110
LCS Estimate: $ 440

No.: 1245
Name: The Cart
Height: 8.5
Current Status: Open issue, permanently retired
Original Issue Year: 1973
Last Year: 1981
Rarity: E
Issue Price: $ 75
High Auction Price: $ 650
LCS Estimate: $ 600

No.: 5807
Name: My Puppies
Height: 8.5
Current Status: Open issue, permanently retired
Original Issue Year: 1991
Last Year: 1993
Rarity: C
Issue Price: $ 325
Last Retail Price: $ 360

No.: 2186
Name: The Greatest Love
Height: 8.5
Current Status: Open issue, currently active
Original Issue Year: 1989
Issue Price: $ 235
Current Retail Price: $ 275

No.: 5603
Name: Close to My Heart
Height: 8.5
Current Status: Open issue, currently active
Original Issue Year: 1989
Issue Price: $ 125
Current Retail Price: $ 155

No.: 2164
Name: My Lost Lamb
Height: 8.5
Current Status: Open issue, currently active
Original Issue Year: 1987
Issue Price: $ 120
Current Retail Price: $ 155

No.: 1010
Name: Girl with Lamb
Height: 8.5
Current Status: Open issue, permanently retired
Original Issue Year: 1969
Last Year: 1993
Rarity: F
Issue Price: $ 26
Last Retail Price: $ 180

No.: 1182
Name: Girl from Manchuria
Height: 8.5
Current Status: Open issue, permanently retired
Original Issue Year: 1971
Last Year: 1975
Rarity: C
Issue Price: $ 60
LCS Estimate: $ 600

No.: 5364
Name: Litter of Fun
Height: 8.5
Current Status: Open issue, currently active
Original Issue Year: 1986
Issue Price: $ 275
Current Retail Price: $ 445

No.: 5761
Name: Out For a Romp
Height: 8.5
Current Status: Open issue, currently active
Original Issue Year: 1991
Issue Price: $ 375
Current Retail Price: $ 390

No.: 5365
Name: Sunday in the Park
Height: 8.5
Current Status: Open issue, currently active
Original Issue Year: 1986
Issue Price: $ 375
Current Retail Price: $ 595

No.: 2254
Name: Step Aside
Height: 8.5
Current Status: Open issue, currently active
Original Issue Year: 1993
Issue Price: 280

No.: 2223
Name: New Lamb
Height: 8.5
Current Status: Open issue, currently active
Original Issue Year: 1992
Issue Price: $ 365
Current Retail Price: $ 365

No.: 7618
Name: Garden Song
Height: 8.75
Current Status: Limited edition, fully subscribed
Original Issue Year: 1992
Last Year: 1992
Rarity: B
Issue Price: $ 295
Current Retail Price: $ 295
Comments: Lladró-Event-Only Special

No.: 5740
Name: Alice in Wonderland
Height: 8.75
Current Status: Open issue, currently active
Original Issue Year: 1991
Issue Price: $ 440
Current Retail Price: $ 460

No.: 2225
Name: Friendly Sparrow
Height: 8.75
Current Status: Open issue, currently active
Original Issue Year: 1992
Issue Price: $ 295
Current Retail Price: $ 295

No.: 2216
Name: Laundry Day
Height: 8.75
Current Status: Open issue, currently active
Original Issue Year: 1991
Issue Price: $ 350
Current Retail Price: $ 365

No.: 2178
Name: Harvest Helpers
Height: 8.75
Current Status: Open issue, currently active
Original Issue Year: 1988
Issue Price: $ 190
Current Retail Price: $ 240

No.: 5908
Name: Just a Little More
Height: 9
Current Status: Open issue, currently active
Original Issue Year: 1992
Issue Price: $ 370
Current Retail Price: $ 370

No.: 7611
Name: Summer Stroll
Height: 9
Current Status: Limited edition, fully subscribed
Original Issue Year: 1991
Last Year: 1992
Rarity: B
Issue Price: $ 195
High Auction Price: $ 275
Comments: LCS Special

No.: 7617
Name: Garden Classic
Height: 9
Current Status: Limited edition, fully subscribed
Original Issue Year: 1991
Last Year: 1991
Rarity: B
Issue Price: $ 295
High Auction Price: $ 625
Comments: LCS Special

No.: 5140
Name: Feeding Her Son
Height: 9
Current Status: Open issue,
  permanently retired
Original Issue Year: 1982
Last Year: 1991
Rarity: E
Issue Price: $ 170
LCS Estimate: $ 340

No.: 1278
Name: Devotion
Height: 9
Current Status: Open issue,
  permanently retired
Original Issue Year: 1974
Last Year: 1990
Rarity: F
Issue Price: $ 140
High Auction Price: $ 500
LCS Estimate: $ 500

No.: 5428
Name: Feeding the Pigeons
Height: 9
Current Status: Open issue,
  permanently retired
Original Issue Year: 1987
Last Year: 1990
Rarity: C
Issue Price: $ 490
High Auction Price: $ 700
LCS Estimate: $ 700

No.: 4812
Name: Little Girl with Goat
Height: 9
Current Status: Open issue,
  permanently retired
Original Issue Year: 1972
Last Year: 1988
Rarity: F
Issue Price: $ 50
LCS Estimate: $ 280

No.: 4918
Name: A Girl at the Pond
Height: 9
Current Status: Open issue,
  permanently retired
Original Issue Year: 1974
Last Year: 1985
Rarity: E
Issue Price: $ 85
High Auction Price: $ 400
LCS Estimate: $ 400

No.: 1103
Name: Girl with Hens
Height: 9
Current Status: Open issue,
  permanently retired
Original Issue Year: 1971
Last Year: 1981
Rarity: E
Issue Price: $ 50
High Auction Price: $ 375
LCS Estimate: $ 350

No.: 4822
Name: Peruvian Girl with Baby
Height: 9
Current Status: Open issue,
  permanently retired
Original Issue Year: 1972
Last Year: 1981
Rarity: E
Issue Price: $ 65
High Auction Price: $ 775
LCS Estimate: $ 750

No.: 4826
Name: Girl Feeding Rabbit
Height: 9
Current Status: Open issue,
  permanently retired
Original Issue Year: 1972
Last Year: 1993
Rarity: F
Issue Price: $ 40
Last Retail Price: $ 185

No.: 5796
Name: Holy Night
Height: 9
Current Status: Open issue, currently
  active
Original Issue Year: 1991
Issue Price: $ 330
Current Retail Price: $ 345

No.: 1052
Name: Girl with Goose
Height: 9
Current Status: Open issue, currently
  active
Original Issue Year: 1969
Issue Price: $ 30
Current Retail Price: $ 195

No.: 2095
Name: Duck Pulling Pigtail
Height: 9.25
Current Status: Open issue, currently
  active
Original Issue Year: 1978
Issue Price: $ 110
Current Retail Price: $ 260

No.: 2253
Name: Noisy Friend
Height: 9.25
Current Status: Open issue, currently
  active
Original Issue Year: 1993
Issue Price: $ 280

No.: 217.08
Name: Nude with Dolphin
Height: 9.5
Current Status: Very rare early issue
Original Issue Year: 1958
Last Year: Not available
Rarity: A
Issue Price: Not available

No.: 4682
Name: Girl with Milk Pail
Height: 9.5
Current Status: Open issue,
permanently retired
Original Issue Year: 1970
Last Year: 1991
Rarity: F
Issue Price: $ 26.50
High Auction Price: $ 350
LCS Estimate: $ 300

No.: 1001
Name: Shepherdess with Goats
Height: 9.5
Current Status: Open issue,
permanently retired
Original Issue Year: 1969
Last Year: 1987
Rarity: F
Issue Price: $ 67.50
High Auction Price: $ 400
LCS Estimate: $ 540

No.: 4576
Name: New Shepherdess
Height: 9.5
Current Status: Open issue,
permanently retired
Original Issue Year: 1969
Last Year: 1985
Rarity: F
Issue Price: $ 37.50
High Auction Price: $ 300
LCS Estimate: $ 300

No.: 1373
Name: Chestnut Seller
Height: 9.5
Current Status: Open issue,
permanently retired
Original Issue Year: 1978
Last Year: 1981
Rarity: C
Issue Price: $ 800
High Auction Price: $ 950
LCS Estimate: $ 950

No.: 4800
Name: Gypsy with Brother
Height: 9.5
Current Status: Open issue,
permanently retired
Original Issue Year: 1972
Last Year: 1979
Rarity: D
Issue Price: $ 36
High Auction Price: $ 400
LCS Estimate: $ 400

No.: 4756
Name: Girl with Goat
Height: 9.5
Current Status: Open issue,
  permanently retired
Original Issue Year: 1971
Last Year: 1978
Rarity: D
Issue Price: $ 50
High Auction Price: $ 450
LCS Estimate: $ 400

No.: 5285
Name: Summer on the Farm
Height: 9.5
Current Status: Open issue, currently
  active
Original Issue Year: 1985
Issue Price: $ 235
Current Retail Price: $ 420

No.: 5034
Name: Goose Trying to Eat
Height: 9.5
Current Status: Open issue, currently
  active
Original Issue Year: 1979
Issue Price: $ 135
Current Retail Price: $ 275

No.: 5416
Name: In the Garden
Height: 9.5
Current Status: Open issue, currently
  active
Original Issue Year: 1987
Issue Price: $ 200
Current Retail Price: $ 310

No.: 5659
Name: Barnyard Scene
Height: 9.5
Current Status: Open issue, currently
  active
Original Issue Year: 1990
Issue Price: $ 200
Current Retail Price: $ 225

No.: 1309
Name: Following Her Cats
Height: 9.5
Current Status: Open issue, currently
  active
Original Issue Year: 1974
Issue Price: $ 120
Current Retail Price: $ 295

No.: 5666
Name: Trino at the Beach
Height: 9.5
Current Status: Open issue, currently active
Original Issue Year: 1990
Issue Price: $ 390
Current Retail Price: $ 440

No.: 4568
Name: Girl with Geese
Height: 9.5
Current Status: Open issue, permanently retired
Original Issue Year: 1969
Last Year: 1993
Rarity: F
Issue Price: $ 45
Last Retail Price: $ 220

No.: 1277
Name: Feeding Time
Height: 9.5
Current Status: Open issue, permanently retired
Original Issue Year: 1974
Last Year: 1993
Rarity: F
Issue Price: $ 120
Last Retail Price: $ 380

No.: 5705
Name: The Swan and the Princess
Height: 9.5
Current Status: Open issue, currently active
Original Issue Year: 1990
Issue Price: $ 350
Current Retail Price: $ 390

No.: 4835
Name: Girl with Lamb
Height: 9.75
Current Status: Open issue, permanently retired
Original Issue Year: 1972
Last Year: 1991
Rarity: F
Issue Price: $ 42
LCS Estimate: $ 170

No.: 1306
Name: "On the Farm"
Height: 9.75
Current Status: Open issue, permanently retired
Original Issue Year: 1974
Last Year: 1990
Rarity: F
Issue Price: $ 130
LCS Estimate: $ 500

No.: 5066
Name: Dutch Girl with Duck
Height: 9.75
Current Status: Open issue,
   permanently retired
Original Issue Year: 1980
Last Year: 1990
Rarity: E
Issue Price: $ 275
High Auction Price: $ 425
LCS Estimate: $ 550

No.: 4816
Name: Girl with Wheelbarrow
Height: 9.75
Current Status: Open issue,
   permanently retired
Original Issue Year: 1972
Last Year: 1981
Rarity: E
Issue Price: $ 50
High Auction Price: $ 375
LCS Estimate: $ 350

No.: 4843
Name: Donkey Ride
Height: 9.75
Current Status: Open issue,
   permanently retired
Original Issue Year: 1973
Last Year: 1981
Rarity: E
Issue Price: $ 86
High Auction Price: $ 700
LCS Estimate: $ 600

No.: 5385
Name: Scarecrow and Lady
Height: 9.75
Current Status: Open issue, currently
   active
Original Issue Year: 1986
Issue Price: $ 350
Current Retail Price: $ 595

No.: 5443
Name: Bedtime
Height: 9.75
Current Status: Open issue, currently
   active
Original Issue Year: 1987
Issue Price: $ 190
Current Retail Price: $ 290

No.: 2113
Name: My Little Duckling
Height: 9.75
Current Status: Open issue,
   permanently retired
Original Issue Year: 1980
Last Year: 1993
Rarity: E
Issue Price: $ 240
Last Retail Price: $ 295

No.: 2179
Name: Sharing the Harvest
Height: 9.75
Current Status: Open issue, currently active
Original Issue Year: 1988
Issue Price: $ 190
Current Retail Price: $ 240

No.: 1311
Name: Little Dogs on Hip
Height: 9.75
Current Status: Open issue, currently active
Original Issue Year: 1974
Issue Price: $ 120
Current Retail Price: $ 325

No.: 4591
Name: Shepherdess with Basket
Height: 9.75
Current Status: Open issue, permanently retired
Original Issue Year: 1969
Last Year: 1993
Rarity: F
Issue Price: $ 20
Last Retail Price: $ 140

No.: 2096
Name: Nosy Puppy
Height: 9.75
Current Status: Open issue, permanently retired
Original Issue Year: 1978
Last Year: 1993
Rarity: F
Issue Price: $ 190
Last Retail Price: $ 410

No.: 5202
Name: Aracely with Pet Duck
Height: 9.75
Current Status: Open issue, permanently retired
Original Issue Year: 1984
Last Year: 1991
Rarity: D
Issue Price: $ 125
LCS Estimate: $ 350

No.: 5287
Name: Winter Frost
Height: 9.75
Current Status: Open issue, currently active
Original Issue Year: 1985
Issue Price: $ 270
Current Retail Price: $ 495

No.: 5201
Name: Josefa Feeding Duck
Height: 10.25
Current Status: Open issue,
  permanently retired
Original Issue Year: 1984
Last Year: 1991
Rarity: D
Issue Price: $ 125

No.: 5272
Name: Biking in the Country
Height: 10.25
Current Status: Open issue,
  permanently retired
Original Issue Year: 1985
Last Year: 1990
Rarity: D
Issue Price: $ 295
High Auction Price: $ 825
LCS Estimate: $ 750

No.: 5078
Name: Teasing the Dog
Height: 10.25
Current Status: Open issue,
  permanently retired
Original Issue Year: 1980
Last Year: 1985
Rarity: D
Issue Price: $ 300
High Auction Price: $ 675
LCS Estimate: $ 650

No.: 4965
Name: Little Red Riding Hood
Height: 10.25
Current Status: Open issue,
  permanently retired
Original Issue Year: 1977
Last Year: 1983
Rarity: D
Issue Price: $ 210
High Auction Price: $ 700
LCS Estimate: $ 700

No.: 4814
Name: Little Girl with Turkey
Height: 10.25
Current Status: Open issue,
  permanently retired
Original Issue Year: 1972
Last Year: 1981
Rarity: E
Issue Price: $ 45
LCS Estimate: $ 320

No.: 5123
Name: Chinese with Baby
Height: 10.25
Current Status: Open issue, currently
  active
Original Issue Year: 1982
Issue Price: $ 150
Current Retail Price: $ 220

No.: 5758
Name: Sunday Best
Height: 10.25
Current Status: Open issue, currently active
Original Issue Year: 1991
Issue Price: $ 725
Current Retail Price: $ 760

No.: 6002
Name: Down You Go
Height: 10.25
Current Status: Open issue, currently active
Original Issue Year: 1993
Issue Price: $ 815

No.: 4920
Name: Mirth in the Country
Height: 10.25
Current Status: Open issue, currently active
Original Issue Year: 1974
Issue Price: $ 165
Current Retail Price: $ 470

No.: 5855
Name: Afternoon Jaunt
Height: 10.5
Current Status: Open issue, permanently retired
Original Issue Year: 1992
Last Year: 1993
Rarity: B
Issue Price: $ 420
Last Retail Price: $ 440

No.: 4505
Name: Girl with Lamb
Height: 10.5
Current Status: Open issue, currently active
Original Issue Year: 1969
Issue Price: $ 20
Current Retail Price: $ 105

No.: 3514
Name: Pensive
Height: 10.5
Current Status: Open issue, currently active
Original Issue Year: 1978
Issue Price: $ 500
Current Retail Price: $ 1000

No.: 4866
Name: Girl with Goose and Dog
Height: 10.5
Current Status: Open issue,
   permanently retired
Original Issue Year: 1974
Last Year: 1993
Rarity: F
Issue Price: $ 33
Last Retail Price: $ 205

No.: 1034
Name: Shepherdess with Dog
Height: 10.5
Current Status: Open issue,
   permanently retired
Original Issue Year: 1969
Last Year: 1991
Rarity: F
Issue Price: $ 30
High Auction Price: $ 275
LCS Estimate: $ 250

No.: 5143
Name: Girl with Motorcycle
Height: 10.5
Current Status: Open issue,
   permanently retired
Original Issue Year: 1982
Last Year: 1988
Rarity: D
Issue Price: $ 575
High Auction Price: $ 1800
LCS Estimate: $ 1725

No.: 5031
Name: Girl with Flowers in Tow
Height: 10.5
Current Status: Open issue,
   permanently retired
Original Issue Year: 1979
Last Year: 1985
Rarity: D
Issue Price: $ 785
High Auction Price: $ 1800
LCS Estimate: $ 1900

No.: 4572
Name: Girl with Piglets
Height: 10.5
Current Status: Open issue,
   permanently retired
Original Issue Year: 1969
Last Year: 1985
Rarity: F
Issue Price: $ 70
High Auction Price: $ 550
LCS Estimate: $ 560

No.: 4590
Name: Girl with Pitcher
Height: 10.5
Current Status: Open issue,
   permanently retired
Original Issue Year: 1969
Last Year: 1981
Rarity: E
Issue Price: $ 47.50
High Auction Price: $ 425
LCS Estimate: $ 400

No.: 4570
Name: Girl with Goat
Height: 10.5
Current Status: Open issue,
  permanently retired
Original Issue Year: 1969
Last Year: 1978
Rarity: E
Issue Price: $ 70
LCS Estimate: $ 630

No.: 5347
Name: Bedtime
Height: 10.5
Current Status: Open issue, currently
  active
Original Issue Year: 1986
Issue Price: $ 300
Current Retail Price: $ 520

No.: 4584
Name: Girl with Lamb
Height: 10.5
Current Status: Open issue,
  permanently retired
Original Issue Year: 1969
Last Year: 1993
Rarity: F
Issue Price: $ 27
Last Retail Price: $ 170

No.: 4510
Name: Girl with Parasol and Geese
Height: 10.5
Current Status: Open issue,
  permanently retired
Original Issue Year: 1969
Last Year: 1993
Rarity: F
Issue Price: $ 37.5
Last Retail Price: $ 245

No.: 6007
Name: The Goddess and the Unicorn
Height: 10.75
Current Status: Open issue, currently
  active
Original Issue Year: 1993
Issue Price: $ 1675

No.: 2217
Name: Gentle Play
Height: 10.75
Current Status: Open issue,
  permanently retired
Original Issue Year: 1991
Last Year: 1993
Rarity: C
Issue Price: $ 380
Last Retail Price: $ 415

No.: 2236
Name: Frosty Outing
Height: 10.75
Current Status: Open issue, currently active
Original Issue Year: 1993
Issue Price: $ 375

No.: 5346
Name: Nature Girl
Height: 11
Current Status: Open issue, permanently retired
Original Issue Year: 1986
Last Year: 1988
Rarity: B
Issue Price: $ 450
High Auction Price: $ 900
LCS Estimate: $ 850

No.: 4813
Name: Girl with Calf
Height: 11
Current Status: Open issue, permanently retired
Original Issue Year: 1972
Last Year: 1981
Rarity: E
Issue Price: $ 50
High Auction Price: $ 650
LCS Estimate: $ 600

No.: 1035
Name: Girl with Geese
Height: 11
Current Status: Open issue, currently active
Original Issue Year: 1969
Issue Price: $ 37.50
Current Retail Price: $ 170

No.: 5284
Name: Glorious Spring
Height: 11
Current Status: Open issue, currently active
Original Issue Year: 1985
Issue Price: $ 355
Current Retail Price: $ 630

No.: 3526
Name: Watching the Dove
Height: 11
Current Status: Open issue, currently active
Original Issue Year: 1982
Issue Price: $ 265
Current Retail Price: $ 515

No.: 1755
Name: Princess and Unicorn
Height: 11
Current Status: Limited edition, currently active
Edition Limit: 1500
Original Issue Year: 1991
Issue Price: $ 1750
Current Retail Price: $ 1800

No.: 1454
Name: Flowers ofthe Season
Height: 11
Current Status: Open issue, currently active
Original Issue Year: 1983
Issue Price: $ 1460
Current Retail Price: $ 2500

No.: 2234
Name: Playful Push
Height: 11.25
Current Status: Open issue, currently active
Original Issue Year: 1992
Issue Price: $ 850
Current Retail Price: $ 850

No.: 2219
Name: Underfoot
Height: 11.25
Current Status: Open issue, currently active
Original Issue Year: 1992
Issue Price: $ 360
Current Retail Price: $ 360

No.: 5874
Name: Off We Go
Height: 11.25
Current Status: Open issue, currently active
Original Issue Year: 1992
Issue Price: $ 365
Current Retail Price: $ 365

No.: 4758
Name: Girl and Sparrow
Height: 11.5
Current Status: Open issue, permanently retired
Original Issue Year: 1971
Last Year: 1979
Rarity: E
Issue Price: $ 35
LCS Estimate: $ 280

No.: 4601
Name: Girl with Swan
Height: 11.5
Current Status: Open issue,
   permanently retired
Original Issue Year: 1969
Last Year: 1972
Rarity: C
Issue Price: $ 65
LCS Estimate: $ 800

No.: 1130
Name: Love of Europe
Height: 11.5
Current Status: Open issue,
   permanently retired
Original Issue Year: 1971
Last Year: 1972
Rarity: B
Issue Price: $ 160
LCS Estimate: $ 1750

No.: 5851
Name: Feathered Fantasy
Height: 11.5
Current Status: Open issue, currently
   active
Original Issue Year: 1992
Issue Price: $ 1200
Current Retail Price: $ 1200

No.: 2151
Name: A Bird on Hand
Height: 11.5
Current Status: Open issue, currently
   active
Original Issue Year: 1985
Issue Price: $ 117.5
Current Retail Price: $ 220

No.: 5798
Name: Milkmaid
Height: 11.5
Current Status: Open issue,
   permanently retired
Original Issue Year: 1991
Last Year: 1993
Rarity: C
Issue Price: $ 450
Last Retail Price: $ 495

No.: 4994
Name: "My Little Pet"
Height: 11.75
Current Status: Open issue,
   permanently retired
Original Issue Year: 1978
Last Year: 1985
Rarity: D
Issue Price: $ 92.5
LCS Estimate: $ 475

No.: 5083
Name: Dutch Mother
Height: 11.75
Current Status: Open issue,
  permanently retired
Original Issue Year: 1980
Last Year: 1983
Rarity: C
Issue Price: $ 485
LCS Estimate: $ 1900

No.: 4953
Name: Woman with Cow and Calf
Height: 11.75
Current Status: Open issue,
  permanently retired
Original Issue Year: 1977
Last Year: 1979
Rarity: B
Issue Price: $ 400
LCS Estimate: $ 2800

No.: 5873
Name: Modern Mother
Height: 11.75
Current Status: Open issue, currently
  active
Original Issue Year: 1992
Issue Price: $ 325
Current Retail Price: $ 325

No.: 2091
Name: Woman with Baby
Height: 12
Current Status: Open issue,
  permanently retired
Original Issue Year: 1978
Last Year: 1981
Rarity: C
Issue Price: $ 125
LCS Estimate: $ 750

No.: 241.10
Name: Lady with Cupid
Height: 12.25
Current Status: Very rare early issue
Original Issue Year: 1958
Last Year: Not available
Rarity: A
Issue Price: Not available

No.: 4815
Name: Girl with Goose
Height: 12.25
Current Status: Open issue,
  permanently retired
Original Issue Year: 1972
Last Year: 1991
Rarity: F
Issue Price: $ 65
LCS Estimate: $ 290

No.: 4986
Name: Attentive Lady
Height: 12.25
Current Status: Open issue, permanently retired
Original Issue Year: 1978
Last Year: 1981
Rarity: C
Issue Price: $ 635
LCS Estimate: $ 3200

No.: 4513
Name: Girl with Calf
Height: 12.25
Current Status: Open issue, permanently retired
Original Issue Year: 1969
Last Year: 1978
Rarity: E
Issue Price: $ 72.5
LCS Estimate: $ 650

No.: 5159
Name: Harmony
Height: 12.25
Current Status: Open issue, currently active
Original Issue Year: 1982
Issue Price: $ 270
Current Retail Price: $ 480

No.: 101.06
Name: Charm
Height: 12.5
Current Status: Very rare early issue
Original Issue Year: 1958
Last Year: Not available
Rarity: A
Issue Price: Not available

No.: 4806
Name: Girl with Dog
Height: 12.5
Current Status: Open issue, permanently retired
Original Issue Year: 1972
Last Year: 1981
Rarity: E
Issue Price: $ 80
High Auction Price: $ 600
LCS Estimate: $ 600

No.: 2189
Name: Mother's Pride
Height: 12.5
Current Status: Open issue, currently active
Original Issue Year: 1990
Issue Price: $ 300
Current Retail Price: $ 330

No.: 358.13
Name: Madonna
Height: 12.75
Current Status: Very rare early issue
Original Issue Year: 1970
Last Year: Not available
Rarity: A
Issue Price: Not available

No.: 5156
Name: Susan and the Doves
Height: 13
Current Status: Open issue, permanently retired
Original Issue Year: 1982
Last Year: 1991
Rarity: E
Issue Price: $ 202.5
LCS Estimate: $ 425

No.: 5431
Name: Midwife
Height: 13
Current Status: Open issue, permanently retired
Original Issue Year: 1987
Last Year: 1990
Rarity: C
Issue Price: $ 175
High Auction Price: $ 400
LCS Estimate: $ 350

No.: 4594
Name: Lady with Greyhound
Height: 13
Current Status: Open issue, permanently retired
Original Issue Year: 1969
Last Year: 1981
Rarity: E
Issue Price: $ 60
LCS Estimate: $ 480

No.: 1769
Name: Frutiful Harvest
Height: 13
Current Status: Open issue, currently active
Original Issue Year: 1993
Issue Price: $ 1300

No.: 5286
Name: Fall Clean-Up
Height: 13
Current Status: Open issue, currently active
Original Issue Year: 1985
Issue Price: $ 295
Current Retail Price: $ 525

No.: 5174
Name: Roaring 20's
Height: 13
Current Status: Open issue,
  permanently retired
Original Issue Year: 1982
Last Year: 1993
Rarity: E
Issue Price: $ 172.5
Last Retail Price: $ 295

No.: 4575
Name: Motherhood
Height: 13
Current Status: Open issue, currently
  active
Original Issue Year: 1969
Issue Price: $ 47.5
Current Retail Price: $ 250

No.: 2187
Name: Jealous Friend
Height: 13
Current Status: Open issue, currently
  active
Original Issue Year: 1989
Issue Price: $ 275
Current Retail Price: $ 325

No.: 2235
Name: Adoring Mother
Height: 13.25
Current Status: Open issue, currently
  active
Original Issue Year: 1993
Issue Price: $ 405

No.: 1537
Name: Stepping Out
Height: 13.25
Current Status: Open issue, currently
  active
Original Issue Year: 1988
Issue Price: $ 230
Current Retail Price: $ 295

No.: 2233
Name: Guess What I Have
Height: 13.25
Current Status: Open issue, currently
  active
Original Issue Year: 1992
Issue Price: $ 340
Current Retail Price: $ 340

No.: 4701
Name: Motherhood
Height: 13.25
Current Status: Open issue, currently active
Original Issue Year: 1970
Issue Price: $ 45
Current Retail Price: $ 290

No.: 1135
Name: Diana
Height: 13.25
Current Status: Open issue, permanently retired
Original Issue Year: 1971
Last Year: 1972
Rarity: B
Issue Price: $ 120
LCS Estimate: $ 1300

No.: 4761
Name: Lady with Dog
Height: 13.75
Current Status: Open issue, permanently retired
Original Issue Year: 1971
Last Year: 1993
Rarity: F
Issue Price: $ 60
Last Retail Price: $ 260

No.: 343.13
Name: Greek Shepherdess
Height: 14.25
Current Status: Very rare early issue
Original Issue Year: 1963
Last Year: Not available
Rarity: A
Issue Price: Not available

No.: 2085
Name: Rosita
Height: 14.25
Current Status: Open issue, permanently retired
Original Issue Year: 1978
Last Year: 1983
Rarity: D
Issue Price: $ 175
High Auction Price: $ 375
LCS Estimate: $ 450

No.: 4658
Name: Bolivian Mother
Height: 14.25
Current Status: Open issue, permanently retired
Original Issue Year: 1969
Last Year: 1972
Rarity: C
Issue Price: $ 70
LCS Estimate: $ 850

No.: 4893
Name: Walk with the Dog
Height: 14.5
Current Status: Open issue, currently active
Original Issue Year: 1974
Issue Price: $ 85
Current Retail Price: $ 200

No.: 1091
Name: Girl and Gazelle
Height: 14.5
Current Status: Open issue, permanently retired
Original Issue Year: 1971
Last Year: 1975
Rarity: C
Issue Price: $ 225
LCS Estimate: $ 1200

No.: 2247
Name: Just Us
Height: 14.75
Current Status: Open issue, currently active
Original Issue Year: 1993
Issue Price: $ 650

No.: 4919
Name: Gypsy Woman
Height: 15
Current Status: Open issue, permanently retired
Original Issue Year: 1974
Last Year: 1981
Rarity: D
Issue Price: $ 165
High Auction Price: $ 1200
LCS Estimate: $ 1160

No.: 1038
Name: Girl with Turkeys
Height: 15
Current Status: Open issue, permanently retired
Original Issue Year: 1969
Last Year: 1978
Rarity: E
Issue Price: $ 95
High Auction Price: $ 450
LCS Estimate: $ 550

No.: 1469
Name: Girl on Carousel Horse
Height: 15
Current Status: Open issue, currently active
Original Issue Year: 1985
Issue Price: $ 470
Current Retail Price: $ 825

No.: 2061
Name: Saint Theresa
Height: 15
Current Status: Limited edition, fully subscribed
Edition Limit: 1200
Original Issue Year: 1977
Issue Price: $ 387.50
High Auction Price: $ 900

No.: 1394
Name: Holy Mary Icon
Height: 15
Current Status: Open issue, currently active
Original Issue Year: 1982
Issue Price: $ 1000
Current Retail Price: $ 1400

No.: 353.13
Name: Country Woman
Height: 15.25
Current Status: Very rare early issue
Original Issue Year: 1965
Last Year: Not available
Rarity: A
Issue Price: Not available

No.: 5802
Name: Elegant Promenade
Height: 15.25
Current Status: Open issue, currently active
Original Issue Year: 1991
Issue Price: $ 775
Current Retail Price: $ 795

No.: 1315
Name: Girl from Scotland
Height: 15.5
Current Status: Open issue, permanently retired
Original Issue Year: 1974
Last Year: 1979
Rarity: D
Issue Price: $ 450
LCS Estimate: $ 3500

No.: 1429
Name: Winter Wonderland
Height: 15.75
Current Status: Open issue, currently active
Original Issue Year: 1982
Issue Price: $ 1025
Current Retail Price: $ 1895

No.: 1297
Name: Swinging
Height: 15.75
Current Status: Open issue,
  permanently retired
Original Issue Year: 1974
Last Year: 1990
Rarity: F
Issue Price: $ 520
High Auction Price: $2150
LCS Estimate: $ 2000

No.: 5086
Name: Mother Amabilis
Height: 15.75
Current Status: Open issue,
  permanently retired
Original Issue Year: 1980
Last Year: 1983
Rarity: C
Issue Price: $ 275
High Auction Price: $ 450
LCS Estimate: $ 500

No.: 1055
Name: Girl with Pheasant
Height: 15.75
Current Status: Open issue,
  permanently retired
Original Issue Year: 1969
Last Year: 1978
Rarity: E
Issue Price: $ 105
LCS Estimate: $ 950

No.: 1036
Name: Horsewoman
Height: 16
Current Status: Open issue,
  permanently retired
Original Issue Year: 1969
Last Year: 1970
Rarity: B
Issue Price: $ 170
LCS Estimate: $ 2000

No.: 2243
Name: Flight of Fancy
Height: 16.25
Current Status: Open issue, currently
  active
Original Issue Year: 1993
Edition Limit: 300
Issue Price: $ 1400

No.: 4514
Name: Diana
Height: 16.5
Current Status: Open issue,
  permanently retired
Original Issue Year: 1969
Last Year: 1981
Rarity: E
Issue Price: $ 65
LCS Estimate: $ 520

No.: 5731
Name: Carousel Charm
Height: 16.5
Current Status: Open issue, currently active
Original Issue Year: 1991
Issue Price: $ 1700
Current Retail Price: $ 1785

No.: 5413
Name: Inspiration
Height: 16.5
Current Status: Limited edition, permanently retired
Edition Limit: 500
Original Issue Year: 1987
Last Year: 1993
Rarity: D
Issue Price: $ 1200
Last Retail Price: $ 2100

No.: 5864
Name: Maternal Joy
Height: 16.5
Current Status: Limited edition, currently active
Edition Limit: 1500
Original Issue Year: 1992
Issue Price: $ 1600
Current Retail Price: $ 1600

No.: 4914
Name: Lady with Shawl
Height: 16.5
Current Status: Open issue, currently active
Original Issue Year: 1974
Issue Price: $ 220
Current Retail Price: $ 650

No.: 4516
Name: Woman on Horse
Height: 17.25
Current Status: Open issue, currently active
Original Issue Year: 1969
Issue Price: $ 170
Current Retail Price: $ 685

No.: 4636
Name: Girl with Child
Height: 7.5
Current Status: Open issue, permanently retired
Original Issue Year: 1969
Last Year: 1979
Rarity: E
Issue Price: $ 13
High Auction Price: $ 275
LCS Estimate: $ 250

No.: 1275
Name: Elizabeth II
Height: 17.75
Current Status: Limited edition, fully
  subscribed
Edition Limit: 250
Original Issue Year: 1974
Last Year: 1985
Rarity: E
Issue Price: $ 3650

No.: 4719
Name: Lady Empire
Height: 18
Current Status: Open issue,
  permanently retired
Original Issue Year: 1970
Last Year: 1979
Rarity: E
Issue Price: $ 150
High Auction Price: $ 850
LCS Estimate: $ 850

No.: 3503
Name: Nude with Dove
Height: 18
Current Status: Limited edition, fully
  subscribed
Edition Limit: 1500
Original Issue Year: 1978
Issue Price: $ 500
Last Year: 1981
Last Retail Price: $ 630

No.: 1272
Name: Thoughts
Height: 19.25
Current Status: Open issue, currently
  active
Original Issue Year: 1974
Issue Price: $ 87.5
Current Retail Price: $ 3050

No.: 3559
Name: Peace Offering
Height: 19.75
Current Status: Open issue, currently
  active
Original Issue Year: 1985
Issue Price: $ 397.5
Current Retail Price: $ 655

No.: 2043
Name: Seated Madonna
Height: 22
Current Status: Limited edition, fully
  subscribed
Edition Limit: 300
Original Issue Year: 1971
Issue Price: $ 400

No.: 1767
Name: Motherly Love
Height: 22.25
Current Status: Open issue, currently
active
Original Issue Year: 1993
Issue Price: $ 1330

No.: 1392
Name: Venus and Cupid
Height: 22.75
Current Status: Limited edition, fully
subscribed
Edition Limit: 750
Original Issue Year: 1981
Rarity: A
Issue Price: $ 1100
High Auction Price: $ 2500

No.: 3545
Name: Adoration
Height: 23.25
Current Status: Limited edition, fully
subscribed
Edition Limit: 150
Original Issue Year: 1983
Issue Price: $ 1050

No.: 2126
Name: Mother Feeding Baby
Height: 23.75
Current Status: Open issue,
permanently retired
Original Issue Year: 1981
Last Year: 1985
Rarity: C
Issue Price: $ 2900
LCS Estimate: $ 8000

No.: 1202
Name: Allegory to Peace
Height: 24
Current Status: Limited edition, fully
subscribed
Edition Limit: 150
Original Issue Year: 1972
Issue Price: $ 550

No.: 3019
Name: True Affection
Height: 24.75
Current Status: Limited edition,
currently active
Edition Limit: 300
Original Issue Year: 1988
Issue Price: $ 750
Current Retail Price: $ 930

No.: 2071
Name: Madonna With Dove
Height: 26.75
Current Status: Open issue,
  permanently retired
Original Issue Year: 1977
Last Year: 1983
Rarity: D
Issue Price: $ 925
High Auction Price: $ 900
LCS Estimate: $ 1000

No.: 2018
Name: Madonna With Child
Height: 28.75
Current Status: Limited edition, fully
  subscribed
Edition Limit: 300
Original Issue Year: 1970
Issue Price: $ 450

No.: 2053
Name: Motherhood
Height: 30
Current Status: Open issue,
  permanently retired
Original Issue Year: 1974
Last Year: 1985
Rarity: E
Issue Price: $ 375
High Auction Price: $ 1050
LCS Estimate: $ 1000

No.: 1503
Name: Neglected
Height: 2.25
Current Status: Open issue,
  permanently retired
Original Issue Year: 1986
Last Year: 1991
Rarity: D
Issue Price: $ 125
LCS Estimate: $ 125

No.: 1505
Name: Nature Boy
Height: 2.5
Current Status: Open issue,
  permanently retired
Original Issue Year: 1986
Last Year: 1991
Rarity: D
Issue Price: $ 100
LCS Estimate: $ 305

No.: 1721
Name: Leprechaun
Height: 3
Current Status: Open issue, currently
  active
Original Issue Year: 1990
Issue Price: $ 1200
Current Retail Price: $ 1325

No.: 1506
Name: A New Friend
Height: 3.25
Current Status: Open issue, permanently retired
Original Issue Year: 1986
Last Year: 1991
Rarity: D
Issue Price: $ 110
LCS Estimate: $ 305

No.: 104.06
Name: Choir Boy
Height: 3.5
Current Status: Very rare early issue
Original Issue Year: 1957
Last Year: Not available
Rarity: A
Issue Price: Not available

No.: 103.06
Name: Choir Boy
Height: 3.5
Current Status: Very rare early issue
Original Issue Year: 1957
Last Year: Not available
Rarity: A
Issue Price: Not available

No.: 1525
Name: Valencian Dreams
Height: 3.5
Current Status: Open issue, permanently retired
Original Issue Year: 1987
Last Year: 1991
Rarity: C
Issue Price: $ 240
LCS Estimate: $ 240

No.: 306.13
Name: Choir Boy
Height: 4
Current Status: Very rare early issue
Original Issue Year: 1961
Last Year: Not available
Rarity: A
Issue Price: Not available

No.: 116.06
Name: Choir Boy
Height: 4
Current Status: Very rare early issue
Original Issue Year: 1956
Last Year: Not available
Rarity: A
Issue Price: Not available

No.: 1508
Name: In The Meadow
Height: 4.25
Current Status: Open issue,
   permanently retired
Original Issue Year: 1986
Last Year: 1991
Rarity: D
Issue Price: $ 100
LCS Estimate: $ 305

No.: 4616
Name: Boy with Drum
Height: 4.25
Current Status: Open issue,
   permanently retired
Original Issue Year: 1969
Last Year: 1979
Rarity: E
Issue Price: $ 16.50
High Auction Price: $ 625
LCS Estimate: $ 550

No.: 1507
Name: Boy and His Bunny
Height: 4.75
Current Status: Open issue,
   permanently retired
Original Issue Year: 1986
Last Year: 1991
Rarity: D
Issue Price: $ 90
LCS Estimate: $ 275

No.: 1509
Name: Spring Flowers
Height: 4.75
Current Status: Open issue,
   permanently retired
Original Issue Year: 1986
Last Year: 1991
Rarity: D
Issue Price: $ 100
LCS Estimate: $ 315

No.: 5399
Name: Time to Rest
Height: 4.75
Current Status: Open issue,
   permanently retired
Original Issue Year: 1987
Last Year: 1993
Rarity: D
Issue Price: $ 175
Last Retail Price: $ 295

No.: 5764
Name: Seeds of Laughter
Height: 4.75
Current Status: Open issue, currently
   active
Original Issue Year: 1991
Issue Price: $ 525
Current Retail Price: $ 550

No.: 5846
Name: All Tuckered Out
Height: 4.75
Current Status: Open issue, currently active
Original Issue Year: 1992
Issue Price: $ 220
Current Retail Price: $ 220

No.: 4613
Name: Boy with Cymbals
Height: 5
Current Status: Open issue, permanently retired
Original Issue Year: 1969
Last Year: 1979
Rarity: E
Issue Price: $ 14
High Auction Price: $ 500
LCS Estimate: $ 550

No.: 5812
Name: Tired Friend
Height: 5
Current Status: Open issue, currently active
Original Issue Year: 1991
Issue Price: $ 225
Current Retail Price: $ 235

No.: 5749
Name: Shepherd Boy
Height: 5
Current Status: Open issue, currently active
Original Issue Year: 1991
Issue Price: $ 225
Current Retail Price: $ 235

No.: 5827
Name: I've Got It!
Height: 5
Current Status: Open issue, currently active
Original Issue Year: 1991
Issue Price: $ 170
Current Retail Price: $ 175

No.: 7619
Name: All Aboard
Height: 5.25
Current Status: Limited edition, fully subscribed
Original Issue Year: 1992
Last Year: 1993
Rarity: B
Issue Price: $ 165
Comments: LCS Special

No.: 1524
Name: Valencian Bouquet
Height: 5.5
Current Status: Open issue,
  permanently retired
Original Issue Year: 1987
Last Year: 1991
Rarity: C
Issue Price: $ 250
LCS Estimate: $ 250

No.: 228.09
Name: Teenage Boy
Height: 5.75
Current Status: Very rare early issue
Original Issue Year: 1958
Last Year: Not available
Rarity: A
Issue Price: Not available

No.: 1024
Name: Boy with Book
Height: 6
Current Status: Open issue,
  permanently retired
Original Issue Year: 1969
Last Year: 1975
Rarity: D
Issue Price: $ 47.50
LCS Estimate: $ 520

No.: 4618
Name: Clown
Height: 6.25
Current Status: Open issue, currently
  active
Original Issue Year: 1969
Issue Price: $ 70
Current Retail Price: $ 395

No.: 4672
Name: Saint Joseph
Height: 6.25
Current Status: Open issue, currently
  active
Original Issue Year: 1969
Issue Price: $ 10.50
Current Retail Price: $ 85

No.: 5290
Name: Little Leaguer, Catcher
Height: 6.5
Current Status: Open issue,
  permanently retired
Original Issue Year: 1985
Last Year: 1990
Rarity: D
Issue Price: $ 150
High Auction Price: $ 600
LCS Estimate: $ 550

No.: 5696
Name: Mandolin Serenade
Height: 6.5
Current Status: Open issue, currently active
Original Issue Year: 1990
Issue Price: $ 300
Current Retail Price: $ 340

No.: 5694
Name: Circus Serenade
Height: 6.5
Current Status: Open issue, currently active
Original Issue Year: 1990
Issue Price: $ 300
Current Retail Price: $ 340

No.: 102.06
Name: Saint Joseph
Height: 6.5
Current Status: Very rare early issue
Original Issue Year: 1959
Last Year: Not available
Rarity: A
Issue Price: Not available

No.: 2057
Name: Short Chinese
Height: 6.5
Current Status: Open issue, currently active
Original Issue Year: 1974
Issue Price: $ 30
Current Retail Price: $ 95

No.: 2159
Name: Pensive Eskimo Boy
Height: 6.5
Current Status: Open issue, currently active
Original Issue Year: 1985
Issue Price: $ 100
Current Retail Price: $ 180

No.: 4673
Name: King Melchior
Height: 6.5
Current Status: Open issue, currently active
Original Issue Year: 1969
Issue Price: $ 11
Current Retail Price: $ 90

No.: 5915
Name: Young Mozart
Height: 6.75
Current Status: Limited edition, currently active
Edition Limit: 2500
Original Issue Year: 1992
Issue Price: $ 500
Current Retail Price: $ 500

No.: 5070
Name: Choir Boy
Height: 6.75
Current Status: Open issue, permanently retired
Original Issue Year: 1980
Last Year: 1983
Rarity: C
Issue Price: $ 240
LCS Estimate: $ 1100

No.: 5813
Name: Having a Ball
Height: 6.75
Current Status: Open issue, currently active
Original Issue Year: 1991
Issue Price: $ 225
Current Retail Price: $ 235

No.: 5476
Name: St. Joseph
Height: 6.75
Current Status: Open issue, currently active
Original Issue Year: 1988
Issue Price: $ 210
Current Retail Price: $ 265

No.: 4714
Name: Boy Jewelry Dish
Height: 7
Current Status: Open issue, permanently retired
Original Issue Year: 1970
Last Year: 1978
Rarity: E
Issue Price: $ 30
LCS Estimate: $ 240

No.: 4566
Name: Student
Height: 7
Current Status: Open issue, permanently retired
Original Issue Year: 1969
Last Year: 1972
Rarity: C
Issue Price: $ 32.5
LCS Estimate: $ 380

No.: 5695
Name: Concertina
Height: 7
Current Status: Open issue, currently
active
Original Issue Year: 1990
Issue Price: $ 300
Current Retail Price: $ 340

No.: 4970
Name: Skier Puppet
Height: 7
Current Status: Open issue,
permanently retired
Original Issue Year: 1977
Last Year: 1983
Rarity: D
Issue Price: $ 85
LCS Estimate: $ 425

No.: 1179
Name: Boy with Concertina
Height: 7
Current Status: Open issue,
permanently retired
Original Issue Year: 1971
Last Year: 1981
Rarity: E
Issue Price: $ 34
High Auction Price: $ 325
LCS Estimate: $ 300

No.: 4503
Name: Seated Harlequin
Height: 7
Current Status: Open issue,
permanently retired
Original Issue Year: 1969
Last Year: 1975
Rarity: D
Issue Price: $ 110
LCS Estimate: $ 1200

No.: 5929
Name: Jazz Drums
Height: 7.25
Current Status: Open issue, currently
active
Original Issue Year: 1992
Issue Price: $ 595
Current Retail Price: $ 595

No.: 5811
Name: Littlest Clown
Height: 7.25
Current Status: Open issue, currently
active
Original Issue Year: 1991
Issue Price: $ 225
Current Retail Price: $ 235

No.: 2209
Name: Long Day
Height: 7.5
Current Status: Open issue, currently active
Original Issue Year: 1991
Issue Price: $ 295
Current Retail Price: $ 300

No.: 2141
Name: Pedro with Jug
Height: 7.5
Current Status: Open issue, currently active
Original Issue Year: 1984
Issue Price: $ 100
Current Retail Price: $ 175

No.: 2153
Name: Chinese Boy
Height: 7.5
Current Status: Open issue, permanently retired
Original Issue Year: 1985
Last Year: 1990
Rarity: D
Issue Price: $ 90
LCS Estimate: $ 180

No.: 5291
Name: Little Leaguer on Bench
Height: 7.5
Current Status: Open issue, permanently retired
Original Issue Year: 1985
Last Year: 1990
Rarity: D
Issue Price: $ 150
High Auction Price: $ 625
LCS Estimate: $ 575

No.: 4614
Name: Boy with Guitar
Height: 7.5
Current Status: Open issue, permanently retired
Original Issue Year: 1969
Last Year: 1979
Rarity: E
Issue Price: $ 19.5
High Auction Price: $ 475
LCS Estimate: $ 550

No.: 4869
Name: Boy Blowing
Height: 7.75
Current Status: Open issue, currently active
Original Issue Year: 1974
Issue Price: $ 13
Current Retail Price: $ 85

No.: 1526
Name: Valencian Flowers
Height: 7.75
Current Status: Open issue,
  permanently retired
Original Issue Year: 1987
Last Year: 1991
Rarity: C
Issue Price: $ 375.5
LCS Estimate: $ 376

No.: 5077
Name: Harlequin C
Height: 7.75
Current Status: Open issue,
  permanently retired
Original Issue Year: 1980
Last Year: 1985
Rarity: D
Issue Price: $ 185
LCS Estimate: $ 560

No.: 4900
Name: Boy with Smoking Jacket
Height: 7.75
Current Status: Open issue,
  permanently retired
Original Issue Year: 1974
Last Year: 1983
Rarity: E
Issue Price: $ 45
LCS Estimate: $ 270

No.: 5203
Name: Little Jester
Height: 7.75
Current Status: Open issue,
  permanently retired
Original Issue Year: 1984
Last Year: 1993
Rarity: E
Issue Price: $ 75
Last Retail Price: $ 140

No.: 4674
Name: King Gaspar
Height: 7.75
Current Status: Open issue, currently
  active
Original Issue Year: 1969
Issue Price: $ 11
Current Retail Price: $ 90

No.: 2056
Name: Tall Chinese
Height: 7.75
Current Status: Open issue, currently
  active
Original Issue Year: 1974
Issue Price: $ 35
Current Retail Price: $ 95

No.: 4967
Name: Soccer Player Puppet
Height: 7.75
Current Status: Open issue,
  permanently retired
Original Issue Year: 1977
Last Year: 1985
Rarity: E
Issue Price: $ 65
LCS Estimate: $ 325

No.: 326.13
Name: Choir Boy
Height: 8
Current Status: Very rare early issue
Original Issue Year: 1965
Last Year: Not available
Rarity: A
Issue Price: Not available

No.: 5076
Name: Harlequin B
Height: 8
Current Status: Open issue,
  permanently retired
Original Issue Year: 1980
Last Year: 1985
Rarity: D
Issue Price: $ 185
High Auction Price: $ 425
LCS Estimate: $ 450

No.: 5877
Name: Guest of Honor
Height: 8
Current Status: Open issue, currently
  active
Original Issue Year: 1992
Issue Price: $ 195
Current Retail Price: $ 195

No.: 4811
Name: Dutch Boy
Height: 8.25
Current Status: Open issue,
  permanently retired
Original Issue Year: 1972
Last Year: 1988
Rarity: F
Issue Price: $ 30
High Auction Price: $ 400
LCS Estimate: $ 350

No.: 4904
Name: Santa Claus
Height: 8.25
Current Status: Open issue,
  permanently retired
Original Issue Year: 1974
Last Year: 1978
Rarity: C
Issue Price: $ 100
LCS Estimate: $ 900

No.: 4905
Name: Santa Claus with Toys
Height: 8.25
Current Status: Open issue,
  permanently retired
Original Issue Year: 1974
Last Year: 1978
Rarity: C
Issue Price: $ 125
High Auction Price: $ 1250
LCS Estimate: $ 1250

No.: 5400
Name: The Wanderer
Height: 8.25
Current Status: Open issue, currently
  active
Original Issue Year: 1987
Issue Price: $ 150
Current Retail Price: $ 235

No.: 4675
Name: King Balthazar
Height: 8.25
Current Status: Open issue, currently
  active
Original Issue Year: 1969
Issue Price: $ 11
Current Retail Price: $ 90

No.: 85.06
Name: The Hunter
Height: 8.25
Current Status: Very rare early issue
Original Issue Year: 1956
Last Year: Not available
Rarity: A
Issue Price: Not available

No.: 5165
Name: Sancho with Bottle
Height: 8.25
Current Status: Open issue,
  permanently retired
Original Issue Year: 1982
Last Year: 1990
Rarity: E
Issue Price: $ 100
High Auction Price: $ 375
LCS Estimate: $ 350

No.: 7610
Name: Can I Play?
Height: 8.25
Current Status: Limited edition, fully
  subscribed
Original Issue Year: 1990
Last Year: 1990
Rarity: B
Issue Price: $ 150
High Auction Price: $ 625
Comments: LCS Special

No.: 7605
Name: Lolo
Height: 8.25
Current Status: Limited edition, fully subscribed
Original Issue Year: 1989
Last Year: 1989
Rarity: B
Issue Price: $ 125
Comments: Rotary Club Special

No.: 4897
Name: Mechanic
Height: 8.25
Current Status: Open issue, permanently retired
Original Issue Year: 1974
Last Year: 1985
Rarity: E
Issue Price: $ 45
LCS Estimate: $ 270

No.: 4899
Name: Punishment
Height: 8.25
Current Status: Open issue, permanently retired
Original Issue Year: 1974
Last Year: 1983
Rarity: E
Issue Price: $ 45
LCS Estimate: $ 270

No.: 5136
Name: Billy Skier
Height: 8.25
Current Status: Open issue, permanently retired
Original Issue Year: 1982
Last Year: 1983
Rarity: B
Issue Price: $ 140
High Auction Price: $ 1000
LCS Estimate: $ 950

No.: 4876
Name: Boy Thinking
Height: 8.25
Current Status: Open issue, permanently retired
Original Issue Year: 1974
Last Year: 1993
Rarity: F
Issue Price: $ 20
Last Retail Price: $ 135

No.: 6004
Name: Bar Mitzvah Day
Height: 8.25
Current Status: Open issue, currently active
Original Issue Year: 1993
Issue Price: $ 460

No.: 2213
Name: Nature's Friend
Height: 8.25
Current Status: Open issue,
  permanently retired
Original Issue Year: 1991
Last Year: 1993
Rarity: C
Issue Price: $ 390
Last Retail Price: $ 420

No.: 5833
Name: Jazz Sax
Height: 8.5
Current Status: Open issue, currently
  active
Original Issue Year: 1991
Issue Price: $ 295
Current Retail Price: $ 295

No.: 5200
Name: Soccer Player
Height: 8.5
Current Status: Open issue,
  permanently retired
Original Issue Year: 1984
Last Year: 1988
Rarity: C
Issue Price: $ 155
High Auction Price: $ 725
LCS Estimate: $ 465

No.: 7602
Name: Little Traveller
Height: 8.5
Current Status: Limited edition, fully
  subscribed
Original Issue Year: 1986
Last Year: 1986
Rarity: B
Issue Price: $ 95
High Auction Price: $ 2100
Comments: LCS Special

No.: 4898
Name: Boy from Madrid
Height: 8.5
Current Status: Open issue, currently
  active
Original Issue Year: 1974
Issue Price: $ 45
Current Retail Price: $ 135

No.: 5472
Name: Circus Sam
Height: 8.5
Current Status: Open issue, currently
  active
Original Issue Year: 1988
Issue Price: $ 175
Current Retail Price: $ 200

No.: 5733
Name: Horticulturist
Height: 8.5
Current Status: Open issue,
  permanently retired
Original Issue Year: 1991
Last Year: 1993
Rarity: C
Issue Price: $ 450
Last Retail Price: $ 495

No.: 5471
Name: Sad Sax
Height: 8.5
Current Status: Open issue, currently
  active
Original Issue Year: 1988
Issue Price: $ 175
Current Retail Price: $ 200

No.: 5928
Name: Jazz Clarinet
Height: 8.5
Current Status: Open issue, currently
  active
Original Issue Year: 1992
Issue Price: $ 295
Current Retail Price: $ 295

No.: 4533
Name: Saint Joseph
Height: 8.5
Current Status: Open issue, currently
  active
Original Issue Year: 1969
Issue Price: $ 14
Current Retail Price: $ 95

No.: 4809
Name: Fisher Boy
Height: 8.5
Current Status: Open issue, currently
  active
Original Issue Year: 1972
Issue Price: $ 30
Current Retail Price: $ 155

No.: 5357
Name: Oration
Height: 8.5
Current Status: Open issue, currently
  active
Original Issue Year: 1986
Issue Price: $ 170
Current Retail Price: $ 265

No.: 4870
Name: Boy Awaking
Height: 8.5
Current Status: Open issue, currently active
Original Issue Year: 1974
Issue Price: $ 13
Current Retail Price: $ 85

No.: 5200.30
Name: Special Male Soccer Player
Height: 8.5
Current Status: Open issue, permanently retired
Original Issue Year: 1984
Last Year: 1988
Rarity: C
Issue Price: $ 150
LCS Estimate: $ 450

No.: 5075
Name: Harlequin A
Height: 8.5
Current Status: Open issue, permanently retired
Original Issue Year: 1980
Last Year: 1985
Rarity: D
Issue Price: $ 217.50
High Auction Price: $ 400
LCS Estimate: $ 450

No.: 5135
Name: Billy Football Player
Height: 8.5
Current Status: Open issue, permanently retired
Original Issue Year: 1982
Last Year: 1983
Rarity: B
Issue Price: $ 140
LCS Estimate: $ 700

No.: 4615
Name: Boy with Double Bass
Height: 8.5
Current Status: Open issue, permanently retired
Original Issue Year: 1969
Last Year: 1979
Rarity: E
Issue Price: $ 22.5
High Auction Price: $ 550
LCS Estimate: $ 550

No.: 5746
Name: St. Joseph
Height: 8.5
Current Status: Open issue, currently active
Original Issue Year: 1991
Issue Price: $ 350
Current Retail Price: $ 365

No.: 5832
Name: Jazz Horn
Height: 8.75
Current Status: Open issue, currently active
Original Issue Year: 1991
Issue Price: $ 295
Current Retail Price: $ 295

No.: 5810
Name: Musically Inclined
Height: 8.75
Current Status: Open issue, permanently retired
Original Issue Year: 1991
Last Year: 1993
Rarity: C
Issue Price: $ 235
Last Retail Price: $ 250

No.: 4966
Name: Tennis Player Puppet
Height: 9
Current Status: Open issue, permanently retired
Original Issue Year: 1977
Last Year: 1985
Rarity: E
Issue Price: $ 60
LCS Estimate: $ 300

No.: 4877
Name: Boy with Flute
Height: 9
Current Status: Open issue, permanently retired
Original Issue Year: 1974
Last Year: 1981
Rarity: D
Issue Price: $ 60
High Auction Price: $ 450
LCS Estimate: $ 400

No.: 4906
Name: Delivery Boy
Height: 9
Current Status: Open issue, permanently retired
Original Issue Year: 1974
Last Year: 1979
Rarity: D
Issue Price: $ 70
LCS Estimate: $ 560

No.: 4896
Name: Boy with Snails
Height: 9
Current Status: Open issue, permanently retired
Original Issue Year: 1974
Last Year: 1979
Rarity: D
Issue Price: $ 50
High Auction Price: $ 600
LCS Estimate: $ 500

No.: 5479
Name: King Melchior
Height: 9
Current Status: Open issue, currently active
Original Issue Year: 1988
Issue Price: $ 210
Current Retail Price: $ 255

No.: 5909
Name: All Dressed Up
Height: 9
Current Status: Open issue, currently active
Original Issue Year: 1992
Issue Price: $ 440
Current Retail Price: $ 440

No.: 5828
Name: Next at Bat
Height: 9
Current Status: Open issue, currently active
Original Issue Year: 1991
Issue Price: $ 170
Current Retail Price: $ 175

No.: 5157
Name: Bongo Beat
Height: 9
Current Status: Open issue, currently active
Original Issue Year: 1982
Issue Price: $ 135
Current Retail Price: $ 220

No.: 5480
Name: King Gaspar
Height: 9
Current Status: Open issue, currently active
Original Issue Year: 1988
Issue Price: $ 210
Current Retail Price: $ 255

No.: 4810
Name: Boy with Yacht
Height: 9
Current Status: Open issue, currently active
Original Issue Year: 1972
Issue Price: $ 30
Current Retail Price: $ 155

No.: 1286
Name: Flower Harvest
Height: 9
Current Status: Open issue, currently active
Original Issue Year: 1974
Issue Price: $ 200
Current Retail Price: $ 470

No.: 6029
Name: Hebrew Scholar
Height: 9.25
Current Status: Open issue, currently active
Original Issue Year: 1993
Issue Price: $ 265

No.: 5115
Name: Little Boy Bullfighter
Height: 9.5
Current Status: Open issue, permanently retired
Original Issue Year: 1982
Last Year: 1985
Rarity: C
Issue Price: $ 122.5
High Auction Price: $ 500
LCS Estimate: $ 490

No.: 5137
Name: Billy Baseball Playr
Height: 9.5
Current Status: Open issue, permanently retired
Original Issue Year: 1982
Last Year: 1983
Rarity: B
Issue Price: $ 140
LCS Estimate: $ 650

No.: 5138
Name: Billy Golfer
Height: 9.5
Current Status: Open issue, permanently retired
Original Issue Year: 1982
Last Year: 1983
Rarity: B
Issue Price: $ 140
LCS Estimate: $ 650

No.: 4548
Name: Troubador
Height: 9.5
Current Status: Open issue, permanently retired
Original Issue Year: 1969
Last Year: 1978
Rarity: E
Issue Price: $ 67.5
LCS Estimate: $ 600

No.: 5762
Name: Checking the Time
Height: 9.5
Current Status: Open issue, currently
active
Original Issue Year: 1991
Issue Price: $ 560
Current Retail Price: $ 585

No.: 5759
Name: Presto!
Height: 9.5
Current Status: Open issue,
permanently retired
Original Issue Year: 1991
Last Year: 1993
Rarity: C
Issue Price: $ 275
Last Retail Price: $ 295

No.: 5676
Name: Wandering Minstrel
Height: 9.5
Current Status: Open issue,
permanently retired
Original Issue Year: 1990
Last Year: 1993
Rarity: C
Issue Price: $ 270
Last Retail Price: $ 310

No.: 5547
Name: Only the Beginning
Height: 9.5
Current Status: Open issue, currently
active
Original Issue Year: 1989
Issue Price: $ 215
Current Retail Price: $ 260

No.: 5395
Name: Valencian Boy
Height: 9.5
Current Status: Open issue,
permanently retired
Original Issue Year: 1986
Last Year: 1991
Rarity: D
Issue Price: $ 200
LCS Estimate: $ 200

No.: 5117
Name: Little Boy Bullfighter
Height: 9.75
Current Status: Open issue,
permanently retired
Original Issue Year: 1982
Last Year: 1985
Rarity: C
Issue Price: $ 122.5
High Auction Price: $ 500
LCS Estimate: $ 490

No.: 4853
Name: Cobbler
Height: 9.75
Current Status: Open issue,
   permanently retired
Original Issue Year: 1973
Last Year: 1985
Rarity: E
Issue Price: $ 100
High Auction Price: $ 600
LCS Estimate: $ 600

No.: 1423.30
Name: King Melchior (White)
Height: 9.75
Current Status: Open issue,
   permanently retired
Original Issue Year: 1983
Last Year: 1985
Rarity: B
Issue Price: $ 132
High Auction Price: $ 135
LCS Estimate: $ 400

No.: 4848
Name: Charm
Height: 9.75
Current Status: Open issue,
   permanently retired
Original Issue Year: 1973
Last Year: 1985
Rarity: E
Issue Price: $ 45
High Auction Price: $ 350
LCS Estimate: $ 300

No.: 4577
Name: New Shepherd
Height: 9.75
Current Status: Open issue,
   permanently retired
Original Issue Year: 1969
Last Year: 1983
Rarity: E
Issue Price: $ 35
High Auction Price: $ 400
LCS Estimate: $ 400

No.: 4968
Name: Olympic Puppet
Height: 9.75
Current Status: Open issue,
   permanently retired
Original Issue Year: 1977
Last Year: 1983
Rarity: D
Issue Price: $ 65
High Auction Price: $ 3800
LCS Estimate: $ 2000

No.: 4726
Name: Little Gardener
Height: 9.75
Current Status: Open issue,
   permanently retired
Original Issue Year: 1970
Last Year: 1978
Rarity: E
Issue Price: $ 40
High Auction Price: $ 400
LCS Estimate: $ 400

No.: 1423
Name: King Melchior
Height: 9.75
Current Status: Open issue, currently active
Original Issue Year: 1982
Issue Price: $ 225
Current Retail Price: $ 420

No.: 5834
Name: Jazz Bass
Height: 10
Current Status: Open issue, currently active
Original Issue Year: 1991
Issue Price: $ 395
Current Retail Price: $ 395

No.: 2007
Name: Eskimo Boy
Height: 10.25
Current Status: Open issue, permanently retired
Original Issue Year: 1970
Last Year: 1990
Rarity: F
Issue Price: $ 30
LCS Estimate: $ 120

No.: 2007.30
Name: Eskimo Boy
Height: 10.25
Current Status: Open issue, permanently retired
Original Issue Year: 1970
Last Year: 1990
Rarity: F
Issue Price: $ 27.5
High Auction Price: $ 250
LCS Estimate: $ 200

No.: 5329
Name: Gentleman Equestrian
Height: 10.25
Current Status: Open issue, permanently retired
Original Issue Year: 1985
Last Year: 1988
Rarity: C
Issue Price: $ 160
High Auction Price: $ 375
LCS Estimate: $ 480

No.: 1424.30
Name: King Gaspar (White)
Height: 10.25
Current Status: Open issue, permanently retired
Original Issue Year: 1983
Last Year: 1985
Rarity: B
Issue Price: $ 142.5
High Auction Price: $ 135
LCS Estimate: $ 400

No.: 5029
Name: The Flower Peddler
Height: 10.25
Current Status: Open issue,
  permanently retired
Original Issue Year: 1979
Last Year: 1985
Rarity: D
Issue Price: $ 675
High Auction Price: $ 1500
LCS Estimate: $ 1500

No.: 5116
Name: Little Boy Bullfighter
Height: 10.25
Current Status: Open issue,
  permanently retired
Original Issue Year: 1982
Last Year: 1985
Rarity: C
Issue Price: $ 122.5
High Auction Price: $ 500
LCS Estimate: $ 490

No.: 4637
Name: Caped Gentleman
Height: 10.25
Current Status: Open issue,
  permanently retired
Original Issue Year: 1969
Last Year: 1972
Rarity: C
Issue Price: $ 25
LCS Estimate: $ 300

No.: 1424
Name: King Gaspar
Height: 10.25
Current Status: Open issue, currently
  active
Original Issue Year: 1982
Issue Price: $ 265
Current Retail Price: $ 450

No.: 4757
Name: Doncel with Roses
Height: 10.5
Current Status: Open issue,
  permanently retired
Original Issue Year: 1971
Last Year: 1979
Rarity: E
Issue Price: $ 35
High Auction Price: $ 400
LCS Estimate: $ 400

No.: 4619
Name: Seminarist
Height: 10.5
Current Status: Open issue,
  permanently retired
Original Issue Year: 1969
Last Year: 1972
Rarity: C
Issue Price: $ 18.50
LCS Estimate: $ 220

No.: 5198
Name: Boy Graduate
Height: 10.5
Current Status: Open issue, currently active
Original Issue Year: 1984
Issue Price: $ 160
Current Retail Price: $ 260

No.: 5768
Name: Academy Days
Height: 10.5
Current Status: Open issue, permanently retired
Original Issue Year: 1991
Last Year: 1993
Rarity: C
Issue Price: $ 280
Last Retail Price: $ 310

No.: 4824
Name: Golfer
Height: 10.5
Current Status: Open issue, currently active
Original Issue Year: 1972
Issue Price: $ 66
Current Retail Price: $ 285

No.: 5088
Name: Cutting Flowers
Height: 10.5
Current Status: Open issue, permanently retired
Original Issue Year: 1980
Last Year: 1988
Rarity: E
Issue Price: $ 645
LCS Estimate: $ 1750

No.: 5128
Name: Lost Love
Height: 10.5
Current Status: Open issue, permanently retired
Original Issue Year: 1982
Last Year: 1988
Rarity: D
Issue Price: $ 400
High Auction Price: $ 700
LCS Estimate: $ 700

No.: 1031
Name: Sancho Panza
Height: 10.5
Current Status: Open issue, permanently retired
Original Issue Year: 1969
Last Year: 1989
Rarity: F
Issue Price: $ 65
High Auction Price: $ 525
LCS Estimate: $ 475

No.: 4969
Name: "Sheriff" Puppet
Height: 10.5
Current Status: Open issue,
 permanently retired
Original Issue Year: 1977
Last Year: 1985
Rarity: E
Issue Price: $ 85
High Auction Price: $ 750
LCS Estimate: $ 700

No.: 5055
Name: Apprentice Seaman
Height: 10.5
Current Status: Open issue,
 permanently retired
Original Issue Year: 1980
Last Year: 1985
Rarity: D
Issue Price: $ 140
High Auction Price: $ 400
LCS Estimate: $ 450

No.: 4894
Name: Tennis Player Boy
Height: 10.5
Current Status: Open issue,
 permanently retired
Original Issue Year: 1974
Last Year: 1980
Rarity: D
Issue Price: $ 75
LCS Estimate: $ 500

No.: 5233
Name: Charlie the Tramp
Height: 11
Current Status: Open issue,
 permanently retired
Original Issue Year: 1984
Last Year: 1991
Rarity: D
Issue Price: $ 150
High Auction Price: $ 850
LCS Estimate: $ 800

No.: 1059
Name: Panchito
Height: 11
Current Status: Open issue,
 permanently retired
Original Issue Year: 1969
Last Year: 1980
Rarity: E
Issue Price: $ 28
LCS Estimate: $ 220

No.: 4688
Name: Gothic King
Height: 11
Current Status: Open issue,
 permanently retired
Original Issue Year: 1970
Last Year: 1975
Rarity: D
Issue Price: $ 20
High Auction Price: $ 350
LCS Estimate: $ 400

No.: 4580
Name: Mardi Gras
Height: 11
Current Status: Open issue, permanently retired
Original Issue Year: 1969
Last Year: 1975
Rarity: D
Issue Price: $ 57.5
LCS Estimate: $ 650

No.: 1090
Name: Lawyer
Height: 11
Current Status: Open issue, permanently retired
Original Issue Year: 1971
Last Year: 1973
Rarity: B
Issue Price: $ 35
LCS Estimate: $ 400

No.: 1089
Name: Lawyer
Height: 11
Current Status: Open issue, permanently retired
Original Issue Year: 1971
Last Year: 1973
Rarity: B
Issue Price: $ 35
LCS Estimate: $ 400

No.: 4718
Name: Cadet
Height: 11
Current Status: Open issue, permanently retired
Original Issue Year: 1970
Last Year: 1971
Rarity: B
Issue Price: $ 25
LCS Estimate: $ 300

No.: 5224
Name: The Quest
Height: 11
Current Status: Open issue, currently active
Original Issue Year: 1984
Issue Price: $ 125
Current Retail Price: $ 260

No.: 5368
Name: Rey de Espadas
Height: 11
Current Status: Limited edition, permanently retired
Edition Limit: 2000
Original Issue Year: 1986
Last Year: 1993
Rarity: E
Issue Price: $ 325
Last Retail Price: $ 600

No.: 5367
Name: Rey de Oros
Height: 11
Current Status: Limited edition,
  permanently retired
Edition Limit: 2000
Original Issue Year: 1986
Last Year: 1993
Rarity: E
Issue Price: $ 325
Last Retail Price: $ 600

No.: 5366
Name: Rey de Copas
Height: 11
Current Status: Limited edition,
  permanently retired
Edition Limit: 2000
Original Issue Year: 1986
Last Year: 1993
Rarity: E
Issue Price: $ 325
Last Retail Price: $ 600

No.: 2002
Name: Gothic King
Height: 11
Current Status: Open issue,
  permanently retired
Original Issue Year: 1970
Last Year: 1975
Rarity: D
Issue Price: $ 25
High Auction Price: $ 300
LCS Estimate: $ 300

No.: 5369
Name: Rey de Bastos
Height: 11
Current Status: Limited edition,
  permanently retired
Edition Limit: 2000
Original Issue Year: 1986
Last Year: 1993
Rarity: E
Issue Price: $ 325
Last Retail Price: $ 600

No.: 5783
Name: Special Delivery
Height: 11.25
Current Status: Open issue, currently
  active
Original Issue Year: 1991
Issue Price: $ 525
Current Retail Price: $ 545

No.: 5661
Name: Travelling Artist
Height: 11.25
Current Status: Open issue, currently
  active
Original Issue Year: 1990
Issue Price: $ 250
Current Retail Price: $ 275

No.: 5204
Name: Sharpening Cutlery
Height: 11.5
Current Status: Open issue,
  permanently retired
Original Issue Year: 1984
Last Year: 1988
Rarity: C
Issue Price: $ 210
LCS Estimate: $ 630

No.: 4684
Name: Hebrew Student
Height: 11.5
Current Status: Open issue,
  permanently retired
Original Issue Year: 1970
Last Year: 1985
Rarity: E
Issue Price: $ 33
High Auction Price: $ 1050
LCS Estimate: $ 800

No.: 5168
Name: King Solomon
Height: 11.5
Current Status: Open issue,
  permanently retired
Original Issue Year: 1982
Last Year: 1985
Rarity: C
Issue Price: $ 205
LCS Estimate: $ 800

No.: 5080
Name: Boy Pottery Seller
Height: 11.5
Current Status: Open issue,
  permanently retired
Original Issue Year: 1980
Last Year: 1985
Rarity: D
Issue Price: $ 320
High Auction Price: $ 750
LCS Estimate: $ 750

No.: 4664
Name: Countryman
Height: 11.5
Current Status: Open issue,
  permanently retired
Original Issue Year: 1969
Last Year: 1979
Rarity: E
Issue Price: $ 50
High Auction Price: $ 500
LCS Estimate: $ 500

No.: 348.13
Name: Prince Charles
Height: 11.5
Current Status: Very rare early issue
Original Issue Year: 1975
Last Year: Not available
Rarity: A
Issue Price: Not available

No.: 2174
Name: Andean Fluteplayer
Height: 11.5
Current Status: Open issue,
  permanently retired
Original Issue Year: 1987
Last Year: 1990
Rarity: C
Issue Price: $ 250
High Auction Price: $ 625
LCS Estimate: $ 500

No.: 5234
Name: Artistic Endeavor
Height: 11.5
Current Status: Open issue,
  permanently retired
Original Issue Year: 1984
Last Year: 1988
Rarity: C
Issue Price: $ 225
High Auction Price: $ 400
LCS Estimate: $ 450

No.: 1400
Name: Valencian Boy
Height: 11.5
Current Status: Open issue,
  permanently retired
Original Issue Year: 1982
Last Year: 1988
Rarity: D
Issue Price: $ 297.50
High Auction Price: $ 500
LCS Estimate: $ 500

No.: 1426
Name: Male Tennis Player
Height: 11.5
Current Status: Open issue,
  permanently retired
Original Issue Year: 1982
Last Year: 1988
Rarity: D
Issue Price: $ 200
High Auction Price: $ 325
LCS Estimate: $ 300

No.: 5273
Name: Civil Guard at Attention
Height: 11.5
Current Status: Open issue,
  permanently retired
Original Issue Year: 1985
Last Year: 1988
Rarity: C
Issue Price: $ 170
LCS Estimate: $ 500

No.: 1235
Name: Buddha
Height: 11.5
Current Status: Open issue,
  permanently retired
Original Issue Year: 1972
Last Year: 1976
Rarity: C
Issue Price: $ 130
LCS Estimate: $ 1300

No.: 4620
Name: Policeman
Height: 11.5
Current Status: Open issue, permanently retired
Original Issue Year: 1969
Last Year: 1972
Rarity: C
Issue Price: $ 16
LCS Estimate: $ 190

No.: 5301
Name: Waiting to Tee Off
Height: 11.5
Current Status: Open issue, currently active
Original Issue Year: 1985
Issue Price: $ 145
Current Retail Price: $ 270

No.: 2212
Name: Patrol Leader
Height: 11.5
Current Status: Open issue, permanently retired
Original Issue Year: 1991
Last Year: 1993
Rarity: C
Issue Price: $ 390
Last Retail Price: $ 420

No.: 5397
Name: The Poet
Height: 11.75
Current Status: Open issue, permanently retired
Original Issue Year: 1986
Last Year: 1988
Rarity: B
Issue Price: $ 425
High Auction Price: $ 750
LCS Estimate: $ 700

No.: 5191
Name: Predicting the Future
Height: 11.75
Current Status: Open issue, permanently retired
Original Issue Year: 1984
Last Year: 1985
Rarity: B
Issue Price: $ 135
High Auction Price: $ 400
LCS Estimate: $ 375

No.: 5194
Name: Roving Photographer
Height: 11.75
Current Status: Open issue, permanently retired
Original Issue Year: 1984
Last Year: 1985
Rarity: B
Issue Price: $ 145
LCS Estimate: $ 725

No.: 5056
Name: Clown with Clock
Height: 11.75
Current Status: Open issue,
  permanently retired
Original Issue Year: 1980
Last Year: 1985
Rarity: D
Issue Price: $ 290
High Auction Price: $ 850
LCS Estimate: $ 900

No.: 1254
Name: Hamlet and Yorick
Height: 11.75
Current Status: Open issue,
  permanently retired
Original Issue Year: 1974
Last Year: 1983
Rarity: E
Issue Price: $ 325
High Auction Price: $ 950
LCS Estimate: $ 950

No.: 1174
Name: Young Sultan
Height: 11.75
Current Status: Open issue,
  permanently retired
Original Issue Year: 1971
Last Year: 1975
Rarity: C
Issue Price: $ 40
LCS Estimate: $ 400

No.: 4646
Name: Pierrot with Mandolin
Height: 11.75
Current Status: Open issue,
  permanently retired
Original Issue Year: 1969
Last Year: 1970
Rarity: B
Issue Price: $ 60
LCS Estimate: $ 720

No.: 1162
Name: Seated Torero
Height: 11.75
Current Status: Open issue,
  permanently retired
Original Issue Year: 1971
Last Year: 1973
Rarity: B
Issue Price: $ 35
High Auction Price: $ 400
LCS Estimate: $ 750

No.: 4854
Name: Quixote Standing Up
Height: 11.75
Current Status: Open issue, currently
  active
Original Issue Year: 1973
Issue Price: $ 40
Current Retail Price: $ 200

No.: 4889
Name: Spanish Policeman
Height: 11.75
Current Status: Open issue, currently active
Original Issue Year: 1974
Issue Price: $ 55
Current Retail Price: $ 295

No.: 5255
Name: Spanish Soldier
Height: 11.75
Current Status: Open issue, permanently retired
Original Issue Year: 1984
Last Year: 1988
Rarity: C
Issue Price: $ 185
High Auction Price: $ 475
LCS Estimate: $ 450

No.: 5944
Name: The Great Adventurer
Height: 12
Current Status: Open issue, currently active
Original Issue Year: 1993
Issue Price: $ 315

No.: 1382
Name: Medieval Boy
Height: 12.25
Current Status: Open issue, permanently retired
Original Issue Year: 1978
Last Year: 1985
Rarity: D
Issue Price: $ 235
High Auction Price: $ 700
LCS Estimate: $ 600

No.: 5253
Name: Cadet
Height: 12.25
Current Status: Open issue, permanently retired
Original Issue Year: 1984
Last Year: 1984
Rarity: B
Issue Price: $ 150
LCS Estimate: $ 750

No.: 1341
Name: Jockey
Height: 12.25
Current Status: Open issue, permanently retired
Original Issue Year: 1977
Last Year: 1979
Rarity: B
Issue Price: $ 120
High Auction Price: $ 500
LCS Estimate: $ 500

No.: 1163
Name: Soldier with Saber
Height: 12.25
Current Status: Open issue,
   permanently retired
Original Issue Year: 1971
Last Year: 1978
Rarity: D
Issue Price: $ 27.5
LCS Estimate: $ 220

No.: 4839
Name: Soldier
Height: 12.25
Current Status: Open issue,
   permanently retired
Original Issue Year: 1973
Last Year: 1976
Rarity: C
Issue Price: $ 65
LCS Estimate: $ 650

No.: 5280
Name: Hiker
Height: 12.25
Current Status: Open issue,
   permanently retired
Original Issue Year: 1985
Last Year: 1988
Rarity: C
Issue Price: $ 195
LCS Estimate: $ 585

No.: 5326
Name: The Tailor
Height: 12.25
Current Status: Open issue,
   permanently retired
Original Issue Year: 1985
Last Year: 1988
Rarity: C
Issue Price: $ 335
High Auction Price: $ 975
LCS Estimate: $ 950

No.: 1167
Name: Soldier with Drum
Height: 12.25
Current Status: Open issue,
   permanently retired
Original Issue Year: 1971
Last Year: 1978
Rarity: D
Issue Price: $ 27.5
LCS Estimate: $ 220

No.: 1164
Name: Soldier with Gun
Height: 12.25
Current Status: Open issue,
   permanently retired
Original Issue Year: 1971
Last Year: 1978
Rarity: D
Issue Price: $ 27.5
LCS Estimate: $ 220

No.: 1165
Name: Soldier with Flag
Height: 12.25
Current Status: Open issue, permanently retired
Original Issue Year: 1971
Last Year: 1978
Rarity: D
Issue Price: $ 27.5
LCS Estimate: $ 220

No.: 1166
Name: Soldier with Cornet
Height: 12.25
Current Status: Open issue, permanently retired
Original Issue Year: 1971
Last Year: 1978
Rarity: D
Issue Price: $ 27.5
LCS Estimate: $ 220

No.: 1161
Name: Little Town Mayor
Height: 12.25
Current Status: Open issue, permanently retired
Original Issue Year: 1971
Last Year: 1973
Rarity: B
Issue Price: $ 30
LCS Estimate: $ 325

No.: 1384
Name: Henry VIII
Height: 12.25
Current Status: Limited edition, permanently retired
Edition Limit: 1200
Original Issue Year: 1978
Last Year: 1993
Rarity: F
Issue Price: $ 650
Last Retail Price: $ 995

No.: 1281
Name: Judge
Height: 12.25
Current Status: Limited edition, fully subscribed
Edition Limit: 1200
Original Issue Year: 1974
Issue Price: $ 325
High Auction Price: $ 1400

No.: 1515
Name: Melchior's Page
Height: 12.25
Current Status: Open issue, permanently retired
Original Issue Year: 1987
Last Year: 1990
Rarity: C
Issue Price: $ 290
LCS Estimate: $ 580

No.: 5289
Name: Little Leaguer Exercising
Height: 12.25
Current Status: Open issue,
permanently retired
Original Issue Year: 1985
Last Year: 1990
Rarity: D
Issue Price: $ 150
High Auction Price: $ 475
LCS Estimate: $ 450

No.: 5214
Name: The Architect
Height: 12.25
Current Status: Open issue,
permanently retired
Original Issue Year: 1984
Last Year: 1990
Rarity: D
Issue Price: $ 140
High Auction Price: $ 500
LCS Estimate: $ 450

No.: 5481
Name: King Balthasar
Height: 12.5
Current Status: Open issue, currently
active
Original Issue Year: 1988
Issue Price: $ 210
Current Retail Price: $ 255

No.: 5976
Name: The Fireman
Height: 12.5
Current Status: Open issue, currently
active
Original Issue Year: 1993
Issue Price: $ 490

No.: 5387
Name: St. Vincent
Height: 12.5
Current Status: Open issue,
permanently retired
Original Issue Year: 1986
Last Year: 1990
Rarity: C
Issue Price: $ 190
LCS Estimate: $ 380

No.: 5404
Name: Cadet Captain
Height: 12.5
Current Status: Open issue,
permanently retired
Original Issue Year: 1987
Last Year: 1990
Rarity: C
Issue Price: $ 175
High Auction Price: $ 325
LCS Estimate: $ 350

No.: 5406
Name: The Bugler
Height: 12.5
Current Status: Open issue,
  permanently retired
Original Issue Year: 1987
Last Year: 1990
Rarity: C
Issue Price: $ 175
High Auction Price: $ 475
LCS Estimate: $ 400

No.: 5405
Name: The Flag Bearer
Height: 12.5
Current Status: Open issue,
  permanently retired
Original Issue Year: 1987
Last Year: 1990
Rarity: C
Issue Price: $ 200
High Auction Price: $ 450
LCS Estimate: $ 400

No.: 5057
Name: Clown Standing
Height: 12.5
Current Status: Open issue,
  permanently retired
Original Issue Year: 1980
Last Year: 1985
Rarity: D
Issue Price: $ 270
LCS Estimate: $ 800

No.: 4844
Name: Pharmacist
Height: 12.5
Current Status: Open issue,
  permanently retired
Original Issue Year: 1973
Last Year: 1985
Rarity: E
Issue Price: $ 70
High Auction Price: $ 2000
LCS Estimate: $ 800

No.: 4977
Name: Harlequin Serenade
Height: 12.5
Current Status: Open issue,
  permanently retired
Original Issue Year: 1977
Last Year: 1979
Rarity: B
Issue Price: $ 185
High Auction Price: $ 675
LCS Estimate: $ 650

No.: 1351
Name: Botanic
Height: 12.5
Current Status: Open issue,
  permanently retired
Original Issue Year: 1978
Last Year: 1979
Rarity: B
Issue Price: $ 400
LCS Estimate: $ 2800

No.: 4983
Name: Courtier Boy
Height: 12.5
Current Status: Open issue,
  permanently retired
Original Issue Year: 1978
Last Year: 1979
Rarity: B
Issue Price: $ 235
LCS Estimate: $ 1600

No.: 1029
Name: Boy with Bowler
Height: 12.5
Current Status: Open issue,
  permanently retired
Original Issue Year: 1969
Last Year: 1970
Rarity: B
Issue Price: $ 37.5
LCS Estimate: $ 450

No.: 5359
Name: El Greco
Height: 12.5
Current Status: Open issue,
  permanently retired
Original Issue Year: 1986
Last Year: 1990
Rarity: C
Issue Price: $ 300
High Auction Price: $ 700
LCS Estimate: $ 600

No.: 5407
Name: At Attention
Height: 12.5
Current Status: Open issue,
  permanently retired
Original Issue Year: 1987
Last Year: 1990
Rarity: C
Issue Price: $ 175
High Auction Price: $ 325
LCS Estimate: $ 350

No.: 5403
Name: The Drummer Boy
Height: 12.5
Current Status: Open issue,
  permanently retired
Original Issue Year: 1987
Last Year: 1990
Rarity: C
Issue Price: $ 225
High Auction Price: $ 550
LCS Estimate: $ 450

No.: 4823
Name: Legionary
Height: 12.5
Current Status: Open issue,
  permanently retired
Original Issue Year: 1972
Last Year: 1978
Rarity: D
Issue Price: $ 55
LCS Estimate: $ 450

No.: 4651
Name: Cellist
Height: 12.5
Current Status: Open issue,
  permanently retired
Original Issue Year: 1969
Last Year: 1978
Rarity: E
Issue Price: $ 70
LCS Estimate: $ 630

No.: 1459
Name: Napoleon Planning the Battle
Height: 13
Current Status: Limited edition,
  currently active
Edition Limit: 1500
Original Issue Year: 1985
Issue Price: $ 825
Current Retail Price: $ 1350

No.: 5195
Name: Say Cheese
Height: 13
Current Status: Open issue,
  permanently retired
Original Issue Year: 1984
Last Year: 1990
Rarity: D
Issue Price: $ 170
High Auction Price: $ 475
LCS Estimate: $ 450

No.: 1514
Name: Gaspar's Page
Height: 13
Current Status: Open issue,
  permanently retired
Original Issue Year: 1987
Last Year: 1990
Rarity: C
Issue Price: $ 275
LCS Estimate: $ 550

No.: 5208
Name: The Professor
Height: 13
Current Status: Open issue,
  permanently retired
Original Issue Year: 1984
Last Year: 1990
Rarity: D
Issue Price: $ 205
High Auction Price: $ 750
LCS Estimate: $ 650

No.: 5196
Name: Music Maestro Please
Height: 13
Current Status: Open issue,
  permanently retired
Original Issue Year: 1984
Last Year: 1988
Rarity: C
Issue Price: $ 135
High Auction Price: $ 375
LCS Estimate: $ 425

No.: 1338
Name: Shakespeare
Height: 13
Current Status: Limited edition, fully subscribed
Edition Limit: 1200
Original Issue Year: 1977
Last Year: 1985
Rarity: E
Issue Price: $ 550
High Auction Price: $ 1850

No.: 1386.30
Name: Saint Joseph (White)
Height: 13
Current Status: Open issue, permanently retired
Original Issue Year: 1983
Last Year: 1985
Rarity: C
Issue Price: $ 167.50
High Auction Price: $ 135
LCS Estimate: $ 500

No.: 4622
Name: Old Man with Violin
Height: 13
Current Status: Open issue, permanently retired
Original Issue Year: 1969
Last Year: 1982
Rarity: E
Issue Price: $ 45
High Auction Price: $ 1100
LCS Estimate: $ 1000

No.: 4923
Name: Serious Clown
Height: 13
Current Status: Open issue, permanently retired
Original Issue Year: 1974
Last Year: 1979
Rarity: D
Issue Price: $ 150
LCS Estimate: $ 1200

No.: 1314
Name: Little Troubador
Height: 13
Current Status: Open issue, permanently retired
Original Issue Year: 1974
Last Year: 1979
Rarity: D
Issue Price: $ 240
LCS Estimate: $ 1900

No.: 4921
Name: Chinese Nobleman
Height: 13
Current Status: Open issue, permanently retired
Original Issue Year: 1974
Last Year: 1978
Rarity: C
Issue Price: $ 325
LCS Estimate: $ 2900

No.: 4600
Name: Man with Heart
Height: 13
Current Status: Open issue,
  permanently retired
Original Issue Year: 1969
Last Year: 1972
Rarity: C
Issue Price: $ 47.5
LCS Estimate: $ 550

No.: 5592
Name: Male Siamese Dancer
Height: 13
Current Status: Open issue,
  permanently retired
Original Issue Year: 1989
Last Year: 1993
Rarity: D
Issue Price: $ 345
Current Retail Price: $ 420

No.: 5213
Name: Attorney
Height: 13
Current Status: Open issue, currently
  active
Original Issue Year: 1984
Issue Price: $ 250
Current Retail Price: $ 495

No.: 1386
Name: St. Joseph
Height: 13
Current Status: Open issue, currently
  active
Original Issue Year: 1981
Issue Price: $ 250
Current Retail Price: $ 375

No.: 2060
Name: Monk
Height: 13
Current Status: Open issue, currently
  active
Original Issue Year: 1977
Issue Price: $ 60
Current Retail Price: $ 120

No.: 5330
Name: Concert Violinist
Height: 13.25
Current Status: Open issue,
  permanently retired
Original Issue Year: 1985
Last Year: 1988
Rarity: C
Issue Price: $ 220
High Auction Price: $ 450
LCS Estimate: $ 450

No.: 4606
Name: Accordion Player
Height: 13.25
Current Status: Open issue, permanently retired
Original Issue Year: 1969
Last Year: 1978
Rarity: E
Issue Price: $ 60
High Auction Price: $ 500
LCS Estimate: $ 540

No.: 4663
Name: Painter
Height: 13.25
Current Status: Open issue, permanently retired
Original Issue Year: 1969
Last Year: 1972
Rarity: C
Issue Price: $ 45
LCS Estimate: $ 550

No.: 5338
Name: Napoleon Bonaparte
Height: 13.25
Current Status: Limited edition, currently active
Edition Limit: 5000
Original Issue Year: 1985
Issue Price: $ 265
Current Retail Price: $ 470

No.: 5489
Name: Justice
Height: 13.25
Current Status: Open issue, permanently retired
Original Issue Year: 1988
Last Year: 1993
Rarity: D
Issue Price: $ 675
Last Retail Price: $ 825

No.: 5934
Name: The Holy Teacher
Height: 13.25
Current Status: Open issue, currently active
Original Issue Year: 1993
Issue Price: $ 385

No.: 3533
Name: Observer
Height: 13.25
Current Status: Limited edition, permanently retired
Edition Limit: 115
Original Issue Year: 1983
Last Year: 1993
Rarity: E
Issue Price: $ 900
Last Retail Price: $ 1650

No.: 5339
Name: Beethoven
Height: 13.25
Current Status: Limited edition,
    permanently retired
Edition Limit: 3000
Original Issue Year: 1985
Last Year: 1993
Rarity: E
Issue Price: $ 760
Last Retail Price: $ 1300

No.: 5206
Name: Yachtsman
Height: 13.25
Current Status: Open issue, currently
    active
Original Issue Year: 1984
Issue Price: $ 110
Current Retail Price: $ 200

No.: 5681
Name: On the Road
Height: 13.5
Current Status: Open issue,
    permanently retired
Original Issue Year: 1990
Last Year: 1991
Rarity: B
Issue Price: $ 320
LCS Estimate: $ 325

No.: 5948
Name: Physician
Height: 13.5
Current Status: Open issue, currently
    active
Original Issue Year: 1993
Issue Price: $ 375

No.: 5896
Name: The Loaves and Fishes
Height: 13.5
Current Status: Open issue, currently
    active
Original Issue Year: 1992
Issue Price: $ 695
Current Retail Price: $ 695

No.: 4887
Name: Violinist
Height: 13.75
Current Status: Open issue,
    permanently retired
Original Issue Year: 1974
Last Year: 1981
Rarity: D
Issue Price: $ 110
LCS Estimate: $ 760

No.: 4933
Name: Fernando of Aragon
Height: 13.75
Current Status: Open issue,
  permanently retired
Original Issue Year: 1974
Last Year: 1981
Rarity: D
Issue Price: $ 525
LCS Estimate: $ 3500

No.: 4927
Name: Minstrel
Height: 13.75
Current Status: Open issue,
  permanently retired
Original Issue Year: 1974
Last Year: 1980
Rarity: D
Issue Price: $ 375
High Auction Price: $ 725
LCS Estimate: $ 800

No.: 1126
Name: Clown with Violin
Height: 13.75
Current Status: Open issue,
  permanently retired
Original Issue Year: 1971
Last Year: 1978
Rarity: D
Issue Price: $ 71
High Auction Price: $ 2350
LCS Estimate: $ 1600

No.: 4558
Name: Sad Harlequin
Height: 13.75
Current Status: Open issue,
  permanently retired
Original Issue Year: 1969
Last Year: 1993
Rarity: F
Issue Price: $ 65
Last Retail Price: $ 510

No.: 5947
Name: General Practitioner
Height: 13.75
Current Status: Open issue, currently
  active
Original Issue Year: 1993
Issue Price: $ 360

No.: 5960
Name: On Patrol
Height: 13.75
Current Status: Open issue, currently
  active
Original Issue Year: 1993
Issue Price: $ 395

No.: 4602.30
Name: Doctor (Reduced)
Height: 13.75
Current Status: Open issue, currently active
Original Issue Year: 1971
Issue Price: $ 33
Current Retail Price: $ 180

No.: 1425
Name: King Balthazar
Height: 13.75
Current Status: Open issue, currently active
Original Issue Year: 1982
Issue Price: $ 315
Current Retail Price: $ 565

No.: 1516
Name: Balthazar's Page
Height: 13.75
Current Status: Open issue, permanently retired
Original Issue Year: 1987
Last Year: 1990
Rarity: C
Issue Price: $ 275
LCS Estimate: $ 550

No.: 4762.30
Name: Dentist (Reduced)
Height: 13.75
Current Status: Open issue, permanently retired
Original Issue Year: 1971
Last Year: 1985
Rarity: E
Issue Price: $ 30
High Auction Price: $ 450
LCS Estimate: $ 450

No.: 1425.30
Name: King Balthazar (Whit)
Height: 13.75
Current Status: Open issue, permanently retired
Original Issue Year: 1983
Last Year: 1985
Rarity: B
Issue Price: $ 142.5
High Auction Price: $ 135
LCS Estimate: $ 400

No.: 5177
Name: Dante
Height: 13.75
Current Status: Open issue, permanently retired
Original Issue Year: 1982
Last Year: 1983
Rarity: B
Issue Price: $ 262.5
High Auction Price: $ 500
LCS Estimate: $ 600

No.: 5132
Name: Miguel de Cervantes
Height: 14.25
Current Status: Open issue,
  permanently retired
Original Issue Year: 1982
Last Year: 1988
Rarity: D
Issue Price: $ 925
LCS Estimate: $ 2800

No.: 5169
Name: Abraham
Height: 14.25
Current Status: Open issue,
  permanently retired
Original Issue Year: 1982
Last Year: 1985
Rarity: C
Issue Price: $ 155
LCS Estimate: $ 625

No.: 4732
Name: Artist
Height: 14.25
Current Status: Open issue,
  permanently retired
Original Issue Year: 1970
Last Year: 1976
Rarity: D
Issue Price: $ 75
High Auction Price: $ 650
LCS Estimate: $ 750

No.: 5167
Name: Jesus
Height: 14.25
Current Status: Open issue, currently
  active
Original Issue Year: 1982
Issue Price: $ 130
Current Retail Price: $ 255

No.: 5239
Name: Wine Taster
Height: 14.25
Current Status: Open issue, currently
  active
Original Issue Year: 1984
Issue Price: $ 190
Current Retail Price: $ 340

No.: 4802
Name: Fisherman
Height: 14.5
Current Status: Open issue,
  permanently retired
Original Issue Year: 1972
Last Year: 1979
Rarity: D
Issue Price: $ 70
LCS Estimate: $ 560

No.: 4657
Name: Sailor
Height: 14.5
Current Status: Open issue,
   permanently retired
Original Issue Year: 1969
Last Year: 1978
Rarity: E
Issue Price: $ 35
LCS Estimate: $ 310

No.: 4656
Name: Woodcutter
Height: 14.5
Current Status: Open issue,
   permanently retired
Original Issue Year: 1969
Last Year: 1978
Rarity: E
Issue Price: $ 80
LCS Estimate: $ 700

No.: 1025
Name: Flute Player
Height: 14.5
Current Status: Open issue,
   permanently retired
Original Issue Year: 1969
Last Year: 1978
Rarity: E
Issue Price: $ 72.5
LCS Estimate: $ 670

No.: 4644
Name: Village Mayor
Height: 14.5
Current Status: Open issue,
   permanently retired
Original Issue Year: 1969
Last Year: 1972
Rarity: C
Issue Price: $ 35
LCS Estimate: $ 400

No.: 4621
Name: Sea Captain
Height: 14.5
Current Status: Open issue,
   permanently retired
Original Issue Year: 1969
Last Year: 1993
Rarity: F
Issue Price: $ 42.5
Last Retail Price: $ 265

No.: 1030
Name: Don Quixote
Height: 14.5
Current Status: Open issue, currently
   active
Original Issue Year: 1969
Issue Price: $ 225
Current Retail Price: $ 1375

No.: 342.13
Name: Greek Shepherd
Height: 14.5
Current Status: Very rare early issue
Original Issue Year: 1963
Last Year: Not available
Rarity: A
Issue Price: Not available

No.: 1247
Name: Happy Harlequin
Height: 14.5
Current Status: Open issue,
  permanently retired
Original Issue Year: 1974
Last Year: 1983
Rarity: E
Issue Price: $ 220
LCS Estimate: $ 1320

No.: 3509
Name: Letters to Dulcinea
Height: 15
Current Status: Limited edition,
  currently active
Original Issue Year: 1978
Issue Price: $ 1000
Current Retail Price: $ 2050

No.: 1455
Name: Reflections of Hamlet
Height: 15
Current Status: Open issue,
  permanently retired
Original Issue Year: 1983
Last Year: 1988
Rarity: D
Issue Price: $ 1000
High Auction Price: $ 1600
LCS Estimate: $1600

No.: 1050
Name: Boy
Height: 15
Current Status: Open issue,
  permanently retired
Original Issue Year: 1969
Last Year: 1978
Rarity: E
Issue Price: $ 65
LCS Estimate: $ 575

No.: 4801
Name: The Teacher
Height: 15
Current Status: Open issue,
  permanently retired
Original Issue Year: 1972
Last Year: 1978
Rarity: D
Issue Price: $ 45
High Auction Price: $ 250
LCS Estimate: $ 250

No.: 1269
Name: Man of La Mancha
Height: 15
Current Status: Limited edition, fully
  subscribed
Edition Limit: 1500
Original Issue Year: 1974
Issue Price: $ 700
High Auction Price: $ 4000

No.: 5933
Name: The Ten Commandments
Height: 15
Current Status: Open issue, currently
  active
Original Issue Year: 1993
Issue Price: $ 930

No.: 345.13
Name: Contemplative Shepherd
Height: 15.25
Current Status: Very rare early issue
Original Issue Year: 1968
Last Year: Not available
Rarity: A
Issue Price: Not available

No.: 344.13
Name: Nanki Poo
Height: 15.5
Current Status: Very rare early issue
Original Issue Year: 1965
Last Year: Not available
Rarity: A
Issue Price: Not available

No.: 5427
Name: Saint Nicholas
Height: 15.5
Current Status: Open issue,
  permanently retired
Original Issue Year: 1987
Last Year: 1991
Rarity: C
Issue Price: $ 425
LCS Estimate: $ 950

No.: 1385
Name: Quixote on Guard
Height: 15.5
Current Status: Open issue,
  permanently retired
Original Issue Year: 1978
Last Year: 1990
Rarity: E
Issue Price: $ 175
High Auction Price: $ 700
LCS Estimate: $ 600

No.: 4653
Name: Orchestra Conductor
Height: 15.5
Current Status: Open issue,
  permanently retired
Original Issue Year: 1969
Last Year: 1979
Rarity: E
Issue Price: $ 95
High Auction Price: $ 900
LCS Estimate: $ 850

No.: 6032
Name: On the Green
Height: 15.5
Current Status: Open issue, currently
  active
Original Issue Year: 1993
Issue Price: $ 645

No.: 5891
Name: The Aviator
Height: 15.5
Current Status: Open issue, currently
  active
Original Issue Year: 1992
Issue Price: $ 375
Current Retail Price: $ 375

No.: 3530
Name: Anxiety
Height: 15.5
Current Status: Limited edition,
  permanently retired
Edition Limit: 125
Original Issue Year: 1983
Last Year: 1993
Rarity: E
Issue Price: $ 1075
Last Retail Price: $ 1875

No.: 2138
Name: Friar Juniper
Height: 15.75
Current Status: Open issue,
  permanently retired
Original Issue Year: 1984
Last Year: 1993
Rarity: E
Issue Price: $ 160
Last Retail Price: $ 275

No.: 4908
Name: The Barrister
Height: 15.75
Current Status: Open issue,
  permanently retired
Original Issue Year: 1974
Last Year: 1985
Rarity: E
Issue Price: $ 100
High Auction Price: $ 425
LCS Estimate: $ 450

No.: 4729
Name: Hamlet
Height: 15.75
Current Status: Open issue,
  permanently retired
Original Issue Year: 1970
Last Year: 1980
Rarity: E
Issue Price: $ 85
High Auction Price: $ 750
LCS Estimate: $ 700

No.: 4602
Name: Doctor
Height: 15.75
Current Status: Open issue,
  permanently retired
Original Issue Year: 1969
Last Year: 1978
Rarity: E
Issue Price: $ 33
LCS Estimate: $ 290

No.: 4762
Name: Dentist
Height: 15.75
Current Status: Open issue,
  permanently retired
Original Issue Year: 1971
Last Year: 1978
Rarity: D
Issue Price: $ 30
High Auction Price: $ 425
LCS Estimate: $ 240

No.: 4924
Name: Languid Clown
Height: 16
Current Status: Open issue,
  permanently retired
Original Issue Year: 1974
Last Year: 1983
Rarity: E
Issue Price: $ 200
LCS Estimate: $ 1200

No.: 4581
Name: Harvester
Height: 16
Current Status: Open issue,
  permanently retired
Original Issue Year: 1969
Last Year: 1975
Rarity: D
Issue Price: $ 60
LCS Estimate: $ 650

No.: 5765
Name: Hats Off to Fun
Height: 16.25
Current Status: Open issue, currently
  active
Original Issue Year: 1991
Issue Price: $ 475
Current Retail Price: $ 495

No.: 1144
Name: Hamlet
Height: 16.5
Current Status: Limited edition, fully subscribed
Edition Limit: 750
Original Issue Year: 1971
Rarity: A
Issue Price: $ 125
High Auction Price: $ 2500

No.: 1343
Name: Wrath of Don Quixote
Height: 16.5
Current Status: Open issue, permanently retired
Original Issue Year: 1977
Last Year: 1990
Rarity: E
Issue Price: $ 250
High Auction Price: $ 850
LCS Estimate: $ 800

No.: 5251
Name: Torch Bearer
Height: 16.5
Current Status: Open issue, permanently retired
Original Issue Year: 1984
Last Year: 1988
Rarity: C
Issue Price: $ 100
High Auction Price: $ 475
LCS Estimate: $ 350

No.: 2084
Name: Don Quixote Dreaming
Height: 16.5
Current Status: Open issue, permanently retired
Original Issue Year: 1978
Last Year: 1985
Rarity: D
Issue Price: $ 550
LCS Estimate: $ 2250

No.: 4940
Name: Torch Bearer
Height: 16.5
Current Status: Open issue, permanently retired
Original Issue Year: 1974
Last Year: 1978
Rarity: C
Issue Price: $ 80
LCS Estimate: $ 725

No.: 5890
Name: The Way of the Cross
Height: 16.5
Current Status: Limited edition, currently active
Edition Limit: 2000
Original Issue Year: 1992
Issue Price: $ 975
Current Retail Price: $ 975

No.: 1741
Name: Columbus Reflecting
Height: 16.5
Current Status: Limited edition, currently active
Edition Limit: 1000
Original Issue Year: 1991
Issue Price: $ 1850
Current Retail Price: $ 1900

No.: 1432
Name: Columbus
Height: 16.5
Current Status: Limited edition, fully subscribed
Edition Limit: 1200
Original Issue Year: 1982
Rarity: A
Issue Price: $ 535
High Auction Price: $ 1500

No.: 5170
Name: Moses
Height: 16.5
Current Status: Open issue, currently active
Original Issue Year: 1982
Issue Price: $ 175
Current Retail Price: $ 340

No.: 1078
Name: Herald
Height: 17
Current Status: Open issue, permanently retired
Original Issue Year: 1969
Last Year: 1970
Rarity: E
Issue Price: $ 110
LCS Estimate: $ 880

No.: 4517
Name: Boy Student
Height: 17
Current Status: Open issue, permanently retired
Original Issue Year: 1969
Last Year: 1978
Rarity: E
Issue Price: $ 57.5
LCS Estimate: $ 520

No.: 1076
Name: Court Jester
Height: 17
Current Status: Open issue, permanently retired
Original Issue Year: 1969
Last Year: 1970
Rarity: B
Issue Price: $ 120
High Auction Price: $ 1450
LCS Estimate: $ 1440

No.: 341.13
Name: Troubador
Height: 17
Current Status: Very rare early issue
Original Issue Year: 1972
Last Year: Not available
Rarity: A
Issue Price: Not available

No.: 3532
Name: Plentitude
Height: 17.25
Current Status: Limited edition, fully subscribed
Edition Limit: 50
Original Issue Year: 1983
Issue Price: $ 1000

No.: 1027
Name: Clown with Concertina
Height: 17.75
Current Status: Open issue, permanently retired
Original Issue Year: 1969
Last Year: 1993
Rarity: F
Issue Price: $ 95
Last Retail Price: $ 735

No.: 1345
Name: Sacristan
Height: 18
Current Status: Open issue, permanently retired
Original Issue Year: 1978
Last Year: 1979
Rarity: B
Issue Price: $ 385
LCS Estimate: $ 2700

No.: 3510
Name: Othello
Height: 18
Current Status: Open issue, permanently retired
Original Issue Year: 1978
Last Year: 1981
Rarity: C
Issue Price: $ 450
LCS Estimate: $ 2200

No.: 5205
Name: Lamplighter
Height: 18.5
Current Status: Open issue, currently active
Original Issue Year: 1984
Issue Price: $ 170
Current Retail Price: $ 340

No.: 4699
Name: Troubador in Love
Height: 19
Current Status: Open issue,
  permanently retired
Original Issue Year: 1970
Last Year: 1975
Rarity: D
Issue Price: $ 60
LCS Estimate: $ 600

No.: 2121
Name: Harpooner
Height: 19.25
Current Status: Open issue,
  permanently retired
Original Issue Year: 1980
Last Year: 1988
Rarity: E
Issue Price: $ 820
High Auction Price: $ 1400
LCS Estimate: $ 1200

No.: 5058
Name: Clown Thinking
Height: 19.25
Current Status: Open issue,
  permanently retired
Original Issue Year: 1980
Last Year: 1985
Rarity: D
Issue Price: $ 290
High Auction Price: $ 425
LCS Estimate: $ 550

No.: 2188
Name: Invincible
Height: 19.25
Current Status: Limited edition,
  currently active
Edition Limit: 300
Original Issue Year: 1990
Issue Price: $ 1100
Current Retail Price: $ 1250

No.: 2065
Name: Chinese Farmer with Staff
Height: 19.75
Current Status: Open issue,
  permanently retired
Original Issue Year: 1977
Last Year: 1985
Rarity: E
Issue Price: $ 340
LCS Estimate: $ 1700

No.: 1615
Name: Jesus of the Rock
Height: 19.75
Current Status: Limited edition,
  currently active
Edition Limit: 1000
Original Issue Year: 1989
Issue Price: $ 1175
Current Retail Price: $ 1450

No.: 1768
Name: Traveller's Respite
Height: 19.75
Current Status: Open issue, currently active
Original Issue Year: 1993
Issue Price: $ 1825

No.: 3554
Name: Stormy Sea
Height: 20
Current Status: Open issue, currently active
Original Issue Year: 1982
Issue Price: $ 675
Current Retail Price: $ 1250

No.: 2139
Name: Aztec Indian
Height: 20.5
Current Status: Open issue, permanently retired
Original Issue Year: 1984
Last Year: 1988
Rarity: C
Issue Price: $ 552.50
High Auction Price: $ 600
LCS Estimate: $ 600

No.: 1740
Name: Columbus, Two Routes
Height: 20.5
Current Status: Limited edition, currently active
Edition Limit: 1000
Original Issue Year: 1991
Issue Price: $ 1500
Current Retail Price: $ 1575

No.: 2068
Name: Chinese Farmer
Height: 20.75
Current Status: Open issue, permanently retired
Original Issue Year: 1977
Last Year: 1985
Rarity: E
Issue Price: $ 340
High Auction Price: $ 1100
LCS Estimate: $ 1700

No.: 2136
Name: The King
Height: 20.75
Current Status: Open issue, permanently retired
Original Issue Year: 1984
Last Year: 1988
Rarity: C
Issue Price: $ 570
High Auction Price: $ 450
LCS Estimate: $ 600

No.: 1522
Name: I Am Don Quixote!
Height: 21.5
Current Status: Open issue, currently active
Original Issue Year: 1987
Issue Price: $ 2600
Current Retail Price: $ 3850

No.: 1486
Name: The New World
Height: 21.5
Current Status: Limited edition, currently active
Edition Limit: 4000
Original Issue Year: 1986
Issue Price: $ 700
Current Retail Price: $ 1300

No.: 4609
Name: Don Juan
Height: 22.5
Current Status: Open issue, permanently retired
Original Issue Year: 1969
Last Year: 1970
Rarity: B
Issue Price: $ 135
LCS Estimate: $ 1600

No.: 2135
Name: Mystical Joseph
Height: 22.75
Current Status: Open issue, permanently retired
Original Issue Year: 1984
Last Year: 1988
Rarity: C
Issue Price: $ 427.5
High Auction Price: $ 700
LCS Estimate: $ 600

No.: 2021
Name: Young Oriental Man
Height: 22.75
Current Status: Limited edition, fully subscribed
Edition Limit: 500
Original Issue Year: 1971
Issue Price: $ 500
High Auction Price: $ 1850

No.: 3017
Name: Muse
Height: 24.5
Current Status: Limited edition, permanently retired
Edition Limit: 300
Original Issue Year: 1988
Last Year: 1993
Rarity: D
Issue Price: $ 650
Last Retail Price: $ 875

No.: 3552
Name: Blue God
Height: 24.75
Current Status: Limited edition,
  currently active
Edition Limit: 1500
Original Issue Year: 1982
Issue Price: $ 900
Current Retail Price: $ 1500

No.: 2143
Name: Aztec Indian
Height: 25.5
Current Status: Open issue,
  permanently retired
Original Issue Year: 1984
Last Year: 1988
Rarity: C
Issue Price: $ 462.5
High Auction Price: $ 550
LCS Estimate: $ 550

No.: 2059
Name: Musketeer
Height: 27.25
Current Status: Open issue,
  permanently retired
Original Issue Year: 1974
Last Year: 1981
Rarity: D
Issue Price: $ 900
High Auction Price: $ 2200
LCS Estimate: $ 3000

No.: 3516
Name: Jesus Christ
Height: 42
Current Status: Open issue,
  permanently retired
Original Issue Year: 1978
Last Year: 1988
Rarity: E
Issue Price: $ 1050
High Auction Price: $ 1450
LCS Estimate: $ 1500

No.: 115.06
Name: Bouquet Ballerina
Height: 3
Current Status: Very rare early issue
Original Issue Year: 1958
Last Year: Not available
Rarity: A
Issue Price: Not available

No.: 215.08
Name: Sea Shell (White)
Height: 3
Current Status: Very rare early issue
Original Issue Year: 1956
Last Year: Not available
Rarity: A
Issue Price: Not available

No.: 96.06
Name: Ballerina Resting
Height: 3.25
Current Status: Very rare early issue
Original Issue Year: 1957
Last Year: Not available
Rarity: A
Issue Price: Not available

No.: 214.08
Name: Little Gypsy
Height: 3.25
Current Status: Very rare early issue
Original Issue Year: 1956
Last Year: Not available
Rarity: A
Issue Price: Not available

No.: 89.06
Name: Sea Shell
Height: 3.25
Current Status: Very rare early issue
Original Issue Year: 1956
Last Year: Not available
Rarity: A
Issue Price: Not available

No.: 5589
Name: Pretty Pose
Height: 3.5
Current Status: Open issue, permanently retired
Original Issue Year: 1989
Last Year: 1993
Rarity: D
Issue Price: $ 185
Current Retail Price: $ 230

No.: 112.06
Name: Girl with Open Book
Height: 3.75
Current Status: Very rare early issue
Original Issue Year: 1958
Last Year: Not available
Rarity: A
Issue Price: Not available

No.: 244.10
Name: Grace
Height: 4
Current Status: Very rare early issue
Original Issue Year: 1958
Last Year: Not available
Rarity: A
Issue Price: Not available

No.: 114.06
Name: Little Lady Sitting
Height: 4
Current Status: Very rare early issue
Original Issue Year: 1958
Last Year: Not available
Rarity: A
Issue Price: Not available

No.: 75.05
Name: Girl in the Garden
Height: 4.25
Current Status: Very rare early issue
Original Issue Year: 1956
Last Year: Not available
Rarity: A
Issue Price: Not available

No.: 5389
Name: Deep in Thought
Height: 4.25
Current Status: Open issue,
  permanently retired
Original Issue Year: 1986
Last Year: 1990
Rarity: C
Issue Price: $ 170
High Auction Price: $ 325
LCS Estimate: $ 340

No.: 5335
Name: Aerobics Floor Exerciser
Height: 4.25
Current Status: Open issue,
  permanently retired
Original Issue Year: 1985
Last Year: 1988
Rarity: C
Issue Price: $ 110
High Auction Price: $ 300
LCS Estimate: $ 330

No.: 5109
Name: Little Ballet Girl
Height: 4.25
Current Status: Open issue,
  permanently retired
Original Issue Year: 1982
Last Year: 1985
Rarity: C
Issue Price: $ 85
LCS Estimate: $ 340

No.: 5041
Name: Girl Kneeling and Tulips
Height: 4.25
Current Status: Open issue,
  permanently retired
Original Issue Year: 1980
Last Year: 1981
Rarity: B
Issue Price: $ 160
LCS Estimate: $ 900

No.: 5664
Name: Giddy Up
Height: 4.25
Current Status: Open issue, currently active
Original Issue Year: 1990
Issue Price: $ 190
Current Retail Price: $ 220

No.: 296.13
Name: Country Girl
Height: 4.5
Current Status: Very rare early issue
Original Issue Year: 1961
Last Year: Not available
Rarity: A
Issue Price: Not available

No.: 5748
Name: Shepherd Girl
Height: 4.75
Current Status: Open issue, currently active
Original Issue Year: 1991
Issue Price: $ 150
Current Retail Price: $ 155

No.: 5391
Name: A Time to Rest
Height: 4.75
Current Status: Open issue, permanently retired
Original Issue Year: 1986
Last Year: 1990
Rarity: C
Issue Price: $ 170
High Auction Price: $ 325
LCS Estimate: $ 340

No.: 5148
Name: "O" is for Olivia
Height: 4.75
Current Status: Open issue, permanently retired
Original Issue Year: 1982
Last Year: 1985
Rarity: C
Issue Price: $ 100
High Auction Price: $ 600
LCS Estimate: $ 450

No.: 5448
Name: Naptime
Height: 4.75
Current Status: Open issue, currently active
Original Issue Year: 1987
Issue Price: $ 135
Current Retail Price: $ 220

No.: 5372
Name: Lolita
Height: 4.75
Current Status: Open issue, permanently retired
Original Issue Year: 1986
Last Year: 1993
Rarity: D
Issue Price: $ 120
Last Retail Price: $ 200

No.: 5383
Name: Petite Maiden
Height: 4.75
Current Status: Open issue, permanently retired
Original Issue Year: 1986
Last Year: 1990
Rarity: C
Issue Price: $ 110
LCS Estimate: $ 220

No.: 5331
Name: Gymnast with Ring
Height: 4.75
Current Status: Open issue, permanently retired
Original Issue Year: 1985
Last Year: 1988
Rarity: C
Issue Price: $ 95
High Auction Price: $ 650
LCS Estimate: $ 450

No.: 5108
Name: Little Ballet Girl
Height: 4.75
Current Status: Open issue, permanently retired
Original Issue Year: 1982
Last Year: 1985
Rarity: C
Issue Price: $ 85
High Auction Price: $ 325
LCS Estimate: $ 340

No.: 5591
Name: Garden Treasures
Height: 4.75
Current Status: Open issue, permanently retired
Original Issue Year: 1989
Last Year: 1993
Rarity: D
Issue Price: $ 185
Last Retail Price: $ 230

No.: 1359
Name: Heather
Height: 5
Current Status: Open issue, permanently retired
Original Issue Year: 1978
Last Year: 1993
Rarity: D
Issue Price: $ 75
Last Retail Price: $ 170

No.: 305.13
Name: Young Valencian Girl
Height: 5
Current Status: Very rare early issue
Original Issue Year: 1963
Last Year: Not available
Rarity: A
Issue Price: Not available

No.: 213.08
Name: Young Ballerina
Height: 5
Current Status: Very rare early issue
Original Issue Year: 1956
Last Year: Not available
Rarity: A
Issue Price: Not available

No.: 2125
Name: Lost in Thought
Height: 5
Current Status: Open issue,
  permanently retired
Original Issue Year: 1981
Last Year: 1990
Rarity: E
Issue Price: $ 105
LCS Estimate: $ 210

No.: 1401
Name: Butterfly Girl
Height: 5
Current Status: Open issue,
  permanently retired
Original Issue Year: 1982
Last Year: 1988
Rarity: D
Issue Price: $ 210
High Auction Price: $ 750
LCS Estimate: $ 500

No.: 5919
Name: Rose Ballet
Height: 5
Current Status: Open issue, currently
  active
Original Issue Year: 1992
Issue Price: $ 210
Current Retail Price: $ 210

No.: 4855
Name: Death of the Swan
Height: 5
Current Status: Open issue, currently
  active
Original Issue Year: 1973
Issue Price: $ 45
Current Retail Price: $ 315

No.: 4855.30
Name: Death of the Swan (White)
Height: 5
Current Status: Open issue,
  permanently retired
Original Issue Year: 1983
Last Year: 1987
Rarity: C
Issue Price: $ 110
LCS Estimate: $ 320

No.: 5373
Name: Carmencita
Height: 5
Current Status: Open issue,
  permanently retired
Original Issue Year: 1986
Last Year: 1993
Rarity: E
Issue Price: $ 120
Last Retail Price: $ 200

No.: 5375
Name: Teresita
Height: 5
Current Status: Open issue,
  permanently retired
Original Issue Year: 1986
Last Year: 1993
Rarity: E
Issue Price: $ 120
Last Retail Price: $ 200

No.: 91.06
Name: Ballerina with Rose
Height: 5.25
Current Status: Very rare early issue
Original Issue Year: 1957
Last Year: Not available
Rarity: A
Issue Price: Not available

No.: 5869
Name: Fallas Queen
Height: 5.25
Current Status: Open issue, currently
  active
Original Issue Year: 1992
Issue Price: $ 420
Current Retail Price: $ 420

No.: 5243
Name: Happy Day Spanish
Height: 5.5
Current Status: Open issue,
  permanently retired
Original Issue Year: 1984
Last Year: 1986
Rarity: B
Issue Price: $ 185
LCS Estimate: $ 740

No.: 5244
Name: Best Wishes
Height: 5.5
Current Status: Open issue,
  permanently retired
Original Issue Year: 1984
Last Year: 1986
Rarity: B
Issue Price: $ 185
High Auction Price: $ 275
LCS Estimate: $ 350

No.: 1087
Name: Little Green-Grocer
Height: 5.5
Current Status: Open issue,
  permanently retired
Original Issue Year: 1969
Last Year: 1981
Rarity: E
Issue Price: $ 40
High Auction Price: $ 325
LCS Estimate: $ 320

No.: 5488
Name: Sandcastles
Height: 5.5
Current Status: Open issue,
  permanently retired
Original Issue Year: 1988
Last Year: 1993
Rarity: D
Issue Price: $ 160
Last Retail Price: $ 220

No.: 5943
Name: World of Fantasy
Height: 5.5
Current Status: Open issue, currently
  active
Original Issue Year: 1992
Issue Price: $ 295

No.: 5374
Name: Pepita
Height: 5.5
Current Status: Open issue,
  permanently retired
Original Issue Year: 1986
Last Year: 1993
Rarity: E
Issue Price: $ 120
Last Retail Price: $ 200

No.: 4523
Name: Little Girl with Slippers
Height: 5.5
Current Status: Open issue,
  permanently retired
Original Issue Year: 1969
Last Year: 1993
Rarity: F
Issue Price: $ 17
Last Retail Price: $ 100

No.: 5867
Name: Serene Valencian
Height: 5.5
Current Status: Open issue, currently
active
Original Issue Year: 1992
Issue Price: $ 365
Current Retail Price: $ 365

No.: 97.06
Name: Tying the Slipper
Height: 5.5
Current Status: Very rare early issue
Original Issue Year: 1957
Last Year: Not available
Rarity: A
Issue Price: Not available

No.: 5390
Name: Spanish Dancer
Height: 5.5
Current Status: Open issue,
permanently retired
Original Issue Year: 1986
Last Year: 1990
Rarity: C
Issue Price: $ 170
High Auction Price: $ 550
LCS Estimate: $ 525

No.: 5245
Name: A Thought for Today
Height: 5.5
Current Status: Open issue,
permanently retired
Original Issue Year: 1984
Last Year: 1986
Rarity: B
Issue Price: $ 180
High Auction Price: $ 325
LCS Estimate: $ 350

No.: 100.06
Name: Hawaiian
Height: 5.75
Current Status: Very rare early issue
Original Issue Year: 1959
Last Year: Not available
Rarity: A
Issue Price: Not available

No.: 98.06
Name: Vanity
Height: 5.75
Current Status: Very rare early issue
Original Issue Year: 1957
Last Year: Not available
Rarity: A
Issue Price: Not available

No.: 5496
Name: Recital
Height: 5.75
Current Status: Open issue, currently active
Original Issue Year: 1988
Issue Price: $ 190
Current Retail Price: $ 250

No.: 5868
Name: Loving Valencian
Height: 5.75
Current Status: Open issue, currently active
Original Issue Year: 1992
Issue Price: $ 365
Current Retail Price: $ 365

No.: 1403
Name: Butterfly Girl
Height: 6
Current Status: Open issue, permanently retired
Original Issue Year: 1982
Last Year: 1988
Rarity: D
Issue Price: $ 210
High Auction Price: $ 550
LCS Estimate: $ 500

No.: 2147
Name: Alida
Height: 6
Current Status: Open issue, currently active
Original Issue Year: 1984
Issue Price: $ 100
Current Retail Price: $ 165

No.: 2161
Name: Fruit Vendor
Height: 6
Current Status: Open issue, currently active
Original Issue Year: 1985
Issue Price: $ 120
Current Retail Price: $ 220

No.: 1178
Name: Girl with Accordion
Height: 6
Current Status: Open issue, permanently retired
Original Issue Year: 1971
Last Year: 1981
Rarity: E
Issue Price: $ 34
LCS Estimate: $ 240

No.: 4596
Name: Girl with Flower
Height: 6
Current Status: Open issue,
    permanently retired
Original Issue Year: 1969
Last Year: 1980
Rarity: E
Issue Price: $ 25
High Auction Price: $ 275
LCS Estimate: $ 200

No.: 5752
Name: Little Virgin
Height: 6
Current Status: Open issue, currently
    active
Original Issue Year: 1991
Issue Price: $ 295
Current Retail Price: $ 310

No.: 4671
Name: Virgin
Height: 6
Current Status: Open issue, currently
    active
Original Issue Year: 1969
Issue Price: $ 10
Current Retail Price: $ 70

No.: 5990
Name: Thoughtful Caress
Height: 6
Current Status: Open issue, currently
    active
Original Issue Year: 1993
Issue Price: $ 245

No.: 1356
Name: Phyllis
Height: 6
Current Status: Open issue,
    permanently retired
Original Issue Year: 1978
Last Year: 1993
Rarity: F
Issue Price: $ 75
Last Retail Price: $ 170

No.: 5499
Name: Pretty Ballerina
Height: 6
Current Status: Open issue, currently
    active
Original Issue Year: 1988
Issue Price: $ 190
Current Retail Price: $ 250

No.: 1479
Name: In a Tropical Garden
Height: 6
Current Status: Open issue, currently active
Original Issue Year: 1985
Issue Price: $ 230
Current Retail Price: $ 420

No.: 95.06
Name: Going For a Walk
Height: 6
Current Status: Very rare early issue
Original Issue Year: 1957
Last Year: Not available
Rarity: A
Issue Price: Not available

No.: 227.09
Name: Teenage Girl
Height: 6
Current Status: Very rare early issue
Original Issue Year: 1958
Last Year: Not available
Rarity: A
Issue Price: Not available

No.: 5412
Name: Isabel
Height: 6
Current Status: Open issue, permanently retired
Original Issue Year: 1987
Last Year: 1990
Rarity: C
Issue Price: $ 225
High Auction Price: $ 350
LCS Estimate: $ 375

No.: 5411
Name: Teresa
Height: 6
Current Status: Open issue, permanently retired
Original Issue Year: 1987
Last Year: 1990
Rarity: C
Issue Price: $ 225
High Auction Price: $ 350
LCS Estimate: $ 375

No.: 5336
Name: Aerobics Scissor Figure
Height: 6
Current Status: Open issue, permanently retired
Original Issue Year: 1985
Last Year: 1988
Rarity: C
Issue Price: $ 110
High Auction Price: $ 375
LCS Estimate: $ 330

No.: 5649
Name: Nothing To Do
Height: 6
Current Status: Open issue, currently
active
Original Issue Year: 1990
Issue Price: $ 190
Current Retail Price: $ 210

No.: 5588
Name: Blustery Day
Height: 6
Current Status: Open issue,
permanently retired
Original Issue Year: 1989
Last Year: 1993
Rarity: D
Issue Price: $ 185
Last Retail Price: $ 230

No.: 2162
Name: Fish Vendor
Height: 6
Current Status: Open issue, currently
active
Original Issue Year: 1985
Issue Price: $ 110
Current Retail Price: $ 195

No.: 2158
Name: Pensive Eskimo Girl
Height: 6.25
Current Status: Open issue, currently
active
Original Issue Year: 1985
Issue Price: $ 100
Current Retail Price: $ 180

No.: 5498
Name: Opening Night
Height: 6.25
Current Status: Open issue, currently
active
Original Issue Year: 1988
Issue Price: $ 190
Current Retail Price: $ 250

No.: 2146
Name: Desiree
Height: 6.25
Current Status: Open issue, currently
active
Original Issue Year: 1984
Issue Price: $ 100
Current Retail Price: $ 165

No.: 5071
Name: Nostalgia
Height: 6.25
Current Status: Open issue,
  permanently retired
Original Issue Year: 1980
Last Year: 1993
Rarity: E
Issue Price: $ 240
Current Retail Price: $ 310

No.: 110.06
Name: Louis XV Lady
Height: 6.25
Current Status: Very rare early issue
Original Issue Year: 1958
Last Year: Not available
Rarity: A
Issue Price: Not available

No.: 2144
Name: Leticia
Height: 6.25
Current Status: Open issue, currently
  active
Original Issue Year: 1984
Issue Price: $ 100
Current Retail Price: $ 165

No.: 2160
Name: Flower Vendor
Height: 6.25
Current Status: Open issue, currently
  active
Original Issue Year: 1985
Issue Price: $ 110
Current Retail Price: $ 190

No.: 2157
Name: Eskimo Girl with Cold Feet
Height: 6.25
Current Status: Open issue, currently
  active
Original Issue Year: 1985
Issue Price: $ 140
Current Retail Price: $ 250

No.: 5221
Name: Sweet Scent
Height: 6.25
Current Status: Open issue, currently
  active
Original Issue Year: 1984
Issue Price: $ 80
Current Retail Price: $ 130

No.: 108.06
Name: Kneeling Ballerina
Height: 6.25
Current Status: Very rare early issue
Original Issue Year: 1958
Last Year: Not available
Rarity: A
Issue Price: Not available

No.: 2145
Name: Gabriela
Height: 6.25
Current Status: Open issue, currently active
Original Issue Year: 1984
Issue Price: $ 100
Current Retail Price: $ 165

No.: 1402
Name: Butterfly Girl
Height: 6.25
Current Status: Open issue, permanently retired
Original Issue Year: 1982
Last Year: 1988
Rarity: D
Issue Price: $ 210
High Auction Price: $ 325
LCS Estimate: $ 500

No.: 5332
Name: Gymnast Balancing Ball
Height: 6.25
Current Status: Open issue, permanently retired
Original Issue Year: 1985
Last Year: 1988
Rarity: C
Issue Price: $ 95
High Auction Price: $ 325
LCS Estimate: $ 285

No.: 1023
Name: Girl with Daisy
Height: 6.25
Current Status: Open issue, permanently retired
Original Issue Year: 1969
Last Year: 1975
Rarity: D
Issue Price: $ 47.5
LCS Estimate: $ 520

No.: 5554
Name: Pretty and Prim
Height: 6.25
Current Status: Open issue, currently active
Original Issue Year: 1989
Issue Price: $ 215
Current Retail Price: $ 260

No.: 5782
Name: My Chores
Height: 6.25
Current Status: Open issue, currently active
Original Issue Year: 1991
Issue Price: $ 325
Current Retail Price: $ 335

No.: 1357
Name: Shelley
Height: 6.25
Current Status: Open issue, permanently retired
Original Issue Year: 1978
Last Year: 1993
Rarity: F
Issue Price: $ 75
Last Retail Price: $ 170

No.: 5678
Name: I Feel Pretty
Height: 6.25
Current Status: Open issue, currently active
Original Issue Year: 1990
Issue Price: $ 190
Current Retail Price: $ 220

No.: 5920
Name: Swan Ballet
Height: 6.25
Current Status: Open issue, currently active
Original Issue Year: 1992
Issue Price: $ 210
Current Retail Price: $ 210

No.: 5859
Name: At the Ball
Height: 6.25
Current Status: Open issue, currently active
Original Issue Year: 1992
Issue Price: $ 295
Current Retail Price: $ 295

No.: 1287
Name: Picking Flowers
Height: 6.25
Current Status: Open issue, currently active
Original Issue Year: 1974
Issue Price: $ 170
Current Retail Price: $ 420

No.: 5193
Name: Juanita
Height: 6.5
Current Status: Open issue, currently active
Original Issue Year: 1984
Issue Price: $ 80
Current Retail Price: $ 145

No.: 5699
Name: Sitting Pretty
Height: 6.5
Current Status: Open issue, currently active
Original Issue Year: 1990
Issue Price: $ 300
Current Retail Price: $ 330

No.: 5173
Name: Pondering
Height: 6.5
Current Status: Open issue, permanently retired
Original Issue Year: 1982
Last Year: 1993
Rarity: E
Issue Price: $ 300
Last Retail Price: $ 495

No.: 4534
Name: Madonna
Height: 6.5
Current Status: Open issue, currently active
Original Issue Year: 1969
Issue Price: $ 15
Current Retail Price: $ 80

No.: 5477
Name: Mary
Height: 6.5
Current Status: Open issue, currently active
Original Issue Year: 1988
Issue Price: $ 130
Current Retail Price: $ 160

No.: 5467
Name: May Flowers
Height: 6.5
Current Status: Open issue, currently active
Original Issue Year: 1988
Issue Price: $ 160
Current Retail Price: $ 195

No.: 5817
Name: Backstage Preparation
Height: 6.5
Current Status: Open issue, currently active
Original Issue Year: 1991
Issue Price: $ 490
Current Retail Price: $ 495

No.: 5548
Name: Pretty Posies
Height: 6.5
Current Status: Open issue, currently active
Original Issue Year: 1989
Issue Price: $ 425
Current Retail Price: $ 515

No.: 5895
Name: Bouquet of Blossoms
Height: 6.5
Current Status: Open issue, currently active
Original Issue Year: 1992
Issue Price: $ 295
Current Retail Price: $ 295

No.: 4841
Name: Valencian Girl
Height: 6.5
Current Status: Open issue, currently active
Original Issue Year: 1973
Issue Price: $ 35
Current Retail Price: $ 195

No.: 5363
Name: Still Life
Height: 6.5
Current Status: Open issue, currently active
Original Issue Year: 1986
Issue Price: $ 180
Current Retail Price: $ 350

No.: 84.06
Name: Balearic Lady
Height: 6.5
Current Status: Very rare early issue
Original Issue Year: 1956
Last Year: Not available
Rarity: A
Issue Price: Not available

No.: 201.07
Name: Lady From Menorca
Height: 6.5
Current Status: Very rare early issue
Original Issue Year: 1956
Last Year: Not available
Rarity: A
Issue Price: Not available

No.: 109.06
Name: Noble Lady
Height: 6.5
Current Status: Very rare early issue
Original Issue Year: 1958
Last Year: Not available
Rarity: A
Issue Price: Not available

No.: 83.06
Name: Regional Dress
Height: 6.5
Current Status: Very rare early issue
Original Issue Year: 1956
Last Year: Not available
Rarity: A
Issue Price: Not available
Comments: Handcrafted personally by
    Vicente Lladró

No.: 7620
Name: Best Friend
Height: 6.5
Current Status: Open issue, currently
    active
Original Issue Year: 1993
Last Year: 1993
Issue Price: $ 195
Comments: LCS Special

No.: 5333
Name: Gymnast Exercising with Ball
Height: 6.5
Current Status: Open issue,
    permanently retired
Original Issue Year: 1985
Last Year: 1988
Rarity: C
Issue Price: $ 95
High Auction Price: $ 325
LCS Estimate: $ 285

No.: 5105
Name: Little Ballet Girl
Height: 6.5
Current Status: Open issue,
    permanently retired
Original Issue Year: 1982
Last Year: 1985
Rarity: C
Issue Price: $ 85
LCS Estimate: $ 340

No.: 4907
Name: Admiration
Height: 6.5
Current Status: Open issue, permanently retired
Original Issue Year: 1974
Last Year: 1985
Rarity: E
Issue Price: $ 165
High Auction Price: $ 750
LCS Estimate: $ 700

No.: 1177
Name: Girl with Ball
Height: 6.5
Current Status: Open issue, permanently retired
Original Issue Year: 1971
Last Year: 1981
Rarity: E
Issue Price: $ 27.5
LCS Estimate: $ 190

No.: 4567
Name: Thinking Girl
Height: 6.5
Current Status: Open issue, permanently retired
Original Issue Year: 1969
Last Year: 1972
Rarity: C
Issue Price: $ 32.5
LCS Estimate: $ 400

No.: 5223
Name: Spring is Here
Height: 6.5
Current Status: Open issue, currently active
Original Issue Year: 1984
Issue Price: $ 80
Current Retail Price: $ 130

No.: 5107
Name: Little Ballet Girl
Height: 6.75
Current Status: Open issue, permanently retired
Original Issue Year: 1982
Last Year: 1985
Rarity: C
Issue Price: $ 85
LCS Estimate: $ 340

No.: 4713
Name: Girl Jewelry Dish
Height: 6.75
Current Status: Open issue, permanently retired
Original Issue Year: 1970
Last Year: 1978
Rarity: E
Issue Price: $ 30
LCS Estimate: $ 240

No.: 5792
Name: Reverent Moment
Height: 6.75
Current Status: Open issue, currently active
Original Issue Year: 1991
Issue Price: $ 295
Current Retail Price: $ 305

No.: 2210
Name: Lazy Day
Height: 6.75
Current Status: Open issue, currently active
Original Issue Year: 1991
Issue Price: $ 240
Current Retail Price: $ 250

No.: 1450
Name: Kiyoko
Height: 7
Current Status: Open issue, currently active
Original Issue Year: 1983
Issue Price: $ 235
Current Retail Price: $ 440

No.: 5590
Name: Spring Breeze
Height: 7
Current Status: Open issue, permanently retired
Original Issue Year: 1989
Last Year: 1993
Rarity: D
Issue Price: $ 185
Last Retail Price: $ 230

No.: 5647
Name: Sara
Height: 7
Current Status: Open issue, currently active
Original Issue Year: 1990
Issue Price: $ 200
Current Retail Price: $ 220

No.: 5211
Name: Angela
Height: 7
Current Status: Open issue, currently active
Original Issue Year: 1984
Issue Price: $ 105
Current Retail Price: $ 195

No.: 5212
Name: Evita
Height: 7
Current Status: Open issue, currently active
Original Issue Year: 1984
Issue Price: $ 105
Current Retail Price: $ 195

No.: 5222
Name: Pretty Pickings
Height: 7
Current Status: Open issue, currently active
Original Issue Year: 1984
Issue Price: $ 80
Current Retail Price: $ 130

No.: 226.09
Name: Girl with Flower Basket
Height: 7
Current Status: Very rare early issue
Original Issue Year: 1958
Last Year: Not available
Rarity: A
Issue Price: Not available

No.: 94.06
Name: Ballet
Height: 7
Current Status: Very rare early issue
Original Issue Year: 1957
Last Year: Not available
Rarity: A
Issue Price: Not available

No.: 2152
Name: Chinese Girl
Height: 7
Current Status: Open issue, permanently retired
Original Issue Year: 1985
Last Year: 1990
Rarity: D
Issue Price: $ 90
LCS Estimate: $ 180

No.: 7607
Name: Flower Song
Height: 7
Current Status: Limited edition, fully subscribed
Original Issue Year: 1988
Last Year: 1988
Rarity: B
Issue Price: $ 175
High Auction Price: $ 700
Comments: LCS Special

No.: 5106
Name: Little Ballet Girl
Height: 7
Current Status: Open issue,
  permanently retired
Original Issue Year: 1982
Last Year: 1985
Rarity: C
Issue Price: $ 85
High Auction Price: $ 450
LCS Estimate: $ 340

No.: 1083
Name: Girl with Doll
Height: 7
Current Status: Open issue,
  permanently retired
Original Issue Year: 1969
Last Year: 1985
Rarity: F
Issue Price: $ 14.50
High Auction Price: $ 350
LCS Estimate: $ 275

No.: 90.06
Name: Regional Dance
Height: 7.5
Current Status: Very rare early issue
Original Issue Year: 1956
Last Year: Not available
Rarity: A
Issue Price: Not available
Comments: Handcrafted personally by
  Vicente Lladró

No.: 1482
Name: Eve
Height: 7.5
Current Status: Open issue,
  permanently retired
Original Issue Year: 1985
Last Year: 1988
Rarity: C
Issue Price: $ 145
High Auction Price: $ 650
LCS Estimate: $ 600

No.: 1084
Name: Girl with Mother's Shoe
Height: .7.5
Current Status: Open issue,
  permanently retired
Original Issue Year: 1969
Last Year: 1985
Rarity: F
Issue Price: $ 14.50
High Auction Price: $ 150
LCS Estimate: $ 150

No.: 5073
Name: Country Flowers
Height: 7.5
Current Status: Open issue,
  permanently retired
Original Issue Year: 1980
Last Year: 1985
Rarity: D
Issue Price: $ 315
LCS Estimate: $ 1000

No.: 1082
Name: Girl Manicuring
Height: 7.5
Current Status: Open issue, permanently retired
Original Issue Year: 1969
Last Year: 1985
Rarity: F
Issue Price: $ 14.5
High Auction Price: $ 275
LCS Estimate: $ 225

No.: 5104
Name: Little Ballet Girl
Height: 7.5
Current Status: Open issue, permanently retired
Original Issue Year: 1982
Last Year: 1985
Rarity: C
Issue Price: $ 85
High Auction Price: $ 350
LCS Estimate: $ 325

No.: 5210
Name: Jolie
Height: 7.5
Current Status: Open issue, currently active
Original Issue Year: 1984
Issue Price: $ 105
Current Retail Price: $ 195

No.: 5608
Name: Baby Doll
Height: 7.5
Current Status: Open issue, currently active
Original Issue Year: 1989
Issue Price: $ 150
Current Retail Price: $ 175

No.: 5605
Name: Floral Treasures
Height: 7.5
Current Status: Open issue, currently active
Original Issue Year: 1989
Issue Price: $ 195
Current Retail Price: $ 240

No.: 4612
Name: Girl Singer
Height: 7.5
Current Status: Open issue, permanently retired
Original Issue Year: 1969
Last Year: 1979
Rarity: E
Issue Price: $ 14
LCS Estimate: $ 550

No.: 5543
Name: Hello, Flowers
Height: 7.5
Current Status: Open issue,
   permanently retired
Original Issue Year: 1989
Last Year: 1993
Rarity: D
Issue Price: $ 385
Last Retail Price: $ 485

No.: 4838
Name: Clean Up Time
Height: 7.5
Current Status: Open issue,
   permanently retired
Original Issue Year: 1973
Last Year: 1993
Rarity: F
Issue Price: $ 36
Last Retail Price: $ 170

No.: 1422
Name: Miss Valencia
Height: 7.5
Current Status: Open issue, currently
   active
Original Issue Year: 1982
Issue Price: $ 175
Current Retail Price: $ 335

No.: 4873
Name: Girl Kissing
Height: 7.5
Current Status: Open issue, currently
   active
Original Issue Year: 1974
Issue Price: $ 13
Current Retail Price: $ 85

No.: 1358
Name: Beth
Height: 7.5
Current Status: Open issue,
   permanently retired
Original Issue Year: 1978
Last Year: 1993
Rarity: F
Issue Price: $ 75
Last Retail Price: $ 170

No.: 4840
Name: Japanese Girl Flower
   Decorating
Height: 7.5
Current Status: Open issue, currently
   active
Original Issue Year: 1973
Issue Price: $ 90
Current Retail Price: $ 490

No.: 2156
Name: Arctic Winter
Height: 7.5
Current Status: Open issue, currently active
Original Issue Year: 1985
Issue Price: $ 75
Current Retail Price: $ 130

No.: 1448
Name: Yuki
Height: 7.5
Current Status: Open issue, currently active
Original Issue Year: 1983
Issue Price: $ 285
Current Retail Price: $ 525

No.: 5643
Name: Cathy
Height: 7.5
Current Status: Open issue, currently active
Original Issue Year: 1990
Issue Price: $ 200
Current Retail Price: $ 225

No.: 5192
Name: Lolita
Height: 7.5
Current Status: Open issue, currently active
Original Issue Year: 1984
Issue Price: $ 80
Current Retail Price: $ 145

No.: 212.08
Name: The Prom
Height: 7.75
Current Status: Very rare early issue
Original Issue Year: 1958
Last Year: Not available
Rarity: A
Issue Price: Not available

No.: 5149
Name: "U" is for Ursula
Height: 7.75
Current Status: Open issue, permanently retired
Original Issue Year: 1982
Last Year: 1985
Rarity: C
Issue Price: $ 100
High Auction Price: $ 600
LCS Estimate: $ 500

No.: 5147
Name: "I" is for Inez
Height: 7.75
Current Status: Open issue,
  permanently retired
Original Issue Year: 1982
Last Year: 1985
Rarity: C
Issue Price: $ 100
High Auction Price: $ 500
LCS Estimate: $ 500

No.: 1175
Name: Girl with Domino
Height: 7.75
Current Status: Open issue,
  permanently retired
Original Issue Year: 1971
Last Year: 1981
Rarity: E
Issue Price: $ 25
High Auction Price: $ 350
LCS Estimate: $ 250

No.: 1176
Name: Girl with Dice
Height: 7.75
Current Status: Open issue,
  permanently retired
Original Issue Year: 1971
Last Year: 1981
Rarity: E
Issue Price: $ 25
High Auction Price: $ 325
LCS Estimate: $ 250

No.: 1058
Name: Lupita
Height: 7.75
Current Status: Open issue,
  permanently retired
Original Issue Year: 1969
Last Year: 1980
Rarity: E
Issue Price: $ 28
LCS Estimate: $ 220

No.: 5218
Name: Autumn
Height: 7.75
Current Status: Open issue, currently
  active
Original Issue Year: 1984
Issue Price: $ 90
Current Retail Price: $ 165

No.: 2251
Name: Noella
Height: 7.75
Current Status: Open issue, currently
  active
Original Issue Year: 1993
Issue Price: $ 405

No.: 5648
Name: Courtney
Height: 7.75
Current Status: Open issue, currently active
Original Issue Year: 1990
Issue Price: $ 200
Current Retail Price: $ 220

No.: 5219
Name: Summer
Height: 7.75
Current Status: Open issue, currently active
Original Issue Year: 1984
Issue Price: $ 90
Current Retail Price: $ 165

No.: 5607
Name: Calling a Friend
Height: 7.75
Current Status: Open issue, currently active
Original Issue Year: 1989
Issue Price: $ 125
Current Retail Price: $ 155

No.: 5814
Name: Curtain Call
Height: 7.75
Current Status: Open issue, currently active
Original Issue Year: 1991
Issue Price: $ 490
Current Retail Price: $ 495

No.: 4871
Name: Girl with Guitar
Height: 7.75
Current Status: Open issue, currently active
Original Issue Year: 1974
Issue Price: $ 13
Current Retail Price: $ 85

No.: 4872
Name: Girl with Hands Akimbo
Height: 7.75
Current Status: Open issue, currently active
Original Issue Year: 1974
Issue Price: $ 13
Current Retail Price: $ 85

No.: 5606
Name: Quiet Evening
Height: 7.75
Current Status: Open issue,
  permanently retired
Original Issue Year: 1989
Last Year: 1993
Rarity: D
Issue Price: $ 125
Last Retail Price: $ 165

No.: 5747
Name: Mary
Height: 7.75
Current Status: Open issue, currently
  active
Original Issue Year: 1991
Issue Price: $ 275
Current Retail Price: $ 285

No.: 5646
Name: Cindy
Height: 8
Current Status: Open issue, currently
  active
Original Issue Year: 1990
Issue Price: $ 190
Current Retail Price: $ 210

No.: 5862
Name: Fragrant Bouquet
Height: 8
Current Status: Open issue, currently
  active
Original Issue Year: 1992
Issue Price: $ 350
Current Retail Price: $ 350

No.: 5644
Name: Susan
Height: 8
Current Status: Open issue, currently
  active
Original Issue Year: 1990
Issue Price: $ 190
Current Retail Price: $ 210

No.: 2093
Name: Girl with Crossed Arms
Height: 8
Current Status: Open issue, currently
  active
Original Issue Year: 1978
Issue Price: $ 90
Current Retail Price: $ 175

No.: 5487
Name: Ingenue
Height: 8
Current Status: Open issue, currently active
Original Issue Year: 1988
Issue Price: $ 110
Current Retail Price: $ 135

No.: 4504
Name: Seated Ballerina
Height: 8.25
Current Status: Open issue, permanently retired
Original Issue Year: 1969
Last Year: 1975
Rarity: D
Issue Price: $ 110
LCS Estimate: $ 1200

No.: 5501
Name: Time to Sew (Blue)
Height: 8.25
Current Status: Open issue, currently active
Original Issue Year: 1988
Issue Price: $ 90
Current Retail Price: $ 105

No.: 1172
Name: Girl with Flowers
Height: 8.25
Current Status: Open issue, permanently retired
Original Issue Year: 1971
Last Year: 1993
Rarity: F
Issue Price: $ 32.5
Last Retail Price: $ 295

No.: 5597
Name: Summer Soiree
Height: 8.25
Current Status: Open issue, currently active
Original Issue Year: 1989
Issue Price: $ 150
Current Retail Price: $ 175

No.: 5686
Name: On the Avenue
Height: 8.25
Current Status: Open issue, currently active
Original Issue Year: 1990
Issue Price: $ 275
Current Retail Price: $ 310

No.: 5687
Name: Afternoon Stroll
Height: 8.25
Current Status: Open issue, currently active
Original Issue Year: 1990
Issue Price: $ 275
Current Retail Price: $ 310

No.: 5598
Name: Bride's Maid
Height: 8.25
Current Status: Open issue, currently active
Original Issue Year: 1989
Issue Price: $ 150
Current Retail Price: $ 175

No.: 4868
Name: Girl with Candle
Height: 8.25
Current Status: Open issue, currently active
Original Issue Year: 1974
Issue Price: $ 13
Current Retail Price: $ 85

No.: 2076
Name: Lonely
Height: 8.25
Current Status: Open issue, currently active
Original Issue Year: 1978
Issue Price: $ 72.5
Current Retail Price: $ 175

No.: 5502
Name: Meditation (Blue)
Height: 8.25
Current Status: Open issue, currently active
Original Issue Year: 1988
Issue Price: $ 90
Current Retail Price: $ 105

No.: 93.06
Name: The Ball
Height: 8.25
Current Status: Very rare early issue
Original Issue Year: 1957
Last Year: Not available
Rarity: A
Issue Price: Not available

No.: 5501.30
Name: Time to Sew (White)
Height: 8.25
Current Status: Open issue,
  permanently retired
Original Issue Year: 1988
Last Year: 1991
Rarity: C
Issue Price: $ 90
LCS Estimate: $ 100

No.: 5502.30
Name: Meditation (White)
Height: 8.25
Current Status: Open issue,
  permanently retired
Original Issue Year: 1988
Last Year: 1991
Rarity: C
Issue Price: $ 90
LCS Estimate: $ 100

No.: 1478
Name: Hawaiian Dancer
Height: 8.25
Current Status: Open issue, currently
  active
Original Issue Year: 1985
Issue Price: $ 230
Current Retail Price: $ 420

No.: 1447
Name: Michiko
Height: 8.25
Current Status: Open issue, currently
  active
Original Issue Year: 1983
Issue Price: $ 235
Current Retail Price: $ 440

No.: 5429
Name: Happy Birthday
Height: 8.25
Current Status: Open issue, currently
  active
Original Issue Year: 1987
Issue Price: $ 100
Current Retail Price: $ 155

No.: 1418
Name: Flower Harmony
Height: 8.25
Current Status: Open issue, currently
  active
Original Issue Year: 1982
Issue Price: $ 130
Current Retail Price: $ 235

No.: 5599
Name: Coquette
Height: 8.25
Current Status: Open issue, currently active
Original Issue Year: 1989
Issue Price: $ 150
Current Retail Price: $ 175

No.: 2155
Name: Dozing
Height: 8.25
Current Status: Open issue, permanently retired
Original Issue Year: 1985
Last Year: 1990
Rarity: D
Issue Price: $ 110
High Auction Price: $ 275
LCS Estimate: $ 275

No.: 7604
Name: School Days
Height: 8.25
Current Status: Limited edition, fully subscribed
Original Issue Year: 1988
Last Year: 1988
Rarity: B
Issue Price: $ 125
High Auction Price: $ 900
Comments: LCS Special

No.: 7603
Name: Spring Bouquets
Height: 8.25
Current Status: Limited edition, fully subscribed
Original Issue Year: 1987
Last Year: 1987
Rarity: B
Issue Price: $ 125
High Auction Price: $ 1200
Comments: LCS Special

No.: 5145
Name: "A" is for Amy
Height: 8.25
Current Status: Open issue, permanently retired
Original Issue Year: 1982
Last Year: 1985
Rarity: C
Issue Price: $ 110
High Auction Price: $ 1300
LCS Estimate: $ 1200

No.: 5146
Name: "E" is for Ellen
Height: 8.25
Current Status: Open issue, permanently retired
Original Issue Year: 1982
Last Year: 1985
Rarity: C
Issue Price: $ 110
LCS Estimate: $ 450

No.: 4836
Name: Rosalinda
Height: 8.25
Current Status: Open issue, permanently retired
Original Issue Year: 1973
Last Year: 1983
Rarity: E
Issue Price: $ 66
High Auction Price: $ 475
LCS Estimate: $ 450

No.: 2089
Name: Girl in Rocking Chair
Height: 8.25
Current Status: Open issue, permanently retired
Original Issue Year: 1978
Last Year: 1981
Rarity: C
Issue Price: $ 235
High Auction Price: $ 375
LCS Estimate: $ 450

No.: 4720
Name: Girl with Tulips
Height: 8.25
Current Status: Open issue, permanently retired
Original Issue Year: 1970
Last Year: 1978
Rarity: E
Issue Price: $ 65
High Auction Price: $ 400
LCS Estimate: $ 450

No.: 1081
Name: Girl with Brush
Height: 8.5
Current Status: Open issue, permanently retired
Original Issue Year: 1969
Last Year: 1985
Rarity: F
Issue Price: $ 14.5
LCS Estimate: $ 120

No.: 5024
Name: Woman with Scarf
Height: 8.5
Current Status: Open issue, permanently retired
Original Issue Year: 1978
Last Year: 1985
Rarity: D
Issue Price: $ 140.90
LCS Estimate: $ 700

No.: 1148
Name: Girl Shampooing
Height: 8.5
Current Status: Open issue, permanently retired
Original Issue Year: 1971
Last Year: 1985
Rarity: E
Issue Price: $ 20
LCS Estimate: $ 120

No.: 1147
Name: Girl with Bonnet
Height: 8.5
Current Status: Open issue,
 permanently retired
Original Issue Year: 1971
Last Year: 1985
Rarity: E
Issue Price: $ 20
High Auction Price: $ 225
LCS Estimate: $ 200

No.: 5158
Name: A Stepping Time
Height: 8.5
Current Status: Open issue, currently
 active
Original Issue Year: 1982
Issue Price: $ 90
Current Retail Price: $ 175

No.: 5462
Name: Practice Makes Perfect
Height: 8.5
Current Status: Open issue, currently
 active
Original Issue Year: 1988
Issue Price: $ 375
Current Retail Price: $ 425

No.: 5604
Name: Spring Token
Height: 8.5
Current Status: Open issue, currently
 active
Original Issue Year: 1989
Issue Price: $ 175
Current Retail Price: $ 220

No.: 5662
Name: May Dance
Height: 8.5
Current Status: Open issue, currently
 active
Original Issue Year: 1990
Issue Price: $ 170
Current Retail Price: $ 185

No.: 5716
Name: Land of the Giants
Height: 8.5
Current Status: Open issue, currently
 active
Original Issue Year: 1990
Issue Price: $ 275
Current Retail Price: $ 300

No.: 4678
Name: Shepherdess with Basket
Height: 8.5
Current Status: Open issue, currently active
Original Issue Year: 1969
Issue Price: $ 13
Current Retail Price: $ 85

No.: 1376
Name: Watering the Flower Pots
Height: 8.5
Current Status: Open issue, permanently retired
Original Issue Year: 1978
Last Year: 1990
Rarity: E
Issue Price: $ 400
High Auction Price: $ 1100
LCS Estimate: $ 1100

No.: 5424
Name: Intermezzo
Height: 8.5
Current Status: Open issue, permanently retired
Original Issue Year: 1987
Last Year: 1990
Rarity: C
Issue Price: $ 325
High Auction Price: $ 575
LCS Estimate: $ 550

No.: 1481
Name: Sunning
Height: 8.5
Current Status: Open issue, permanently retired
Original Issue Year: 1985
Last Year: 1988
Rarity: C
Issue Price: $ 145
High Auction Price: $ 425
LCS Estimate: $ 435

No.: 5028
Name: Flowers in Pot
Height: 8.5
Current Status: Open issue, permanently retired
Original Issue Year: 1980
Last Year: 1985
Rarity: D
Issue Price: $ 325
High Auction Price: $ 550
LCS Estimate: $ 600

No.: 5026
Name: Planning the Day
Height: 8.5
Current Status: Open issue, permanently retired
Original Issue Year: 1980
Last Year: 1985
Rarity: D
Issue Price: $ 90
High Auction Price: $ 325
LCS Estimate: $ 360

No.: 1285
Name: My Goodness
Height: 8.5
Current Status: Open issue, currently active
Original Issue Year: 1974
Issue Price: $ 190
Current Retail Price: $ 395

No.: 1211
Name: Girl with Doll
Height: 8.5
Current Status: Open issue, permanently retired
Original Issue Year: 1972
Last Year: 1993
Rarity: F
Issue Price: $ 72
Last Retail Price: $ 440

No.: 5671
Name: Little Dutch Gardener
Height: 8.5
Current Status: Open issue, permanently retired
Original Issue Year: 1990
Last Year: 1993
Rarity: C
Issue Price: $ 400
Last Retail Price: $ 475

No.: 5685
Name: Promenade
Height: 8.5
Current Status: Open issue, currently active
Original Issue Year: 1990
Issue Price: $ 275
Current Retail Price: $ 310

No.: 5254
Name: Making Paella
Height: 8.5
Current Status: Open issue, permanently retired
Original Issue Year: 1984
Last Year: 1993
Rarity: E
Issue Price: $ 215
Last Retail Price: $ 400

No.: 5122
Name: August Moon
Height: 8.5
Current Status: Open issue, permanently retired
Original Issue Year: 1982
Last Year: 1993
Rarity: E
Issue Price: $ 185
Last Retail Price: $ 310

No.: 1284
Name: My Flowers
Height: 8.5
Current Status: Open issue, currently active
Original Issue Year: 1974
Issue Price: $ 200
Current Retail Price: $ 525

No.: 3512
Name: Girl with Two Pails
Height: 8.5
Current Status: Open issue, currently active
Original Issue Year: 1978
Issue Price: $ 140
Current Retail Price: $ 270

No.: 3025
Name: Resting Nude
Height: 8.5
Current Status: Limited edition, fully subscribed
Edition Limit: 200
Original Issue Year: 1991
Last Year: 1992   **Rarity:** B
Issue Price: $ 650
Current Retail Price: $ 650
High Auction Price: $ 650

No.: 5852
Name: Easter Bonnets
Height: 8.75
Current Status: Open issue, permanently retired
Original Issue Year: 1992
Last Year: 1993
Rarity: B
Issue Price: $ 265
Last Retail Price: $ 275

No.: 5663
Name: Spring Dance
Height: 8.75
Current Status: Open issue, currently active
Original Issue Year: 1990
Issue Price: $ 170
Current Retail Price: $ 185

No.: 5858
Name: Waiting to Dance
Height: 8.75
Current Status: Open issue, currently active
Original Issue Year: 1992
Issue Price: $ 295
Current Retail Price: $ 295

No.: 5775
Name: Gift of Beauty
Height: 8.75
Current Status: Open issue, currently active
Original Issue Year: 1991
Issue Price: $ 850
Current Retail Price: $ 890

No.: 5790
Name: Carefree
Height: 8.75
Current Status: Open issue, currently active
Original Issue Year: 1991
Issue Price: $ 300
Current Retail Price: $ 315

No.: 5176
Name: Lady Lying on Divan
Height: 9
Current Status: Open issue, permanently retired
Original Issue Year: 1982
Last Year: 1985
Rarity: C
Issue Price: $ 325
High Auction Price: $ 1150
LCS Estimate: $ 1100

No.: 5025
Name: A Clean Sweep
Height: 9
Current Status: Open issue, permanently retired
Original Issue Year: 1980
Last Year: 1985
Rarity: D
Issue Price: $ 100
LCS Estimate: $ 400

No.: 5134
Name: Lilly Football Player
Height: 9
Current Status: Open issue, permanently retired
Original Issue Year: 1982
Last Year: 1983
Rarity: B
Issue Price: $ 140
High Auction Price: $ 900
LCS Estimate: $ 865

No.: 5327
Name: Nippon Lady
Height: 9
Current Status: Open issue, currently active
Original Issue Year: 1985
Issue Price: $ 325
Current Retail Price: $ 520

No.: 5172
Name: Chinese in Market
Height: 9
Current Status: Open issue, currently active
Original Issue Year: 1982
Issue Price: $ 190
Current Retail Price: $ 365

No.: 5160
Name: Rhumba
Height: 9
Current Status: Open issue, currently active
Original Issue Year: 1982
Issue Price: $ 112.5
Current Retail Price: $ 180

No.: 3549
Name: Reposing
Height: 9
Current Status: Limited edition, fully subscribed
Edition Limit: 80
Original Issue Year: 1983
Issue Price: $ 425

No.: 5009
Name: Curious
Height: 9
Current Status: Open issue, currently active
Original Issue Year: 1978
Issue Price: $ 55
Current Retail Price: $ 130

No.: 1361
Name: Julia
Height: 9
Current Status: Open issue, permanently retired
Original Issue Year: 1978
Last Year: 1993
Rarity: F
Issue Price: $ 75
Last Retail Price: $ 170

No.: 4650
Name: Girl with Flowers
Height: 9
Current Status: Open issue, currently active
Original Issue Year: 1969
Issue Price: $ 16.5
Current Retail Price: $ 130

No.: 1480
Name: Aroma of the Islands
Height: 9
Current Status: Open issue, currently
  active
Original Issue Year: 1985
Issue Price: $ 260
Current Retail Price: $ 455

No.: 1360
Name: Laura
Height: 9
Current Status: Open issue,
  permanently retired
Original Issue Year: 1978
Last Year: 1993
Rarity: F
Issue Price: $ 75
Last Retail Price: $ 170

No.: 4972
Name: Sitting Girl with Lillies
Height: 9
Current Status: Open issue, currently
  active
Original Issue Year: 1977
Issue Price: $ 65
Current Retail Price: $ 165

No.: 5614
Name: Startled
Height: 9
Current Status: Open issue,
  permanently retired
Original Issue Year: 1989
Last Year: 1991
Rarity: B
Issue Price: $ 265
LCS Estimate: $ 265

No.: 5334
Name: Aerobics Pull-Ups
Height: 9
Current Status: Open issue,
  permanently retired
Original Issue Year: 1985
Last Year: 1988
Rarity: C
Issue Price: $ 110
High Auction Price: $ 500
LCS Estimate: $ 450

No.: 5164
Name: Cat Girl
Height: 9
Current Status: Open issue,
  permanently retired
Original Issue Year: 1982
Last Year: 1985
Rarity: C
Issue Price: $ 125
High Auction Price: $ 500
LCS Estimate: $ 500

No.: 1077
Name: Dutch Girl
Height: 9.25
Current Status: Open issue, permanently retired
Original Issue Year: 1969
Last Year: 1981
Rarity: E
Issue Price: $ 57.5
High Auction Price: $ 575
LCS Estimate: $ 550

No.: 5038
Name: Girl Bowing
Height: 9.25
Current Status: Open issue, permanently retired
Original Issue Year: 1979
Last Year: 1981
Rarity: B
Issue Price: $ 185
LCS Estimate: $ 1100

No.: 5857
Name: Grand Entrance
Height: 9.25
Current Status: Open issue, currently active
Original Issue Year: 1992
Issue Price: $ 265
Current Retail Price: $ 265

No.: 5789
Name: The Flirt
Height: 9.25
Current Status: Open issue, currently active
Original Issue Year: 1991
Issue Price: $ 185
Current Retail Price: $ 195

No.: 5709
Name: Between Classes
Height: 9.25
Current Status: Open issue, permanently retired
Original Issue Year: 1990
Last Year: 1993
Rarity: C
Issue Price: $ 280
Last Retail Price: $ 315

No.: 5894
Name: Precious Petals
Height: 9.5
Current Status: Open issue, currently active
Original Issue Year: 1991
Issue Price: $ 395
Current Retail Price: $ 395

No.: 1449
Name: Mayumi
Height: 9.5
Current Status: Open issue, currently active
Original Issue Year: 1983
Issue Price: $ 235
Current Retail Price: $ 440

No.: 5865
Name: Dressing for the Ballet
Height: 9.5
Current Status: Open issue, currently active
Original Issue Year: 1992
Issue Price: $ 395
Current Retail Price: $ 395

No.: 5490
Name: Floral Maria
Height: 9.5
Current Status: Open issue, currently active
Original Issue Year: 1988
Issue Price: $ 500
Current Retail Price: $ 610

No.: 2175
Name: Andean Country Girl
Height: 9.5
Current Status: Open issue, permanently retired
Original Issue Year: 1987
Last Year: 1990
Rarity: C
Issue Price: $ 230
High Auction Price: $ 325
LCS Estimate: $ 400

No.: 2171
Name: Island Girl
Height: 9.5
Current Status: Open issue, permanently retired
Original Issue Year: 1987
Last Year: 1990
Rarity: C
Issue Price: $ 150
High Auction Price: $ 375
LCS Estimate: $ 375

No.: 1354
Name: Girl Watering
Height: 9.5
Current Status: Open issue, permanently retired
Original Issue Year: 1978
Last Year: 1988
Rarity: E
Issue Price: $ 242.5
LCS Estimate: $ 725

No.: 5084
Name: A Good Book
Height: 9.5
Current Status: Open issue,
permanently retired
Original Issue Year: 1980
Last Year: 1985
Rarity: D
Issue Price: $ 175
LCS Estimate: $ 630

No.: 5162
Name: Mouse Girl
Height: 9.5
Current Status: Open issue,
permanently retired
Original Issue Year: 1982
Last Year: 1985
Rarity: C
Issue Price: $ 125
High Auction Price: $ 300
LCS Estimate: $ 400

No.: 5040
Name: Girl Walking
Height: 9.5
Current Status: Open issue,
permanently retired
Original Issue Year: 1979
Last Year: 1981
Rarity: B
Issue Price: $ 150
LCS Estimate: $ 900

No.: 4847
Name: Classic Dance
Height: 9.5
Current Status: Open issue,
permanently retired
Original Issue Year: 1973
Last Year: 1985
Rarity: E
Issue Price: $ 80
High Auction Price: $ 575
LCS Estimate: $ 500

No.: 1026
Name: Girl with Mandolin
Height: 9.5
Current Status: Open issue,
permanently retired
Original Issue Year: 1969
Last Year: 1978
Rarity: E
Issue Price: $ 52.5
LCS Estimate: $ 470

No.: 5708
Name: My First Class
Height: 9.5
Current Status: Open issue,
permanently retired
Original Issue Year: 1990
Last Year: 1993
Rarity: C
Issue Price: $ 280
Last Retail Price: $ 315

No.: 1304
Name: Valncian Girl with Flower
Height: 9.5
Current Status: Open issue, currently active
Original Issue Year: 1974
Issue Price: $ 200
Current Retail Price: $ 595

No.: 2170
Name: Andalucian Dancer
Height: 9.5
Current Status: Open issue, currently active
Original Issue Year: 1987
Issue Price: $ 225
Current Retail Price: $ 300

No.: 5321
Name: Parisian Lady
Height: 9.75
Current Status: Open issue, currently active
Original Issue Year: 1985
Issue Price: $ 192.5
Current Retail Price: $ 310

No.: 5027
Name: Flowers in Basket
Height: 9.75
Current Status: Open issue, currently active
Original Issue Year: 1979
Issue Price: $ 230
Current Retail Price: $ 450

No.: 5006
Name: Naughty Girl
Height: 9.75
Current Status: Open issue, currently active
Original Issue Year: 1978
Issue Price: $ 55
Current Retail Price: $ 130

No.: 54.04
Name: Valencian Girl
Height: 9.75
Current Status: Very rare early issue
Original Issue Year: 1957
Last Year: Not available
Rarity: A
Issue Price: Not available

No.: 5615
Name: Bathing Beauty
Height: 9.75
Current Status: Open issue,
   permanently retired
Original Issue Year: 1989
Last Year: 1991
Rarity: B
Issue Price: $ 265
LCS Estimate: $ 265

No.: 5064
Name: Dutchgirl, Hands Akimbo
Height: 9.75
Current Status: Open issue,
   permanently retired
Original Issue Year: 1980
Last Year: 1990
Rarity: E
Issue Price: $ 255
LCS Estimate: $ 525

No.: 5328
Name: Lady Equestrian
Height: 9.75
Current Status: Open issue,
   permanently retired
Original Issue Year: 1985
Last Year: 1988
Rarity: C
Issue Price: $ 160
High Auction Price: $ 375
LCS Estimate: $ 480

No.: 5063
Name: Dutchgirl with Braids
Height: 9.75
Current Status: Open issue,
   permanently retired
Original Issue Year: 1980
Last Year: 1985
Rarity: D
Issue Price: $ 265
LCS Estimate: $ 875

No.: 1387.30
Name: Mary (White)
Height: 9.75
Current Status: Open issue,
   permanently retired
Original Issue Year: 1983
Last Year: 1985
Rarity: B
Issue Price: $ 150
High Auction Price: $ 135
LCS Estimate: $ 300

No.: 4686
Name: Girl's Head with Cap
Height: 9.75
Current Status: Open issue,
   permanently retired
Original Issue Year: 1970
Last Year: 1984
Rarity: E
Issue Price: $ 25
LCS Estimate: $ 175

No.: 5039
Name: Candid
Height: 9.75
Current Status: Open issue,
  permanently retired
Original Issue Year: 1979
Last Year: 1981
Rarity: B
Issue Price: $ 145
LCS Estimate: $ 875

No.: 5010
Name: Prissy
Height: 9.75
Current Status: Open issue, currently
  active
Original Issue Year: 1978
Issue Price: $ 55
Current Retail Price: $ 130

No.: 5199
Name: Girl Graduate
Height: 9.75
Current Status: Open issue, currently
  active
Original Issue Year: 1984
Issue Price: $ 160
Current Retail Price: $ 260

No.: 5546
Name: Reaching the Goal
Height: 9.75
Current Status: Open issue, currently
  active
Original Issue Year: 1989
Issue Price: $ 215
Current Retail Price: $ 260

No.: 3547
Name: Reclining Nude
Height: 9.75
Current Status: Limited edition, fully
  subscribed
Edition Limit: 75
Original Issue Year: 1983
Issue Price: $ 650

No.: 1387
Name: Virgin Mary
Height: 9.75
Current Status: Open issue, currently
  active
Original Issue Year: 1981
Issue Price: $ 240
Current Retail Price: $ 365

No.: 5008
Name: The Dreamer
Height: 9.75
Current Status: Open issue, currently active
Original Issue Year: 1978
Issue Price: $ 55
Current Retail Price: $ 130

No.: 5707
Name: After School
Height: 9.75
Current Status: Open issue, permanently retired
Original Issue Year: 1990
Last Year: 1993
Rarity: C
Issue Price: $ 280
Last Retail Price: $ 315

No.: 5007
Name: Bashful
Height: 9.75
Current Status: Open issue, currently active
Original Issue Year: 1978
Issue Price: $ 55
Current Retail Price: $ 130

No.: 4828
Name: Cinderella
Height: 9.75
Current Status: Open issue, currently active
Original Issue Year: 1972
Issue Price: $ 47
Current Retail Price: $ 220

No.: 5127
Name: Girl Sitting with Roses
Height: 10
Current Status: Open issue, permanently retired
Original Issue Year: 1982
Last Year: 1985
Rarity: C
Issue Price: $ 255
LCS Estimate: $ 1000

No.: 5062
Name: Kristina
Height: 10
Current Status: Open issue, permanently retired
Original Issue Year: 1980
Last Year: 1985
Rarity: D
Issue Price: $ 255
High Auction Price: $ 375
LCS Estimate: $ 350

No.: 5118
Name: Girl in Green Dress
Height: 10
Current Status: Open issue,
  permanently retired
Original Issue Year: 1982
Last Year: 1985
Rarity: C
Issue Price: $ 170
LCS Estimate: $ 675

No.: 5092
Name: After the Dance
Height: 10
Current Status: Open issue,
  permanently retired
Original Issue Year: 1980
Last Year: 1983
Rarity: C
Issue Price: $ 165
High Auction Price: $ 350
LCS Estimate: $ 350

No.: 5095
Name: Ballet Bowing
Height: 10
Current Status: Open issue,
  permanently retired
Original Issue Year: 1980
Last Year: 1983
Rarity: C
Issue Price: $ 165
High Auction Price: $ 275
LCS Estimate: $ 300

No.: 5866
Name: Final Touches
Height: 10
Current Status: Open issue, currently
  active
Original Issue Year: 1992
Issue Price: $ 395
Current Retail Price: $ 395

No.: 1531
Name: Malia
Height: 10.25
Current Status: Open issue,
  permanently retired
Original Issue Year: 1987
Last Year: 1990
Rarity: C
Issue Price: $ 275
LCS Estimate: $ 550

No.: 5298
Name: Girl Sitting Under Trellis
Height: 10.25
Current Status: Open issue,
  permanently retired
Original Issue Year: 1985
Last Year: 1988
Rarity: C
Issue Price: $ 340
High Auction Price: $ 650
LCS Estimate: $ 750

No.: 5163
Name: Bunny Girl
Height: 10.25
Current Status: Open issue, permanently retired
Original Issue Year: 1982
Last Year: 1985
Rarity: C
Issue Price: $ 125
High Auction Price: $ 425
LCS Estimate: $ 450

No.: 5500
Name: Prayerful Moment (Blue)
Height: 10.25
Current Status: Open issue, currently active
Original Issue Year: 1988
Issue Price: $ 90
Current Retail Price: $ 105

No.: 4981
Name: Ironing Time
Height: 10.25
Current Status: Open issue, permanently retired
Original Issue Year: 1977
Last Year: 1985
Rarity: E
Issue Price: $ 80
High Auction Price: $ 375
LCS Estimate: $ 400

No.: 5119
Name: Girl in Bluish Dress
Height: 10.25
Current Status: Open issue, permanently retired
Original Issue Year: 1982
Last Year: 1985
Rarity: C
Issue Price: $ 170
LCS Estimate: $ 680

No.: 5120
Name: Girl in Pink Dress
Height: 10.25
Current Status: Open issue, permanently retired
Original Issue Year: 1982
Last Year: 1985
Rarity: C
Issue Price: $ 170
LCS Estimate: $ 680

No.: 4860
Name: Dutch Girl
Height: 10.25
Current Status: Open issue, permanently retired
Original Issue Year: 1974
Last Year: 1985
Rarity: E
Issue Price: $ 45
High Auction Price: $ 250
LCS Estimate: $ 250

No.: 1213
Name: Girl Offering Ceramic
Height: 10.25
Current Status: Open issue,
 permanently retired
Original Issue Year: 1972
Last Year: 1975
Rarity: C
Issue Price: $ 55
LCS Estimate: $ 550

No.: 1214
Name: Country Girl
Height: 10.25
Current Status: Open issue,
 permanently retired
Original Issue Year: 1972
Last Year: 1975
Rarity: C
Issue Price: $ 55
LCS Estimate: $ 550

No.: 1159
Name: Girl with Traditional Dress and
 Bowl
Height: 10.25
Current Status: Open issue,
 permanently retired
Original Issue Year: 1971
Last Year: 1975
Rarity: C
Issue Price: $ 40
LCS Estimate: $ 400

No.: 5011
Name: Coy
Height: 10.25
Current Status: Open issue, currently
 active
Original Issue Year: 1978
Issue Price: $ 55
Current Retail Price: $ 130

No.: 4989
Name: Sayonara
Height: 10.25
Current Status: Open issue, currently
 active
Original Issue Year: 1978
Issue Price: $ 125
Current Retail Price: $ 285

No.: 4851
Name: Golf Player Woman
Height: 10.25
Current Status: Open issue, currently
 active
Original Issue Year: 1973
Issue Price: $ 70
Current Retail Price: $ 245

No.: 5787
Name: Sophisticate
Height: 10.25
Current Status: Open issue, currently active
Original Issue Year: 1991
Issue Price: $ 185
Current Retail Price: $ 195

No.: 5324
Name: English Lady
Height: 10.25
Current Status: Open issue, currently active
Original Issue Year: 1985
Issue Price: $ 225
Current Retail Price: $ 390

No.: 1419
Name: A Barrow of Blossoms
Height: 10.25
Current Status: Open issue, currently active
Original Issue Year: 1982
Issue Price: $ 390
Current Retail Price: $ 650

No.: 1451
Name: Teruko
Height: 10.25
Current Status: Open issue, currently active
Original Issue Year: 1983
Issue Price: $ 235
Current Retail Price: $ 440

No.: 5322
Name: Viennese Lady
Height: 10.25
Current Status: Open issue, currently active
Original Issue Year: 1985
Issue Price: $ 160
Current Retail Price: $ 285

No.: 5788
Name: Talk of the Town
Height: 10.25
Current Status: Open issue, currently active
Original Issue Year: 1991
Issue Price: $ 185
Current Retail Price: $ 195

No.: 5551
Name: Call to Prayer (Blue)
Height: 10.25
Current Status: Open issue,
  permanently retired
Original Issue Year: 1989
Last Year: 1993
Rarity: D
Issue Price: $ 100
Last Retail Price: $ 135

No.: 5500.30
Name: Prayerful Moment (White)
Height: 10.25
Current Status: Open issue,
  permanently retired
Original Issue Year: 1988
Last Year: 1991
Rarity: C
Issue Price: $ 90
LCS Estimate: $ 100

No.: 5552.30
Name: Morning Chores (White)
Height: 10.25
Current Status: Open issue,
  permanently retired
Original Issue Year: 1989
Last Year: 1991
Rarity: B
Issue Price: $ 115
LCS Estimate: $ 115

No.: 5551.30
Name: Call to Prayer (White)
Height: 10.25
Current Status: Open issue,
  permanently retired
Original Issue Year: 1989
Last Year: 1991
Rarity: B
Issue Price: $ 100
LCS Estimate: $ 100

No.: 5065
Name: Ingrid
Height: 10.25
Current Status: Open issue,
  permanently retired
Original Issue Year: 1980
Last Year: 1990
Rarity: E
Issue Price: $ 370
High Auction Price: $ 900
LCS Estimate: $ 750

No.: 2172
Name: Island Beauty
Height: 10.25
Current Status: Open issue,
  permanently retired
Original Issue Year: 1987
Last Year: 1990
Rarity: C
Issue Price: $ 150
LCS Estimate: $ 300

No.: 1530
Name: Leilani
Height: 10.25
Current Status: Open issue,
permanently retired
Original Issue Year: 1987
Last Year: 1990
Rarity: C
Issue Price: $ 275
High Auction Price: $ 525
LCS Estimate: $ 550

No.: 5552
Name: Morning Chores (Blue)
Height: 10.25
Current Status: Open issue,
permanently retired
Original Issue Year: 1989
Last Year: 1993
Rarity: D
Issue Price: $ 115
Last Retail Price: $ 140

No.: 5323
Name: Milanese Lady
Height: 10.25
Current Status: Open issue, currently
active
Original Issue Year: 1985
Issue Price: $ 180
Current Retail Price: $ 325

No.: 5957
Name: The Glass Slipper
Height: 10.25
Current Status: Open issue, currently
active
Original Issue Year: 1993
Issue Price: $ 475

No.: 5054
Name: Little Senorita
Height: 10.5
Current Status: Open issue,
permanently retired
Original Issue Year: 1980
Last Year: 1985
Rarity: D
Issue Price: $ 235
High Auction Price: $ 500
LCS Estimate: $ 450

No.: 1379
Name: Debbie and Her Doll
Height: 10.5
Current Status: Open issue,
permanently retired
Original Issue Year: 1978
Last Year: 1985
Rarity: D
Issue Price: $ 215
High Auction Price: $ 1000
LCS Estimate: $ 700

No.: 5053
Name: Festival Time
Height: 10.5
Current Status: Open issue,
  permanently retired
Original Issue Year: 1980
Last Year: 1985
Rarity: D
Issue Price: $ 250
High Auction Price: $ 450
LCS Estimate: $ 500

No.: 5079
Name: Woman Painting Vase
Height: 10.5
Current Status: Open issue,
  permanently retired
Original Issue Year: 1980
Last Year: 1985
Rarity: D
Issue Price: $ 300
LCS Estimate: $ 1100

No.: 4912
Name: Young Lady in Trouble
Height: 10.5
Current Status: Open issue,
  permanently retired
Original Issue Year: 1974
Last Year: 1985
Rarity: E
Issue Price: $ 110
LCS Estimate: $ 650

No.: 5121
Name: Girl in Blue Dress
Height: 10.5
Current Status: Open issue,
  permanently retired
Original Issue Year: 1982
Last Year: 1985
Rarity: C
Issue Price: $ 170
LCS Estimate: $ 680

No.: 5093
Name: A Dancing Partner
Height: 10.5
Current Status: Open issue,
  permanently retired
Original Issue Year: 1980
Last Year: 1983
Rarity: C
Issue Price: $ 165
High Auction Price: $ 600
LCS Estimate: $ 500

No.: 4987
Name: Sweet Girl
Height: 10.5
Current Status: Open issue,
  permanently retired
Original Issue Year: 1978
Last Year: 1980
Rarity: B
Issue Price: $ 110
High Auction Price: $ 425
LCS Estimate: $ 400

No.: 4985
Name: Mimi
Height: 10.5
Current Status: Open issue,
  permanently retired
Original Issue Year: 1978
Last Year: 1980
Rarity: B
Issue Price: $ 110
LCS Estimate: $ 660

No.: 1216
Name: Hindu Dancer
Height: 10.5
Current Status: Open issue,
  permanently retired
Original Issue Year: 1972
Last Year: 1975
Rarity: C
Issue Price: $ 60
LCS Estimate: $ 600

No.: 4799
Name: Japanese Woman
Height: 10.5
Current Status: Open issue,
  permanently retired
Original Issue Year: 1972
Last Year: 1975
Rarity: C
Issue Price: $ 45
LCS Estimate: $ 450

No.: 1215
Name: Hindu Goddess
Height: 10.5
Current Status: Open issue,
  permanently retired
Original Issue Year: 1972
Last Year: 1975
Rarity: C
Issue Price: $ 110
LCS Estimate: $ 1100

No.: 1173
Name: Sultanita
Height: 10.5
Current Status: Open issue,
  permanently retired
Original Issue Year: 1971
Last Year: 1975
Rarity: C
Issue Price: $ 40
LCS Estimate: $ 400

No.: 3000
Name: Dawn
Height: 10.5
Current Status: Limited edition,
  currently active
Edition Limit: 300
Original Issue Year: 1983
Issue Price: $ 325
Current Retail Price: $ 525

No.: 3536
Name: Relaxation
Height: 10.5
Current Status: Limited edition, fully subscribed
Edition Limit: 100
Original Issue Year: 1983
Issue Price: $ 525

No.: 2154
Name: Hawaian Flower Vendor
Height: 10.5
Current Status: Open issue, currently active
Original Issue Year: 1985
Issue Price: $ 245
Current Retail Price: $ 400

No.: 1395
Name: Full of Mischief
Height: 10.5
Current Status: Open issue, currently active
Original Issue Year: 1982
Issue Price: $ 420
Current Retail Price: $ 730

No.: 5903
Name: Down the Aisle
Height: 10.5
Current Status: Open issue, currently active
Original Issue Year: 1992
Issue Price: $ 295
Current Retail Price: $ 295

No.: 5550
Name: Serene Moment (Blue)
Height: 10.5
Current Status: Open issue, permanently retired
Original Issue Year: 1989
Last Year: 1993
Rarity: D
Issue Price: $ 115
Last Retail Price: $ 150

No.: 5816
Name: Prima Ballerina
Height: 10.5
Current Status: Open issue, currently active
Original Issue Year: 1991
Issue Price: $ 490
Current Retail Price: $ 495

No.: 1396
Name: Appreciation
Height: 10.5
Current Status: Open issue, currently active
Original Issue Year: 1982
Issue Price: $ 420
Current Retail Price: $ 730

No.: 5550.30
Name: Serene Moment (White)
Height: 10.5
Current Status: Open issue, permanently retired
Original Issue Year: 1989
Last Year: 1991
Rarity: B
Issue Price: $ 115
LCS Estimate: $ 115

No.: 1399
Name: Dutch Girl
Height: 10.5
Current Status: Open issue, permanently retired
Original Issue Year: 1982
Last Year: 1988
Rarity: D
Issue Price: $ 750
High Auction Price: $ 700
LCS Estimate: $ 750

No.: 1417
Name: Nature's Bounty
Height: 10.5
Current Status: Open issue, currently active
Original Issue Year: 1982
Issue Price: $ 160
Current Retail Price: $ 295

No.: 5141
Name: Balloon Seller
Height: 10.5
Current Status: Open issue, currently active
Original Issue Year: 1982
Issue Price: $ 145
Current Retail Price: $ 240

No.: 5818
Name: On Her Toes
Height: 10.5
Current Status: Open issue, currently active
Original Issue Year: 1991
Issue Price: $ 490
Current Retail Price: $ 495

No.: 1397
Name: Second Thoughts
Height: 10.5
Current Status: Open issue, currently active
Original Issue Year: 1982
Issue Price: $ 420
Current Retail Price: $ 730

No.: 1416
Name: Budding Blossoms
Height: 10.5
Current Status: Open issue, currently active
Original Issue Year: 1982
Issue Price: $ 140
Current Retail Price: $ 260

No.: 1398
Name: Reverie
Height: 10.5
Current Status: Open issue, currently active
Original Issue Year: 1982
Issue Price: $ 490
Current Retail Price: $ 860

No.: 1374
Name: Waiting in the Park
Height: 10.75
Current Status: Open issue, permanently retired
Original Issue Year: 1978
Last Year: 1993
Rarity: F
Issue Price: $ 235
Last Retail Price: $ 450

No.: 1313
Name: Exquisite Scent
Height: 11
Current Status: Open issue, permanently retired
Original Issue Year: 1974
Last Year: 1990
Rarity: F
Issue Price: $ 200
High Auction Price: $ 650
LCS Estimate: $ 600

No.: 1512
Name: Hawaiian Beauty
Height: 11
Current Status: Open issue, permanently retired
Original Issue Year: 1987
Last Year: 1990
Rarity: C
Issue Price: $ 575
High Auction Price: $ 725
LCS Estimate: $ 700

No.: 1427
Name: Female Tennis Player
Height: 11
Current Status: Open issue,
   permanently retired
Original Issue Year: 1982
Last Year: 1988
Rarity: D
Issue Price: $ 200
LCS Estimate: $ 300

No.: 1378
Name: Suzy and Her Doll
Height: 11
Current Status: Open issue,
   permanently retired
Original Issue Year: 1978
Last Year: 1985
Rarity: D
Issue Price: $ 215
High Auction Price: $ 650
LCS Estimate: $ 700

No.: 5094
Name: Ballet First Step
Height: 11
Current Status: Open issue,
   permanently retired
Original Issue Year: 1980
Last Year: 1983
Rarity: C
Issue Price: $ 165
High Auction Price: $ 350
LCS Estimate: $ 350

No.: 4978
Name: In the Garden
Height: 11
Current Status: Open issue,
   permanently retired
Original Issue Year: 1977
Last Year: 1981
Rarity: C
Issue Price: $ 160
LCS Estimate: $ 1000

No.: 4939
Name: Milk Maid
Height: 11
Current Status: Open issue,
   permanently retired
Original Issue Year: 1976
Last Year: 1981
Rarity: D
Issue Price: $ 70
High Auction Price: $ 350
LCS Estimate: $ 350

No.: 4689
Name: Gothic Queen
Height: 11
Current Status: Open issue,
   permanently retired
Original Issue Year: 1970
Last Year: 1975
Rarity: D
Issue Price: $ 20
LCS Estimate: $ 200

No.: 2003
Name: Gothic Queen
Height: 11
Current Status: Open issue, permanently retired
Original Issue Year: 1970
Last Year: 1975
Rarity: D
Issue Price: $ 25
LCS Estimate: $ 250

No.: 1158
Name: Shepherdess with Traditional Dress
Height: 11
Current Status: Open issue, permanently retired
Original Issue Year: 1971
Last Year: 1975
Rarity: C
Issue Price: $ 35
LCS Estimate: $ 350

No.: 4865
Name: Embroiderer
Height: 11
Current Status: Open issue, currently active
Original Issue Year: 1974
Issue Price: $ 115
Current Retail Price: $ 615

No.: 5275
Name: Weary Ballerina
Height: 11
Current Status: Open issue, currently active
Original Issue Year: 1985
Issue Price: $ 175
Current Retail Price: $ 285

No.: 5030
Name: Girl and Basket of Flowers
Height: 11
Current Status: Open issue, currently active
Original Issue Year: 1979
Issue Price: $ 360
Current Retail Price: $ 670

No.: 5044
Name: Pulling Doll's Carriage
Height: 11
Current Status: Open issue, currently active
Original Issue Year: 1980
Issue Price: $ 115
Current Retail Price: $ 210

No.: 111.06
Name: Lady With Umbrella
Height: 11
Current Status: Very rare early issue
Original Issue Year: 1958
Last Year: Not available
Rarity: A
Issue Price: Not available

No.: 1532
Name: Lehua
Height: 11
Current Status: Open issue,
   permanently retired
Original Issue Year: 1987
Last Year: 1990
Rarity: C
Issue Price: $ 275
High Auction Price: $ 575
LCS Estimate: $ 550

No.: 302.13
Name: Virgin
Height: 11.25
Current Status: Very rare early issue
Original Issue Year: 1958
Last Year: Not available
Rarity: A
Issue Price: Not available

No.: 5045
Name: Belinda with Her Doll
Height: 11.25
Current Status: Open issue, currently
   active
Original Issue Year: 1980
Issue Price: $ 115
Current Retail Price: $ 195

No.: 2008.30
Name: Eskimo Girl
Height: 11.5
Current Status: Open issue,
   permanently retired
Original Issue Year: 1970
Last Year: 1990
Rarity: F
Issue Price: $ 27.5
High Auction Price: $ 275
LCS Estimate: $ 225

No.: 1529
Name: Momi
Height: 11.5
Current Status: Open issue,
   permanently retired
Original Issue Year: 1987
Last Year: 1990
Rarity: C
Issue Price: $ 275
LCS Estimate: $ 550

No.: 5240
Name: Lady from Majorca
Height: 11.5
Current Status: Open issue,
  permanently retired
Original Issue Year: 1984
Last Year: 1990
Rarity: D
Issue Price: $ 120
High Auction Price: $ 425
LCS Estimate: $ 400

No.: 5126
Name: Medieval Lady
Height: 11.5
Current Status: Open issue,
  permanently retired
Original Issue Year: 1982
Last Year: 1990
Rarity: E
Issue Price: $ 185
High Auction Price: $ 750
LCS Estimate: $ 650

No.: 2008
Name: Eskimo Girl
Height: 11.5
Current Status: Open issue,
  permanently retired
Original Issue Year: 1970
Last Year: 1990
Rarity: F
Issue Price: $ 30
LCS Estimate: $ 120

No.: 1339
Name: Girl with Watering Can
Height: 11.5
Current Status: Open issue,
  permanently retired
Original Issue Year: 1977
Last Year: 1988
Rarity: E
Issue Price: $ 162.5
High Auction Price: $ 550
LCS Estimate: $ 500

No.: 4665
Name: Girl with Basket
Height: 11.5
Current Status: Open issue,
  permanently retired
Original Issue Year: 1969
Last Year: 1979
Rarity: E
Issue Price: $ 50
LCS Estimate: $ 450

No.: 1160
Name: Shephrdess with Traditional
  Dress
Height: 11.5
Current Status: Open issue,
  permanently retired
Original Issue Year: 1971
Last Year: 1975
Rarity: C
Issue Price: $ 35
High Auction Price: $ 400
LCS Estimate: $ 750

No.: 4988
Name: Oriental Spring
Height: 11.5
Current Status: Open issue, currently active
Original Issue Year: 1978
Issue Price: $ 125
Current Retail Price: $ 310

No.: 5050
Name: Dancer
Height: 11.5
Current Status: Open issue, currently active
Original Issue Year: 1979
Issue Price: $ 85
Current Retail Price: $ 185

No.: 4990
Name: Chrysanthemum
Height: 11.5
Current Status: Open issue, currently active
Original Issue Year: 1978
Issue Price: $ 125
Current Retail Price: $ 295

No.: 1601
Name: Rock Nymph
Height: 11.5
Current Status: Open issue, currently active
Original Issue Year: 1989
Issue Price: $ 665
Current Retail Price: $ 785

No.: 5660
Name: Sunning in Ipanema
Height: 11.5
Current Status: Open issue, permanently retired
Original Issue Year: 1990
Last Year: 1993
Rarity: C
Issue Price: $ 370
Last Retail Price: $ 420

No.: 5081
Name: Girl Pottery Seller
Height: 11.75
Current Status: Open issue, permanently retired
Original Issue Year: 1980
Last Year: 1985
Rarity: D
Issue Price: $ 300
High Auction Price: $ 675
LCS Estimate: $ 750

No.: 5061
Name: Girl Bending
Height: 11.75
Current Status: Open issue,
  permanently retired
Original Issue Year: 1980
Last Year: 1983
Rarity: C
Issue Price: $ 370
High Auction Price: $ 650
LCS Estimate: $ 650

No.: 4842
Name: Viola Lesson
Height: 11.75
Current Status: Open issue,
  permanently retired
Original Issue Year: 1973
Last Year: 1981
Rarity: E
Issue Price: $ 66
LCS Estimate: $ 460

No.: 1271
Name: Pleasure
Height: 11.75
Current Status: Open issue,
  permanently retired
Original Issue Year: 1974
Last Year: 1981
Rarity: D
Issue Price: $ 65
LCS Estimate: $ 450

No.: 1242
Name: Lady at Dressing Table
Height: 11.75
Current Status: Open issue,
  permanently retired
Original Issue Year: 1973
Last Year: 1978
Rarity: D
Issue Price: $ 320
High Auction Price: $ 3750
LCS Estimate: $ 2880

No.: 4645
Name: Meditating
Height: 11.75
Current Status: Open issue,
  permanently retired
Original Issue Year: 1969
Last Year: 1975
Rarity: D
Issue Price: $ 50
LCS Estimate: $ 550

No.: 1236
Name: Disciple of Buddha
Height: 11.75
Current Status: Open issue,
  permanently retired
Original Issue Year: 1972
Last Year: 1975
Rarity: C
Issue Price: $ 70
LCS Estimate: $ 700

No.: 5815
Name: In Full Relave
Height: 11.75
Current Status: Open issue, currently active
Original Issue Year: 1991
Issue Price: $ 490
Current Retail Price: $ 520

No.: 4991
Name: Madame Butterfly
Height: 11.75
Current Status: Open issue, currently active
Original Issue Year: 1978
Issue Price: $ 125
Current Retail Price: $ 285

No.: 5439
Name: The Black Bride
Height: 11.75
Current Status: Open issue, currently active
Original Issue Year: 1987
Issue Price: $ 250
Current Retail Price: $ 375

No.: 5898
Name: Spring Splendor
Height: 11.75
Current Status: Open issue, currently active
Original Issue Year: 1992
Issue Price: $ 440
Current Retail Price: $ 440

No.: 3022
Name: Daydreaming
Height: 11.75
Current Status: Limited edition, currently active
Edition Limit: 500
Original Issue Year: 1990
Issue Price: $ 600
Current Retail Price: $ 730

No.: 1381
Name: Medieval Girl
Height: 11.75
Current Status: Open issue, permanently retired
Original Issue Year: 1978
Last Year: 1985
Rarity: D
Issue Price: $ 195
LCS Estimate: $ 975

No.: 2220
Name: Free Spirit
Height: 12
Current Status: Open issue, currently active
Original Issue Year: 1992
Issue Price: $ 235
Current Retail Price: $ 235

No.: 5773
Name: Graceful Offering
Height: 12
Current Status: Open issue, currently active
Original Issue Year: 1991
Issue Price: $ 850
Current Retail Price: $ 885

No.: 2221
Name: Spring Beauty
Height: 12
Current Status: Open issue, currently active
Original Issue Year: 1992
Issue Price: $ 285
Current Retail Price: $ 285

No.: 3507
Name: Girl Carrying Flower
Height: 12.25
Current Status: Open issue, permanently retired
Original Issue Year: 1978
Last Year: 1988
Rarity: E
Issue Price: $ 230
High Auction Price: $ 350
LCS Estimate: $ 500

No.: 1380
Name: Cathy and Her Doll
Height: 12.25
Current Status: Open issue, permanently retired
Original Issue Year: 1978
Last Year: 1985
Rarity: D
Issue Price: $ 215
High Auction Price: $ 775
LCS Estimate: $ 700

No.: 4979
Name: Milkmaid with Wheelbarrow
Height: 12.25
Current Status: Open issue, permanently retired
Original Issue Year: 1977
Last Year: 1981
Rarity: C
Issue Price: $ 220
LCS Estimate: $ 1300

No.: 1125
Name: Pelusa
Height: 12.25
Current Status: Open issue,
  permanently retired
Original Issue Year: 1971
Last Year: 1978
Rarity: D
Issue Price: $ 70
LCS Estimate: $ 560

No.: 2025
Name: Oriental Dancer
Height: 12.25
Current Status: Open issue,
  permanently retired
Original Issue Year: 1971
Last Year: 1975
Rarity: C
Issue Price: $ 45
LCS Estimate: $ 450

No.: 4520
Name: Flamenco Dancer
Height: 12.25
Current Status: Open issue,
  permanently retired
Original Issue Year: 1969
Last Year: 1970
Rarity: B
Issue Price: $ 70
LCS Estimate: $ 850

No.: 5682
Name: Breezy Afternoon
Height: 12.25
Current Status: Open issue, currently
  active
Original Issue Year: 1990
Issue Price: $ 180
Current Retail Price: $ 195

No.: 4807
Name: Geisha
Height: 12.25
Current Status: Open issue,
  permanently retired
Original Issue Year: 1972
Last Year: 1993
Rarity: F
Issue Price: $ 190
Last Retail Price: $ 440

No.: 5171
Name: Our Lady with Flowers
Height: 12.25
Current Status: Open issue, currently
  active
Original Issue Year: 1982
Issue Price: $ 172.5
Current Retail Price: $ 295

No.: 3539
Name: Daintiness
Height: 12.25
Current Status: Limited edition, fully
  subscribed
Edition Limit: 100
Original Issue Year: 1983
Issue Price: $ 1000

No.: 4879
Name: Aranjuez Little Lady
Height: 12.25
Current Status: Open issue, currently
  active
Original Issue Year: 1974
Issue Price: $ 48
Current Retail Price: $ 285

No.: 5003
Name: A Sunny Day
Height: 12.25
Current Status: Open issue,
  permanently retired
Original Issue Year: 1978
Last Year: 1993
Rarity: F
Issue Price: $ 192.5
Last Retail Price: $ 360

No.: 5297
Name: Girl Standing Under Trellis
Height: 12.25
Current Status: Open issue,
  permanently retired
Original Issue Year: 1985
Last Year: 1988
Rarity: C
Issue Price: $ 340
High Auction Price: $ 750
LCS Estimate: $ 750

No.: 5417
Name: Artist Model
Height: 12.5
Current Status: Open issue,
  permanently retired
Original Issue Year: 1987
Last Year: 1990
Rarity: C
Issue Price: $ 425
High Auction Price: $ 550
LCS Estimate: $ 550

No.: 3508
Name: Girl with Geranium
Height: 12.5
Current Status: Open issue,
  permanently retired
Original Issue Year: 1978
Last Year: 1988
Rarity: E
Issue Price: $ 230
High Auction Price: $ 375
LCS Estimate: $ 500

No.: 3506
Name: Maiden
Height: 12.5
Current Status: Open issue,
  permanently retired
Original Issue Year: 1978
Last Year: 1988
Rarity: E
Issue Price: $ 230
High Auction Price: $ 375
LCS Estimate: $ 500

No.: 4511.30
Name: Nude in White
Height: 12.5
Current Status: Open issue,
  permanently retired
Original Issue Year: 1983
Last Year: 1985
Rarity: B
Issue Price: $ 150
LCS Estimate: $ 580

No.: 4875
Name: The Jug Carrier
Height: 12.5
Current Status: Open issue,
  permanently retired
Original Issue Year: 1974
Last Year: 1985
Rarity: E
Issue Price: $ 40
High Auction Price: $ 350
LCS Estimate: $ 325

No.: 4511
Name: Nude
Height: 12.5
Current Status: Open issue,
  permanently retired
Original Issue Year: 1969
Last Year: 1985
Rarity: F
Issue Price: $ 115
LCS Estimate: $ 920

No.: 4999
Name: Miss Teresa
Height: 12.5
Current Status: Open issue,
  permanently retired
Original Issue Year: 1978
Last Year: 1983
Rarity: D
Issue Price: $ 150
High Auction Price: $ 400
LCS Estimate: $ 400

No.: 4798
Name: Girl Tennis Player
Height: 12.5
Current Status: Open issue,
  permanently retired
Original Issue Year: 1972
Last Year: 1981
Rarity: E
Issue Price: $ 50
High Auction Price: $ 375
LCS Estimate: $ 350

No.: 4599
Name: He Loves Me
Height: 12.5
Current Status: Open issue,
  permanently retired
Original Issue Year: 1969
Last Year: 1972
Rarity: C
Issue Price: $ 47.5
LCS Estimate: $ 550

No.: 4938
Name: Baby's Outing
Height: 12.5
Current Status: Open issue, currently
  active
Original Issue Year: 1976
Issue Price: $ 250
Current Retail Price: $ 695

No.: 1602
Name: Spring Nymph
Height: 12.5
Current Status: Open issue, currently
  active
Original Issue Year: 1989
Issue Price: $ 665
Current Retail Price: $ 785

No.: 357.13
Name: Girl with Pigtails
Height: 12.5
Current Status: Very rare early issue
Original Issue Year: 1970
Last Year: Not available
Rarity: A
Issue Price: Not available

No.: 5345
Name: A New Hat
Height: 12.5
Current Status: Open issue,
  permanently retired
Original Issue Year: 1986
Last Year: 1990
Rarity: C
Issue Price: $ 200
High Auction Price: $ 475
LCS Estimate: $ 600

No.: 5125
Name: Goya Lady
Height: 12.5
Current Status: Open issue,
  permanently retired
Original Issue Year: 1982
Last Year: 1990
Rarity: E
Issue Price: $ 130
LCS Estimate: $ 260

No.: 310.13
Name: Behind the Screen
Height: 12.75
Current Status: Very rare early issue
Original Issue Year: 1966
Last Year: Not available
Rarity: A
Issue Price: Not available

No.: 4501
Name: A Basket of Goodies
Height: 13
Current Status: Open issue, permanently retired
Original Issue Year: 1969
Last Year: 1985
Rarity: F
Issue Price: $ 37.5
LCS Estimate: $ 300

No.: 2120
Name: Girl from Majorca
Height: 13
Current Status: Open issue, permanently retired
Original Issue Year: 1978
Last Year: 1982
Rarity: C
Issue Price: $ 250
LCS Estimate: $ 1200

No.: 1157
Name: Woman with Traditional Dress
Height: 13
Current Status: Open issue, permanently retired
Original Issue Year: 1971
Last Year: 1975
Rarity: C
Issue Price: $ 25
LCS Estimate: $ 250

No.: 1028
Name: Girl with Heart
Height: 13
Current Status: Open issue, permanently retired
Original Issue Year: 1969
Last Year: 1970
Rarity: B
Issue Price: $ 37.5
LCS Estimate: $ 450

No.: 5593
Name: Siamese Dancer
Height: 13
Current Status: Open issue, permanently retired
Original Issue Year: 1989
Last Year: 1993
Rarity: D
Issue Price: $ 345
Last Retail Price: $ 420

No.: 2190
Name: To The Well
Height: 13
Current Status: Open issue, currently active
Original Issue Year: 1990
Issue Price: $ 255
Current Retail Price: $ 285

No.: 5209
Name: School Marm
Height: 13
Current Status: Open issue, permanently retired
Original Issue Year: 1984
Last Year: 1990
Rarity: D
Issue Price: $ 205
High Auction Price: $ 800
LCS Estimate: $ 775

No.: 4916
Name: Chinese Noblewoman
Height: 13
Current Status: Open issue, permanently retired
Original Issue Year: 1974
Last Year: 1978
Rarity: C
Issue Price: $ 300
LCS Estimate: $ 2700

No.: 5197
Name: Female Physician
Height: 13.25
Current Status: Open issue, currently active
Original Issue Year: 1984
Issue Price: $ 120
Current Retail Price: $ 230

No.: 4936
Name: Spring Breeze
Height: 13.25
Current Status: Open issue, currently active
Original Issue Year: 1974
Issue Price: $ 145
Current Retail Price: $ 390

No.: 5742
Name: Bridal Portrait
Height: 13.25
Current Status: Open issue, currently active
Original Issue Year: 1991
Issue Price: $ 480
Current Retail Price: $ 495

No.: 5651
Name: Musical Muse
Height: 13.25
Current Status: Open issue, currently active
Original Issue Year: 1990
Issue Price: $ 375
Current Retail Price: $ 420

No.: 3023
Name: After the Bath
Height: 13.25
Current Status: Limited edition, fully subscribed
Edition Limit: 300
Original Issue Year: 1990
Last Year: 1991
Rarity: B
Issue Price: $ 350
High Auction Price: $ 850

No.: 3505
Name: Fiesta
Height: 13.25
Current Status: Open issue, permanently retired
Original Issue Year: 1978
Last Year: 1988
Rarity: E
Issue Price: $ 230
High Auction Price: $ 475
LCS Estimate: $ 500

No.: 4934
Name: Dainty Lady
Height: 13.25
Current Status: Open issue, permanently retired
Original Issue Year: 1974
Last Year: 1985
Rarity: E
Issue Price: $ 60
LCS Estimate: $ 360

No.: 5060
Name: Clown with Trumpet
Height: 13.25
Current Status: Open issue, permanently retired
Original Issue Year: 1980
Last Year: 1985
Rarity: D
Issue Price: $ 290
High Auction Price: $ 500
LCS Estimate: $ 475

No.: 5283
Name: Socialite of the Twenties
Height: 13.25
Current Status: Open issue, currently active
Original Issue Year: 1985
Issue Price: $ 175
Current Retail Price: $ 330

No.: 5378
Name: Time for Reflection
Height: 13.25
Current Status: Open issue, currently active
Original Issue Year: 1986
Issue Price: $ 425
Current Retail Price: $ 710

No.: 3534
Name: In The Distance
Height: 13.25
Current Status: Limited edition, fully subscribed
Edition Limit: 75
Original Issue Year: 1983
High Auction Price: $ 750
Issue Price: $ 525

No.: 5774
Name: Nature's Gifts
Height: 13.25
Current Status: Open issue, currently active
Original Issue Year: 1991
Issue Price: $ 900
Current Retail Price: $ 940

No.: 1568
Name: Grand Dame
Height: 13.25
Current Status: Open issue, currently active
Original Issue Year: 1987
Issue Price: $ 290
Current Retail Price: $ 380

No.: 359.13
Name: Insular Lady
Height: 13.75
Current Status: Very rare early issue
Original Issue Year: 1969
Last Year: Not available
Rarity: A
Issue Price: Not available

No.: 4922.30
Name: Wind Blown Girl (White)
Height: 13.75
Current Status: Open issue, permanently retired
Original Issue Year: 1983
Last Year: 1985
Rarity: B
Issue Price: $ 155
LCS Estimate: $ 600

No.: 4951
Name: "Missy"
Height: 13.75
Current Status: Open issue, permanently retired
Original Issue Year: 1976
Last Year: 1985
Rarity: E
Issue Price: $ 300
High Auction Price: $ 750
LCS Estimate: $ 750

No.: 4502
Name: Marketing Day
Height: 13.75
Current Status: Open issue, permanently retired
Original Issue Year: 1969
Last Year: 1985
Rarity: F
Issue Price: $ 40
LCS Estimate: $ 320

No.: 4932
Name: Isabel of Castilla
Height: 13.75
Current Status: Open issue, permanently retired
Original Issue Year: 1974
Last Year: 1981
Rarity: D
Issue Price: $ 525
LCS Estimate: $ 3500

No.: 4976
Name: Agustine of Aragon
Height: 13.75
Current Status: Open issue, permanently retired
Original Issue Year: 1977
Last Year: 1979
Rarity: B
Issue Price: $ 475
High Auction Price: $ 1800
LCS Estimate: $ 1750

No.: 4586
Name: Madonna
Height: 13.75
Current Status: Open issue, permanently retired
Original Issue Year: 1969
Last Year: 1979
Rarity: E
Issue Price: $ 32.5
LCS Estimate: $ 300

No.: 4922
Name: Sea Breeze
Height: 13.75
Current Status: Open issue, currently active
Original Issue Year: 1974
Issue Price: $ 150
Current Retail Price: $ 355

No.: 1431
Name: The Debutante
Height: 13.75
Current Status: Open issue, currently active
Original Issue Year: 1982
Issue Price: $ 115
Current Retail Price: $ 240

No.: 1428
Name: Afternoon Tea
Height: 13.75
Current Status: Open issue, currently active
Original Issue Year: 1982
Issue Price: $ 115
Current Retail Price: $ 245

No.: 4559
Name: Waiting Backstage
Height: 13.75
Current Status: Open issue, permanently retired
Original Issue Year: 1969
Last Year: 1993
Rarity: F
Issue Price: $ 110
Last Retail Price: $ 440

No.: 3525
Name: Class Water Carrier
Height: 14.25
Current Status: Open issue, currently active
Original Issue Year: 1981
Issue Price: $ 360
Current Retail Price: $ 595

No.: 4603.30
Name: Nurse (Reduced)
Height: 14.25
Current Status: Open issue, currently active
Original Issue Year: 1971
Issue Price: $ 35
Current Retail Price: $ 185

No.: 1270
Name: Reminiscing
Height: 14.25
Current Status: Open issue, permanently retired
Original Issue Year: 1974
Last Year: 1988
Rarity: E
Issue Price: $ 975
High Auction Price: $ 1000
LCS Estimate: $ 1000

No.: 4995
Name: Coquetry
Height: 14.25
Current Status: Open issue,
   permanently retired
Original Issue Year: 1978
Last Year: 1979
Rarity: B
Issue Price: $ 140
LCS Estimate: $ 1000

No.: 4997
Name: Frustrated Walk
Height: 14.25
Current Status: Open issue,
   permanently retired
Original Issue Year: 1978
Last Year: 1979
Rarity: B
Issue Price: $ 130
LCS Estimate: $ 900

No.: 5000
Name: Reading
Height: 14.25
Current Status: Open issue, currently
   active
Original Issue Year: 1978
Issue Price: $ 150
Current Retail Price: $ 245

No.: 5756
Name: Ashley
Height: 14.25
Current Status: Open issue,
   permanently retired
Original Issue Year: 1991
Last Year: 1993
Rarity: C
Issue Price: $ 265
Last Retail Price: $ 290

No.: 5755
Name: Claudette
Height: 14.25
Current Status: Open issue,
   permanently retired
Original Issue Year: 1991
Last Year: 1993
Rarity: C
Issue Price: $ 265
Last Retail Price: $ 285

No.: 5470
Name: Tea Time
Height: 14.25
Current Status: Open issue, currently
   active
Original Issue Year: 1988
Issue Price: $ 260
Current Retail Price: $ 345

No.: 4700
Name: Dressmaker
Height: 14.25
Current Status: Open issue,
  permanently retired
Original Issue Year: 1970
Last Year: 1993
Rarity: F
Issue Price: $ 40
Last Retail Price: $ 360

No.: 298.13
Name: Lady from Valencia
Height: 14.5
Current Status: Very rare early issue
Original Issue Year: 1963
Last Year: Not available
Rarity: A
Issue Price: Not available

No.: 2081
Name: Fisher Woman
Height: 14.5
Current Status: Open issue,
  permanently retired
Original Issue Year: 1978
Last Year: 1985
Rarity: D
Issue Price: $ 550
LCS Estimate: $ 2600

No.: 5048
Name: Teacher Woman
Height: 14.5
Current Status: Open issue,
  permanently retired
Original Issue Year: 1980
Last Year: 1981
Rarity: B
Issue Price: $ 115
High Auction Price: $ 600
LCS Estimate: $ 600

No.: 4928
Name: Medieval Lady
Height: 14.5
Current Status: Open issue,
  permanently retired
Original Issue Year: 1974
Last Year: 1980
Rarity: D
Issue Price: $ 275
High Auction Price: $ 825
LCS Estimate: $ 800

No.: 2026
Name: Oriental Woman
Height: 14.5
Current Status: Open issue,
  permanently retired
Original Issue Year: 1971
Last Year: 1975
Rarity: C
Issue Price: $ 45
LCS Estimate: $ 450

No.: 4698
Name: Lady with Fan
Height: 14.5
Current Status: Open issue,
permanently retired
Original Issue Year: 1970
Last Year: 1975
Rarity: D
Issue Price: $ 75
LCS Estimate: $ 750

No.: 5377
Name: A Touch of Class
Height: 14.5
Current Status: Open issue, currently
active
Original Issue Year: 1986
Issue Price: $ 475
Current Retail Price: $ 785

No.: 1495
Name: A Lady of Taste
Height: 14.5
Current Status: Open issue, currently
active
Original Issue Year: 1986
Issue Price: $ 575
Current Retail Price: $ 995

No.: 2231
Name: Afternoon Verse
Height: 14.5
Current Status: Open issue, currently
active
Original Issue Year: 1992
Issue Price: $ 580
Current Retail Price: $ 580

No.: 4565
Name: Oriental Lady
Height: 15
Current Status: Open issue,
permanently retired
Original Issue Year: 1969
Last Year: 1972
Rarity: C
Issue Price: $ 65
LCS Estimate: $ 800

No.: 3544
Name: Reflections
Height: 15
Current Status: Limited edition,
currently active
Edition Limit: 75
Original Issue Year: 1983
Issue Price: $ 650
Current Retail Price: $ 975
High Auction Price: $ 500

No.: 4850
Name: Aesthetic Pose
Height: 15
Current Status: Open issue, permanently retired
Original Issue Year: 1973
Last Year: 1985
Rarity: E
Issue Price: $ 110
High Auction Price: $ 900
LCS Estimate: $ 800

No.: 1049
Name: Girl
Height: 15
Current Status: Open issue, permanently retired
Original Issue Year: 1969
Last Year: 1978
Rarity: E
Issue Price: $ 60
LCS Estimate: $ 540

No.: 5175
Name: Lady Grand Casino
Height: 15.25
Current Status: Open issue, currently active
Original Issue Year: 1982
Issue Price: $ 185
Current Retail Price: $ 345

No.: 2062
Name: Day Dream
Height: 15.5
Current Status: Open issue, permanently retired
Original Issue Year: 1977
Last Year: 1985
Rarity: E
Issue Price: $ 400
LCS Estimate: $ 2000

No.: 2074
Name: Water Carrier
Height: 15.5
Current Status: Open issue, permanently retired
Original Issue Year: 1977
Last Year: 1985
Rarity: E
Issue Price: $ 500
High Auction Price: $ 1900
LCS Estimate: $ 2000

No.: 1040
Name: Girl with Letter
Height: 15.5
Current Status: Open issue, permanently retired
Original Issue Year: 1969
Last Year: 1978
Rarity: E
Issue Price: $ 57.5
LCS Estimate: $ 520

No.: 3020
Name: Demureness
Height: 15.5
Current Status: Limited edition, currently active
Edition Limit: 300
Original Issue Year: 1989
Issue Price: $ 525
Current Retail Price: $ 525

No.: 1466
Name: Classic Fall
Height: 15.75
Current Status: Limited edition, fully subscribed
Edition Limit: 1500
Original Issue Year: 1985
Issue Price: $ 620
High Auction Price: $ 1000

No.: 4518
Name: Girl Student
Height: 15.75
Current Status: Open issue, permanently retired
Original Issue Year: 1969
Last Year: 1978
Rarity: E
Issue Price: $ 57.5
LCS Estimate: $ 520

No.: 4603
Name: Nurse
Height: 15.75
Current Status: Open issue, permanently retired
Original Issue Year: 1969
Last Year: 1978
Rarity: E
Issue Price: $ 35
LCS Estimate: $ 310

No.: 4582
Name: Harvester
Height: 15.75
Current Status: Open issue, permanently retired
Original Issue Year: 1969
Last Year: 1975
Rarity: D
Issue Price: $ 55
LCS Estimate: $ 600

No.: 1465
Name: Classic Spring
Height: 15.75
Current Status: Limited edition, fully subscribed
Edition Limit: 1500
Original Issue Year: 1985
Issue Price: $ 620
High Auction Price: $ 1650

No.: 336.13
Name: Nude
Height: 16
Current Status: Very rare early issue
Original Issue Year: 1972
Last Year: Not available
Rarity: A
Issue Price: Not available

No.: 3010.70
Name: Isabel La Catolica
Height: 16
Current Status: Limited edition, fully
  subscribed
Edition Limit: 350
Original Issue Year: 1986
Issue Price: $ 1375

No.: 1421
Name: Mariko
Height: 16
Current Status: Open issue, currently
  active
Original Issue Year: 1982
Issue Price: $ 860
Current Retail Price: $ 1500

No.: 3010.60
Name: Isabel La Catolica
Height: 16
Current Status: Limited edition, fully
  subscribed
Edition Limit: 350
Original Issue Year: 1986
Issue Price: $ 1375

No.: 3010.20
Name: Isabel La Catolica
Height: 16
Current Status: Limited edition, fully
  subscribed
Edition Limit: 350
Original Issue Year: 1986
Issue Price: $ 1375

No.: 3010.10
Name: Isabel La Catolica
Height: 16
Current Status: Limited edition, fully
  subscribed
Edition Limit: 350
Original Issue Year: 1986
Issue Price: $ 1375

No.: 3535
Name: Slave
Height: 16.25
Current Status: Limited edition, fully
  subscribed
Edition Limit: 50
Original Issue Year: 1983
High Auction Price: $ 750
Issue Price: $ 950

No.: 2181
Name: Bathing Nymph
Height: 16.5
Current Status: Open issue, currently
  active
Original Issue Year: 1988
Issue Price: $ 560
Current Retail Price: $ 725

No.: 5005
Name: Eloise
Height: 16.5
Current Status: Open issue,
  permanently retired
Original Issue Year: 1978
Last Year: 1981
Rarity: C
Issue Price: $ 175
High Auction Price: $ 475
LCS Estimate: $ 500

No.: 2034
Name: St. Elizabeth of Hungary
Height: 16.5
Current Status: Open issue,
  permanently retired
Original Issue Year: 1971
Last Year: 1973
Rarity: B
Issue Price: $ 40
LCS Estimate: $ 450

No.: 2069
Name: Thai Dancer
Height: 17
Current Status: Open issue, currently
  active
Original Issue Year: 1977
Issue Price: $ 300
Current Retail Price: $ 690

No.: 2244
Name: The Awakening
Height: 17
Current Status: Open issue, currently
  active
Original Issue Year: 1993
Edition Limit: 300
Issue Price: $ 1200

No.: 2080
Name: Woman
Height: 17.25
Current Status: Open issue,
   permanently retired
Original Issue Year: 1978
Last Year: 1985
Rarity: D
Issue Price: $ 625
High Auction Price: $ 750
LCS Estimate: $ 750

No.: 3542
Name: Yoga
Height: 17.25
Current Status: Limited edition, fully
   subscribed
Edition Limit: 125
Original Issue Year: 1983
Issue Price: $ 650
High Auction Price: $ 800

No.: 2229
Name: Seasonal Gifts
Height: 17.5
Current Status: Open issue, currently
   active
Original Issue Year: 1992
Issue Price: $ 450
Current Retail Price: $ 450

No.: 2079
Name: Nude with Rose
Height: 18
Current Status: Open issue,
   permanently retired
Original Issue Year: 1978
Last Year: 1979
Rarity: B
Issue Price: $ 210
LCS Estimate: $ 1475

No.: 2023
Name: Girl to the Fountain
Height: 18.5
Current Status: Open issue,
   permanently retired
Original Issue Year: 1971
Last Year: 1979
Rarity: E
Issue Price: $ 35
High Auction Price: $ 375
LCS Estimate: $ 280

No.: 2182
Name: Daydreamer
Height: 18.5
Current Status: Open issue, currently
   active
Original Issue Year: 1988
Issue Price: $ 560
Current Retail Price: $ 725

No.: 3517.30
Name: Nude with Rose
Height: 18.5
Current Status: Open issue,
  permanently retired
Original Issue Year: 1978
Last Year: 1985
Rarity: D
Issue Price: $ 215
LCS Estimate: $ 950

No.: 3518
Name: Lady Macbeth
Height: 18.5
Current Status: Open issue,
  permanently retired
Original Issue Year: 1980
Last Year: 1981
Rarity: B
Issue Price: $ 385
High Auction Price: $ 600
LCS Estimate: $ 600

No.: 3517
Name: Nude With Rose
Height: 18.5
Current Status: Open issue, currently
  active
Original Issue Year: 1978
Issue Price: $ 225
Current Retail Price: $ 725

No.: 3541
Name: Tranquility
Height: 19
Current Status: Limited edition, fully
  subscribed
Edition Limit: 75
Original Issue Year: 1983
Issue Price: $ 1000

No.: 4805
Name: Woman with Umbrella
Height: 19.25
Current Status: Open issue,
  permanently retired
Original Issue Year: 1972
Last Year: 1981
Rarity: E
Issue Price: $ 100
High Auction Price: $ 850
LCS Estimate: $ 700

No.: 3548
Name: Serenity
Height: 19.25
Current Status: Limited edition,
  permanently retired
Edition Limit: 300
Original Issue Year: 1983
Last Year: 1993
Rarity: E
Issue Price: $ 925
Last Retail Price: $ 1550

No.: 3014
Name: The Nymph
Height: 19.25
Current Status: Limited edition, currently active
Edition Limit: 250
Original Issue Year: 1987
Issue Price: $ 1000
Current Retail Price: $ 1350

No.: 3537
Name: Dreaming
Height: 19.75
Current Status: Limited edition, fully subscribed
Edition Limit: 250
Original Issue Year: 1983
Issue Price: $ 475

No.: 3013
Name: Youthful Innocence
Height: 20
Current Status: Limited edition, currently active
Edition Limit: 500
Original Issue Year: 1987
Issue Price: $ 1300
Current Retail Price: $ 1650

No.: 2083
Name: Carmen
Height: 20.75
Current Status: Open issue, permanently retired
Original Issue Year: 1978
Last Year: 1981
Rarity: C
Issue Price: $ 275
High Auction Price: $ 750
LCS Estimate: $ 700

No.: 2032
Name: Tahitiana
Height: 21
Current Status: Limited edition, fully subscribed
Edition Limit: 200
Original Issue Year: 1971
Issue Price: $ 295

No.: 2022
Name: Woman from Altamira
Height: 21.25
Current Status: Open issue, permanently retired
Original Issue Year: 1971
Last Year: 1979
Rarity: E
Issue Price: $ 40
LCS Estimate: $ 325

No.: 1330
Name: Woman with Hat
Height: 21.25
Current Status: Limited edition, fully
  subscribed
Edition Limit: 750
Original Issue Year: 1976
Issue Price: $ 900

No.: 3012
Name: Classic Beauty
Height: 21.5
Current Status: Limited edition,
  currently active
Edition Limit: 500
Original Issue Year: 1987
Issue Price: $ 1300
Current Retail Price: $ 1650

No.: 3002
Name: Waiting
Height: 21.5
Current Status: Limited edition, fully
  subscribed
Edition Limit: 125
Original Issue Year: 1983
Issue Price: $ 1550

No.: 2016
Name: Girl With Guitar
Height: 21.5
Current Status: Limited edition, fully
  subscribed
Edition Limit: 750
Original Issue Year: 1970
Issue Price: $ 325

No.: 2039
Name: Aida
Height: 21.5
Current Status: Open issue,
  permanently retired
Original Issue Year: 1971
Last Year: 1979
Rarity: E
Issue Price: $ 65
LCS Estimate: $ 525

No.: 3546
Name: African Woman
Height: 22
Current Status: Limited edition, fully
  subscribed
Edition Limit: 50
Original Issue Year: 1983
Issue Price: $ 1300

No.: 3018
Name: Cellist
Height: 23.25
Current Status: Limited edition,
  permanently retired
Edition Limit: 300
Original Issue Year: 1988
Last Year: 1993
Rarity: D
Issue Price: $ 650
Last Retail Price: $ 875

No.: 1461
Name: Youthful Beauty
Height: 23.5
Current Status: Limited edition,
  currently active
Edition Limit: 5000
Original Issue Year: 1985
Issue Price: $ 750
Current Retail Price: $ 1150

No.: 2049
Name: Country Woman
Height: 23.5
Current Status: Limited edition, fully
  subscribed
Edition Limit: 750
Original Issue Year: 1973
Issue Price: $ 200

No.: 2137
Name: Fairy Ballerina
Height: 23.5
Current Status: Open issue,
  permanently retired
Original Issue Year: 1984
Last Year: 1988
Rarity: C
Issue Price: $ 500
LCS Estimate: $ 1500

No.: 5386
Name: Pastoral Scene
Height: 23.5
Current Status: Limited edition,
  currently active
Edition Limit: 750
Original Issue Year: 1986
Issue Price: $ 1100
Current Retail Price: $ 2000

No.: 3553
Name: Fire Bird
Height: 23.5
Current Status: Limited edition,
  currently active
Edition Limit: 1500
Original Issue Year: 1982
Issue Price: $ 800
Current Retail Price: $ 1250

No.: 3538
Name: Youth
Height: 23.5
Current Status: Limited edition, fully subscribed
Edition Limit: 250
Original Issue Year: 1983
High Auction Price: $ 1200
Issue Price: $ 525.5

No.: 2123
Name: Dancer
Height: 23.75
Current Status: Open issue, permanently retired
Original Issue Year: 1980
Last Year: 1985
Rarity: D
Issue Price: $ 790
LCS Estimate: $ 2350

No.: 3026
Name: Unadorned Beauty
Height: 25.5
Current Status: Limited edition, currently active
Edition Limit: 200
Original Issue Year: 1991
Issue Price: $ 1700
Current Retail Price: $ 1750

No.: 3003
Name: Indolence
Height: 26
Current Status: Limited edition, fully subscribed
Edition Limit: 150
Original Issue Year: 1983
Issue Price: $ 1465
High Auction Price: $ 1000

No.: 4942
Name: Portrait
Height: 28.25
Current Status: Open issue, permanently retired
Original Issue Year: 1976
Last Year: 1985
Rarity: E
Issue Price: $ 650
High Auction Price: $ 1000
LCS Estimate: $ 1000

No.: 3005
Name: Venus in the Bath
Height: 28.25
Current Status: Limited edition, fully subscribed
Original Issue Year: 1983
Issue Price: $ 1175
High Auction Price: $ 750

No.: 3558
Name: Innocence
Height: 28.25
Current Status: Open issue,
  permanently retired
Original Issue Year: 1984
Last Year: 1991
Rarity: D
Issue Price: $ 960
High Auction Price: $ 800
LCS Estimate: $ 850

No.: 3558.30
Name: Innocence
Height: 28.25
Current Status: Open issue,
  permanently retired
Original Issue Year: 1984
Last Year: 1987
Rarity: C
Issue Price: $ 960
LCS Estimate: $ 2700

No.: 2029
Name: Eve at the Tree
Height: 28.75
Current Status: Limited edition, fully
  subscribed
Edition Limit: 600
Original Issue Year: 1971
High Auction Price: $ 2000
Issue Price: $ 450

No.: 3502
Name: Native
Height: 28.75
Current Status: Open issue, currently
  active
Original Issue Year: 1978
Issue Price: $ 700
Current Retail Price: $ 2350

No.: 3540
Name: Pose
Height: 31.75
Current Status: Limited edition, fully
  subscribed
Edition Limit: 100
Original Issue Year: 1983
Issue Price: $ 1250

No.: 3015
Name: Dignity
Height: 33
Current Status: Limited edition,
  currently active
Edition Limit: 150
Original Issue Year: 1987
Issue Price: $ 1400
Current Retail Price: $ 1800

No.: 3543
Name: Demure
Height: 33
Current Status: Limited edition, fully subscribed
Edition Limit: 100
Original Issue Year: 1983
Issue Price: $ 1250
High Auction Price: $ 850

No.: 2015
Name: Knowledge
Height: 35
Current Status: Open issue, permanently retired
Original Issue Year: 1970
Last Year: 1985
Rarity: E
Issue Price: $ 325
LCS Estimate: $ 1950

No.: 2031
Name: Lyric Muse
Height: 45.5
Current Status: Limited edition, fully subscribed
Edition Limit: 400
Original Issue Year: 1971
Issue Price: $ 750
High Auction Price: $ 1900

Indexes

Throughout this book we have tried to make it easy for you to locate the Lladró figurines you are trying to identify. We've used:

Form Spoons versus full-length figurines versus vases versus heads, busts and torsos versus lamps, and so on.

Subject Within figurines, we've used one female, one male, groups of people, birds, animals and so on as dividers to help you find your pieces.

Height Within many large categories, we've used height

Now, at the end of this research, we have further indexed the collection into eighteen themes which, from the early 1940s to the present, appear over and over again.

But first, Lladró's 4-digit production numbers have dominated the Spanish classification system up to this time. If you know your object by its 4-digit number, we have indexed them by the pages in which they appear.

The eighteen themes are:

Afro-Americans, America's Black Heritage 46, 215, 230, 231, 263, 264, 272, 283, 286, 294, 299, 301, 312, 320, 325, 329, 358, 372, 407, 427, 443, 450, 476, 498.

Hawaiians, Asians and Polynesians 8, 47, 105, 216, 234, 235, 239, 240, 245, 247, 251, 253, 255, 261, 269, 270, 282, 295, 311, 312, 337, 360, 363, 364, 379, 381, 393, 394, 402, 408, 409, 410, 419, 422, 423, 431, 432, 435, 436, 442, 447, 449, 450, 451, 453, 459, 461, 462, 463, 464, 466, 467, 469, 472, 474, 476, 477, 478, 482, 483, 485, 489, 490, 493, 494, 497, 499, 500.

Ballerinas 10, 49, 50, 52, 126, 228, 229, 232, 238, 240, 246, 249, 250, 281, 288, 289, 291, 292, 294, 297, 298, 299, 302, 304, 306, 307, 308, 310, 313, 317, 320, 411, 412, 413, 415, 416, 417, 419, 420, 421, 423, 425, 426, 428, 429, 430, 432, 433, 434, 435, 438, 440, 450, 451, 453, 454, 459, 465, 467, 468, 470, 471, 476, 482, 487, 499.

Clowns 112, 113, 114, 116, 214, 243, 246, 252, 263, 264, 266, 267, 268, 269, 278, 302, 355, 357, 358, 359, 361, 362, 368, 369, 374, 380, 385, 390, 393, 397, 404, 407, 408, 484.

Don Quixote and Friends 17, 33, 116, 118, 120, 123, 188, 244, 247, 275, 279, 280, 366, 369, 378, 380, 385, 400, 401, 402, 405, 410.

Eskimos 242, 255, 256, 262, 264, 282, 283, 286, 298, 301, 308, 341, 360, 376, 423, 424, 431, 436, 472, 473.

Harlequins 11, 21, 50, 114, 120, 125, 126, 254, 256, 266, 287, 308, 310, 362, 364, 365, 370, 373, 375, 385, 390, 397, 401.

Jesus Christ 9, 10, 35, 203, 209, 210, 211, 212, 241, 243, 244, 245, 253, 267, 274, 297, 300, 306, 331, 353, 355, 395, 396, 399, 405, 408, 411.

Lladró Collectors Society Member-only Specials

Addendum

These final 1993 issue prices arrived too late for inclusion with their photos in the book. When you see a figure introduced in 1993, check here for final prices in all cases.

No.	Title	Issue Price (US Dollars)	No.	Title	Issue Price (US Dollars)
1762	Paella Valenciano	10000	5934	The Holy Teacher	375
1763	Trusting Friend	1200	5935	Nutcracker Suite	620
1764	He's My Brother	1500	5936	Little Skipper	320
1765	Course of Adventure	1625	5941	Riding the Waves	405
1766	Ties That Bind	1700	5942	The Blessing	1345
1767	Motherly Love	1330	5943	World of Fantasy	295
1768	Traveller's Respite	1825	5944	The Great Adventurer	325
1769	Fruitful Harvest	1300	5946	A Mother's Way	1350
1770	Gypsy Dancers	2250	5947	General Practicioner	360
1771	Country Doctor	1475	5948	Physician	360
1772	Back to Back	1450	5949	Candleholder-Lyre	225
1773	Michevious Musician	975	5950	Candleholder-Tambourine	225
1774	A Treasured Moment	950	5951	Our Lady of Rocio	3500
1775	Oriental Garden	22500	5952	Where To, Sir?	5250
2235	Adoring Mother	405	5953	Sounds of Summer	125
2236	Frosty Outing	375	5954	Sounds of Winter	125
2237	The Old Fishing Hole	625	5955	Sounds of Fall	125
2238	Learning Together	500	5956	Sounds of Spring	125
2239	Valencian Courtship	880	5957	The Glass Slipper	475
2240	Winged Love	285	5958	Country Ride	2850
2241	Winged Harmony	285	5959	It's Your Turn	365
2242	Away to School	465	5960	On Patrol	395
2243	Flight of Fancy	1400	5961	The Great Teacher	850
2244	The Awakening	1200	5964	The Great Voyage	50
2245	Inspired Voyage	4800	5965	The Clipper Ship	240
2246	Lion Tamer	375	5966	Flowers Forever	4150
2247	Just Us	650	5967	Discovery Mug 1992	90
2248	Days of Yore	2050	5968	Honeymoon Ride	2750
2249	Holiday Glow	750	5970	Bow Clock	195
2250	Autumn Glow	750	5971	A Special Toy	815
2251	Noella	405	5972	Before the Dance	3550
2252	Waiting for Father	660	5973	Angelic Time	1050
2253	Noisy Friend	280	5974	Family Outing	4275
2254	Step Aside	280	5975	Up and Away	2850
2255	Humble Grace	2150	5976	The Fireman	395
5932	Jester's Serenade	1995	5977	Revelation-White	310
5933	The Ten Commandments	930	5978	Revelation-Black	310

No.	Title	Issue Price (US Dollars)	No.	Title	Issue Price (US Dollars)
5979	Revelation-Sand	310	6008	Joyful Event	825
5980	The Past-White	310	6011	Monday's Child Boy	245
5981	The Past-Black	310	6012	Monday's Child Girl	260
5982	The Past-Sand	310	6013	Tuesday's Child Boy	225
5983	Deity-White	310	6014	Tuesday's Child Girl	245
5984	Deity-Black	310	6015	Wednesday's Child Boy	245
5985	Deity-Sand	310	6016	Wednesday's Child Girl	245
5986	Sunday Sermon	425	6017	Thursday's Child Boy	225
5987	Talk To Me	145	6018	Thursday's Child Girl	245
5988	Taking Time	145	6019	Friday's Child Boy	225
5989	A Mother's Touch	470	6020	Friday's Child Girl	225
5990	Thoughtful Caress	225	6021	Saturday's Child Boy	245
5991	Love Story	2800	6022	Saturday's Child Girl	245
5992	Time For Love	760	6023	Sunday's Child Boy	225
5993	Unicorn and Friend	355	6024	Sunday's Child Girl	225
5994	Meet My Friend	695	6025	Barnyard See Saw	500
5995	Soft Meow	480	6026	My Turn	515
5996	Bless the Child	465	6027	Hanukah Lights	345
5997	One More Try	715	6028	Mazel Tov!	380
5998	Looking Out	38	6029	Hebrew Scholar	225
5999	Swinging	38	6030	Maidenhead Vase	1350
6000	Duck Plate	38	6031	On the Go	475
6001	My Dad	550	6032	On the Green	645
6002	Down You Go	815	6033	Graceful Moment	1475
6003	Ready to Learn	650	6034	Monkey Business	745
6004	Bar Mitzvah Day	395	6035	The Hand of Justice	1250
6005	Christening Day	1425	6036	Young Princess	240
6006	Oriental Column	1875	7522	Courage	195
6007	The Goddess & Unicorn	1675	7620	Best Friend	195

1992 Disney Exclusive Soars in Value

Tinkerbell, Lladró's portrayal of Peter Pan's magic guardian.
Chosen by the Disney Co. as a 1992 collectible special.

In 1992, the officials at Walt Disney World in Orlando staged a large collectibles convention, personally inviting several thousand known collectors of Disney memorabilia. Lladró was one of the few companies selected to produce an exclusive collectible, available only at the convention. A Disney 1992 convention emblem is fired permanently into the base of each figurine. Available only in a small edition of 1500 at a $350 issue price, *Tinkerbell* sold out during the first hours of the show.

Word quickly spread to both the Lladró and Disney collecting worlds and the latest trading range being quoted by secondary market dealers is $2,500/2,600, the current LCS estimate.

Disney is a registered trademark of The Disney Co.